Between Mass Death and Individual Loss

Studies in German History
Published in Association with the German Historical Institute, Washington, DC

General Editors:
Hartmut Berghoff, Director of the German Historical Institute, Washington, DC
Uwe Spiekermann, Deputy Director of the German Historical Institute, Washington, DC

Volume 1
Nature in German History
Edited by Christof Mauch

Volume 2
Coping with the Nazi Past: West German Debates on Nazism and Generational Conflict, 1955–1975
Edited by Philipp Gassert and Alan E. Steinweis

Volume 3
Adolf Cluss, Architect: From Germany to America
Edited by Alan Lessoff and Christof Mauch

Volume 4
Two Lives in Uncertain Times: Facing the Challenges of the 20th Century as Scholars and Citizens
Wilma Iggers and Georg Iggers

Volume 5
Driving Germany: The Landscape of the German Autobahn, 1930–1970
Thomas Zeller

Volume 6
The Pleasure of a Surplus Income: Part-Time Work, Gender Politics, and Social Change in West Germany, 1955–1969
Christine von Oertzen

Volume 7
Between Mass Death and Individual Loss: The Place of the Dead in Twentieth-Century Germany
Edited by Alon Confino, Paul Betts, and Dirk Schumann

BETWEEN MASS DEATH AND INDIVIDUAL LOSS

The Place of the Dead in Twentieth-Century Germany

Edited by

Alon Confino

Paul Betts

and

Dirk Schumann

Berghahn Books
NEW YORK • OXFORD

Published in 2008 by
Berghahn Books
www.berghahnbooks.com

© 2008, 2011 Alon Confino, Paul Betts, Dirk Schumann
First paperback edition published in 2011

All rights reserved.
Except for the quotation of short passages
for the purposes of criticism and review, no part of this book
may be reproduced in any form or by any means, electronic or
mechanical, including photocopying, recording, or any information
storage and retrieval system now known or to be invented,
without written permission of the publisher.

Library of Congress Cataloging-in-Publication Data

Between mass death and individual loss : the place of the dead in twentieth-century Germany / edited by Alon Confino, Paul Betts and Dirk Schumann.
　p. cm.
Includes bibliographical references.
ISBN 978-1-84545-397-8 (hbk) -- ISBN 978-0-85745-169-9 (pbk)
　1. Germany—Social life and customs—20th century. 2. Death—Germany—History—20th century. 3. Cemeteries—Germany—History. 4. Funeral rites and ceremonies—Germany—History—20th century. 5. Collective memory—Germany. I. Confino, Alon. II. Betts, Paul. III. Schumann, Dirk.

DD239.B48 2008
306.90943'0904—dc22

2007030712

British Library Cataloguing in Publication Data

A catalogue record for this book is available from the British Library.

Printed in the United States on acid-free paper

ISBN 978-1-84545-397-8 (hardback)
ISBN 978-0-85745-169-9 (paperback)
ISBN 978-0-85745-384-6 (ebook)

The world is rich with wonders,
Yet none more baffling than man.

...

Anything he can meet—
Only death he will never master.

Antigone, Sophocles

Contents

List of Illustrations ... ix

Introduction: Death and Twentieth-Century Germany ... 1
Paul Betts, Alon Confino, Dirk Schumann

I. Bodies

1. How the Germans Learned to Wage War: On the Question of Killing in the First and Second World Wars ... 25
   Michael Geyer

2. The Shadow of Death in Germany at the End of the Second World War ... 51
   Richard Bessel

3. Reburying and Rebuilding: Reflecting on Proper Burial in Berlin after "Zero Hour" ... 69
   Monica A. Black

II. Disposal

4. Fanning the Flames: Cremation in Late Imperial and Weimar Germany ... 93
   Simone Ameskamp

5. Disposing of the Dead in East Germany, 1945–1990 ... 113
   Felix Robin Schulz

6. Death at the Munich Olympics ... 129
   Kay Schiller

7. When Cold Warriors Die: The State Funerals of Konrad Adenauer and Walter Ulbricht 151
Paul Betts

III. Subjectivity

8. A Common Experience of Death: Commemorating the German-Jewish Soldiers of the First World War, 1914–1923 179
Tim Grady

9. Laughing about Death? "German Humor" in the Two World Wars 197
Martina Kessel

10. Death, Spiritual Solace, and Afterlife: Between Nazism and Religion 219
Alon Confino

11. Yizkor! Commemoration of the Dead by Jewish Displaced Persons in Postwar Germany 232
Gabriel N. Finder

IV. Ruins

12. The Imagination of Disaster: Death and Survival in Postwar West Germany 261
Svenja Goltermann

13. European Melancholy and the Inability to Listen: Sebald, Politics, and Death 275
Daniel Steuer

14. A Cemetery in Berlin 298
Peter Fritzsche

Notes on Contributors 314

Select Bibliography 317

Index 322

List of Illustrations

Figure 7.1.	Border Guard Officers escorting Adenauer's coffin from his private residence in Rhöndorf, Germany	154
Figure 7.2.	Konrad Adenauer Lying-in-State in the Great Cabinet Hall, Cologne, Germany, 1967	155
Figure 7.3.	Adenauer Lying-in-State, Cologne Dome, Cologne, Germany, 1967	156
Figure 7.4.	Adenauer Lying-in-State, Cologne Dome, Cologne, Germany, 1967	157
Figure 7.5.	Demonstrators on Adenauerdamm, Berlin, 1967	162
Figure 7.6.	Erich Honecker Congratulating Walter Ulbricht on the Occasion of his 78th Birthday, 30 June 1971, Berlin	164
Figure 7.7.	Erich Honecker, Friedrich Ebert and Willi Stoph Accompanying Ulbricht's Coffin, Berlin, 1973	166
Figure 7.8.	Ulbricht's Funeral Procession, Berlin, 1973	168
Figure 7.9.	Ulbricht's Funeral Procession, Berlin, 1973	169
Figure 7.10.	Newspaper Cartoon, "Ehrenplatz," or "Square of Honor" (Artist: Hicks)	173
Figure 11.1.	Survivors from Vilna gather for a memorial service in Munich in 1948.	241

Figure 11.2. Group portrait of Jewish DPs from Makow Mazowiecki convened to commemorate the community's victims of Nazism on the anniversary of the liquidation of its ghetto; December 15, 1947.   243

Figure 11.3. Cover of Radom *yizker* book, *Dos yidishe Random in khurves* (Stuttgart, 1948).   245

Figure 11.4. Jewish DPs march to Mittenwald for a memorial observance, May 14, 1947.   250

Introduction

DEATH AND TWENTIETH-CENTURY GERMANY

Paul Betts, Alon Confino, and Dirk Schumann

As the twentieth century begins to shift from experience to memory, historians are trying to understand what it has brought and left us. Like Benjamin's Angel of History, they have trained their gaze on the accumulated wreckage of miscarried dreams and man-made catastrophes that have plagued the globe since the outbreak of the Great War. That the century is seen to have started in 1914 with political assassination in Sarajevo and to have ended in the very same city with the outbreak of the Yugoslav Wars following the events of 1989 may be too Eurocentric for some, but it does reflect a common feeling that violent killing was its indelible signature.[1] Little wonder that Eric Hobsbawm, in his popular 1995 overview of the century, *Age of Extremes*, uses the words of Isaiah Berlin, who had lived through most of the century, as an epigram: "I remember it only as the most terrible century in Western history."[2] And in a century characterized by war, mass death, and genocide, Germany predictably occupies a special place.[3] While some have contended that the last century's global violence, brutal population transfers, genocides, and "radical evil" are still disproportionately framed by Hitler's Germany and Stalin's Soviet Union,[4] there is no denying that mass death and Germany are still closely associated terms in the minds of many. The flood of popular histories, television docudramas, and academic assessments on the "Age of Catastrophe" that accompanied the turn of the millennium often put Germany (and in particular the Third Reich) at the very center of twentieth century retrospectives. Indeed, Paul Celan's famous line that "Death is a Master from Germany" has become a favorite epithet of the "German century" as a whole, precisely because it is seen as describing something fundamental about Germany's national experience.[5]

But what exactly? No doubt we are all familiar with Germany's responsibility for both world wars and the Holocaust, actions that brought untold suffering and

---

Notes for this chapter begin on page 18.

grief to millions of soldiers and civilians, Germany's among them. Composing a meaningful narrative that makes sense of this legacy of death and destruction is not as easy as it first appears, though. For one thing, it is not obvious how or why the brutality and decimation that disfigured the first half of the century can or should stand in as somehow representative of the entire period. In regard to Germany, the problem goes far beyond simply better integrating the warring and bloody first half of the century with the relatively peaceful and bloodless second.[6] The deeper question is how to better grasp the place and significance of death across the century. For if the twentieth century is earmarked by the experience of mass death and destruction, then how have the dead impinged upon the lives of the living? That judges, undertakers, psychiatrists, and insurance adjusters have had to deal firsthand with the aftermath of mass death and destruction is plain enough, but it is still surprising that historians have been so reluctant to explore the social meaning of this legacy beyond a Versailles and Nuremberg logic of sitting in judgment about crime, punishment, and the (in)ability to "master the past." Efforts to identify perpetrators and victims of violent misdeeds, important as they are, have provided little in the way of explaining something that is no less urgent to all sides, namely how people—as opposed to states—relate to the dead.

Admittedly, the German case is complicated. Much of this stems from the fact that the cultural place of the dead in Germany has relatively little to do with Germany as a place of death. That is, much of the twentieth-century German experience of death and destruction did not occur in Germany at all. Hardly a shot was fired by enemy soldiers in Germany during the First World War; moreover, most of the annihilation perpetrated by the German military in the Second World War was carried out outside German borders. It was only during the endgame of the war in 1944/45 that the ferocity of what Germany had unleashed on the killing fields of Eastern Europe boomeranged back on Germany and the Germans with such devastating intensity. What this meant was that a large percentage of German war dead, especially soldiers, died outside the homeland, only rarely receiving any proper burial. The alienation of the fallen from the homeland is not so unusual in itself—the same holds true for British, Canadian, American, and Japanese soldiers over the course of the last century; the Australians even fashioned their modern national identity around the distant and lost campaign of Gallipoli in 1916. Indeed, the numerous pilgrimages organized by families and charitable organizations after 1918 in all of the countries that participated in the war (with the exception of the new Soviet Union) underlined the Great War's deeply-felt dislocation of death, nation, and homeland.

For Germans, the Second World War was both a continuation with and a break from this First World War legacy. As in the Great War, many German soldiers died on foreign soil, though this time on the Eastern Front. And while many Germans (including civilians) died on German soil during the ferocious fighting at the very end of World War II, it hardly mattered that they had died at home. Most were quickly interred in so-called "emergency cemeteries" in which neither sacred place nor public thanksgiving played any role whatsoever (see the contributing essays in Part I). The upshot is that these sacrificial deaths—in both cases in service to the Fatherland—went essentially unmarked and that mourning them either proved to be highly divisive, as after World War I, or was postponed and privatized, as after World War II. The collapse of the "symbolic fathers" behind the tragic war campaigns—the Kaiser and Hitler, respectively—only made it more difficult to put these sacrifices in any meaningful narrative framework. Two lost world wars, revolution, and the desperate desire of each postwar German regime to distance itself from its wartime predecessor made it clear to all that the dead, and with them the immediate past, were to be buried as quickly and unceremoniously as possible.

But what about the people? How did they try to come to terms with this confrontation with mass death? In this context Marx's famous sentence from *The 18th Brumaire* comes to mind: "The tradition of all the dead generations weighs like a nightmare on the brain of the living." But what Germany's twentieth-century experience has revealed, especially in light of the world wars, is that Marx's abstract idea of the weight of "dead generations" had become the more pressing burden of encountering real dead bodies in their midst. This was the twentieth century's version of the "nightmare on the brain of the living." The dead exerted a new presence for twentieth-century Germans, haunting their lives and memories like furies in a manner not seen since the Thirty Years' War.

How Germans dealt with the dead over the course of the century is the main question of this volume. It has been suggestively opened up—even if not very satisfactorily—by the publication of W. G. Sebald's *On the Natural History of Destruction*. His is an extended essay published in 1999 on wartime German death from, and postwar reaction to, the Allied bombing campaign in the final years of the war.[7] In it Sebald recounts facts that beggar the imagination: Allied saturation bombing included 131 cities and towns, leaving 600,000 civilians dead.[8] In Dresden, the rubble piled up to 42.8 cubic meters per inhabitant, while 6865 corpses burned in SS funeral pyres raging in the city in February 1945. Everywhere were smoking corpses, melted flesh, and scenes of apocalyptic carnage and suffering. Sebald is disturbed by what he sees as Germans' intentional amnesia of this part of their history, most notably the silence of German writers who were unable or unwilling to confront this matter.

Almost immediately the book attracted great attention and enjoyed wide readership, in no small measure as a result of Sebald's elegiac prose. A dominant interpretation of the book among scholars and general readers has viewed it within the context of Germans' memories of Second World War victimhood, memories that found common expression during the 1990s.[9] Much of this commentary criticized Sebald's book as well as works by Günter Grass and Jörg Friedrich for supposedly harboring revisionist tendencies.[10] But it is misleading to read Sebald's elegy of the mass death of Germans in this narrow context. In fact, Sebald, Grass, and Friedrich could raise the horrors of death of Germans precisely because for over twenty years now scholarship and the arts have focused justifiably on the horrors of death caused by Germans. At the end of the twentieth century, the mass death perpetrated by Germans, in Germany's name, through the machinery of the German state and with horrendous consequences for victims as well as for the nation of killers, dominates the way we think of death in modern Germany.

What is so striking is how little of this was present at the beginning of the century. Consider for example Thomas Mann's famous 1911 novella *Death in Venice*, which chronicled the celebrated poet and holidaymaker Gustave von Aschenbach. In the memorable final scene, Aschenbach's object of affection, the Polish boy Tadzio, dreamily stands waist-high in the waves as the "pale and lovely Summoner," seemingly beckoning the frail and forlorn artist out to sea to join him "in an immensity of richest expectation." Despite the novella's title, death hardly figures much in it (the word is only mentioned four times), and remains to the very end strangely unremarked, hidden, bloodless and singular. The utter solitude of von Aschenbach's death (like his life) is further punctuated by the story's final three sentences: "Some minutes passed before anyone hastened to the aid of the elderly man sitting there collapsed in his chair. They bore him to his room. And before nightfall a shocked and respectful world received the news of his decease."[11] This image of death on a Venetian shore stands in impossible tension with the numbing figures of mass death caused and suffered by Germans just three years later.

How are we to write a history of death in modern Germany that combines long-term sensibilities and short-term cataclysmic violence? The texts of Sebald and Mann serve as a good starting point to show that the two are complementary, not contradictory. *On the Natural History of Destruction* caused such a furor precisely because it connected bourgeois mores, Nazism, and postwar amnesia. It referred to Alexander and Margarete Mitscherlich's famous 1967 book on the German "inability to mourn," which described this mental and emotional incapacity as the result of the Germans' attempt to sever radically the psychological bond to the father-figure Hitler without "working through" his profound influence on them in the first place.[12] "This scandalous deficiency," Sebald writes about the inability to mourn, "reminded me that I had grown up with the feeling that something was being kept from me: at home, at school, and by the German writers whose books I read hoping to glean information about the monstrous events in the background of my own life." This "something" was connected to a German mentality that was central to family life as well as to Nazism: the inability to mourn "make[s] one at least suspect some connection between the German catastrophe ushered in under Hitler's regime and the regulation of intimate feelings within the German family."[13] What began as a story of impersonal horror, numbing facts, and mass death is revealed as a family tale: mass death was related to private life as much as it was to the nation and to ideology.

It is precisely this tension between mass death and individual loss that warrants our attention. German society, like any society, had multiple perceptions of death—private and public, peaceful and violent—that interacted, were in conflict with, and influenced one another. We cannot assume that mass death was an outcome of the context of war with no connections to larger perceptions of death in society before and after the battles. But while we know a great deal about the death cults and killing fields of Nazi-occupied Europe, the broader understanding and meaning of death for Germans both before and after the Nazi period—with the possible exception of the soldier's experiences in, and the apocalyptic imagery of, the First World War—are still quite unknown.

The aim of this book, therefore, is to think through major issues in the history of death in twentieth-century Germany. How and when was death politicized, how and when privatized? Did these changes necessarily and always follow political events? What were the rituals of death in the private sphere, in the family, in cemeteries? How important were the churches and synagogues—that is, religion—in framing these changing understandings of death? What specific developments and forms did death take over the decades? The challenge of this book, then, is to link long-term patterns of mourning, burial, and grief with the short-term cataclysmic violence of the world wars; to link mentalities and emotions with swift historical and ideological changes. This collection of essays, which grew out of a conference at the University of Virginia at Charlottesville in the fall of 2003, seeks to go beyond making another contribution to the vast literature on death, trauma, and memory. Its purpose is to think through some of the possibilities of a cultural and social history of death in modern German history, with a view toward presenting starting points and ideas for future research.

I.

To make clear what was new about the twentieth century, it pays to sketch briefly the pre-1914 context. In this regard, Mann's literary representation of death was perfectly in keeping with some the broader trends in the "culture of death" in the Western world over the course of the nineteenth century. As Philippe Ariès has argued, the nineteenth century witnessed a gradual secularization of death and its attendant commemorative rituals. In part this was due to the loosening of the churches' long-time monopoly over the rites and rhetoric involved in properly seeing off the departed. But such changes were also linked to a gradual "privatization of death," best seen in the decline of public mourning and communal participation in a member's passing. Increasingly the bereaved family turned inward, and grieving was driven indoors as nineteenth-century European society grew more distant and indifferent toward the death of neighbors and fellow townsmen.[14] In a similar development, capital punishment was transformed from a public spectacle into an administrative act performed behind closed doors.[15] To be sure, the bourgeois trend toward large gravestones and funereal statuary across Europe marked this inward shift, arising as compensation for the once rich social pageantry surrounding the death of community notables. The growing theatricality surrounding the burial of royals and military leaders, fallen soldiers and newly minted "national heroes," was an effort to provide a new collective framework for individual death by inventing fresh traditions of secular service, patriotic sacrifice, and national belonging.[16] Nevertheless, it was the newly felt alienation of the individual shorn of the comforts of history and community that earmarked much of nineteenth-century thought and cultural life.[17]

The Romantic preoccupation with sentimental "sublime death" was also in many ways a reaction against what was seen as a growing cultural apathy toward individual life and death. In this sense, von Aschenbach's demise neatly drew on what had become by then a well-known model of artistic death, underlining as it did the poet's utter loneliness (which notably was no better back home in Munich, where he "grew up solitary and without comradeship") and estrangement from others. That the grief of his death would be felt only by his distant fans ("a shocked and respectable world") upon reading his obituary in the next day's newspaper—rather than in the midst of family and friends—dramatized the fundamentally modern quality of his passing.[18] Indeed, one could read Mann's novella as primarily a meditation on the meaning of immortality itself, juxtaposing the poet's quest for "the eternal" with the tawdry allures and deadening effects of literary fame.

What is so intriguing here is just how decisively the European imagery of and cultural contact with death changed with the outbreak of the First World War. The distant, abstract quality of death in Mann's story now took on sharp immediacy and palpable presence. The daily confrontation with mortality on the fighting front and the harrowing effects of industrialized mass killing there radically shaped the experiences and memories of all involved, as death became a strangely familiar fixture of combat life everywhere. Paul Fussell's famous thesis that the First World War forever killed off the Victorian world of martial dreams and delusions (be it about the glories of "civilization," military valor, the wisdom of commanding officers, or the hypocrisy of the old recruiting clincher "dulce et decorum est pro patria mori") is less widely accepted than it once was. No doubt there is some truth to Fussell's claim that the war brokered a new "ironic" sensibility among the war generation, one in which a host of modernist modes of expression were given a fresh lease to describe a brave new world of Industrial Age warfare and its gruesome consequences.[19] But he is less convincing about the supposed shared feeling of malaise and despondency among common soldiers on all sides toward war and mass killing. More recently, scholars have countered that many soldiers actually adjusted quite well to the new circumstances, even so far as enjoying the "pleasures of war" and the ruthless slaughter amid these "storms of steel."[20] Others have taken aim at the notion of the Great War's modernizing effect on cultural sensibilities, showing that the war in no way shattered nineteenth-century structures of meaning in the face of wartime loss and devastation. On the contrary, traditional and especially Christian imagery (above all, the Apocalypse) was commonly used as comfort and guidance in making sense of unrelenting destruction and terror.[21] New case studies have confirmed the extent to which soldiers were able to cope with the experience of mass death in the trenches by means of religious faith and communication with their loved ones at home through a steady stream of letter-writing.[22] But even if the structures of meaning remained quite traditional, the industrial-scale "murder in our midst" was not.[23]

War of course was no stranger to culture. In the German case, there is a long tradition of war literature, dating back to Grimmelshausen's *Adventures of Simplicius Simplicissimus* on the Thirty Years' War, to Büchner's *Danton's Death* after the Napoleonic Wars, to C. D. Grabbe's *Napoleon, or the 100 Days*. Death itself became a favorite theme of German literature and philosophy over the course of the nineteenth century, and the concept of man-made mass death even featured prominently in Hegel's thought.[24] What is so interesting, however, is that this tradition was hardly invoked at all during the Great War as compass, context, or consolation. No doubt some of this had to do with the "long peace" of the nineteenth century itself, which was relatively bloodless compared to its seventeenth- and eighteenth-century predecessors. After all, the longest war of the century between 1815 and 1914 in the Western world was the American Civil War, in which some 600,000 Americans lost their lives in the new republic's traumatic "fratricide" of the early 1860s. That war and death lost their traumatic quality in German culture may also be the result of success, as German (more precisely, Prussian) military campaigns—at least after 1813—were relatively quick, decisive, and triumphant. After the War of Liberation against Napoleon, the virtues of the citizen-soldier and his sacrifice for the nation came to occupy a prominent place in public discourse across the German lands, as noted in the writings of Theodor Koerner and Ernst Moritz Arndt.[25] Moreover, associations of war veterans, which sprang up all over the country in Imperial Germany following the Unification Wars of 1864–1871, helped popularize an image of war that downplayed the horrors of dying against the gallantry of the warrior.[26] Tales of wartime sacrifice and honor were then enlisted for the nationalist cause, as the glories of the Prussian Army were to become the bedrock of German national pride and identity.[27]

But in the effort to convert Prussian military triumphs into new national history, stories of loss and suffering enjoyed little prominence. This contrasted markedly with those countries that suffered from German invasion, such as France. As Ariès observes, it "was in France after 1870 that the memory of the dead came to be more precisely preserved and the dead venerated."[28] For France, whose national identity had then been badly wounded, linked to pain and death, a traumatized "culture of defeat" was now motivated by redeeming the dead in a future revenge campaign against the hated Germans.[29] Yet such anti-Prussian feeling could be felt within Germany as well, as the effort to turn the new nation into an enlarged Prussian barracks with goose-stepping pomp and circumstance met with skepticism and contempt among Catholic and anti-Prussian provinces such as Baden, Württemberg, and Bavaria. Nowhere was this more apparent than in the failure to make Sedan Day into a true celebratory national holiday, as identities in life and death largely remained regional and religious.[30] Thus in terms of its commemorative culture of death, Germany was still very much a "nation of provincials."[31] The construction of alternative pantheons to remember and honor "anti-Bismarckian" heroes, such the revolutionary martyrs of 1848 and key socialist leaders, further vitiated any "nationalization of death" based on common sacrifice and a shared canon of great Germans past.[32] The German army's colonial adventures in Africa and Asia, including the brutal suppression of the Herero in Southwest Africa during 1904–1907, may have provided cause for national pride in a mass-mediated Age of Imperialism. But even in these far-flung engagements, the fallen played no real great role in the national imagination.[33] The larger point is that over the course of the nineteenth century, the dead were quite remote from the meaning and maintenance of the German nation.

With the end of the First World War, all that changed. The dead were now omnipresent, haunting the Weimar Republic from its very beginning. In large measure this of course was due to the lost war effort and the infamous "stab in the back" legend, as the fallen comrades were seen by many disgruntled survivors (and not just the military and right-wing) as having been betrayed by the new Socialist government. The harsh "Carthaginian Peace" imposed by the Allies at the Paris Peace Conference and the creation of a shaky new republic as the "evil fruit" of national loss and humiliation did nothing to put the war dead to rest. On the contrary, the widely perceived illegitimacy of the Weimar state coupled with the unleashing of popular nationalism—itself a byproduct of the war— further fueled Germany's own "culture of defeat" across the political spectrum.[34] And if John Keane is right in saying that "[a]s a rule, crises are times during which the living do battle for the hearts, minds and souls of the dead,"[35] then there is no better example than the Weimar Republic. If nothing else, the wave of political assassinations in the early 1920s, the militarization of politics, and the real fear that civil war might become the consequence of the lost world war dramatized to what extent the unredeemed war dead lorded over interwar politics.[36] The presence of the dead was equally manifest in Weimar literature and art, as well as in popular picture books about the war.[37] Death emerged as a favorite theme in German philosophy and cultural criticism (as noted in the work of Heidegger, Bloch, Benjamin, and Adorno among others) as never before.[38] War memoirs and letters from soldiers describing life and death on the front were reprinted and became best-sellers at the time.[39] Not least, the ubiquity of the First World War statuary, gravestones, and popular pilgrimages to battle sites further underlined this new civic cult of the fallen soldier after 1918.[40] As was shown by the ultimately inconclusive debate about the site and aesthetic form of a central memorial for the German war dead, however, Germans were deeply divided over the political meaning of their sacrifice.[41]

Hitler's assumption of power in 1933 ushered in a new understanding of the place of the dead in German political life. On one level, the Third Reich's new order was an extension of Mussolini's own conception of "trenchocracy" and the fascist romance with the Great War's fighting front. At stake, though, was much more than the widely shared conviction that the First World War, despite its outcome, was the genuine birth of the German nation, or that the political world should be remade according to the spirit and solidarity of trench life. What fueled a good deal of Nazi ideology was the notion that the soldiers of the First World War had died in vain, and that their sacrifice still had to be redeemed for the good of the nation. For Nazis, it was bad enough that the objects of wartime self-sacrifice—king and empire—were no more; worse, however, was that the postwar social-democratic government, in its desperate effort to distance itself from the *Kaiserreich* and the failed war effort, was seen to have done precious little in the way of honoring and integrating the defenders of the Fatherland, living or dead.

To make good on his promise to undo the shame and dishonor of the "republican interregnum," Hitler vastly expanded the pageantry surrounding the hallowed dead. The elaborate commemorations, bestowed on both the heroes of the First World War and the NSDAP's own stormtrooper martyrs killed during the 1920s and 1930s in street clashes with their leftist opponents, neatly illustrated how the fallen were enlisted as honorary members of the Third Reich, overseeing and inspiring its expansionist "politics of revenge."[42] Hitler's high-profile 1933 closure of the Prosecuting Office at Leipzig, which was formally created on Allied insistence to investigate German war crimes during the First World War, thus was more than simply withdrawing Germany from the League of Nations as an assertion of national sovereignty. It pivoted on restoring the honor of the German soldiers past and present. His 1940 command to his troops occupying Belgium to raze any and all Belgian monuments commemorating civilian victims of First World War German atrocities also reflected his abiding concern for keeping alive the spirit of the dead in the name of unity and justice.[43]

The Second World War radicalized the German relationship between the living and the dead. Hitler's symbolic desire to revive the dead went hand in hand with killing many of the living, as German war and occupation turned all of Europe into an immense killing field of lethal proportions. By 1939 the genocidal war was already well under way in Poland as the first *Einsatzgruppen* shot thousands of Jews and members of the Polish elites;[44] revealingly, the term that Poles used to try to describe Nazi-occupied Poland was Germany's "Todesraum," or "Death Space."[45] Three years later the Holocaust was unfolding with harrowing intensity.

But it was not only this brutal racism and systematic politics of extermination that distinguished the Second World War from its forerunner. Devastating as it was, the First World War was predominantly a rural conflict, one that left cities and their civilian populations largely intact. In the Second World War, by contrast, urban civilians were not only terrorized by total war, but eventually became the very targets of military destruction. In other words, however much war haunted the Weimar Republic and early Nazi years, it was largely confined to the experiences and memories of men, and soldiers at that. After 1918 this fissure between soldiers and civilians was thus the main dividing line of German society, undergirded as it was by a sacred and exclusionary notion of the "front generation." The Second World War in turn widened the direct experience of the terror of combat, as industrial modern war itself was now brought into everyone's life. With it came a new and everyday familiarity with death, even for children.[46]

The invocation of the dead for continued sacrifice and killing even in the face of mounting corpses and imminent national defeat drove home the extent to which "the dead had come to rule the living." Goebbels himself had noted this in December 1942, when he wrote—with a note of pride—that "we cannot even imagine today the powers which the dead possess over the living."[47] This will to kill and self-sacrifice—be it for reasons of ideological commitment, religious devotion, or more personal motives of familial obligation—was part of the claim that the dead exacted on the living, and may have been the defining moment that underpinned the collective "German catastrophe." As Konrad Jarausch and Michael Geyer put it: "[i]f there was something like a collective experience, it was the encounter with mass death, with irretrievable loss."[48]

The twentieth century's encounter with mass death was, of course, not limited to Germany. While large parts of Eastern Europe in the first half of the century went through a harrowing sequence of war, civil war, oppression, and war again, Russia also had to endure famines as well as various waves of persecutions and purges, before facing the onslaught and devastating retreat of the German military machine. China, struggling through a civil war since the late 1920s, found itself, along with other parts of Southeast Asia, brutally attacked and occupied by Japan. Decolonization, new civil wars, and ideologically motivated persecution left millions dead in Asia and Africa in the decades after 1945. What may have set Germany apart was the rapid succession of experiences of peace and prosperity, then war and violence in the fairly short timespan of less than forty years, coupled with the responsibility it bore for both wars and the Holocaust.

The collapse of the Third Reich and the physical destruction of Germany altered the relationship between individual death and the nation. To be sure, this was hardly limited to Germany, as antiwar sentiment was deeply felt across war-torn Europe after the cease-fire.[49] In fact, one could argue that the wartime myth of heroism and brotherhood at the front was in many ways one of the casualties of the Second World War. Even so, this revulsion toward martial values and the fusion of war and national identity enjoyed unique resonance in Germany, where the *Wehrmacht* was completely dissolved by the Allies and a decade passed before new military forces were set up under close supervision by the same Allies. The rejection of a national identity grounded in military virtues was especially pronounced in the Federal Republic. This could also be seen in the disinclination to build war memorials and collective cemeteries. As Mosse noted, "[i]n spite of outward appearance of the war cemeteries, which looked like those of the First World War, there was a new attempt to emphasize the individual dead, in keeping with postwar liberalism."[50] While this "denationalization" of death was a common trend across Western Europe,[51] the cultural inability, or unwillingness, to commemorate the war dead--especially soldiers—in any meaningful, postfascist collective framework was a distinctive trait of West German society.[52] Similar tendencies could even be detected in West German death announcements, whose language was markedly low-key, family-based, and shorn of the old rhetorical conventions of social standing, sacrificial honor, and redemptive pathos.[53] For

Sebald, this "inability to mourn" the dead was in many ways the foundational moment of West German society, based as it was on the "well-kept secret of the corpses built into the foundations of our [West German] state, a secret that bound all Germans together in the postwar years, and indeed still binds them, more closely than any positive goal such as the realization of democracy ever could."[54] How secret or silent this postwar sensibility really was has of course been the subject of recent debate. But what Sebald seems to have correctly identified is his country's broken kinship between the living and the dead.

But this is not to say that there was not a great deal of talk about the lost war after 1945. Obviously there was, even if it was not nearly as contrite as Allied re-education authorities and victims of Nazism wished it to be. In this regard, Robert Moeller's pioneering 2001 book, *War Stories,* has furnished a revealingly different account of West German storytelling about the war. What Moeller has persuasively shown is how adept West Germans were in developing their own rhetoric of victimization to go alongside the mythmaking being produced en masse in France, Belgium, Holland, and elsewhere.[55] Indeed, a new language of victimhood replaced the language of heroism that accompanied the ceasefire of 1918. It was in this respect that the German expellees and POWs still imprisoned in the Soviet Union (some of whom were not released until 1955) proved so instrumental in a West Germany's postfascist discourse of suffering and victimhood. Their pain and suffering (and anticommunist credentials) in Soviet camps became transposed into a story of the suffering nation as a whole.[56] But unlike the situation following the First World War, these new "rhetorics of victimization" did not fuel any revanchist fantasies or demands for retribution. Unconditional surrender, the Nuremberg Trials, Allied Occupation, and the emerging Cold War—wherein issues of the past were subordinated to the speedy integration of each rival German republic into its respective Cold War orbit—all combined to discourage the formation of any toxic "Stalingrad syndrome" that might mobilize postwar passions. What further distinguished post-1945 sensibilities from the interwar period is that virtually all of the feelings of kinship and concern were projected onto living soldiers in captivity. By comparison the public's emotional connection to the dead soldiers—which after the First World War had been so decisive for this "politics of revenge"—was noticeably absent. While the presence of the POWs in the East along with the difficult integration of the expellees—about half a million of whom had died on the way—indicated that there was still a good deal of unfinished business from the Second World War, the dead no longer ruled the living.

The East German case is very different. Given the shaky beginnings and shallow historical roots of the GDR, it is no great surprise that the new regime used a range of socialist luminaries to write a new, redemptive history of German communism. The SED, East Germany's ruling Communist Party, wasted little time in constructing a new pantheon of German and Soviet communists to whom the new republic owed its inspiration and direction. The great communist struggle against fascism became the bedrock of the new state, and its victory over "Western imperialism" was the touchstone myth of the new socialist society. Such commemoration dominated the political calendar, street parades, school system and cultural world;[57] so strong was the GDR's ancestor worship that GDR playwright Heiner Mueller once called the GDR "a state dominated by the dead" (*ein Staat der Toten*), not least because the "dead provided the legitimation of the GDR."[58] True, not all of the dead were counted as witnesses to socialist victory; neither Jewish victims of Nazi genocidal racism nor Christian resisters found any resonance in the GDR's new socialist cosmos of antifascist heroes.[59]

But how was this official relationship between the living the dead received, and how did it change? While there is still not much material on this theme, it is safe to say that the SED's injunction to honor great socialists past as moral compass for the future faded with time, especially among youth, who were disinclined toward such ancestor worship. The increasing presence of religion in the GDR not only offered an alternative worldview and a vital haven of dissent, it also provided different answers to the larger questions about life and death. Our knowledge of citizen attitudes toward death in the GDR is still scant; what we have usually comes from the world of literature and the arts. But as Felix Schulz shows in his contribution to this volume, the study of funeral and burial rites in East Germany affords new insights into the changing attitude toward death among common citizens beyond the prescriptions of state socialism.

German Reunification in 1990 also brought with it a changed attitude toward the dead. With the dismantling of the Berlin Wall, not only was the Cold War reduced to new museum objects, but the enduring power and presence of World War II—including its dead—within postwar German identity politics also became instant history.[60] This may seem puzzling to some readers, given for example the passionate discussion about the new capital's Jewish Museum and the Holocaust Memorial, which were commonly seen as key litmus tests for Germany's post-Reunification attitude toward the Nazi period and its victims.[61] In the 1990s German cultural attention also focused on the end of Second World War, and especially the Allied bombing campaigns against German civilians. If nothing else, the popularity of the books by Sebald, Grass, and Friedrich reflected the ongoing fascination with the war and its legacy, and seemed to have put the lie to the worry that a reunified Germany would suffer from collective amnesia and "memory deficit." The statuary of atonement for German war crimes has now been placed in the very heart of the capital.

But commemoration is not necessarily the same thing as remembrance; as Robert Musil once remarked, "there is nothing in the world as invisible as monuments." Leaving aside the whole question of the utility of such monumentalized memory, the 1990s memory boom seems to confirm the long-standing rightwing view that "only a united Germany can take on the task of mourning properly."[62] However one interprets this, the main point is that the dead in no way seem to haunt the "Berlin Republic." Indeed, it could be argued that instead of invoking the spirit of the dead, these new memorials have helped lay the dead to rest in the public imagination. Whether the ghosts of the past will stay buried is anyone's guess. But Sebald's perception that the dead are just beneath the smooth floorboards of the "economic miracle"—unburied and unatoned, and still wandering among the living—apparently belongs to another age.

II.

This volume is dedicated to exploring many of these issues from a variety of perspectives. It may not be surprising that out of the fourteen essays in this book, eight deal directly with the First and Second World Wars. But this only raises the question: How are we to understand the mass death within a larger context of ongoing sensibilities about death in German society? How was the history of funerals, rituals, or burial sites connected to wartime mass death, if at all? The focus on mass death has kept a wide range of other, troubling questions about the presence of death in German life from being asked. Our collection of essays proposes to go beyond the focus on wartime death, its memory, and its ideological usage. The aim is to explore how notions of death operated in German culture and society before, during, and after the world wars. We ask: What was the place of death in German society? What was the status of the dead in society, their place in emotional, physical terms? What obligations did the living owe the dead? How did the dead threaten the living? How did the living exploit the dead for their own social, cultural, political, personal, emotional needs? Differently put, what was the "exchange and interaction between the living and the dead"[63] in an age of mass death?

To be sure, medievalists have been at the forefront of investigating many of these issues in recent years, and those of us specializing in the modern period would do well to follow their lead in thinking more carefully about the role and significance of the dead in modern life.[64] After all, the twentieth century hardly enjoys a monopoly on mass death and destruction. New research has begun to consider the place of the twentieth century in a much broader historical context. One recent volume, for example, sets out to compare the twentieth century with the fourteenth and seventeenth centuries—which witnessed the Black Death and Hundred Years' War on one hand, and the gruesome Thirty Years' War on the other—as kindred centuries of "power, violence and mass death" in their own right.[65] Alas, the twentieth century was unique both in the scale and intensity of killing, as this text has already pointed out at various times.

For the purposes of presentation, we chose to focus on two main themes. The first, Part I and II on "bodies" and "disposals," emphasizes the materiality the dead leave behind, such as the body, the burial, and the cemetery and especially the centrality of the body in the spatial and cultural surrounding. The second, Parts III and IV on "subjectivity" and "ruins," explores how the living interact with dead by imagining them. It takes its inspiration from the simple yet profound insight that whatever is said and practiced about death is not a result of experiencing it. This is a topic that calls for a study of the imagination.

Part I, "Bodies," addresses how mass killing was militarily produced and how Germans coped with their landscape of destroyed bodies after 1945. Giving meaning to mass death was linked to the circumstances under which it occurred, and to how the dead could be buried and their graves cared for. New forms of mourning had to be found and old ones adapted. Michael Geyer opens the discussion by exploring the links between the fear of death and killing in the First World War and their ramifications for the Second. In contrast to commonly held assumptions, Geyer contends that instead of decreasing, German soldiers' will to fight increased over the course of the war. German soldiers also killed much more effectively than their counterparts. Drawing upon field manuals and military reports, Geyer shows how the German army learned to overcome the key problem of modern warfare, dealing with an enemy's tremendous firepower. Breaking up military units into small groups of soldiers who moved with a high degree of independence on the battlefield, jointly operating highly lethal weapons such as machine guns and flame throwers, made each soldier's survival dependent, paradoxically, on his aggressiveness. Thus, Geyer concludes, the "principle of permanent tactical self-defense" became, in ideology and practice, the driving force of the German way to make war.

The experience of death and attitudes toward it in 1945 is the focus of Richard Bessel's contribution. Bessel points out that never before had Germans been confronted with death on the scale of the last months of the war, when almost one million German soldiers and civilians died on German soil as a result of the Allied offensives and bombing campaigns, as well as the regime's executions of alleged defeatists. Hundreds of thousands died as they attempted to flee the advancing Soviet troops or were expelled from their homes in the East. Thousands of people committed suicide as Nazi rule collapsed, and countless civilians in the East became the victims of rape. As the German landscape was littered with corpses, coming across unburied dead became an everyday occurrence. When the Allies attempted to confront the Germans with the death they had wrought in the concentration camps, the general German response was a heightened sense of the Germans' own victimhood.

Monica Black takes up the various ways in which, long after the death and killing associated with the war were over, death continued to stalk the Berlin landscape and the imaginations of Berliners. Emergency burial sites outside of regular cemeteries became part of the city landscape in 1945. While during the "Third Reich" non-Aryan Germans often had been denied a "proper burial," now many ordinary Germans were buried in irregular ways. How Berliners came to terms with this experience, Black argues, was indicative of their complex relationship with the Nazi past. By rejecting the construction of mass graves, formerly reserved for racial "others" and now imposed by occupation authorities, Berliners claimed to continue Germany's tradition of a *Kulturvolk* and to distance themselves from the Nazi past. At the same time, protecting emergency burial sites from dissolution contributed to a sense of German victimhood.

The four essays in Part II, "Disposal," explore how the living disposed of the dead, focusing on the changes in burial practices from the late nineteenth to the late twentieth century in the private and the public sphere.

Simone Ameskamp's contribution examines the rise of cremation. The first crematorium in modern Germany was built in Gotha in 1878. The urban Protestants who constituted the backbone of the cremation movement emphasized the modernity, cleanliness, and dignity of the practice, and linked it to German values. Catholics until 1963 were supposed to heed a papal decree banning it. Proponents and opponents of the practice disagreed on whether nature should run its course or not, on whether cremation meant a regression to paganism or an embrace of modernity, and on what constituted the self. Drawing upon statistical evidence that indicated a steady growth of cremation, Ameskamp shows that the world wars had little impact on its success. The rise of cremationism, as she points out, also militates against Philippe Ariès' argument that the Enlightenment paved the way for the denial and repression of death.

Felix Robin Schulz discusses the changing burial practices in East Germany after 1945. Why were these practices, so notoriously resistant to change, so thoroughly transformed under the Communist regime? The war, argues Schulz, had little impact on them, as they returned to traditional forms almost immediately after the war had ended. While there was a desire in the SED to create burial practices that were socialist in content, Schulz suggests that the dramatic changes that eventually occurred in East Germany (resulting, for example, in the development of *Urnengemeinschaftsgräber*) were largely caused by material constraints rather than ideological motives. East German burial practices were chiefly oriented toward disposing of the dead as efficiently as possible, and they met with lukewarm responses in rural areas and complaints about the bleak way burials were conducted.

Kay Schiller examines the conflict between the intended image of the 1972 Olympic Games and the tragedy of the Israeli athletes' massacre. He sees the perception and interpretation of the event as a transitory stage in West German attempts to come to terms with the Nazi past. The Munich Games used an aesthetic approach that eschewed politics in its attempt to overcome the 1936 Berlin Olympics precedent. The image projected at the Munich Olympics stressed a cosmopolitan, peace-loving Germany, and wedded technology to aesthetics to emphasize clarity, lightness, and transparency. This aesthetic was the inversion of the monumental, ponderous scale of Berlin in 1936. In the aftermath of the murder of the Israeli athletes, Schiller argues, the discourse that arose conflated the victims and their Olympic hosts, but it also contributed to the much more intense examination of the Nazi past after 1990.

Paul Betts explores a different perspective of the official postwar culture of death in his essay on the funerals of Adenauer and Ulbricht as means of state self-representation. Adenauer's funeral allowed for a public confirmation of West Germany's Western integration, rapprochement with France, and *Wiedergutma-*

chung with Israel. Adenauer was styled as a redeemer, but more importantly, as a civil servant of the state to which he bore allegiance. In the case of Ulbricht, although at the time of his death he had fallen from the party's grace and become an *Unperson*, the resonance of his death with the people of the GDR was remarkable and had to be recognized by the SED. His funeral affirmed his place in the history of German communism and confirmed his status as a private citizen devoted to public work. Significantly, narratives of aggrieved nationalism, tragedy, and heroism were absent in both funerals. In the end, these ceremonies were not about nation-building; rather, they represented the internalization of the division of Germany and the allegiance of each political patriarch to his cherished state.

Part III, "Subjectivity," captures the attempt to imagine death through humor, solace, and grief. When Germans laughed about death and mourned the dead, traditions mattered, as did community bonds and local customs. And yet, both humor and grief helped "normalize" the new violence of the world wars.

Tim Grady explores how mourning served as a common denominator in a divided society: how Germans commemorated during and immediately after 1918 the German-Jewish soldiers of the First World War. Wartime death had a profound emotional impact on all sections of German-Jewish life. Grady gives this argument an innovative interpretation: against the common historiographical view that sees the war as marking a negative turning point in German Jewish/non-Jewish relations, Grady shows that Jewish and non-Jewish war dead had been commemorated after 1918 together in the same remembrance sites, thus creating "a common experience of death." Focusing on the cities of Hamburg and Würzburg, Grady analyzes the many areas in which Jews crossed religious and ethnic divides to remember the war dead together with non-Jewish Germans.

Martina Kessel discusses how humor served as an instrument to cope with death. Over the course of the nineteenth century, she argued, a particular German concept of humor had developed that explicitly rejected irony and focused on telling the truth. The humorous soldier became part of this concept from the 1860s on. In the First World War, German propaganda used jokes to counter stories of German atrocities and to help soldiers come to terms with the unpredictability of death by inverting the stereotypes used by enemy propaganda and emphasizing the value of order. Following the Nazi stormtroopers' cultivation of this tradition of humor during the Weimar Republic, Nazi propaganda in the Second World War II largely avoided referring to the difficult character of the present war. At the same time, a culture of oral jokes (Flüsterwitze) emerged among the population that included addressing the murderous policy of the regime, albeit indirectly.

Alon Confino's essay explores the tension and the commingling between the Nazi attempt to build a revolutionary cultural system and the traditional, mostly religious, rites of death that were notoriously resistant to change. As the Second World War became protracted and the losses mounted, who and what provided spiritual sustenance to the bereaved? Here, argues Confino, were the limits of

Nazi ideology and death rituals: the Party offered a general truth and a national, collective cause, but for many religious Germans it could not quite offer personal redemption and promise of an afterlife. The Nazis could not monopolize the spiritual element in death in a society that was largely religious, whereas the church provided spiritual assistance in death, but in language that often provided support to the regime. The point is not that Nazism "lost" or "won" against religion; it is rather that lived Nazism—the way people actually experienced it—successfully commingled Nazi and religious practices.

Gabriel Finder examines how the Jewish tradition of mourning the dead was adapted by Jewish "Displaced Persons" (DPs) and took on a political thrust in the immediate postwar years. While *yizkor*, the traditional communal memorial service for the dead, remained the prevailing form of commemoration among the surviving religious and nonreligious Jewish DPs alike, mass death and the anonymity of its victims did not allow for the ceremonies that traditionally guided a family's gradual separation from their dead. *Landsmanshaftn*, associations of survivors from the same localities, took care of burials and published memorial books as virtual gravestones for those communities annihilated by Nazi Germany. Public remembrances of the dead became coupled with calls for creating a safe Jewish homeland in Palestine. As Israel was being founded, a day of remembrance and liberation that Jewish DPs established in May faded in competition with the date of the Warsaw uprising.

Finally, Part IV, "Ruins," focuses on the psychological scars of mass death. The three chapters in this section investigate how those were represented in language, how people came to terms with them, and how this differed between the public and the private sphere.

Svenja Goltermann explores the tortuous mix of acknowledgment and denial of mass death during the 1950s in West Germany. Goltermann criticizes historians for treating the concept of trauma as self-evident, for the concept has a history and postwar contemporaries did not yet refer to it. Drawing upon psychiatric case files of former soldiers, women on the homefront, and Jewish survivors, she demonstrates how memories of the war experience were constructs mediated by postwar language, imagination, and *ex post* knowledge. In addition to the conflicting emotions of guilt and suffering, the pressures of maintaining family bonds and keeping to ideals of manliness also had an impact on these memories. German society in the 1950s, Goltermann argues, was a "society driven by angst" but expressing it in multiple and dissonant voices, including silence.

Daniel Steuer explores the writings of the late W. G. Sebald, in particular his *On the Natural History of Destruction*. Sebald, argues Steuer, presents us with a unique case of a German writer who was able—through the use of an aesthetic strategy that Steuer refers to as "critical melancholy"—to write from the perspective of the victims of Nazi terror. Steuer criticizes Sebald, however, for unreservedly subscribing to the Mitscherlich's thesis of the Germans' "inability to mourn," and he contrasts it with Adorno's more complex view of the causes of guilt and the modes of expressing it. Steuer sees Sebald's position as akin to that of the '68 generation: their members failed to listen to the war generation and then accused it of not having anything to say about the Nazi past.

Finally, Peter Fritzsche critically addresses the resurgence of interest in German suffering during and after the Second World War since the 1990s. Drawing upon two recent novels by Reinhard Jirgl and Stephan Wackwitz, he warns against interpreting it as a "conventional normalization" of the Nazi past. This renewed interest, Fritzsche argues, is not characterized by the self-righteousness of either the immediate postwar years and their insistence on German victimhood, or the '68 movement and its unequivocal condemnation of the father-generation. Instead, he points out, it represents a shift to an acknowledgment of the complexity of guilt and suffering that breaks down the dichotomy between ordinary Germans and Nazi perpetrators.

These essays together make a strong case for what is known but rarely comprehensively analyzed, namely that a social and cultural history of death in modern Germany is important and deserves much more scholarly attention. Given the country's twentieth-century experience, it is no wonder that death figures at its very center. As an interpretative whole, the essays suggest that Philippe Ariès may have been right when he emphasized that long-term trends in the history of death are not directly affected by political events. Neither the two world wars and the Holocaust nor the changes in political regimes seem to have fundamentally changed burial practices and the language and rites of mourning. "Dignity" remained the key value. What these essays also show, however, in one way or another, is that the dead were very much alive in the minds of the living for most the century, so much so that at times the bonds with the dead were maintained at the expense of solidarity with the living. Reconsidering the presence of these ghosts is central to this volume. In this regard, we should give credence to a mid-1960s diary entry by West German writer Peter Weiss that posits that writing is an attempt "to preserve our equilibrium among the living with all our dead within us, as we lament the dead and with our death before our eyes."[66] And for most Germans who lived through the twentieth century, such a view was commonly shared.

Notes

1. Alf Lüdtke and Bernd Weisbrod, eds., *No Man's Land of Violence: Extreme Wars in the 20th Century* (Göttingen, 2006).
2. Eric Hobsbawm, *The Age of Extremes* (New York, 1995), 1.
3. Dan Diner, *Das Jahrhundert verstehen: Eine universalhistorische Deutung* (Munich, 1999) and Omer Bartov, Atina Grossman and Mary Nolan, eds., *Crimes of War: Guilt and Denial in the Twentieth Century* (New York, 2002).
4. Mark Mazower, "Violence and the State in the 20th Century," *American Historical Review* 107, no. 2 (October 2002): 1158–1178.

5. Eberhard Jäckel, *Das deutsche Jahrhundert: Eine historische Bilanz* (Stuttgart, 1996).
6. On this theme, see the special issue on "Histories and Memories of 20th Century Germany" edited by Alon Confino, *History and Memory* 17, nos. 1/2 (fall, 2005) as well as Paul Betts and Greg Eghigian, eds., *Pain and Prosperity: Reconsidering Twentieth Century German History* (Palo Alto, 2003).
7. The text was first delivered as a series of lectures in Zurich in 1997 and published in German in 1999 entitled "Airwar and Literature" and in English as *On the Natural History of Destruction. With Essays on Alfred Andersch, Jean Améry and Peter Weiss*, trans. Anthea Bell (London, 2003). The original German edition did not contain the essays on Améry and Weiss.
8. Recent research has given a lower figure (around 400,000). See Ralf Blank, 'Kriegsalltag und Luftkrieg an der "Heimatfront,"' in Jörg Echternkamp, ed., *Die Deutsche Kriegsgesellschaft 1939 bis 1945* (Munich, 2004), 357–461.
9. Bill Niven, ed., *Germans as Victims* (London, 2006).
10. For a good analysis, Robert Moeller, "Sinking Ships, the Lost Heimat and Broken Taboos: Günter Grass and the Politics of Memory in Contemporary Germany," *Contemporary European History* 12 (2003): 1–35.
11. Thomas Mann, *Death in Venice and Seven Other Stories*, trans. H.T. Lowe-Porter (New York, 1954), 75.
12. Alexander and Margarete Mitscherlich, *Die Unfähigkeit zu Trauern: Grundlagen kollektiven Verhaltens* (Munich, 1967), English edition, *The Inability to Mourn: Principles of Collective Behavior*, trans. Beverley R. Placzek (New York, 1975).
13. Sebald, *Natural History*, 84.
14. Phillippe Ariès, *The Hour of Our Death*, trans. Helen Weaver (Oxford, 1981), 409–616. A more contradictory view can be found in Michelle Perrot, ed., *A History of Private Life, vol. 4: From the Fires of the Revolution to the Great War* (Cambridge, 1990), 331–337. For England, see Geoffrey Gorer, *Death, Grief and Mourning in Contemporary Britain* (Garden City, NJ, 1965).
15. Richard J. Evans, *Rituals of Retribution. Capital Punishment in Germany, 1600–1987* (Oxford, 1996).
16. David Cannadine, "The Context, Performance and Meaning of Ritual: The British Monarchy and the 'Invention of Tradition', c. 1820–1877," in Eric Hobsbawm and Terence Ranger, eds., *The Invention of Tradition* (Cambridge, 1983), 101–164.
17. Peter Fritzsche, *Stranded in the Present* (Cambridge, Mass, 2004).
18. On this theme, Norbert Elias, *The Loneliness of Dying*, trans. Edmund Jephcott (London, 1985).
19. Paul Fussell, *The Great War and Modern Memory* (Oxford, 1975). See also Samuel Hynes, *A War Imagined: The Great War and English Culture* (London, 1991).
20. Joanna Bourke, *An Intimate History of Killing: Face to Face Killing in Twentieth Century Warfare* (New York, 1999).
21. Jay Winter, *Sites of Memory, Sites of Mourning: The Great War in European Cultural History* (Cambridge, 1995) and *Facing Armegeddon: The First World War Experienced*, eds. Hugh Cecil and Peter H. Liddle (London, 1996). In this regard, it is worth noting that Ariès's thesis about the secularization of death is not all that applicable to Germany. Despite partial de-Christianization, in particular in the Socialist labor movement, burial rites were still largely the domain of the churches; in fact, recent research shows that the number of Protestant burials even increased in Prussia and Württemberg between 1880 and 1914. Gerhard Ritter and Klaus Tenfelde, *Arbeiter im Deutschen Kaiserreich 1871–1914* (Bonn, 1992), 176–77.
22. Benjamin Ziemann, *Front und Heimat: Ländliche Kriegserfahrungen im südlichen Bayern 1914–1923* (Essen, 1997).
23. Omer Bartov, *Murder in Our Midst: The Holocaust, Industrial Killing and Representation* (New York, 1996), esp. 33–52.
24. Edith Wyschogrod, *Spirit in Ashes: Hegel, Heidegger and Man-Made Mass Death* (New Haven, 1985).

25. Karen Hagemann, *"Männlicher Muth und teutsche Ehre": Nation, Krieg und Geschlecht in der Zeit der antinapoleonischen Kriege Preußens* (Paderborn, 2002) and Rene Schilling, *"Kriegshelden": Deutungsmuster heroischer Männlichkeit in Deutschland 1813–1945* (Paderborn, 2002).
26. Thomas Rohkrämer, *Der Militarismus der "kleinen Leute". Die Kriegervereine im deutschen Kaiserreich 1871–1914* (Munich, 1990); Dirk Schumann, "Der brüchige Frieden: Kriegserinnerungen, Kriegsszenarien und Kriegsbereitschaft," in Ute Frevert, ed., *Das neue Jahrhundert: Europäische Zeitdiagnosen und Zukunftsentwürfe um 1900* (Göttingen, 2000), 113–145.
27. Sabine Behrenbeck and Alexander Nützenadel, "Politische Feiern im Nationalstaat: Perspektiven eines Vergleichs zwischen Italien und Deutschland," in their edited *Inszenierungen des Nationalstaats: Politische Feiern in Italien und Deutschland seit 1860/1871* (Cologne, 2000), 9–26.
28. Ariès, *Death*, 549.
29. Wolfgang Schivelbusch, *The Culture of Defeat: On National Trauma, Mourning and Recovery* (London, 2001), esp. 103–188.
30. Alon Confino, *The Nation as a Local Metaphor: Württemberg, Imperial Germany, and National Memory 1871–1918* (Chapel Hill, NC, 1997).
31. Celia Applegate, *A Nation of Provincials: The German Idea of Heimat* (Berkeley, 1990).
32. Manfred Hettling, *Totenkult statt Revolution: 1848 und seine Opfer* (Frankfurt, 1998).
33. Isabel V. Hull, *Absolute Destruction: Military Culture and the Practice of War in Imperial Germany* (Ithaca and London, 2005).
34. Schivelbusch, *Defeat*, 189–288.
35. John Keane, "More Theses on the Philosophy of History," in James Tully, ed., *Meaning and Context: Quentin Skinner and His Critics* (Cambridge, 1988), 204, quoted in Jan-Werner Mueller, ed., *Memory and Power in Post-War Europe* (Cambridge, 2002), 3.
36. Dirk Schumann, *Politische Gewalt in der Weimarer Republik, 1918–1933: Kampf um die Straße und Furcht vor dem Bürgerkrieg* (Essen, 2001). According to George Mosse, there were 324 assassinations committed by the Right between 1919–1923 and 22 by the extreme Left. George Mosse, *Fallen Soldiers: Reshaping the Memory of the World Wars* (New York, 1990), 169.
37. Maria Tatar, *Lustmord* (Cambridge, MA, 1995) and Eva Karcher, *Eros und Tod im Werk von Otto Dix : Studien zur Geschichte des Korpers in den zwanziger Jahren* (Münster, 1984). Mann's 1923 bestseller, *The Magic Mountain,* was of course another meditation on disease and death, but this time the themes were much more central to the narrative of the book.
38. Hubert Dreyfus and Mark Wrathall, eds., *Heidegger Re-Examined: Volume 1: Dasein, Authenticity and Death* (London, 2002); Domenico Losurdo, *Die Gemeinschaft, der Tod, das Abendland: Heidegger und die Kriegsideologie* (Stuttgart, 1995); Rainer Marten, *Der menschliche Tod: Eine philosophische Revision* (Paderborn, 1987); Ernst Bloch, "Karl Marx, Death and the Apocalypse," in his *The Spirit of Utopia* (Palo Alto, 2000 [1923]), 233–278; Walter Benjamin, "The Storyteller," in his *Reflections* (New York, 1969), 83–110; and Theodor Adorno, *Kierkegaard: Construction of the Aesthetic* (Minneapolis, 1989 [1933]).
39. Philipp Witkop, ed., *German Students' War Letters,* trans. A.F. Wedd (Philadelphia, 2002). This book was originally published in German in 1929, and translated into English that same year. More generally, Wolfgang Natter, *Literature at War: Representing the "Time of Greatness" in Germany* (New Haven, 1999).
40. Reinhart Koselleck and Michael Jeismann, eds., *Der politische Totenkult: Kriegerdenkmäler in der Moderne* (Munich, 1994).
41. Benjamin Ziemann, "Die deutsche Nation und ihr zentraler Erinnerungsort: Das 'Nationaldenkmal für die Gefallenen des Weltkrieges' und die Idee des Unbekannten Soldaten 1914–1935," in Helmut Berding, Klaus Heller, and Winfried Speitkamp, eds., *Krieg und Erinnerung: Fallstudien zum 19. und 20. Jahrhundert* (Göttingen, 2000), 67–91; see also the essays by Jürgen Tietz, Ursel Berger, and Martina Weinland in Rainer Rother, ed., *Die letzten Tage der Menschheit: Bilder des Ersten Weltkriegs* (Berlin, 1994).

42. Sabine Behrenbeck, *Der Kult um die toten Helden: Nationalsozialistische Mythen, Riten und Symbole, 1923–1945* (Greifswald, 1996); Jay W. Baird, *To Die For Germany: Heroes in the Nazi Pantheon* (Bloomington, IN, 1990); and Volker Ackermann, *Nationale Totenfeiern in Deutschland: Von Wilhelm I. bis Franz-Josef Strauss* (Stuttgart, 1990).
43. James F. Willis, *Prologue to Nuremberg: The Politics and Diplomacy of Punishing War Criminals during the First World War* (Westport, CT, 1982), 146 and John Horne and Alan Kramer, *German Atrocities: A History of Denial* (New Haven, 2001), 404. For discussion, see Paul Betts, "Germany, International Justice and the 20th Century," in *History and Memory*, 17, nos. 1/2 (Fall 2005): 45–86.
44. Jochen Böhler, *Auftakt zur Vernichtungskrieg: Die Wehrmacht in Polen 1939* (Frankfurt, 2006).
45. Francis Aldor, *Germany's 'Death Space': The Polish Tragedy* (London, 1940).
46. Nicholas Stargardt, *Witnesses of War: Children's Lives Under the Nazis* (London, 2005) and *Abends wenn wir essen fehlten uns immer einer: Kinder schreiben an die Väter, 1939–1945* (Frankfurt, 2000).
47. Michael Geyer, "'There is a Land Where Everything Is Pure: Its Name Is Death': Some Observations on Catastrophic Nationalism," in Greg Eghigian and Matthew Paul Berg, eds., *Sacrifice and National Belonging in 20th Century Germany* (College Station, TX, 2002), 139.
48. Konrad H. Jarausch and Michael Geyer, *Shattered Past: Reconstructing German Histories* (Princeton, 2003), 353.
49. George Mosse, *Fallen Soldiers: Reshaping the Memory of the World Wars* (New York, 1990).
50. Mosse, *Fallen Soldiers*, 216.
51. For example, a 1946 French law stipulated that the "army provide free transport and delivery of bodies of soldiers and victims of the war. After World War II the French people refused to turn their dead soldiers over to the large national cemeteries like those of World War I; they preferred to keep them in family graves." Ariès, *Death*, 556. Such practices had an older tradition; embalming was often used during the American Civil War to allow the bodies of slain soldiers to be brought back home to be buried in their family or church graveyards. Jessica Mitford, *The American Way of Death* (New York, 1963), 200–201.
52. Edgar Wolfrum, "Die Unfähigkeit zu feiern? Der 8. Mai und der 17. Juni in der bundesrepublikanischen Erinnerungskultur," in Behrenbeck and Nützenadel, *Inszenierungen*, 221–241.
53. Stella Baum, *Ploetzlich und Unerwartet: Todesanzeigen* (Düsseldorf, 1980).
54. Sebald, *Natural History*, 13.
55. Robert Moeller, *War Stories: The Search for a Usable Past in the Federal Republic of Germany* (Berkeley and Los Angeles, 2001). For the wider West European experience, Pieter Lagrou, *The Legacy of Nazi Occupation: Patriotic Memory and National Recovery in Western Europe, 1945–1965* (Cambridge, 2000). See also Alon Confino, "Remembering the Second World War, 1945–1965: Narratives of Victimhood and Genocide," *Cultural Analysis: An Interdisciplinary Forum on Folklore and Popular Culture*, vol. 4, 2005: http://ist-socrates.berkeley.edu/~caforum/volume4/vol4_article3.html with responses by Robert Moeller and Jay Winter.
56. Frank Biess, *Homecomings: Returning POWs and the Legacies of Defeat in Postwar Germany* (Princeton, 2006).
57. Monika Gibas, "'Aufgestanden aus Ruinen und der Zukunft zugewandt!' Politische Feier- und Gedenktage der DDR," in Behrenbeck and Nützenadel, 191–220.
58. "Verwaltungsakte produzieren keine Erfahrungen:" Heiner Müller im Gespräch mit Hendrik Werner, 7 May 1995, Berlin, www.hydra.umn.edu/mueller/hendrik.html, 8.
59. This point is made most forcefully by Jeffrey Herf, *Divided Memory: The Nazi Past in the Two Germanys* (Cambridge, MA., 1997).
60. John Keegan, *The Battle for History: Refighting World War II* (London, 1997).
61. Silke Wenk, "Sacrifice and Victimization in the Commemorative Practices of Nazi Genocide after German Unification – Memorials and Visual Metaphors," in Eghigian and Berg, *Sacrifice*, 196–226. The German reception of Daniel Jonah Goldhagen's 1996 *Hitler's Willing Execution-*

ers could also be seen as a test case of the new Berlin Republic's understanding of its Third Reich past. See Geoff Eley, ed., *The Goldhagen Effect: History, Memory, Nazism—Facing the German Past* (Ann Arbor, 2000).

62. Jan-Werner Mueller, *Another Country: German Intellectuals, Unification and National Identity* (New Haven, 2000), 258.
63. Patrick Geary, "Exchange and Interaction between the Living and the Dead in early Medieval Society," in *Living With the Dead in the Middle Ages* (Ithaca, 1994), 77–94.
64. Bruce Gordon and Peter Marshall, eds., *The Place of the Dead : Death and Remembrance in Late Medieval and Early Modern Europe* (Cambridge, 2000), 2–3. See also A. N. Galpern "The Legacy of Late Medieval Religion in Sixteenth-Century Champagne," in C. Trinkaus and H. O. Oberman, eds., *The Pursuit of Holiness in Late Medieval and Renaissance Religion* (Leiden, 1974).
65. Joseph Canning, Hartmut Lehmann and Jay Winter, eds., *Power, Violence and Mass Death in Pre-Modern and Modern Times* (London, 2004).
66. Peter Weiss, *Notizbücher, 1960–1971* (Frankfurt, 1982), vol. II, 813, cited in Sebald, *Natural History*, 172–173.

Part I

BODIES

Chapter 1

HOW THE GERMANS LEARNED TO WAGE WAR
On the Question of Killing in the First and Second World Wars

Michael Geyer

The short answer to the question posed in the title—how the Germans learned to wage war—consists in this: Germans learned to wage war by learning anew how to fight in the course of the First World War. What they learned was an extraordinarily aggressive form of warfare, unprecedented both in its lethality and in the efficacy as well as efficiency of its means. In what follows, I will briefly detail and explain this particularly German form of warfare, as it emerged from circumstances in the practice of the German Field Army during the First World War.*

A Preliminary Remark about Discourse and Practice

Only the briefest of remarks must suffice to give some depth and focus to the present enquiry. It concerns the German war experience and the language of war and its correspondence, or rather non-correspondence, to actual fighting and killing. Recent German scholarship agrees that German soldiers wrote very little about killing; rather, they reminisced about the overwhelming omnipresence of death. Few desired to confront the lethality of their own actions, and fewer still wished to convey such realities to their loved ones or even their comrades. Or so it is said. However, there are a couple of strange contradictions.

While very few soldiers wrote about killing, an indubitable fascination with violence runs through the entire war literature. This fascination grows, as wartime experience gives way to the memory of, and to a literature on, war. Narrative conventions develop—we may think of them as "noir" versions of adventure narratives—that capture the act and the emotions of fighting, even if they "cut," as it were, rather abruptly from fighting to its consequence, dead and wounded

---

Notes for this chapter begin on page 46.

bodies or splattered body parts. While brief, the portrayal is graphic and extolls the abject horror of war so as to highlight either the virtue or the suffering, and always the sublime nature, of violence in war. The descriptions here, including those in the antiwar literature, are drastic and border on the pornographic.[1] By the same token, there is other evidence, for example the many photographs—intriguing that it should be photographs—of executions, especially on the Eastern Front, and on the degradation of human life through hunger, forced labor, or unsettlement.[2] It is not clear why there should be so many photos. Is it that the practice was unusually pervasive? Or is it that these degradations were perceived as a degeneration of war that reminded the literate viewer of early modern images? Further, it is not at all evident what is empathetic and what is punitive in this images. In any case, there exists a pictorial language—in my view it is a penal gaze—and to some extent also a rhetoric that deals not just with death, but with the act of killing. It seems that a second, more skeptical look is warranted at the "simultaneity of a taboo on [the representation of] killing and the fascination with violence."[3]

This is all the more the case, since recent French studies have come to similar and quite striking conclusions regarding French soldiers and their articulation of the readiness to kill.[4] They confirm the discursive taboo, but also point to a far more explicit furor of killing than hitherto acknowledged. In the French case, the latter is articulated in the inventiveness and, so one might say, loving care with which infantry soldiers armed themselves with weapons for hand-to-hand combat. This is all the more intriguing given that, statistically, relatively few German soldiers died as a result of close combat and that, if anything, they feared the English or Canadian handguns more than French daggers and clubs. Even stranger, the only recorded German equivalent, trench art, highlights rather homely items.[5] These studies tend to point in a direction similar to that stressed by Joanna Bourke in her *Intimate History of Killing* with reference to American and British soldiers: namely, a clear and unmistakable willingness, even zeal and enthusiasm, to kill in combat, and only the slightest hesitation to celebrate their enemies' death and treat their corpses as trophies—meanwhile treating one's own deaths as representations of the horrors of war, to be overcome one way or another.[6]

But let us assume for the sake of convention that when it came to articulating their own acts of killing, German soldiers were rather more easily shamed and hesitant.[7] And in the absence of a critical new look at the evidence, let us presume that French and German battle-field behavior were unequal. (My sense is that the real difference is in the articulation of aggressive sentiment rather than in aggressivity as such.[8]) In any case, if the conventional wisdom prevails it would become even more remarkable that these same soldiers were such decidedly effective killers—more effective, evidently, than all other combatants combined. Here, too, we need not believe everything that has been proposed and surely should not trust the German soldiers' widespread sense of their own superiority in infantry combat (certainly compared to the English, although less so with regard to the French, and not at all with regard to Canadians). However, the statistical trends suggest that Niall Ferguson is basically right.[9] German losses in both world wars were staggeringly large, but the corresponding Allied numbers were significantly higher. In the First World War, on the Western Front alone, there were 376 Germans wounded per thousand compared to around 482 per thousand Allied soldiers, and 53 per thousand German dead compared to 86 dead on the French and British side.[10] Up until the fall of 1918, there was not a single month in which German forces did not inflict higher losses on the Allies than they themselves had incurred.[11] Allied losses on the Eastern and Southern fronts were even more imbalanced, and in some battles, especially on the Russian front, they amounted to mass slaughter.

This reality should make us pause to think. Not only were German soldiers remarkably effective, but they became more lethal as the German situation worsened. To begin with, the Allies held a decided material advantage over the Central Powers, if not initially, then at the latest by the Battle of the Somme in the summer of 1916. But all the same, Allied casualties went up in 1917, while German casualties went down or stabilized. Moreover, German battle fatigue appears to have developed in an inverse relationship with lethality—the highest rates of English casualties occurred in 1918.[12] Indeed, despite the increasing superiority of Allied matériel and the increasing battle fatigue of the Germans, Allied losses continued to increase from year to year both in absolute terms, and relative to the total losses of all participants in the war.[13] The German field army may have lost the war, but considering the magnitude of Allied losses, they fought hard and went down fighting more effectively, with depleted ranks killing ever more enemy combatants despite a growing gap in terms of quantity and quality of matériel. Even if we recall the old battlefield wisdom that offensive wars are more deadly than defensive ones and that the Allies had been on the offense ever since early 1915, the question remains: How and why did German soldiers fight so hard and, in fighting, prove to be so extraordinarily lethal?

And this is only half the story. While hesitant to talk or write about its peculiar "success," German society at large did not partake in the pacifist turn that followed the war throughout the West during the 1920s. Instead, out of sync with the cycle, German war literature and, more generally, a public mobilized for revenge paved the way for a new, radical culture of violence.[14] Twenty years after the defeat of 1918, the Wehrmacht began to fight a new war with even greater intensity and effectiveness, and with a brutality beyond all moral bounds that ended in total defeat. As in World War I, all three factors contributing to the lethality of the German forces—intensity, effectiveness, and brutality of fighting—tended to increase, rather than decrease. That is to say, the German forces started at a higher level of lethality than did their foes and, against all prevailing assumptions about a let-down, they fought the Second World War with a growing lethality. The latter reached its zenith only during the last year of the war, not only in terms of German casualties, but also and especially in terms of Allied battle losses. Once again, German soldiers, as war-weary as they may ever have been, continued to fight with extraordinary efficacy, even as the Wehrmacht's firepower and its mobility declined—not only relatively, compared to the Western and Eastern Allies, but also in absolute terms.[15]

It is not quite by chance that this effectiveness elicited something of a postwar myth—and certainly an extensive sociological and historical literature—about the German soldier. The more scholarly literature focused on the nature and role of small groups in the army. Popular culture, particularly in the Anglo-American world, developed a veritable cult of German military paraphernalia that faithfully reflects the way in which the Nazi state dressed up its own obsessions with killing. But neither of these infatuations has been able to uncover the cool "kill – kill – kill" attitude that a more recent literature attributes to the rise of the West, which, for all intents and purposes, should have the German army and its lethal infantry soldiers, rather than the ancient Greeks, as their model. Of course, the Germans lost their wars, which somewhat dents the entire argument about "warrior-culture," but they fought with extraordinary ferocity.[16] Then again, the historically serious literature discovers a link between killing and the deep investment in a sense of *Kameradschaft,* male bonding, that focuses more on the care and concern for fellow soldiers than on the paraphernalia of Nazi war culture.[17] It also discovers a military culture that is obsessed with outcomes, which it seeks to achieve at any cost.[18]

This said, we are confronted, in World War II, with a far wider spectrum of deadly force. For one thing, the chief arena of combat had shifted from the relatively narrow, band-like battlefield of the Western Front to a battle space that encompassed all of Eastern Europe and the European portion of the Soviet Union up to the Caucasus—where the distinction between advancing armies, the deep front (no longer a line, but an extensive zone of combat), and the rear dissolved. In part this was a result of the guerilla war waged behind the front, but it was also a consequence of mobile combat that was fought, not along a line as in the nineteenth century, but in battle space(s). If we add to this the long retreat from the Volga and the Caucasus with its systematic scorched-earth tactics between 1943 and 1944/45, we might indeed say that the entire Soviet and Eastern European arena became a zone of death, for combat extended beyond fighting the enemy to ecological destruction (infrastructure, housing, habitation, wells, etc.). Thus, the greater part of the Wehrmacht's lethality was indirect—a crisis of food, health, and shelter that overwhelmed the remaining, and the returning, civilian population. The effect of this "ecological" war was, above all, a systematic urbicide that depopulated entire urban areas and effectively destroyed an older Russian and eastern European urban culture.[19]

This way of waging war was deliberate. From the very start the Wehrmacht fought(to varying degrees in the central, western, southern, and eastern regions) a war of annihilation against hostile societies (or, at the least, against presumed hostile elements within them) rather than against enemy armies.[20] Thus, the German army—or, in any case, elements in it—separated and eliminated black soldiers in the French army, a blatant case of racial warfare.[21] Despite individual protests, it supported a war of utter destruction against Polish society and it fought a highly ideologized war of conquest against the Soviet Union. These campaigns were, as far as the Wehrmacht was concerned, premeditated. They reflected, in the Wehrmacht's view, the changing nature of warfare. The latter encompassed not only the recognition of the "total," that is all-encompassing nature of modern war that mobilized men, women, and children alike, but also the emotional or, if you wish, ideological dimensions of war. Not least, the nature of the warfare fit the radical war aims, especially of the eastern wars—conquest and subordination. Because resistance was expected from entire populations, the resolution was that war, in order to be successful, would have to encompass a surveillance and policing, counterinsurgency dimension. War was, deliberately and from the start, a war against civilians as well.

Whether or not premeditated genocide, in particular of the European Jewry, was part and parcel of this warfare against entire populations—or whether it took place under the guise of war—is controversial.[22] My sense is that the "war against Jews" was indeed a war against the Jews; that is, it was an integral aspect, a specific, even crucial, theater of National Socialist warfare.[23] National Socialist warfare, as interpreted by its proponents, was "biological" war quite literally in that its enemy were entire populations whose survival constituted a mortal threat.[24] The Wehrmacht partook in this war, partly because it shared Nazi proclivities and partly because its own military sense of what constituted a threat had shifted from enemy armies to enemy societies to "absolute enemies," peoples and ideologies beyond subordination and incorporation. The convenient figure for the latter was the "partisan," but the partisan was less this or that guerilla group than a new kind of "principled" enemy engaged in a life-and-death struggle.[25] Of course, the latter was the Nazi (and, arguably, the Wehrmacht) view of war rather than that of the people they killed. What they engaged in, in actual fact, was plain mass murder, genocide, of civilian, non-combatant populations. But the point here is that the "war against Jews" was a war. Therefore, while the specific targeting and the calculated murder of the Jews as mortal enemy stands out as the most lethal killing field of the war, the Judaeocide is not an extrinsic, but an intrinsic aspect (if a separate theater) of the war the Nazis waged. It was a theater of war in which the Wehrmacht was a supporting actor, the main force in this particular theater being the SS. But not only was there no military resistance against this murderous war; it also fit into the more general campaigns of societal annihilation that the Wehrmacht fought.[26]

It is now commonly assumed that there is a subterranean connection between the German way of waging war in the First World War and the war of annihilation, genocide and Judaeocide in the Second World War.[27] Were we to accept as an effective metaphor the generic characterization of the entire period as an "age of extremes" or a "thirty-year war," this connection would have to be made explicit. However, the holistic view of both wars leaves much to be desired. Foremost among such views is the thesis that war became more brutal because life had become cheap in the human slaughterhouse of World War I, resulting in a coarsening of social norms and standards of behavior, and the breakdown of international legal and "civilizational" norms and agreements on humanitarian conduct—not only within the military, but throughout the nation. A competing approach stresses the totalization of the war, referring above all to the paralysis of political controls in the face of escalating violence—whereby in the more recent literature arguments about organizational or technological imperatives have tended to be replaced by cultural considerations (such as the mobilization of emotions like hatred, which cannot be turned off and on at will). Total wars unleash emotions and ideologies to produce an phantasmagoric world in which the all-out fight-to-death replaces an older "strategic" culture of warfare.[28] A third type of argument tries to establish a link between the way war was fought in World War I and the Holocaust. The general claim here is that, despite genocidal tendencies prior to 1914, World War I was a decisive threshold—either in the sense of demonstrating for the first time the possibility of complete annihilation in its full reality, or in the sense that with the mobilization of society, the genocidal strain of thought spread rapidly and established itself as the central idea of radical nationalism. Another, more recent line of inquiry emphasizes the "return of the repressed"—of colonial and peripheral warfare right in the center of Europe. There is surely not a lack of arguments.

However, there is an awkward lack of studies on German combat—in stark contrast to the British and French experience. The problem is that the common-sense argument about the destructiveness and dehumanization in World War I opening up the way to genocidal warfare in World War II does not look at the most immediate issue at stake, killing in combat, and proceeds from generalities about modern warfare to even more general conclusions about genocidal violence. It seems to me, on the contrary, indispensable for our understanding to examine closely the practice of war, and the act of killing itself, if we want to understand what links World War I with World War II and what constitutes continuities and discontinuities in the German way of waging war.[29]

In practical terms, the question is how all the modern national armies of the nineteenth and twentieth centuries managed to mold members of a diverse and differentiated male population into homogenous soldiers and warriors with uniform reactions in combat.[30] In our case, the more specific issue is the way in which the German army molded the German nation in arms into such extraordinarily effective, indeed, ferocious warriors that commanded—and command—a certain uncanny respect due to their utter readiness to fight both in victory and defeat, and what, if anything, this way of waging war has to do with the annihilationist murderous campaigns in World War II.

The ultimate goal is to comprehend a culture of war that began to reorganize fighting in the First World War and by the Second had stripped it radically of its limits and turned it, within the context of a war against entire societies, into systematic, directed genocide. The various stages and dimensions of this development cannot be fused or run together. There will always be a difference—between the First and Second World Wars, between war and genocide. But perhaps, gathering clues one by one, we may begin to understand this German culture of war—and in this context especially the role of small groups, their initiative and competency—in the era of world wars. It seems that there is no better way to start than to explore how, in actual fact, German soldiers fought war and how they learned to kill so effectively.

The New German Way of War

How, then, can we understand the waging of war, if the soldiers themselves are so tentative about describing their trade? Looking at the articulation of combat experience in German diaries and letters as a first line of interpretation is not the solution. However, we can assume that the military itself had an interest in training and deploying recruits so that they would fight, and fight successfully. And of course there is a specialized corpus of knowledge, coded in specifically military terms, that is concerned predominantly with the questions of converting civilians into soldiers and deploying soldiers as combatants in battle. Naturally, one would expect a certain discrepancy between knowledge and practice (and one would always want to countenance the likelihood of the military getting things wrong), but in as much as this corpus of knowledge reflects a changing practice of fighting wars, it gives us unique access to the question of how soldiers kill in war. In case of doubt, soldiers act the way they are trained.

This corpus of knowledge about killing in war can be found mainly in the areas of tactics and training. Of course, tactics and training serve merely as guidelines for practice. They say virtually nothing about how soldiers actually act(ed). But, at least for the German field army, we can observe an increasingly intimate relationship between theory/guidelines and practice/execution, especially after the devastating battles of matériel in 1916 at Verdun and at the Somme. This is confirmed by the numerous debates surrounding standard regulations, reports from the field of battle, large and small, training courses for units and entire formations behind the front lines, the introduction of new procedures that were repeatedly tested for efficiency, and so forth.[31] For the soldiers, the ceaseless training sessions seemed like prolonging their drudgery by other means, while the staff officers were irritated by the increasing amount of paperwork caused by the continual demands for reports. The result, however, was a new way to conduct training for war and a new way of fighting wars, which may not have been practiced everywhere and all the time (because old habits die hard) but did become widespread practice nonetheless. Whether this new way of fighting was an extension of an older military culture, as Isabel Hull would suggest, or whether a wholly new way of waging war emerged, is impossible to argue out on the basis of the material I present here. I think the latter is the case. But for the time being, I am concerned with showing why, and at what costs, German soldiers became such lethally effective soldiers.

With regard to wartime training, three points merit consideration. First, questions of "proper" training, which had already been discussed intensely prior to the war, took on their true significance only during the course of the war itself—for in the face of dwindling reserves, the period of basic training for new recruits shrank down to two or three months, and any further training was shifted to recruit depots behind the front, in the army's rearward zone. At the same time, it was clear to everyone involved that the war of matériel had exponentially increased the mental and physical strain of combat.[32] Thus, making soldiers combat-ready involved teaching many more skills—and, perhaps more importantly, teaching skills in the first place—and teaching them in a much shorter time than had been the case in the prewar period.

Second, in order to achieve this aim, a long-standing argument was brought to a close (despite quite considerable resistance) in conjunction with the "Infantry Training Manual" ("Ausbildungsvorschrift für Fußtruppen [A.V.F]") of December 1916. In contrast to the French army, the German and especially the Prussian armies, had never thought much of the "power of emotion" on the battlefield and therefore did not particularly stress the soldier's martial zeal. There was, however, an intense debate about the respective advantages of close-order drill vs. combat training, which was resolved in favor of the latter.[33] The close-order drill created a clear hierarchy between superior and subordinate. Making this chain of command routine was intended to guarantee obedience on the battlefield as well. Combat training, on the other hand, put the emphasis on the soldier's inner discipline (or disciplining)—on a kind of internalized, repetitive compulsion to act that is virtually "in the blood," and is meant to standardize procedures into a system of automatic (but precisely *not* autonomous) combat responses.[34] The salient point of combat-based training was to have the soldiers involuntarily act as one in order to achieve the assigned objective.

In addition, there was a third element, which was observed in the First World War only to a limited extent. The decision between the choices of close-order drill and combat training rested on two different conceptions of how and why soldiers would fight in battle. The proponents of the close-order drill articulated the view that the military must instill obedience in the soldier so that he could and would follow orders, and carry them out as unreflectively as possible, even under extreme battle conditions. They understood the will and readiness to fight as a finite resource that they must somehow supply to the soldier to carry into battle. They fully expected this resource of drilled action to be used up quite literally in combat. Troops were not just physically but also morally and mentally burnt out; hence the resource of drilled, involuntary action had to be renewed. Divisions were rotated in and out of the battlefront. In the rear, they were not inactive. Instead, their drill regiment, and therefore their resolve, was replenished much as the dead and the wounded were replaced. According to this notion, "the corrosive effect of position warfare" especially undermined discipline and authority.[35] Therefore, the formal and outward demonstration of discipline during wartime and in the rear was considered to be more important than ever. Additives to close-order drill were sought in, for instance, the patriotic indoctrination of the field troops. But the basic assumption remained the same: if the soldiers could be sent into battle bolstered by a fresh reserve of (patriotic) motivation, and with their well-honed discipline renewed, they would be more likely to hold out.[36]

The alternate conception, which was embraced only by a minority within the Kaiser's field army, gained ascendancy in the Wehrmacht.[37] It developed out of the practice of combat-oriented training. As it turned out, a soldier trained for efficiency in battle would, if need be, fight entirely on his own—and continue to the point of collapse. If the soldier was endowed with the requisite capacities for fighting, so the argument went, then he would fight. Moreover, despite returning from battle physically and psychologically exhausted, his overall combat readiness would not be worn down, as was traditionally assumed. Quite to the contrary, combat enhanced readiness, notwithstanding physical and psychological exhaustion.[38] A good combat soldier needed care, rest, and recreation in order to replenish his body and soul, but he did not require re-disciplining, because combat had sharpened his fighting skills.

The "new look" at soldiers and their training, then, consisted in reassessing the effects of battle upon soldiers. Whereas the older idea assumed the erosion of combat readiness to the point of the exhaustion and the collapse of fighting discipline, the newer version wagered that successful fighting (and the training it required) would increase combat readiness and fighting ability because the latter was a matter of skills.[39] The more soldiers could be trained to act as skilled and self-willed fighters within a unit—and, for that matter, within entire formations—the stronger their faith in and reliance upon their squad or unit would be; conversely, the more they perceived themselves as having an existential duty to their fellow comrades, the more willing they would be to fight against all odds. Thus, individual skills, self-willed action, and small group practice developed hand-in-hand. They turned drilled soldiers into skilled "warriors." Obviously, warrior units also got burnt out fast, but burnt out fighting; and the survivors did not lose, but rather accumulated, fighting experience and passed it on.

The result of such considerations was the recognition that simply breaking the (civilian) will of the recruit was insufficient to the task of creating an effective military instrument. Rather, both his civilian will *and his fighting spirit* would have to be "converted" into an alternative martial state.[40] This martial state originated not in subordination but, ultimately, in the self-willed, if internalized and hence involuntary operation of the soldier, in the control over his own powers required by his training, and in the cold-blooded readiness to risk his own life in fraternity with others and carry on the waging of the war.[41] In this way, even— or especially—the "little man" could become a hero, or at a minimum his own (imaginary) champion and self-motivated defender of the national or military cause.[42] What we can observe here is the development of a military practice in which the conscripted soldier is remade into an instinctive warrior, if we understand that "instinct" is a complex artifact that combines discipline, skills, and experience. In 1940, this was articulated quite concisely: "Combat training should mold the soldier into a fighter capable of acting towards the common goal even without orders."[43]

As important as training was for the socialization of the new warrior-type, one who could take war-making and survival into his own hands, the new war-making regime attained full potential mainly in the "how" of combat—that is, in the tactical guidelines for unit and group deployment. (Actually, training in "combined operations" of entire formations also mattered greatly; but consideration of this matter would only distract.) This was certainly not a German issue alone, and a more detailed study would reveal that the Germans learned quite a bit from the French, much as they put down British tactics. In any case, all nations were faced with the problem that the prewar doctrine of infantry (as well as artillery) deployment inevitably led to certain death or the utter immobilization of the deeply dug-in soldiers. The German solution, which initially had been copied from the French in 1915/16, consisted of pushing the infantry out from their deep dugouts of the first line to create staggered zones in which small, mobile groups could engage in combat; artillery doctrine, in turn, shifted away from the mass barrage and toward precision bombardment and duel-like confrontation with enemy artillery (in as much as the latter was at all possible, given Germany's quantitative and qualitative inferiority with regard to artillery). With a breathtaking immediacy, such combat practice made self-willed killing into the prerequisite for survival. In order to fight, the soldier had to move, and in order to move, he had to move in tandem with all others in the midst of mayhem. And he had to coordinate his movements with artillery support, which waged its own war, trying to knock out superior Allied long-range guns through careful forward observation. (The most exposed spot in the entire system of German fighting was the forward artillery observation post.) The turn to combat practice led not just to an escalation in fighting but to direct confrontation with the enemy, aiming at his complete destruction at close quarters.

On the face of it, the consequences of such action are quite stunning and contradict what we seem to know about combat in World War I. Where we expect anonymity, we find, in fact, an increase in face-to-face action. Where we expect soldiers acting as automatons, we find the self-willed warrior. The key to all this is that the Kaiser's field army recognized the potential of soldiers as self-willed warriors and discovered in due course that if they were formed into small enough units they would strike out more effectively than an army of drilled soldiers or, for that matter, of enthusiasts. The Langemarck volunteers and their heroic self-sacrifice were a civilian myth for which there was not much room in the field army. In fact, everything pointed in the opposite direction. Preventing Langemarck-like situations became the basic rationale of combat tactics and training, irrespective of the celebration of the Langemarck spirit. Military practice and representation turned out to be two quite different things.

In practice, this new approach was never entirely successful—nor could it have been. In active combat, the soldiers could not be prevented from clumping together in large groups, thus reducing their mobility, and from digging themselves in.[44] Frequently, they became paralyzed with terror.[45] There were entire divisions that for one or the other reason proved incapable, or unwilling, to change.

More tellingly, because the training of raw recruits back home never caught up, quite commonly it had to be repeated up-front. But certainly, something did happen—for otherwise, in the face of ever increasing impact of materiél, German losses would not have diminished in absolute and relative terms while those of the Allies continued to rise. This something, this tendency, was precisely what could not be acknowledged about the war experience of the "little man"—at least not to himself or his loved ones. In order to maximize the probability of his survival, the new tactical doctrine turned him into an effective warrior, or, in actual fact, into a self-willed killer.

Let us examine this practice more closely. For the sake of simplicity, I will restrict myself to the manuals that defined the new practice of war-making—above all, the "Regulations for Position Warfare for All Armed Services" ("Vorschrift für den Stellungskrieg für alle Waffen") and especially part 8, "Principles of Command in the Defensive Battle in Position Warfare" (1 December 1916, revised 1 September 1917) and part 14, "The Attack in Position Warfare" (1 January, 1918), and bracket, for the sake of brevity, the numerous first-hand reports at the regiment, battalion, and company levels. The latter tells us in great detail how doctrine, actual knowledge, and experience intersected. Suffice it to say here that they did; the manuals were adapted in practice, and adapted quite differently from division to division and Army Corps to Army Corps; in turn, practice changed knowledge and doctrine and, in turn, transformed the manuals far beyond their initial text. Entire formations were pulled from the front line, in 1917/18, in order to be retrained in new battle tactics behind the front by specially earmarked training divisions. Officer training was intensified, although many officers, and not just older ones, just did not "get it." Within divisions, and especially within Army Corps, "best practice" and the failure of it were continually and critically debated with reference to set-pieces (like the disastrous battle of Arras in early 1917, where the new tactics failed), and changing Allied tactics, as well as to ongoing divisional and Corps action. All of this happened as standard practice in addition to the formation of storm troops, which have come to exert such fascination on American military historians.

To make a long story short, the new way of waging war can be distinguished by three principles, none of them entirely new, but unprecedented in their combination: defense of terrain, emptiness of the battlefield, and quickness of response.[46]

The fundamental idea underlying this tactical regime was simple. In order to escape the superior power of artillery fire, the regulations elevated evasive maneuvers within the respective boundaries of each combat sector to a principle. Rather than holding a line at all cost, the control of a battle sector was of the essence. In accordance with this tactic, the defense of terrain relied emphatically on in-depth formation and the elasticity of one's own forces. The latter meant that units would try to elude enemy fire by constantly shifting around (in the trenches, of course, but also in the pockmarked landscape of "no-man's land") in order to fend off the enemy's advances with their own.[47]

Therefore movement and encounter, rather than stasis and distance, characterized the microcosm of the war of matériel. Concessions to actual combat had to be made.[48] Nonetheless, behind the "storm of steel" we discover an endless multiplication of duels of squads and units—infantry as well as artillery. All of this was played out in the smallest possible space, involving a series of risky micromovements. Although one rarely saw the enemy up close and in person, in hand-to-hand combat, he was far from anonymous, but rather an entirely tangible opponent engaged in the same micro-movements and struggling for the same small territorial advantages and for survival. Certainly there were also a good number of mutual, temporary understandings at work in this deadly dance.[49] But after the first phase of the position war, with its fixed trench lines, this space for understandings, for a mutual containment of violence, became increasingly smaller due to the growing flexibility of the tactical units. Instead of the trench warfare system of "live and let live," there developed a regime of fighting for survival—or at least, as the English microhistories on the subject demonstrate, a regime of engagement that was nearly permanent and was indeed practiced with some determination.[50] Thus, one may conclude that fighting in zones (rather than lines) made enmity more inexorable, because one side's micro-advantage in its control of terrain was now the other side's disadvantage. Of course, the front itself did not move at all. But each sector of the front was in permanent movement—movement that depended largely on unit tactics and small group decisions over how to gain and maintain local advantage.

The pressure to move went hand in hand with the in-depth staggering of available forces, which led to the "emptying of the battlefield"—an observation that was commonly made but is not well understood.[51] In practical terms, this meant that the massive scale of linear deployment was abandoned in favor of a number of smaller, relatively independent units and groups, which would spread out like a honeycomb and ensconce themselves in a series of shifting shelter positions in order to, on the one hand, evade enemy fire, and on the other, to provide effective cover for one another. The smallest units, even companies, columns, and groups, determined (within the scope of their orders) their own positions in their respective sectors of the battle zone. That is the reason why the entire principle is commonly referred to as an "individualization of tactics."[52] Every group or unit made do for itself, albeit within the context of a specific mission and of an overall effort that "combined" various types infantry and artillery units. The effect of this nonlinear, ultimately formless dislocation was that the massive scale of (prewar) linear formation broke up into a multitude of local, mobile positions that interacted in a complex system of mutual support.[53]

Here too, one would want to make considerable concessions to reality, whether due to the difficulty of the terrain, the obstinacy of the commanding officers and their traditional schematics, or competition between the units, which jostled for the slightest advantage. Nonetheless, the general effect was astonishing. The giant, outstretched line of the massive field army of 1914 was transformed into a dense network of sections—common metaphors included fabric, spider web, honeycomb, chessboard, and many more—that functioned interactively and, for good or ill, were dependent on one another.

This, in fact, was precisely the salient point of the system. In formal terms, the objective was to dissolve units into multiple groups, each of which would attempt to evade enemy fire in order to throw themselves all the more effectively into the hot spots of the battle. In technical terms, the objective was to gather the masses of prewar infantry around each unit's available, "organic" crew-served weapons, *Truppwaffen* in German, such as machine guns, flamethrowers, and trench mortars, and coordinate their deployment, so that the squads organized around these weapons formed a sort of collective person.[54] But most decisive for combat was the fact that, within the confines of his section, each group and each soldier within a group was made responsible for the survival of all the rest. The consequence was breathtaking. It was as though the entire burden of the battle now fell on the individual warrior-soldier and his small group.[55]

To summarize: "front-line" soldiers were left with no choice but to emerge from their dugouts, move out into the open, and fight and risk death if they did not wish to endanger others, and ultimately themselves, by being over-run. Often, they were moving barely 100–200 yards forward or sideways, but move they did. One way or another, there were plenty of opportunities to be killed. But survival was possible only by killing, and killing depended in turn on movement in cooperation with others. The duty and responsibility was toward the unit—or, as it would later be called in the war literature, the "community of the front"—which itself was the only guarantee for survival. Soldiers died each one for himself, but they needed the group in order to survive. And in order to survive there was no way out but to fight. This is so, because the best chance to survive (against artillery fire) was to move forward into the face of the enemy infantry.

The physical, and especially the mental, strain of this kind of war-making was extraordinary. If the correspondence of the soldiers is to be believed, they wished (if at all) to be led, or commanded into war, but certainly not to be made responsible for their own and their comrades' survival.[56] Yet it was precisely this notion that constituted (though perhaps not by design) the moral and military essence of a small infantry unit's cohesiveness and training. In practice, this principle turned out to function astoundingly well. Once the soldiers arrived at the front, they fought doggedly until utter exhaustion.[57] Combat fatigue was expressed in the increasing difficulty of getting soldiers—or, more precisely, entire units—to the front.[58] In 1918, this fatigue rose quite sharply, not least because the tactical "system" functioned so well even without any prospect of military success. This was only possible because the group compulsion to take on the responsibility for the respective whole (the comrades in the squad, the column, the company, the battalion, the regiment) and to fight to that end was overwhelming.

The only way out—which many chose in 1918, and which was closed down in 1939/40—was to not get drawn into the fighting system in the first place. Desertions rose, and war-trauma cases increased exponentially with the overwhelming obligation to fight that came with the new battle tactics. Typically, deserters did not run away from the front, but on the way to the front; trauma was not sustained at the front, but on the way to it. Fighting exhausted units and burnt them out, but getting there tested their morale. Once a soldier was at the front there was no exit—except to kill and die. (The typical break-down up-front was "panic" or mass-fright, a situation of a rapidly radiating, local "system's break-down," which emerged in tandem with the new combat practice.) Only toward the end of the war did soldiers surrender—and they always surrendered as a group.

By late fall, 1918, the third principle of the new tactics, the quickness of response or striking force (*Schlagkraft*) had become largely paralyzed due to the pressing superiority of the enemy. With the paralysis of *Schlagkraft* the German way of fighting war imploded, for the entire tactical system had been guided by the principle of effective counter-strike by strike forces. In formal terms, striking force refers to the combination of firepower and movement needed to achieve an objective; the question of combat readiness is involved inasmuch as the successful achievement of an objective is dependent on the soldier's will to overpower the enemy—and to kill him.

The coordination of firepower and movement was an old problem, that, in the face of the destructive force of modern machine weapons, had already posed itself with renewed urgency prior to the First World War. The main question then had been how to regain striking force, and with it the soldiers' readiness to fight a war of position, in the face of the Allies' increasing superiority of matériel. The resolution of this problem was complex. The bottom line consisted in placing the soldiers in tactical situations in which they had little choice but to fight back on their own initiative if they wanted to survive. This principle of permanent tactical self-defense became both the practical and ideological core of the German combat practice.

Since German offensive operations on the Western Front remained an exception after the Battle of the Marne, and particularly after the battles of 1916, offensive action out of a defensive position became the norm. Additionally, the fundamental principles of defense in position warfare prescribed that every enemy attack was to be parried by an (immediate) counterstrike, or in a larger battle, by a counterattack or a deliberate counteroffensive—and specifically, in such a manner as to not only win back the lost terrain, but to beat back the opposing forces while inflicting the greatest possible damage.[59] When this principle was given up in September 1918, the war was in fact already lost in military terms.[60]

In order to understand the initial capacity to strike, we must examine tactical procedures in conjunction with the operative defensive more closely. By focusing on movement and mobility, the "Principles of Command in the Defensive Battle in Position Warfare" determined that the point and purpose of every movement was to evade enemy fire *with the purpose of a counterstrike* or counterattack. The dissolution of fixed lines, the chessboard-like distribution of detachments, and the corresponding layout of trenches and mine fields were meant to provide the flexibility to destroy enemy advances through (often flanking) counterattacks in just such a way that the (seeming) success of the enemy offensive would lead into a trap that was all the more deadly. Thus, in the place of the unfolding of the line and the frontal blocking of the enemy in the line of battle, there emerged a staccato-like interaction of detachments, units, or groups—depending on the scale—in a system of deceleration and acceleration of action, and in evading and striking the enemy. Ideally, enemy units were not blocked off but cut off into pockets, enveloped, and overwhelmed. In place of a central command structure, there emerged the decentralized mobilization of local units, all striving to achieve the same objective: to strike at the enemy from a tactical, or operative, defensive position and, by eluding his fire, to annihilate him all the more effectively in a counterstrike.

Even the regulations for offensive action—"The Attack in Position Warfare" of 1 January 1918—pointed in the same direction. According to the regulations, infiltrations or incursions backed by artillery were directed toward relatively weakly defended zones and interstices; they strove for envelopment on a small scale, which could then be expanded in a flexible manner with the additional use of infantry and heavy artillery.[61] Here too, the principle was that the enemy should be goaded (in this case, through infiltration) into movement, which would then be lethally countered through dexterous and unexpected action and temporarily superior man- and fire-power. The aim of infiltration consisted in breaking open the enemy's compact, deep formation and splitting it into its component parts, which could then be "finished off" one at a time. This necessitated the ability to make decisions and maintain an overview even in the smallest areas. But above all, it required a great degree of aggressively mobile action, in advancing and retreating, in order to draw out and engage the enemy. Remarkably, the German side, in contrast, for instance, to the French, was rather less concerned with hand-to-hand combat. It happened, but it was not the climactic moment of combat for German soldiers. Rather, their main concern was to move into a position of local superiority in order to deploy the destructive power of machine weapons (machine guns, flame throwers) against the enemy's disintegrating sector advances. In other words, they did not aim at the individual kill, but at wholesale, if face-to-face annihilation. The deadly encounter was no less direct, but it was mediated by machines.

Infiltration and incursion tactics developed out of counterstrike tactics and maintained their basic principles. The devastating (counter-) strike was the essence of both the defensive and the offensive doctrine. The concept of annihilation takes on a new, or at least a specific, significance in this situation, for the implication now is no longer simply that the enemy is to be overpowered in order to achieve a given objective, but rather the enemy is to be annihilated in each sector of combat. *Schlagkraft* was never simply a doctrine of striking back, but it was the capacity, and the readiness, to overwhelm and to annihilate in place after place. The enemy was not pushed back or enveloped en masse, but parceled off into small pieces to be more effectively destroyed. The imperative and the decision to fight and kill was thus effectively decentered. It clearly put the burden of killing on the individual soldier or, in actual fact, on the group or unit with its machine-weapons. (One of the unanticipated consequences of these new tactics consisted in the much criticized practice of ordinary infantry soldiers relying on accompanying machine weapons instead of using their own rifles.) This is just one of the many indications that practice actually changed, even if not entirely with the intended effect. It appears that soldiers knew instinctively that the better they performed their new warrior role, the likelier it was that they would get killed.

The German field army turned its soldiers into warriors and made the small units they fought in the linchpin for fighting and killing. To that end they handed down the obligation and the decision—and, in a perverse, way: the freedom—to act, that is, to kill. This happened on a remarkable scale. In any case, it was never limited to specifically designated storm troops, although not all units, possibly not even the majority, pursued the new tactic in quite the way they were intended to. While all divisions adopted the new combat practice, only a minority were able to live up to them, or so it seems after an initial survey of some of the internal evaluations. There is an interesting history to be had as to why certain units, including rather lowly reserve units, performed so much better than others, including crack units like guard divisions, but it is not one I am able to pursue here.[62] Rather, the curious thing about the new tactics is that they were not the way soldiers wanted to remember the war; possibly, they did not even "experience" the war with the tactics in mind. In articulating their war experience, the soldier as warrior and agent of his own destiny gave way to the soldier not exactly as victim, but as survivor under overwhelming duress. The small unit transmogrified into a "community" welded together by overwhelming, external force—which is the opposite of what it was (namely a solidarity, built around organic crew weapons) and evokes the opposite of what they soldiers in order to survive as a group—for in actual fact, they set out to kill in order to survive.

It seems a reasonable conjecture that this compulsion to kill was also the main reason why so many soldiers and officers, especially older ones, hated the new tactics or plainly could not deal with them. If they did reflect on the novel way of fighting, they did not remember warrior-tactics, but their own poor selves as representatives of the nation and its struggle for survival against overwhelming force. To be sure, there were others who celebrated themselves as "men of steel." But for all the literature and all the excitement among historians they generated, they were quite as far from reality as those soldiers who saw themselves as victims when in fact they were uncannily lethal warriors. What both sides neglect to mention (and military practice reflects only indirectly) is not, as we might expect, the act of killing. Rather, it is the sheer fright and terror that killing induced.

Ferocity and Fright

The problem with the soldiers' (lack of) memory is the curious ambiguity of soldiers felt about their role as warriors—as self-willed actors, within a group, whose skill was to strike back in order to kill. In one way, we may think of this problem within the context of a civilizational taboo on killing, which only a small, self-proclaimed elite—led by the writings of Ernst Jünger—dared to break, and which a postwar generation and subsequent generations of historians idolized.[63] The pervasiveness of the image of the German soldier as a man of steel, as opposed to a rather more treacherous and ambivalent reality, is a problem. The readiness, especially of literary scholars, to draw far-reaching conclusions not simply about an image, but about experience and practice, is an outright headache, even when and where the literary analysis is compelling.[64] However, while all of this deserves scrutiny, there is a far more important issue at stake: the peculiar nature of German ferocity.

The historically more pertinent question really is: Where, in a war-weary army, would the fighting strength and endurance come from? In World War I, ideology barely played a role, the fear of punishment was equally insignificant, and the (supposedly) bright and eager bellicosity of the cult of the 1914 offensive was surely smashed to pieces in 1916. The two grand battles of 1916, at Verdun and at the Somme, effectively demolished Wilhelmine, belligerent manliness—and not only by wiping out active soldiers, NCOs, and a lower officer corps that had managed to survive the exorbitant casualties of 1914/15.[65] These battles taught German soldiers to fear the enemy and loath the war—and there can be no doubt that they did.[66] Nonetheless, the new regulations for defense and attack in 1917/18—as well as the postwar regulation, *Führung und Gefecht der verbundenen Waffen* (1921/22)—quite deliberately made military operations dependent on the unfettered use of force on the tactical level and on empowering small units to act on their own. Combat was made dependent on small group action in the overall context of advancing both theory and practice of combined operations (most highly developed in, but not limited to, the interplay between infantry and artillery). In other words, it was made dependent on soldiers, who were anything but ready to fight. In fact, in 1916/17, fighting was made dependent on soldiers who had repeatedly given indications—in break-downs of authority, refusals to go over the top, and insubordinations that were not all that dissimilar from what happened on the French side in 1917—that they might well refuse to fight.[67]

In some ways, this was less a contradiction than it may appear. While the Germans always admired the French and their emphasis on the élan of the ordinary soldier, they really never trusted soldiers, and certainly not recruits, in order to expect anything but fear as a primary response to fire. Therefore the question always was how to overcome fear. The prewar answer was close-order drill, a system of training that never disappeared. In fact, there is an argument to be made that close-order drill became more prominent in basic training at home. At the front, the lay of the land was more complicated, with some divisions reducing close-order drill in favor of combat training while others increased it in order to maintain discipline, and yet others tried to do both, thus turning periods of recuperation into living hell for the soldiers.

Still, looking at the development of training between 1915/16 and 1918 overall, there is a distinct reorientation toward combat-oriented training, especially behind the front. However, even when and where training was insufficient, combat practice had changed with the effect of empowering independent unit action and, in that context, removing restraints on killing and on facing up to the enemy directly. The difference in training had the consequence that some of the more traditional units were simply less prepared for the new way of fighting, which is the reason, as far as I can see, why some of the Wilhelmine elite divisions performed badly compared to some of the reserve divisions. Again, this would be better dealt with in a more systematic and empirical analysis of training and unit behavior. What I am after here is something else: For it seems strange that quite evidently frightened men did their job of fighting so remarkably well. What makes frightened men fight so ferociously?

The answer is, in some part, combat training. But for the most part it has to do with tactics—getting soldiers into a position in which they could not but fight back, and providing them (in principle, if not always in practice) with the skills, the means (*Truppwaffen*, forward artillery observation), and the sanction to do whatever it took to annihilate the enemy, before he got a chance to annihilate them. Training clearly helped, although it occasionally confused and tired out soldiers. The new way of fighting favored more athletic and, for the most part, younger men. It also required new skills of moving and firing, which were extremely difficult to inculcate. But above all, it required developing a group-sense—and this latter aspect was driven home time and again. Some thought that soccer might help; others thought that peasants would never get it and that it took workers and artisans to instinctively "understand" combat; still others firmly believed that it took a community of fate or blood, a kind of mystical higher unity, to make it work. The training behind the front taught soldiers how to move as a group in conjunction with other groups and how to position themselves in order to inflict maximum destruction. There is a whole world of related experience that awaits further study. The bottom line is that, even if we are skeptical about the effects of the new tactics, there was more and more self-activated group- and unit-involvement in killing than had been when and where a prewar sense of manly belligerence ruled supreme. New, successful combat was tied to the principle of ruthless retaliation. The principle was to react, fight back, aggressively. Enemy forces advanced under massive artillery barrages, while German units were supposed to evade the destructive fire in order to strike back. And strike back they did, with extraordinary ferocity—not everywhere and all the time, but enough to see the new tactics work.

The counterstrike and, on the level of formations, the counterattack principle was simple in theory but difficult to realize in practice, all the more since space for movement was limited and the appearance of tanks increased the fear of exposure. However, the main problem was distinctly human. Commanding officers did not, for the most part, possess the operational cunning and courage to stage a counterstrike or launch a counterattack, even if reserves were appropriately deployed. Soldiers were loath to yield their trenches and dug-outs in order to strike back, because it exposed them to enemy fire. And yet, the principle became basic military doctrine. It was the main inspiration for German combined operations (which started out as a practice of flexibly linking fire and movement in the context of defensive and offensive operations in trench warfare). It was writ large in the offensive operations in 1918, where the limits of mobility and of individualized tactics became painfully obvious. Nonetheless, the doctrine was once more further expanded and refined in the basic manual of 1921/22, the *Führung und Gefecht mit verbundenen Waffen*. Eventually, it would become the reality behind the propaganda facade of "Blitzkrieg," which was nothing other than a system of tactical aggression staged on a grand scale by the National Socialist propaganda machine.[68] In the beginning, though, were the defensive tactics of 1916/17 in the face of Allied superiority in men and weapons.

In one sense, there was nothing new about counterstrikes and counterattacks. The attack from the position of operative defense has a long and illustrious history.[69] However, the attempt to find a way out of the impasse created by the war in the trenches did have its own unique features. We have seen how the mass character of infantry warfare had been replaced by a differentiated network in which the unit's crew-served weapons (machine gun, flamethrower, trench mortar) occupied the most sensitive points, as well as how the infantry's conduct in combat was characterized by flexible evasion of the main thrust of the enemy's attack.[70] But because of their concentrated firepower, they—as well as the shock troops—were also in particular danger. The success of each enemy offensive depended on whether precisely these small detachments, fighting from their often fortified positions, could be subdued and eliminated. If nothing else, the Allied lore about heroism and sacrifice in clearing these positions and the baleful pleasure of having them blown to bits suggest that counterstrike combat took its toll. In turn, counterstrike and counterattack were not for the faint-hearted—and surely were inappropriate for older soldiers, who were seen as unfit for front-line duty.[71] The best chance for a combatants' survival lay in the elastic ability to elude the enemy's main assault so as to strike back with as much destructive force as possible in order to avoid being overrun or crushed. Thus, the initial flexibility of evading the enemy (or drawing him out into offensive action) only exacerbated the predicament: in order to survive, the evading side would have to attack sooner or later—or be forced to flee.[72] Preventing evasive maneuvers from becoming permanent retreats thus became one of the chief concerns (and one of the chief points of contention) of the field army's leadership. I do not wish to go into it in detail here, but it involved determining the fictitious zone, the *Hauptkampflinie*, where there could no longer be any backward, forward, or lateral movement and the only option was to destroy the enemy under whatever circumstances prevailed. Micro-panics happened all the time. Entire divisions collapsed more rarely, but they did. These were the vulnerabilities of a tactical and operational practice which, on the whole worked well in that an ever smaller number of front-line troops withstood Allied attacks into the fall of 1918 and collapsed only in October of that year. It also reduced death-tolls quite dramatically, especially in 1917, although this advantage was squandered in the 1918 German offensive, which demonstrated that the Kaiser's field army, while set for defensive warfare, was not particularly good at offensive fighting.

The tactics of the counterstrike built on ordinary soldiers' willingness to move, and to expose themselves to fire in movement, in order to strike. It necessitated fierce, concentrated bursts of fire. Because there was no room for making prisoners in the combination of movement and fire, annihilation became the order of the day. But there was no room for error either, or one was most assuredly dead. The fighting turned extraordinarily bitter–quite literally a "kill-or-die" and often enough a "kill-and-die" system for friend and foe. The various elements of the counterstrike, undertaken to destroy an overwhelming threat elicited by one's own actions, are best exemplified in the elaboration of the principles of tank defense.[73] The ultimate form of the German tank defense in 1918—or the defense against "tank terror," as it was repeatedly called—consisted in the following: the infantry detachments, or the lighter elements of the field artillery, emerged (or, at least, were supposed to emerge) from their cover into the direct line of fire to duel with individual tanks. It was either do or die. The salient point was that in this situation aggression offered not only the sole possibility of survival, but also the best method of overcoming one's own terror. It took a while for the staffs—and, as always, there is an ample debate on the matter—to discover that the best way for soldiers to deal with fright was to confront the source of it head-on. And confrontation meant annihilation. In describing how they torched, mutilated, incapacitated, and tortured tanks and their crews, German soldiers expressed the same kind of bile-ful pleasure that Allied soldiers showed over eliminating the fortified strongholds of the Germans. Annihilation—of a pillbox or a tank and their crews—quite literally liberated the combatant from a deadly threat. If the French did not have the word jouissance for the resulting sentiment, it would have to be invented. Soldiers' language for the lust to kill in order to escape deadly danger is, of course, a lot more plastic and cruder.

The basic concept behind the principle of a counterstrike-force thus consisted in this: to strike back with all available means, to repulse an overwhelming threat with a crushing blow, and in doing so, to undo one's own terror in the face of impending death. What emerged was a system of calculated, staged self-defense (when everything went according to plan, which was rarely the case) that turned cutting off, with the goal of annihilating the enemy, into the precondition of survival. Soldiers fought, and they fought ferociously as statistics of lethality suggest, because they fought back. This way of fighting no longer had much to do with patriotic spirit or heroic zeal. It had little to do with command authority either, certainly less than in the old-fashioned line- or trench-formations of the first two years of the war. Instead, it had a great deal to do with group cohesion and solidarity. The killing was "intimate," but the basic emotion was one of fright overcome by group rage and aggression. While the prevalence of emotions is harder to prove than the basic pattern of military practice, I have come to think that fear and rage were the basic emotions that kept front-line troops fighting. Inasmuch as soldiers talked, they spoke of their quality work well done, and it took an intellectual like Ernst Jünger to imbue this satisfaction with a "cold" emotional language of its own.

There were soldiers at the front for whom killing was distasteful, just as there were those who enjoyed it. Some became so brutal as to be unrecognizable to their comrades, and others were so traumatized they could no longer recognize themselves. But the system of the elastic defense (and attack) worked, because so long as any one of the men was placed in this tactical combat situation, they all fought—and in 1917/18, fighting meant moving from defense to assault in a situation of allied superiority in terms of men, weapons, and surveillance of the terrain. It meant to push artillery and infantry counterstrikes in full knowledge that the enemy knew where you were and had the superior means to destroy you.

This system was absolutely terrifying: the hunter was always also the hunted, and vice versa. The soldiers' conduct entirely depended on the ability of the individual and the collective to overcome fear and panic. One prerequisite for this was, as we have seen, training through drill—whereby the precise form and purpose of the drill were a matter of tremendous contention. But in order to really make soldiers fight, and hence to turn them into warriors, more was necessary. German battle tactics first turned the fear and panic into movement (evasive maneuvers) instead of frozen stasis, and then converted this movement into all-out aggression. The preferred depiction for this kind of soldier was the steel-helmeted hard face with flaming eyes and pursed lips. But photographs provide us with a somewhat different image. We see gaunt soldiers, with their thousand-yard stare, slumping over in exhaustion. If they were not killed or wounded, they were physically and emotionally burnt out by battle. Both images matter, because the soldiers themselves, and especially the youngsters who emulated them, wanted to see themselves as toughened by war and unconditionally committed to their task. Unconditionality (*Unbedingtheit*), though, was clearly a mask—a mask for soldiers who were scared to death and therefore killed unconditionally.[74]

From the vantage point of theory (and contemporary speculation), the transformation of fear into aggression was nothing particularly extraordinary. In practice, however, something did have to happen after all to effect the transformation. The reordering of group solidarities was one answer; a new decentered command structure was another. A new emotion of fighting war, fear and rage, may yet emerge as a third dimension. The irony of the system consisted in the fact that every individual soldier could get the impression that he and his unit would survive only if they possessed sufficient skills and aggression. Statistics spoke to the contrary, but those who survived could nonetheless believe that they did so by dint of their own effort and skill—and thanks to providence, the sheer luck of the survivor who made it by going after and hitting back at the enemy. These soldiers did not collapse in grief, but carried within them the deep ambiguity of an unmistakable sense of superiority on the one hand, and a feeling of existential threat on the other. This became the German way of waging war.

Does the emerging combat practice between 1916 and 1918 explain the way the Wehrmacht would fight in World War II? In some ways, it does because what was novel in World War I became routine in World War II. The end effect was a peculiar ferocity in fighting that only increased with the long retreat in the East, the South, and the West. It also makes sense of the sheer emotive force, the abandon, with which German soldiers fought. But there is no straight line that leads from the annihilation tactics to a war of annihilation. While compelling in a superficial way, the idea of human carnage in the war of materiél and the debasement of human life is not the best starting point from which to make sense of the mixture of ferocity and superiority that is so central to the brutalization of soldiers in World War II. A more persuasive factor is fear and the rage it engenders of striking to wipe out anything and everything that might kill you.

The latter, as is well known, was not only the German way of waging war, but also the self-proclaimed Nazi way of life and death. To get from one to the other, we would have to look much more carefully at the coding of violence—at the ways in which the soldiers and the nation came to grips with the war they had fought and the war they had lost.[75] They knew that they were invincible and firmly believed that as such they were entitled to be victorious—and if that were not to be, that they would go down in flames, but not before bringing down those who knew the secret of their vulnerability. This is where a way of fighting gave way to myth, to a militant antisemitism, and to phantasmagorias of all-out annihilation, and where killing in war gave way to genocide.

Notes

* I would like to acknowledge the careful editorial work of Barry Haneberg and the insightful comments by Dwight Phillips as well as by the anonymous reviewer of the manuscript.

1. The most important influence on this continues to be Klaus Theweleit, *Männerphantasien*, vol. 1: *Frauen, Fluten, Körper, Geschichte*. Frankfurt/Main: Roter Stern, 1977 and Klaus Theweleit, *Männerphatasien*, vol. 2: *Männerkörper: Zur Psychoanalyse des Weißen Terror* (Frankfurt am Main, 1978).
2. See, for example, *Wehrlos hinter der Front: Leiden der Völker im Krieg: 144 Bilddokumente* (Frankfurt am Main, 1931). Anton Holzer, *Die andere Front: Fotografie und Propaganda im Ersten Weltkrieg* (Darmstadt, 2007).
3. Thorsten Bonacker, "Zuschreibungen der Gewalt: Zur Sinnförmigkeit interaktiver, organisierter und gesellschaftlicher Gewalt," *Soziale Welt* 53 (2002): 31–48, here 35.
4. Stéphane Audoin-Rouzeau, "Pratiques et objects de la cruauté sur le champ de bataille," *14–18 aujourd'hui* 2 (1999): 105–114. Bruno Cabanes, *La victoire endeuillée : la sortie de guerre des soldats français, 1918–1920* (Paris, 2004).
5. Projektgruppe 'Trench Art'—Kreativität des Schützengrabens, ed., *Kleines aus dem Großen Krieg: Metamorphosen militärischen Mülls* (Tübingen, 2002).

6. Joanna Bourke, *An Intimate History of Killing: Face-to-Face Killing in Twentieth-Century Warfare* (New York, 1999).
7. The problem lies with the anthropology of the German war. German war practice, unlike the French, tended quite deliberately to dampen élan as a source for action.
8. For France, see Leonard V. Smith, *The Embattled Self: French Soldiers' Testimony of the Great War* (Ithaca and London, 2007).
9. Niall Ferguson, *The Pity of War* (New York, 1999). See also James McRandle and James Quirk, "The Blood Test Revisited: A New Look at German Casualty Counts in World War I," *Journal of Military History* 70, no. 3 (2006): 667–701.
10. Heeres-Sanitätsinspektion des Reichskriegsministeriums, *Sanitätsbericht über das Deutsche Heer (Deutsches Feld- und Besatzungsheer) im Weltkriege 1914/18*, 3 vols. (Berlin, 1934–1938), vol. 3, 66.
11. Ferguson, *Pity of War,* 300.
12. The highest casualty rates were suffered by the British forces during the defense against the major German assault between 25 March and 3 April 1918, with 6,325 officers lost, and in the last great Allied offensive between 25 September and 2 October 1918, with 3,017 officers lost. The losses in the Battle of the Somme were lower (2456), and were comparable to those in the week of 28 August 1918 (namely, 2,478) and of 1 May 1918 (2,201). War Office, *Statistics of the Military Effort of the British Empire during the Great War, 1914/1920* (London, 1922), 253, Table 3.
13. War Office, *Statistics of the Military Effort,* 253–271, Table 3(casualties by months in France). Brief information about French losses may be found in Leonard V. Smith, Stéphane Audoin-Rouzeau and Annette Becker; *France and the Great War, 1914–1918* (Cambridge and New York, 2003), 68–71.
14. Volker Berghahn, *Europa im Zeitalter der Weltkriege: Die Entfesselung und Entgrenzung der Gewalt* (Frankfurt am Main, 2002).
15. If this point is more controversial than it needs to be, that is above all because the second half of the war—1942–1945—has been studied much less than the first. In any case, the theory of the dematerialization and demodernization of the Wehrmacht between 1942 and 1944, which is advocated above all by Omer Bartov, does not withstand closer scrutiny. Omer Bartov, *Hitler's Army: Soldiers, Nazis, and War in the Third Reich* (New York, 1991).
16. Victor David Hanson, *Carnage and Culture: Landmark Battles in the Rise of Western Power* (New York, 2001).
17. Thomas Kühne, *Kameradschaft: Die Soldaten des nationalsozialistischen Krieges und das 20. Jahrhundert* (Göttingen, 2006).
18. Isabel V. Hull, *Absolute Destruction: Military Culture and the Practice of War in Imperial Germany* (Ithaca and London, 2005). While I am in agreement with many aspects of this important study, I have given up on the idea that the military culture of the empire is capable of explaining the lethality (and brutality) of German fighting in the Second World War or, for that matter, in World War I. If anything, I have come to appreciate ever more the extraordinary inventiveness of the German military, even as it involves a learning curve with devastating effect. My own efforts in this direction go back to Michael Geyer,"German Strategy in the Age of Machine Warfare, 1914–1945," in Peter Paret, ed., *Makers of Modern Strategy from Machiavelli to the Nuclear Age* (Princeton, NJ, 1985), 527–597.
19. Stefan Kaufmann, "Raumrevolution: Die militärischen Raumauffassungen zwischen dem Ersten und dem zweiten Weltkrieg," in Rainer Rother, ed., *Der Weltkrieg 1914–1918: Ereignis und Erinnerung* (Berlin, 2004), 42–49.
20. Alexander B. Rossino, *Hitler Strikes Poland: Blitzkrieg, Ideology, and Atrocity* (Lawrence, KS, 2003). Klaus-Michael Mallmann and Bogdan Musial, eds., *Genesis des Genozids : Polen 1939–1941* (Darmstadt, 2004).

21. Raffael Scheck, "They Are Just Savages": German Massacres of Black Soldiers from the French Army in 1940," *Journal of Modern History* 77, no. 2 (2005): 325–344.
22. Christopher R. Browning, ed., *The Origins of the Final Solution: The Evolution of Nazi Jewish Policy, September 1939–March 1942* (Lincoln, NE and Jerusalem, 2004).
23. Konrad H. Jarausch and Michael Geyer, *Shattered Past: Reconstructing German Histories* (Princeton, N.J., 2003).
24. Jeffrey Herf, *The Jewish Enemy: Nazi Propaganda during World War II and the Holocaust* (Cambridge, Mass., 2006).
25. Walter Manoschek, "'Wo der Partisan ist, ist der Jude, und wo der Jude ist, ist der Partisan'": Die Wehrmacht und die Shoah," in Gerhard Paul, ed., *Die Täter der Shoah: Fanatische Nationalsozialisten oder ganz normale Deutsche?* (Göttingen, 2002), 167–185.
26. Jürgen Förster, "Wehrmacht, Krieg und Holocaust," in Rolf-Dieter Müller and Erich Volkmann, eds., *Die Wehrmacht: Mythos und Realität* (Munich,1999), 948–63.
27. The most effective advocate is Omer Bartov, *Mirrors of Destruction: War, Genocide, and Modern Identity* (Oxford and New York, 2000). See also Alan Kramer, *Dynamics of Destruction: Culture and Mass Killing in the First World War* (Oxford, 2007).
28. Leonard V. Smith, Stephane Audoin-Rouzeau, and Annette Becker, *France and the Great War 1914-1918* (Cambridge and New York,, 2003).
29. Benjamin Ziemann, "Die Eskalation des Tötens in zwei Weltkriegen" in Richard von Dülmen, ed., *Erfindung des Menschen: Schöpfungsträume und Körperbilder 1500–2000* (Vienna and Cologne, 1998), 411–429. Anne Duménil. "1918, l'année de la "Grand Bataille": Les facteurs militaires de la défaite allemande," in Nicolas Beaupré, Anne Duménil and Christian Ingrao, eds., *1914–1945: L'ère de la guerre - violence, mobilisations, deuil* (Paris, 2004), 229–255.
30. Ute Frevert, *A Nation in Barracks: Modern Germany, Military Conscription, and Civil Society.* (Oxford and New York, 2004).
31. A preliminary look at the large variety of these documents may be found in Duménil, "1918." My own research confirms Duménil's insights. However, this essay affords little space for exploring the issue in depth. Suffice it to say that there is a genuine learning process in the way of fighting war, a process of adaptation in which this knowledge was translated into practice, and a system of after-battle reports that discuss systematically the application of new tactics. The somewhat surprising thing is that, although this process is a prominent feature in the record of all units and formations, historians have not really looked at it.
32. This point had already been addressed before the war, above all in the works of Johann von Bloch, who believed, however, that the effectiveness of the weapons would eradicate war. See, for example, his short essay "Die Fortschritte der Waffentechnik müssen die Kriege verschwinden lassen," *Deutsche Revue* 26 (1901): 83–94.
33. Hugo Freiherr von Freytag-Loringhoven, "Die Exerzier-Reglements für die Infanterie von 1812, 1847, 1888, und 1906. Ein Jahrhundert taktischer Entwicklung," *Beiheft zum Militär-Wochenblatt*, no. 1 (1907): 27–40. See also his account, *Das Exerzier-Reglement für die Infanterie vom 29. Mai 1906 kriegsgeschichtlich erläutert* (Berlin, 1907). For the inter-war years, see Robert M. Citino, *The Path to Blitzkrieg: Doctrine and Training in the German Army, 1920–1939* (Boulder, 1999).
34. Ulrich Bröckling, *Disziplin: Soziologie und Geschichte militärischer Gehorsamsproduktion* (Munich, 1997).
35. The quote comes from: A.O.K. 7 Ia/IIa Nr. 711 geh. V. 13.9. 1917, gez. von Boehn: Anlage 8C in "Entwicklung der Ausbildung in der Heimat und in den Rekrutendepots hinter der Front," Bundesarchiv-Militärarchiv (BA-MA) W-10/50725.
36. Benjamin Ziemann, *Front und Heimat: Ländliche Kriegserfahrung im südlichen Bayern* (Essen, 1997), 120–138.
37. Hew Strachan, "Ausbildung, Kampfgeist und die zwei Weltkriege," in Bruno Thoß and Hans-Erich Volkmann, eds., *Erster Weltkrieg — Zweiter Weltkrieg: Krieg, Kriegserlebnis, Kriegserfahrung in Deutschland* (Paderborn, 2002), 265–286.

38. See "Wiederherstellung der Kampfkraft und die Erstellung einheitlicher, neuzeitlicher Verfahren," BA-MA W-10/50 747. "Stimmung des Heeres 1918," BA-MA W-10/51 833.
39. OTL Engelmann, "Die Ausbildungsvorschrift für Fußtruppen" (A.V.F.), December 1916 and the first and second drafts of the "Ausbildungsvorschrift für die Fußtruppen im Kriege" (A.V.F.), 1917 and January 1918, BA-MA W-10/50 151.
40. See, for instance, the study by Georg Soldan, *Der Mensch und die Schlacht der Zukunft* (Oldenburg i.O., 1925).
41. This became a major theme of German war literature. Ann P. Linder, *Princes of the Trenches: Narrating the German Experience of the First World War* (Columbia, SC, 1996).
42. René Schilling, *"Kriegshelden:" Deutungsmuster heroischer Männlichkeit in Deutschland 1813–1945* (Paderborn, 2002), although he focuses on the hero as martyr. See also OT Mahlmann, "Der Entschluß: Erziehung und Ausbildung von Soldaten," BA-MA W-10/50 149.
43. (Wilhelm) Reibert, *Der Dienstunterricht im Heer: Ausgabe für den Schützen der Schützenkompagnie*, rev. 12th ed. (Berlin, 1940).
44. See, for instance, Chef des Generalstabes des Feldheeres IA/II Nr. 6578 geh, op. 16. 2. 1918, gez. Ludendorff, with complaints, among others, that the troops would run through to a forward position, huddle together ("brings unnecessary losses"), shoot senselessly from the hip ("thoughtful exploitation of the weapon's effect vital"), and "fail to coordinate their actions with the machine guns. "Angriff-Abwehr 1918," BA-MA W-10/50 836.
45. Klaus Latzel, "Die Soldaten des industrialisierten Krieges: 'Fabrikarbeiter der Zerstörung': Eine Zeugenbefragung zu Gewalt, Arbeit und Gewöhnung," in Rolf Spilker and Bernd Ulrich, eds., *Der Tod als Maschinist: Der industrialisierte Krieg 1914–1918* (Bramsche, 1998), 125–141. Paul Lerner, "Psychiatry and Casualties of War in Germany, 1914–18," *Journal of Contemporary History* 35, no. 1 (2001): 13–28.
46. Martin Samuels, *Command or Control? Command, Training and Tactics in the British and German Armies 1888–1918* (London, 1995).
47. For a summary, see OTL Engelmann, "Grundsätze für die Führung in der Abwehrschlacht im Stellungskrieg," BA-MA W-10/50 168.
48. Gerhard P. Groß, "Das Dogma der Beweglichkeit: Überlegungen zur Genese der deutschen Heerestaktik im Zeitalter der Weltkriege," in Thoß and Volkmann, *Erster Weltkrieg—Zweiter Weltkrieg*, 143–166.
49. Ziemann, *Front und Heimat,* 192–205.
50. Tony Ashworth, *Trench Warfare 1914–1918: The Live and Let Live System* (New York, 1980). Tim Travers, *How the War Was Won: Command and Technology in the British Army on the Western Front, 1917–1918* (London, 1992). Paddy Griffith, *Battle Tactics on the Western Front: The British Army's Art of Attack, 1916–1918* (New Haven and London, 1994).
51. Antulio J. Echevarria, *After Clausewitz: German Military Thinkers Before the Great War* (Lawrence, KS, 2000), 70, 123.
52. Groß, "Dogma der Beweglichkeit," 152.
53. See the comparative study, "Über Gefechtsausdehnungen," BA-MA W-10/50 132.
54. Timothy T. Lupfer, *The Dynamics of Doctrine: The Changes in Tactical Doctrine during the First World War* (Fort Leavenworth, KS, 1981).
55. I am grateful to Anne Duménil for this apt formulation.
56. Benjamin Ziemann, "'Macht der Maschine' — Mythen des industriellen Krieges," in Spilker and Ulrich, *Der Tod als Maschinist,* 176–189.
57. As evidenced, for instance, in "Divisionen 14.7.1917–4.11.1918 (Zustandsmeldungen, Verlustlisten," "Verluste 17.6.1917–30.10.1918," "OQu Mob 5.5.1918–19.10.1918 (Rückzug)," and "Lagekarten und Schriftverkehr 29.8.1918–31.10.1918," in Bayerisches Hauptstaatsarchiv IV, Militärarchiv, Heeresgruppe Kronprinz Ruprecht, Bund 153.
58. Christoph Jahr, *Gewöhnliche Soldaten: Desertion und Deserteure im deutschen und britischen Heer 1914–1918* (Göttingen, 1998), 149–66.
59. See Samuels, *Command or Control?*, p. 167–69, expressly on this point.

60. Michael Geyer, "People's War: The German Debate about a *Levée en Masse* in October 1918," in Daniel Moran and Arthur Waldron, eds., *The People in Arms: Military Myth and National Mobilization since the French Revolution* (New York and Cambridge, 2002), 124–158.
61. Dr. W. Solger, "Die Vorschrift "Der Angriff im Stellungskrieg" vom 1. Januar 1918," BA-MA W-10/50 587 and "Die Entwicklung des deutschen Angriffsverfahrens bis zum Beginn der "Großen Schlacht von Frankreich" [March/April 1940], BA/MA W-10/50 588.
62. The amount of surviving documentation, especially in the two state archives in Stuttgart and Munich, is stunning. In many ways, the most interesting records concern the units and formations that were unable to perform according to the new standards. Breakdowns occurred on every conceivable level, from the common solider to the commanding officer.
63. Klaus Latzel, *Deutsche Soldaten—nationalsozialistischer Krieg? Kriegserlebnis—Kriegserfahrung 1939–1945* (Paderborn, 1998).
64. Eva Horn, "Die Mobilmachung des Körpers." *Transit* 16 (1998/99): 92–107.
65. Michael Geyer, "Vom massenhaften Tötungshandeln, oder: Wie die Deutschen das Krieg-Machen lernten," in Peter Gleichmann and Thomas Kühne, eds., *Massenhaftes Töten: Kriege und Genozide im 20. Jahrhundert* (Essen, 2004), 105–42, with statistical evidence on the deleterious 1914/15 campaigns.
66. Gerhard Hirschfeld, Gerd Krumeich, and Irina Renz, eds. *Die Deutschen an der Somme 1914–1918: Krieg, Besatzung, Verbrannte Erde* (Essen, 2006).
67. This is a rather difficult issue, which requires further scrutiny. The first one to point to the resistant behavior of German soldiers in 1916 and 1917 was Benjamin Ziemann, "Verweigerungsformen von Frontsoldaten in der deutschen Armee 1914–1918," in Andreas Gestrich, ed., *Gewalt im Krieg: Ausübung, Erfahrung und Verweigerung von Gewalt in Kriegen des 20. Jahrhunderts* (Münster, 1996), 99–122.
68. Karl-Heinz Frieser, *Blitzkrieg-Legende: Der Westfeldzug 1940* (Munich, 1995). Omer Bartov, "From Blitzkrieg to Total War: Controversial Links between Image and Reality," in Ian Kershaw and Moshe Lewin, eds., *Stalinism and Nazism: Dictatorships in Comparison* (Cambridge and New York, 1997), 158–84.
69. The father of this idea is none other than Clausewitz. Whether Schlieffen also belongs in this genealogy is one of the issues currently being debated among American military intellectuals. See Terence Zuber, *Inventing the Schlieffen Plan: German War Planning 1871–1914* (Oxford, 2002).
70. The clearest picture emerges from "Sturmbataillone," BA-MA W-10/50 793.
71. Evidence in Geyer, "Vom massenhaften Töten."
72. Flight was the more lethal alternative. Defection was hardly an option, for the Allies did not trust the extremely dangerous German troops. See Ferguson, *Pity of War,* 367–394.
73. See especially "Kampfwagenabwehr," BA-MA W-10/50 769. Extensive documents relating to this development may be found in "Tankabwehr 29.3.1917–29.9. 1918," in Bayerisches Hauptstaatsarchiv IV, Militärarchiv, Heeresgruppe Kronprinz Ruprecht, Bund 126.
74. Michael Wildt, *Generation des Unbedingten: Das Führungskorps des Reichssicherheitshauptamtes* (Hamburg, 2002).
75. Michael Geyer, "Insurrectionary Warfare: The German Debate about a Levée en Masse in October 1918," *Journal of Modern History* 73, no 3 (2001): 459–527.

Chapter 2

THE SHADOW OF DEATH IN GERMANY AT THE END OF THE SECOND WORLD WAR

Richard Bessel

> Death is a problem of the living.
> —Norbert Elias

During the last year of the Second World War, more Germans died than in any other year before or since. In 1945 Germany became a land of the dead, a "Totenland."[1] In the middle of a century in which death became less and less public, in which the dying increasingly were found in hospitals, old people's homes, and hospices (a process described by Norbert Elias as a "tacit removal of ... the dying from the community of the living"[2]) and the dead disposed of beyond the public gaze by "paid specialists,"[3] in which "the sight of the dying and the dead ... no longer is an everyday occurrence"[4] and death became hidden and repressed, Germans suddenly were confronted publicly by death and by corpses as never before in their modern history. For a short period, death—violent death—was at the center of public as well as private life in Germany. Never before or since had Germans come face to face with death in so extensive and shocking a manner. One may debate whether or in what respects 1945 was Germany's "Zero Hour," but it certainly was the hour of the corpse.

The greatest cause of death in Germany in early 1945 was military action on the ground, which claimed the lives of astronomical numbers of soldiers in the final stages of the war. Although it is well known that the last year of the war had terrible consequences for the German people, the sheer scale of the bloodshed and loss of life, and the implications that flow from this, often are not fully appreciated. While German losses during the preceding war years had been enormous, what took place in the last months of the conflict overshadows even previous horrors and may be described as a veritable killing frenzy. For the Germans the

---

Notes for this chapter begin on page 63.

greatest loss of life came not in the first four years of war, but during 1944 and 1945. Spurred on to fight by fear of the Russians on the one hand and of Wehrmacht military "justice" on the other,[5] often placed in positions where there was no possibility of retreat, and left to face the overwhelming firepower amassed by Allied forces—more German soldiers lost their lives during the last months of the war than ever before.

The very worst of the killing took place in early 1945, and this occurred largely as a result of fighting *within* Germany. In the first five months of 1945 alone, Germany's military losses were greater than those in 1942 and 1943 put together. That is to say, it was neither "Barbarossa," nor the fighting at the gates of Moscow in the winter of 1941/42, nor the great offensives in 1942, nor the battles of Stalingrad or Kursk, that brought the Wehrmacht its greatest losses; its greatest losses were the consequence of the bitter battles of the last months of the war—battles which largely took place inside Germany. In January 1945, the month when the great Soviet offensive along a front from East Prussia to southern Poland effectively broke the back of the Wehrmacht, the numbers of German military dead reached their peak of over 450,000: in each of the next three months the number of German soldiers killed was more than 280,000—that is to say, far in excess of the 185,000 Wehrmacht members who died in January 1943, the month of the defeat at Stalingrad.[6] Allied casualties—the overwhelming majority of which were Soviet soldiers battling their way into the Reich from the East—were by all accounts even greater than German; in the battle for Berlin alone the Soviet Army, whose tactics hardly were designed to minimize its own losses, suffered more than 300,000 casualties in the space of just three weeks.[7] Never before had so many people been killed in Germany in so short a time.

To the colossal numbers of deaths arising from military action on the ground were added fatalities resulting from the Allied bombing. At the same time that military casualties were at their highest, the bombing campaign against Germany reached its peak. In the final months of the war—when cities across Germany were bombed day and night and Magdeburg (in January 1945), Pforzheim and Dresden (in February), and Swinemünde and Würzburg (in March) were destroyed as the whole of Germany came within range of British and American bombers—a greater tonnage of bombs was dropped on the Reich per month than ever before: between January 1945 and Germany's surrender in May, on average over 1,000 people were killed daily by the bombing—roughly 130,000 altogether.[8] In contrast to the end of the First World War, when German troops still stood well beyond the borders of the Reich at the time Germany's military effort collapsed, in the last battles of the Second World War both German soldiers and civilians were fighting and dying within Germany. The dead of 1945 fell not in France or Russia but in Berlin and Breslau, and they were not just male soldiers but also female civilians, not just Germans but also foreigners compelled to work in the Nazi war economy.

The massive numbers of deaths during the last months of the war were the result not only of Allied military action. The Nazi murder machine did not cease operation just because Germany was losing a world war. As Allied armies approached the concentration-camp empire, tens of thousands of desperately hungry and ill prisoners were forced onto evacuation marches, often in the middle of winter, which left huge numbers dead: of the 714,211 concentration-camp inmates registered on 15 January 1945, at least a third and perhaps as many as half died in the next four months.[9] Many were shot by their guards along the roadside during forced marches, often for minor infractions such as taking too long to urinate or defecate; others starved or fell victim to the terrible epidemics that were a feature of the camps in the last months before the war ended. Leaving aside the mass murder by gas that had taken place earlier in extermination camps set up specifically for that purpose, the death marches, starvation, and disease probably claimed the lives of half of all the victims of the wartime concentration camps during the last months of the war.

It was not just Jews and other camp inmates who fell victim. As its end drew near and the prospect of imminent defeat (and the futility of continuing to fight) became blindingly obvious, the Nazi regime also turned viciously on its own people. Wehrmacht soldiers who retreated were, if caught, to be executed and (as in the "Fortress" Schneidemühl at the beginning of 1945) publicly hanged with signs hanging from their bodies reading "This is what happens to all cowards."[10] The Wehrmacht high command demanded that the "most drastic measures" be leveled against looters, who either were to be shot on the spot or, where they came before courts-martial, were subject to harsh sentences to be "carried out immediately and in the most visible manner": looters were to be shot "as far as possible at the entrances and exits of towns."[11] The results were summed up well in a headline in the last-ever issue of the newspaper *Stargarder Tageblatt* on 17 18 February 1945: "On Adolf-Hitler-Square the Hanged are Swinging in the Wind."[12]

During the last weeks of the war, civilians (especially in the west) increasingly urged German soldiers to cease fighting and thus prevent the physical destruction of their communities, and in numerous cases greeted Allied forces with white flags.[13] The Nazi regime responded to such "defeatism" in characteristic fashion: according to the decree issued by Heinrich Himmler (in his capacity as Supreme Commander of the Replacement Army) on 12 April 1945, "all male persons" found "in any house from which a white flag appears" were "to be shot."[14] Far from seeking to hide the dead from public view, in its last months the Nazi regime made a point of displaying the corpses of "cowards" so that all could see. Over sixty years later, in the interview in which he revealed his membership, as a 17-year-old, in the Waffen-SS, Günter Grass recalled: "The first dead that I saw were not Russians, but Germans. They were hanging from the trees, many of them were my age."[15]

Not only was death meted out publicly in order to intimidate and to terrorize; it also was offered as a goal, to inspire future generations that someday might again take up the struggle.[16] The Nazi regime embraced death as had no other. As the Third Reich reached its end, the Nazi leadership could offer the German people only death as a way out of the nightmare that National Socialism had created. Joseph Goebbels put it in a nutshell in a diary entry in mid-March 1945, six weeks before his own suicide and that of his "Führer," when he wrote: "We must always lead the German people back to the basic thesis of how we wage war and make it clear to them that they have no other choice but to fight or to die."[17] However, by March 1945 the Nazi leadership was not offering the choice of fighting *or* dying so much as the prospect of fighting *and* dying. During the last weeks of the war, German military formations were led into positions where they were encircled and annihilated, as in the bloody battles in the forests at Halbe to south of Berlin (where roughly 60,000 members of the Wehrmacht were killed),[18] around Elbing in West Prussia, in Berlin, in the "Fortress Breslau," and in dozens of other cities that were declared "fortresses," whose remaining inhabitants were expected to fight to the last breath. German cities and towns became littered with corpses—of "criminals" who had been hanged for alleged petty offenses, defeatism, or cowardice, of soldiers who had fallen in battle, of victims of the bombing who often were so burned that they no longer could be identified.

Many Germans grasped only too well the choice that Goebbels articulated in March 1945 and, like the Minister for Propaganda and Enlightenment and "Plenipotentiary for Total War," chose to kill themselves once the Third Reich went down in flames. Even Karl Dönitz, soon to become Hitler's successor as head of state, spoke at the end of April of his intention to "seek death in a last battle in order to remove for all time any suspicion of personal cowardice."[19] The wave of suicides that accompanied German defeat encompassed not just much of the erstwhile political leadership of the Third Reich—including Hitler, Goebbels, Göring, Himmler, Thierack, and Ley—but also many second-ranking Nazi leaders (including the *Gauleiter* Paul Giesler, Wilhelm Murr, Bernhard Rust, Gustav Simon, Jacob Sprenger, Otto Telchow and Josef Terboven), military commanders (including Hans Krebs, Walter Model, and Hans Georg von Friedeburg), and minor functionaries of the National Socialist regime, as well as thousands of ordinary people who killed themselves as Allied forces smashed their way into the Reich and occupied the country.[20]

Fear of retribution, fear of rape, desolation at the loss of home and family, lack of a future perspective, and anger at what had occurred combined to fuel a massive suicide wave without parallel in modern German history.[21] According to a report of the German Security Service about popular opinion and morale in early 1945, "Many are getting used to the idea of making an end of it all. Everywhere there is great demand for poison, for a pistol and other means for ending one's life. Suicides due to genuine depression about the catastrophe which certainly is expected are an everyday occurrence."[22] In late January, shortly before Breslau was surrounded by Soviet military forces, the priest Paul Peikert reported that "the number of suicides in our city has increased tremendously"; he went on: "A police officer from one station told me that in his precinct 60 suicides were recorded in the last ten days. In my parish as well some families were found asphyxiated by gas in their flats."[23] The sight that greeted American soldiers when they arrived at the *Neues Rathaus* in Leipzig—littered with the bodies of Nazi officials who had killed themselves and their families[24]—was but a rather spectacular example of a widespread phenomenon during the first half of 1945.

As the German military effort collapsed, in some areas suicide became almost a mass phenomenon. In Berlin 3,881 people were recorded as having killed themselves in April 1945 and another 977 in May.[25] Perhaps the most extreme case is that of the Pomeranian district town of Demmin, where roughly 5 percent of the entire population killed themselves in 1945.[26] In Teterow, a town in Mecklenburg numbering fewer than ten thousand inhabitants in 1946, the burial register included a "Continuation of the Appendix for the Suicide Period Early May 1945" containing details of 120 suicides, listing how the act had been carried out: people shot themselves, hanged themselves, drowned themselves, poisoned themselves; frequent reports noted how fathers killed their entire families and then themselves.[27] In the Sudetenland, where alongside expulsion from their homes Germans now faced some of the most extreme violence meted out to the former masters of Europe, "whole families would dress up in their Sunday best, surrounded by flowers, crosses, and family albums, and then kill themselves by hanging or poison."[28] The wave of suicides did not subside when the deportees returned to what remained of Germany; according to General Ivan Alexandrovich Serov (head of the Soviet secret police in the Soviet Occupation Zone) in June 1945, "with their futures ruined and having no hope for anything better, many of them end their lives by suicide, cutting their wrists."[29] In Frankfurt an der Oder, which had been leveled in the fighting when the Russians took the city in February 1945, one refugee (from the district of Züllichau-Schwiebus) noted that when she arrived in June the bridge over the Oder was littered with loaded wagons and containers; their owners—about 70 families of a "trek" from the East—had just killed themselves by jumping into the river.[30]

Bombing, murder, terror, suicide, intense battles, mass flight, and deportation created a landscape of death in Germany in 1945. In city after city, town after town, the violence of the last days and weeks of the war left behind not just a destroyed physical environment but also numerous corpses. One example among many is provided by the fate of Cottbus, an important site of armaments production (in particular, of the Focke-Wulf FW-190 fighter plane) a little over 100 kilometers southeast of Berlin. Cottbus had been the target of severe bombing, culminating in a raid by more than 400 American B-17s that killed almost a thousand people and made roughly 13,000 homeless on 15 February 1945. Declared a "fortress" in early 1945, Cottbus became a battlefield when the Soviet Army made its final, successful assault and captured the city on 22 April. When the fighting was finished, fewer than 8,000 civilians were left in a city that before the war had contained more than 50,000 inhabitants; more than 1,200 German soldiers had been killed in the final, senseless battle for the city, and 187 civilians had taken their own lives.[31] Cottbus had been reduced to a field of rubble surrounded by mass graves.

The fate of the Silesian capital of Breslau and its inhabitants was even worse. There the final battle in 1945 lasted not for a few days but for three months. As the Soviet Army closed in on the city in January 1945, a large portion of the civilian population fled, with appalling consequences. Panic among crowds desperately trying to get aboard the last trains out of Breslau reportedly led to 60–70 children being crushed to death at the main railway station.[32] The exodus of tens of thousands of the city's inhabitants in freezing temperatures led to huge numbers of casualties, particularly among children and the aged, with search parties subsequently burying hundreds of frozen children and adults found in ditches alongside the roads.[33] When the weather finally warmed, special "corpse-recovery commandos" were sent out along the roads where the refugees had fled westward and where (according to the Breslau priest Paul Peikert) "one says that in Silesia alone some 90,000 corpses were found."[34] Within the "Fortress" Breslau, which was surrounded by Soviet forces on 15 February, corpses became a ubiquitous part of the landscape. A young Polish woman, a forced laborer in the besieged city, noted in her diary on 4 April 1945: "A common cart picked up the dead from yesterday. They are thrown in like chunks of meat."[35] By the time that the German forces in the "Fortress" Breslau surrendered on 6 May (four days after Berlin had fallen to Soviet forces), some 60 percent of the city had been destroyed; German military fatalities were in the region of 6,000 and Soviet military deaths were an estimated 8,000; civilians who died in the "fortress" city have been estimated at roughly 20,000 (with estimates ranging from 10,000 to 80,000, including 3,000 suicides).[36] For more than three months, violence, death, and the sight of corpses framed the daily experiences of those trapped in the doomed city.

Public encounters with the dead, with corpses, occupy a significant place in accounts of what occurred in Germany during the first half of 1945. Franz Scholz, a priest at the Catholic parish of St. Bonifatius in the east of Görlitz (which during the war was the site of the city's army barracks and after the war part of Poland), wrote in his diary (published in the 1970s) about conditions in the city during the last weeks of the war:

> The mortuary at the municipal cemetery is bursting at the seams. For some time now the dead no longer could be accommodated. Therefore only the countless corpses of children are brought there. The huge hall of the Nikolai Church is used for the corpses of the adults. Some 100 corpses, placed temporarily in boxes, await burial. … In the entrance hall one sees a pile of the dead, taller than a man and covered with sackcloth, barely two metres long and two metres wide. At one end a tangle of naked feet, at the other hair and people's heads.[37]

More recently, the Jewish violinist Michael Wieck has published memoirs of his childhood and adolescence in Königsberg, in which he vividly describes his experiences as a 16-year-old in the East Prussian capital after it had been occupied by Soviet forces:

> The city still was littered with unburied dead. They buried soldiers, but the troops did not regard themselves as responsible for civilians. So it now was our task to search houses and cellars, courtyards and gardens for corpses, in order to "dispose of" them.

One could not really describe it as burying. I have to bring myself to describe what we did: The first removal was of a partly naked young woman with dried streams of blood around the vagina and the mouth, lying on the ground floor of a half-burned-out house. She had a delicate, tender face. We carried her with gloves - which they gave to us - by the arms and legs out to the street; we had to throw her into the nearest bomb crater. Others brought a man who had been shot. They threw him on top of the woman. The corpses were about a week old, and already began to decompose. We worked much too slowly and took too much trouble for the Russians. They developed a new method: We were given ropes which had a noose at one end. The nooses would be placed around the feet or the hands, and now a corpse could be dragged into the nearest bomb crater by just one person, that went much faster. I can still remember almost all of these poor murdered women and men; I see not just their faces but also their various positions and sometimes also the objects that surrounded them. Children as well as old people; most of them shot, some stabbed or strangled. There also were a number of suicides. They had taken poison or hanged themselves on the staircase. In one case there was an entire family that had killed themselves. In [the district of] Hufen there was one street with an especially large bomb crater - I have forgotten the name of the street. Into this crater I dragged people who had been shriveled up by the heat of the house that had burned down on top of them.[38]

In the documentary collection on "The Expulsion of the Germans from the Regions east of the Oder-Neiße" edited by Theodor Schieder during the 1950s, one also finds numerous descriptions of encounters with the dead, with corpses, after the Soviet Army had occupied the eastern Prussian provinces. One example is the account by Fritz Schmidt, a vicar from Marschwitz in Kreis Ohlau in Lower Silesia, of his "Heimat" after the fighting had ended, of shot-up and burnt-out houses, of streets littered with broken agricultural machinery and smashed domestic possessions, of "dead soldiers and cadavers," and of being compelled by the Russians to remove and bury the rotting corpses left after the fighting.[39] Another vicar, Georg Gottwald, described the scene in the Lower Silesian town of Grünberg: he testified that he had buried the corpses of women who had been horribly mutilated, and wrote that of the 4,000 inhabitants (out of a former population of 35,000) who remained in the city after the surrender, "in the first 14 days [after the Russians arrived] over 500 people (entire families, men, women and children) ended their lives by suicide, including doctors, senior court officials, factory owners and prosperous citizens. The corpses of those who had killed themselves must have remained unburied for two weeks. They [the corpses] had to remain in people's flats or were left on the pavement in order to frighten others."[40]

The Western Allies too sometimes left corpses in public view as a warning to those who might be tempted to continue to resist.[41] In the first half of 1945 carrying out everyday tasks, searching for food, or visiting friends and relatives frequently meant encountering corpses on the streets—corpses of soldiers, of civilians, of strangers, of acquaintances, of people who no longer could be recognized. As never before, death had become part of everyday life.

In addition to those who met a violent end in 1945, many more died as a consequence of cold, malnutrition, and disease. The fact that the mass exodus of

Germans from the East ahead of the Soviet Army was precipitated in the dead of winter—when the great Soviet military offensive during the second half of January 1945 brought Russian troops from the Vistula to the Oder in less than three weeks—exposed millions to the elements at the coldest time of year. Early estimates of the casualties among the approximately twelve million Germans altogether who fled or were expelled from their homes in the East exceeded one million dead. This probably was an overestimate, made by a West German government keen during the 1950s to emphasize the suffering of the German people. More recent calculations have put the number at about 500,000, but it is clear that flight and expulsion left many corpses in their wake.[42]

Within what remained of Germany—as the bombing and the fighting on the ground left German cities and towns without water, gas, electricity, telecommunications, working transport systems, or functioning health-care and medical infrastructure—disease was rampant. To take one example, that of Kleve near the Dutch border, which was captured by British troops after fierce combat in March 1945: more than twice as many civilians (367) died of disease in the internment camp set up by the British in nearby Bedburg after the fighting than had died as a direct result of the military action (147); the majority of those who died in the camp (215 of the 367) were over sixty years of age, alongside 57 children (the majority of whom died of diphtheria).[43] Typhus was a serious concern for the occupying Allied forces in Germany in the spring and summer of 1945, most acutely in and around liberated concentration camps.[44] Even worse were conditions in areas east of the Oder-Neiße, which came under Polish and Soviet control and where the collapse of public-health facilities and a massive typhus epidemic in East Prussia had dire consequences. According to one doctor's estimate, of the roughly 100,000 people remaining in Königsberg when the commandant of the surrounded "fortress" city finally capitulated to the Soviet Army on 9 April 1945, nearly three quarters had died due to malnutrition and disease by the spring of 1947.[45]

As the infrastructure of industrial society—water, gas, electricity, transport, hospitals—crumbled and the numbers of civilian dead rose, it no longer was possible, in a country where order had been so cherished, to dispose of the dead in an orderly and dignified manner. There were countless instances—such as when the bodies of people killed on a train from Frankfurt that had been strafed were laid out on the station platform once it arrived in Fürth[46]—where the dead were left in full public view. In Cologne, for example, after the last major bombing raid on the city on 2 March 1945, hundreds of corpses were left in the streets.[47] The most shocking case was that of Dresden after the bombing raids of 13–14 February 1945, which resulted in some 35,000 dead: the numbers of corpses left after the attacks were so great that the city administration ordered that bodies be burned in the *Altmarkt* in the center of the city. Between 20 February and 5 March 6,865 corpses were burned on iron grates in a huge funeral pyre amidst a landscape of bombed-out buildings—a terrible scene that, as one who witnessed it later testified, those who were there "will never forget"; the mountain of corpses thus was transformed into ten cubic meters of ash and subsequently buried.[48] According to one observer, searching for his father after the Dresden bombing, there were corpses everywhere: "They lie alone and in clumps on the streets, which are no longer streets. ... Corpses so mutilated, that I don't sense them as corpses, rather spirits that come out of Hell and are thrown away here. The Great Garden [the huge park adjacent to the center of Dresden], the Great Corpse Garden, with mangled trees, burning pavilions, corpses, corpses."[49]

Whereas dead soldiers usually could be identified (thanks to their identification tags), dead civilians or members of other formations (such as youthful members of Labor Service brigades called upon to fight in the last battles)[50] often could not.[51] During the last months of the war, with the bombing campaign at its peak and battles being fought on German soil, German casualties increasingly were civilians who had been so burned and/or mutilated that they could not be identified.[52] Local-government authorities kept card files recording the human remains found in bombed-out flats, containing descriptions such as "unidentified corpse = only remains of bones."[53] After bombing raids, corpses often were buried in mass graves without coffins (which were in short supply); cemetery personnel were insufficient to dig all the necessary graves; cremations were limited by lack of fuel due to the coal shortage.[54] Cemeteries ran out of space; individual private burials often became impossible; mass burials were the order of the day.[55] Mortuaries were no less liable to be destroyed in the bombings than were other buildings.[56] Parks were turned into makeshift graveyards, and the dead of previous times were unearthed when bombs fell on established cemeteries.[57]

When Germans buried their dead in the last months of the war, the rituals normally associated with death and disposal—rituals that were and remain integral parts of a social culture and meet important social and psychological needs—had to be abbreviated or cast aside. In Würzburg after the bombing on 16 March 1945, when more than 4,500 of the city's inhabitants were killed, one curate reported: "People bring their dead relatives on stretchers, handcarts, two-wheeled carts and push-carts. They hand the corpses over for individual burial. I help dig out a grave here and there, especially if it is only women who bring the deceased. I lay [the corpse] down—always without a casket of course—and cover the grave over again after I have completed the church rites. Now and then people bring the remains of their relatives in battered buckets, tin bathtubs and other containers." The vast majority of the Würzburg dead, however, were buried in mass graves: "After being received [for burial], the dead are carried by foreigners on medical stretchers out to the mass grave. Rolled over onto the stretcher in the usual manner, they arrive lying on their backs or on their bellies or half on the side. The stretcher-bearers step up to the edge of the grave with their burden, tip the stretcher over a bit in the direction of the pit, and the dead person rolls off and flops over sideways with arms spread out into the abyss. Once several corpses are lying there, a few spadesful of lime are thrown on top, then this is covered with earth and one begins with the next layer or the next section of the grave. Of respect for the dead there is not a trace."[58] As one woman was heard to say in a public bomb shelter in Berlin in late March 1945, commenting on rumors that the dead were being cremated *en masse* without coffins or ceremony: "Many too many people are dying. Where should one find the time for proper burials."[59] Burnt corpses, anonymous ashes of human remains, and mass burials do not lend themselves to elaborate or comforting funeral ritual.

The immediate, physical confrontation with the dead, in conditions of extreme disorder and within Germany, provides a striking contrast with what occurred at the end of the First World War. During the 1914–1918 conflict, the overwhelming majority of German dead were soldiers; violent death was something that occurred far away, on the battlefield, beyond the borders of the Reich. The war dead of the First World War also often were disposed of in a shocking manner, but this was done out of the sight of the civilian population.[60] Germans in the "Heimat" received notices of war deaths, but they did not see the corpses (although the social and psychological consequences of the 1918 influenza epidemic within Germany remain to be investigated fully). In 1945 the experiences of Germans on the home front were very different indeed.

Germans' encounters with corpses in 1945 were not limited to those killed as a result of the bombing and the final battles on the ground. They had another very important component—the forced encounters with the dead of the concentration camps. Allied military personnel were deeply shocked and angered at what they found when they arrived in Germany toward the end of the war, upon entering camps in which there had been, in addition to unspeakable cruelty and deliberate mass murder, dreadful overcrowding, rampant disease, and a breakdown of provisioning during the early months of 1945.[61] Consequently they compelled Germans from nearby towns to view the corpses piled up at concentration camps which had been liberated—at Bergen-Belsen, Weimar/Buchenwald, Dachau and elsewhere—or left behind after massacres committed by the SS.[62]

Townspeople, both men and women, frequently were conscripted to bury the corpses found in the newly liberated camps; the burials, in accordance with Eisenhower's standing instructions, were carried out in the most prominent suitable location in the nearest town.[63] For example, in Ludwigslust (between Berlin and Hamburg) at the beginning of May, the commander of the American 82nd Airborne Division, General James Gavin, ordered all the town's inhabitants over ten years of age to view the horrors on display at the nearby camp at Wöbbelin (a satellite of the Neuengamme concentration camp); then the able-bodied male residents were made to exhume some 200 corpses from mass graves and rebury them in individual graves at a cemetery near the palace in the middle of town.[64] After the liberation of Bergen-Belsen, according to an inhabitant of a nearby village, "every day 100 men and women were sent to Belsen in order to bury corpses, clean toilets, etc."[65] Forcing Germans to acknowledge the crimes of the Nazi regime meant forcing them to bury the corpses that the regime had left in its wake.

Photographs of encounters with the corpses of victims of the Nazi regime were given wide circulation, as Eisenhower insisted that they should be, and they continue to frame the ways in which we visualize the liberation of the camps.

Newspapers under Allied control printed articles about the camps; the walls of German cities and towns were covered with photographs of piles of corpses (with admonitions such as "You are guilty of this" or titles such as "German Culture 1945"); pamphlets filled with shocking images of the concentration-camp dead were distributed widely; radio programs were devoted to the atrocities in the camps. German cinema-goers were treated to film of the liberated camps in weekly newsreels and, most famously, in the 22-minute film *Todesmühlen* (Death Mills), which was based on Allied documentary footage of the liberation of numerous camps and was distributed to cinemas in 1946.[66]

In the immediate aftermath of the war, Germans were to be reeducated through exposure to corpses. According to evidence of an Allied survey in June 1945: "Within four weeks after V-E Day, almost every German had had direct and repeated contact with our campaign to present the facts [about the atrocities]."[67] It was an experience they never would forget, and one that often surfaced in Germans' reminiscences decades later.[68] However, these forced encounters with evidence of Nazi atrocities did not necessarily have the desired effect. Rather than expressing guilt and repentance, as Allied reeducators may have hoped they would, Germans tended often to emerge with a sense that they had been accused unfairly by occupiers who did not appreciate conditions in a dictatorship at war. Forced exposure to the "death mills" left Germans not so much convinced of their guilt as endowed with a heightened sense that they were victims. In the spring of 1945, by the time Allied commanders made them view the dead of the concentration camps, Germans already had been exposed to death and corpses in ample quantity—corpses of people with whom they identified: their friends, their neighbors, their loved ones. That experience not only was not appreciated by the victorious Allies, whose attempts at reeducation proved to be rather short-lived, but it also had resulted in large measure from military action taken by those very Allies who now marched the Germans in front of the corpses of *others*. Both sets of encounters with corpses in 1945—public exposure to the corpses of Germans and public exposure to the corpses of concentration-camp prisoners—served to reinforce Germans' sense of their own victimhood.[69]

The shadow of death hanging over Germany at the end of the war was, if anything, deepened by the fact that so many of the dead in effect had disappeared. This was partly a consequence of the territorial losses Germany suffered in 1945. It now is largely forgotten that the region of pre-1938 Germany that suffered proportionally the greatest number of deaths was the Neumark, the eastern region of Brandenburg, east of the Oder, which became part of Poland after 1945; there, of a population of 644,834 before the outbreak of war in 1939 (and about 660,000 in 1944), an estimated 257,000—roughly two fifths—had died by 1945 as a result of military action, flight, and expulsion.[70] Beyond the frontiers of post-1945 Germany, where there no longer were German communities to register and bury those who died, the dead effectively disappeared. More generally, German society and culture after the war were affected deeply by the enormous numbers of missing people—the hundreds of thousands whose deaths had gone unconfirmed or unrecorded at the front, in the bombing, in the course of flight from the East, in the battles waged on German soil during the last months of the conflict. Huge numbers of soldiers had been reported "missing in action";[71] family members had been separated during the desperate flight ahead of the Soviet Army in early 1945; men, women and children had been blown apart or burned beyond recognition in the bombings, leaving no verifiable trace.

After the war Germans were haunted by the missing, and by the fear that the missing were indeed dead. The immediate postwar period saw a desperate search for information about the missing. Newspapers contained advertisements by families searching for news of loved ones; railway stations were filled with noticeboards on which pictures of the missing were displayed in the hope that someone passing through might recognize a face and provide news; churches, welfare organizations, and cemeteries busied themselves with inquiries about whether missing persons were alive or dead. The absence of the dead did not signify an absence of death. In cemeteries not only were the dead buried, but gravestones were erected for the missing as well.[72] In a country where roughly half the population had lost a family member during the war,[73] death was ever-present, even—perhaps especially—where the dead were absent.

The confrontations with extreme violence and death in 1945 left their stamp on Germans' consciousness far into the postwar period. As a result of their terrible experiences particularly in the last months and weeks of the war, Germans emerged with a powerful sense of their own victimhood from a war launched by a Germany that had invaded and conquered much of the European continent, enslaved millions of people, destroyed cities and towns from Rotterdam to Minsk, caused the deaths of millions of soldiers, and murdered innocent civilians on a hitherto unimaginable scale. After the shock of their experiences during the last days of the Reich, Germans emerged preoccupied almost exclusively with their own problems and sorrows, and hardly possessed the mental energy to concern themselves with the problems and sorrows of others. In this the Germans were not unique. In Japan too "a pervasive victim consciousness took root, leading many Japanese to perceive themselves as the greatest sufferers from the recent war"; there too "the preoccupation with their own misery ... led most Japanese to ignore the suffering they had inflicted on others."[74] Victim consciousness after mass death and total defeat, in Japan as well as Germany, profoundly affected the ways in which people constructed their postwar identities.

Hannah Arendt, in her oft-quoted "report from Germany" in 1950, wrote of the "feverish busyness" which she observed amongst the Germans: "Watching the Germans busily stumble through the ruins of a thousand years of their own history, shrugging their shoulders at the destroyed landmarks or resentful when reminded of the deeds of horror that haunt the whole surrounding world, one comes to realize that busyness has become their chief defense against reality. And one wants to cry out: But this is not real—real are the ruins, real are the past horrors, real are the dead whom you have forgotten."[75] However, insightful though it is, this cry is too simple, and perhaps tells us as much about the observer as it does about the observed. For there were a great many dead whom the Germans had *not* forgotten—their own! What Arendt labeled a "defense against reality" may also have been a welcome path to what widely was regarded as normality—to a world in which death again was a nonviolent, essentially private affair and in which the dead were identifiable individuals who could be laid to rest with the appropriate rituals, not anonymous corpses left on the streets or piled up in concentration camps who then were cremated *en masse* or dumped unceremoniously into mass graves.

Mass, public death at the end of the Second World War presented a shock to Germans that was both traumatic and opportune. On the one hand, it made a deep imprint on the mentalities of Germans and left a dark shadow lingering over German society and culture during the postwar years.[76] On the other hand, it offered a handy way out from under the political and psychological rubble left by Nazism and war: by focusing on their terrible suffering during the last year of the war, Germans could avoid facing their involvement, large and small, in the criminality of the Third Reich. The shock of violence and death on a hitherto unimaginable scale and on ghastly public display was central to how Germans emerged into a postwar world where their country was occupied, divided, and positioned at the center of the Cold War. The price they paid was incredibly high, but Germans eventually were able to build "normal" lives in quite abnormal circumstances and out of the most terrible physical, social, and moral wreckage ever known to a modern nation, and to construct a surprisingly successful and peaceful society during the second half of the twentieth century.

Notes

1. Robert Jungk, "Aus einem Totenland," in *Die Weltwoche*, vol. 13 (Zürich, 1945), 9.
2. Norbert Elias, *Über die Einsamkeit der Sterbenden*, 8.
3. Elias, *Über die Einsamkeit der Sterbenden*, 48.
4. Elias, *Über die Einsamkeit der Sterbenden*, 17.
5. See Manfred Messerschmidt and Fritz Wüllmer, *Die Wehrmachtjustiz im Dienste des Nationalsozialismus* (Baden-Baden, 1987); Steven R. Welch, "'Harsh but Just'? German Military Justice in the Second World War: A Comparative Study of the Court-Martialling of German and US Deserters," *German History*, 17, no. 3 (1999): 369–399.
6. Rüdiger Overmans, *Deutsche militärische Verluste im Zweiten Weltkrieg* (Munich, 1999), 265–266.
7. John Erickson, *The Road to Berlin* (London, 2003, first published 1983), 622. According to Erickson, of the roughly half million military and civilian casualties resulting from the Battle of Berlin, the three Soviet Fronts (army groups) involved in the fighting lost 304,887 men killed, wounded, and missing between 16 April and 8 May 1945.
8. Manfred Overesch, *Das III. Reich 1939. Eine Tageschronik der Politik, Wirtschaft, Kultur* (Augsburg, 1991), 622; Jörg Friedrich, *Der Brand. Deutschland im Bombenkrieg 1940–1945* (Munich, 2002), pp. 150, 168.

9. Martin Broszat, "Nationalsozialistische Konzentrationslager 1933–1945," in Hans Buchheim, Martin Broszat, Hans-Adolf Jacobsen, and Helmut Krausnick, *Anatomie des SS-Staates,* vol. 2 (Munich, 1979), 132–133; Yehuda Bauer, "The Death-Marches, January–May 1945," *Modern Judaism* 3, no. 1 (Feb. 1983): 2; Daniel Blatman, "Die Todesmärsche—Entscheidungsträger, Mörder und Opfer," in Ulrich Herbert, Karin Orth, and Christoph Dieckmann, eds., *Die nationalsozialistischen Konzentrationslager. Entwicklung und Struktur,* vol. 2 (Göttingen, 1998), 1066–1068. For a detailed description of a death march in early 1945, see Reinhard Henkys, "Ein Todesmarsch in Ostpreußen," *Dachauer Hefte,* no. 20 (Oct. 2004): 3–21.
10. See Andreas Kunz, "Die Wehrmacht in der Agonie der nationalsozialistischen Herrschaft 1944/45. Eine Gedankenskizze," in Jörg Hillmann and John Zimmermann, eds., *Kriegsende 1945 in Deutschland* (Munich, 2002), 109.
11. Bundesarchiv-Militärarchiv Freiburg (hereafter, BA-MA), RW 4, Nr. 722, f. 74: Oberkommando der Wehrmacht, Chef des Wehrmachtstreifendienstes, 14 Feb. 1945.
12. Quoted in Hans-Martin Stimpel, *Widersinn 1945. Aufstellung, Einsatz und Untergang eines militärischen Verbandes* (Göttingen, 1998), 68.
13. See, for example, BA-MA, RW 4, Nr. 495, f. 28: Anlage Nr. 1 zu: Chef des NS-Führungsstabes, "Truppenbesuch im Bereich OB West und Ersatzheer," 19 March 1945.
14. Quoted in Rudolf Absolon, ed., *Die Wehrmacht im Dritten Reich* (Band 6: 19. Dezember bis 9. Mai 1945) (Boppard am Rhein, 1995), 604.
15. "Warum ich nach sechzig Jahren mein Schweigen breche. Eine deutsche Jugend: Günter Grass spricht zum ersten Mal über sein Erinnerungsbuch und seine Mitgliedschaft in der Waffen-SS," *Frankfurter Allgemeine Zeitung,* no. 186, 12 Aug. 2006, 33.
16. See Bernd Wegner, "Hitler, der Zweite Weltkrieg und die Choreographie des Untergangs," *Geschichte und Gesellschaft,* 26, no. 3 (2000), 492–518.
17. Elke Fröhlich, ed., *Die Tagebücher von Joseph Goebbels. Teil II Diktate 1941–1945. Band 15, Januar–April 1945* (Munich, 1995), 478 (entry for 12 March 1945). Shortly thereafter Goebbels secured Hitler's agreement for a plan to send 300 German fighter planes on suicide missions against Allied bombers. See Christian Goeschel, "Suicide in Weimar and Nazi Germany" (PhD thesis, University of Cambridge, 2006), 194.
18. Klaus Scheel, "Veränderungen der Lebenslage der deutschen Zivilbevölkerung in der Provinz Brandenburg vor dem Kriegsende 1945," in Fritz Petrick (Hg.), *Kapitulation und Befreiung. Das Ende des II. Weltkriegs in Europa* (Münster, 1997), p. 46.
19. See Walter Lüdde-Neurath, *Regierung Dönitz. Die letzten Tage des Dritten Reiches* (Göttingen, 1951), 43.
20. See Klaus-Dietmar Henke, *Die amerikanische Besetzung Deutschlands* (Munich, 1995), 964–965. Altogether 8 of 41 Gauleiter, 7 of 47 Higher SS and Police Leaders, 53 of 554 Army generals, 14 of 98 Luftwaffe generals, and 11 of 53 admirals killed themselves. See Goeschel, "Suicide in Weimar and Nazi Germany," 200.
21. See Goeschel, "Suicide in Weimar and Nazi Germany," 196–216. See also Richard Bessel, "Hatred after War. Emotion and the Postwar History of East Germany," *History and Memory* 17, nos. 1/2 (2005): 199–203.
22. BA-MA, RW 44, Nr. I/11: "Volk und Führung" (dated in pencil 16/1 [1945]). This report is printed in Heinz Boberach ed., *Meldungen aus dem Reich. Die geheimen Lageberichte des Sicherheitsdienstes der SS 1938–1945,* vol. 17 (Herrsching, 1984), 6734–6740 (quotation on 6737); there it is given as a "Bericht aus den Akten der Geschäftsführenden Reichsregierung Dönitz von Ende März 1945."
23. Paul Peikert, *"Festung Breslau" in den Berichten eines Pfarrers 22. Januar bis 6. Mai 1945,* ed. Karol Jonca and Alfred Konieczny (Berlin, 1971), 37.
24. Rainer Behring, "Das Kriegsende 1945," in Clemens Vollnhals, ed., *Sachsen in der NS-Zeit* (Leipzig, 2002), 236.
25. Goeschel, "Suicide in Weimar and Nazi Germany," 209.

26. Mecklenburgisches Landeshauptarchiv Schwerin, Kreistag/Rat des Kreises Demmin, Nr. 46, ff. 62–4: [Der Landrat] des Kreises Demmin to the Präsident des Landes Mecklenburg-Vorpommern, Abteilung Innere Verwaltung, "Tätigkeitsbericht," [Demmin], 21 Nov. 1945. See also Ursula Baumann, *Vom Recht auf den eigenen Tod. Die Geschichte des Suizids vom 18. bis zum 20. Jahrhundert* (Weimar, 2001), 376–378.
27. Damian van Melis, *Entnazifizierung in Mecklenburg-Vorpommern. Herrschaft und Verwaltung 1945–1948* (Munich, 1999), 23–24.
28. Norman M. Naimark, *Fires of Hatred. Ethnic Cleansing in Twentieth-Century Europe* (Cambridge, MA, and London, 2001), 117.
29. Letter of General Serov to Beria, 8 June 1945, quoted in Naimark, *Fires of Hatred*, 117.
30. Bundesministerium für Vertriebe, Flüchtlingen und Kriegsgeschädigte and Theodor Schieder, eds., *Die Vertreibung der deutschen Bevölkerung aus den Gebieten östlich der Oder-Neiße*, Band I/2 (Augsburg, 1993), 687: Erlebnisbericht der Frau Isabella von Eck, Rittergut Birkholz, Kreis Züllichau-Schwiebus in Brandenburg, 26 May 1951.
31. Heinz Petzold, "Cottbus zwischen Januar und Mai 1945," in Werner Stang and Kurt Arlt, eds., *Brandenburg im Jahr 1945. Studien* (Potsdam 1995), 124–125.
32. Peikert, *"Festung Breslau,"* 30; Andreas Hofmann, *Die Nachkriegszeit in Schlesien, Gesellschafts- und Bevölkerungspolitik in den polnischen Siedlungsgebieten 1945–1948* (Cologne, Weimar, and Vienna, 2000), 22.
33. Peikert, *"Festung Breslau,"* 31.
34. Peikert, *"Festung Breslau,"* 270. See also Hofmann, *Die Nachkriegszeit in Schlesien*, 22–23. Of the 530,000 civilian inhabitants of Breslau in the autumn of 1944, only 150,000–180,000 still were in the city when it was cut off by Soviet forces in February 1945.
35. Quoted in Norman Davies and Roger Moorhouse, *Microcosm. Portrait of a Central European City* (London, 2003), 33.
36. Hofmann, *Die Nachkriegszeit in Schlesien*, 18; Davies and Moorhouse, *Microcosm*, 33.
37. Franz Scholz, *Wächter, wie tief die Nacht? Görlitzer Tagebuch 1945/46*, 3rd ed. (Eltville, 1986), 17–18 (entry from 12 Feb. 1945).
38. Michael Wieck, *Zeugnis vom Untergang Königsbergs, Ein "Geltungsjude" berichtet* (Munich, 2005), 238–239.
39. *Die Vertreibung der deutschen Bevölkerung aus den Gebieten östlich der Oder-Neiße*, Band I/2, 380: Erlebnisbericht des Pfarrers Fritz Schmidt aus Marschwitz, Kreis Ohlau i. Niederschles. Original, 3 October 1949.
40. *Die Vertreibung der deutschen Bevölkerung aus den Gebieten östlich der Oder-Neiße*, Band I/2, 349: Erlebnisbericht des Pfarrers Georg Gottwald, Dechant von Grünberg i. Niederschles. Original, 15 June 1949.
41. See, for example, the photo of British soldiers examining a corpse displayed along a street next to a sign reading "This man shot at our sentry during the night of 3 to 4 May," in Charles Whiting, *Norddeutschland Stunde Null April–September 1945. Ein Bild/Text-Band* (Düsseldorf, 1980), 167.
42. According to rough calculations made by the West German government in the 1950s, as of late 1950 1,390,000 people who had lived in the former eastern regions of Germany were unaccounted for, presumed dead as a consequence of the fighting in the last months of war, of the deportations carried out by the Soviet authorities, or of the dreadful conditions that had characterized the move westward. See Statistisches Bundesamt, ed., *Die deutschen Vertreibungsverluste. Bevölkerungsbilanzen für die deutschen Vertreibungsgebiete 1939/50* (Wiesbaden, 1958) 37. For more recent, and more reliable estimates, see Rüdiger Overmans, "Personelle Verluste der deutschen Bevölkerung durch Flucht und Vertreibung," *Dzieje najnowsze* 16, no. 2 (1994): 51–65.
43. Wilhelm Michels and Peter Sliepenbeck, *Niederrheinisches Land im Krieg. Ein Beitrag zur Geschichte des Zweiten Weltkrieges im Landkreis Kleve* (Kleve, 1964), 164.

44. See Paul Julian Weindling, *Epidemics and Genocide in Eastern Europe 1890–1945* (Oxford, 2000), 393–399. As a result of disease and undernourishment, some 13,000 internees died at the Belsen camp after liberation and in August 1945 over 15,000 cases of typhus were reported in Germany.
45. Wilhelm Starlinger, *Grenzen der Sowjetmacht im Spiegel einer Ost-West-Begegnung hinter Palisaden, von 1945–1954. Mit einem Bericht der deutschen Seuchenkrankenhäuser York und St. Elisabeth über das Leben und Sterben in Königsberg von 1945–1947* (Kitzingen, 1954), 38, 53. Cited in Manfred Zeidler, *Kriegsende im Osten. Die Rote Armee und die Besetzung Deutschlands östlich von Oder und Neiße* (Munich, 1996), 204. In his memoirs, Michael Wieck gives the figure of 20,000 survivors out of 130,000. Wieck, *Zeugnis vom Untergang Königsbergs*, 264–5.
46. Wolfram Wette, Ricarda Bremer, and Detlef Vogel, eds., *Das letzte halbe Jahr. Stimmungsberichte der Wehrmachtpropaganda 1944/45* (Essen, 2001) 372: 2. Bericht des Wehrmacht-Propaganda-Offiziers im Wehrkreiskommando XIII, Nürnberg, Major Müller, für die Zeit vom 1.3. bis 15.3.1945.
47. Friedrich, *Der Brand*, 260.
48. Bundesministerium für Vertriebene, Flüchtline und Kriesbeschädigte, ed., *Dokumente deutscher Kriegsschäden. Evakuierte, Kriegsgeschädigte, Währungsgeschichte. Die geschichtliche und rechtliche Entwicklung*, Bd. II, 1, 443. See also Rainer Behring, "Das Kriegsende 1945," in Clemens Vollnhals, ed., Sachsen in der NS-Zeit (Leipzig, 2002), 227; Friedrich, Der Brand, 431; Almut Hielscher, "Wir haben ja nichts mehr," in Stephan Burghoff and Christian Habbe, eds., *Als Feuer vom Himmel fiel* (Munich, 2005), 193.
49. Quoted in Edward N. Peterson, *The Many Faces of Defeat. The German People's Experience in 1945* (New York, 1990), 233.
50. On the use of young Labor Service members to form military units in the final months of the war, see Kiran Klaus Patel, *"Soldaten der Arbeit." Arbeitsdienst in Deutschland und den USA 1933–1945* (Göttingen, 2003), 374–375.
51. For example, the 39 young men who died in the fighting in Parchim, in Mecklenburg, on 3 May 1945. See the account by Joachim Göllnitz, printed in Kurt Studemann, *Parchimer Heimathefte Nr. 19. Parchim 1945 - Am Rande des Abgrundes* (Barsbüttel, 1994), 46.
52. See Friedrich, *Der Brand*, for example 110–111.
53. Gerd R. Ueberschär, *Freiburg im Luftkrieg 1939–1945* (Freiburg im Breisgau, 1990), 284.
54. E.g., in Freiburg after the raids on 27 November 1944. See Ueberschär, *Freiburg im Luftkrieg*, 284.
55. See, e.g., Jörg Friedrich's discussion of raids on Munich and Würzburg, in Friedrich, *Der Brand*, 332, 433.
56. As, for example, in the Altstadt-Friedhof in Aschaffenburg in January 1945. See Alois Stadtmüller, *Aschaffenburg im Zweiten Weltkrieg. Bombenangriffe - Belagerung - Übergabe*, 2nd ed. (Aschaffenburg, 1971) 93.
57. As in "Festung Breslau" in April 1945. See Hugo Hartung, *Schlesien 1944/45. Aufzeichnungen und Tagebücher* (Munich, 1976), 79: diary entry for 6 April 1945.
58. "Aufzeichnungen von Herrn Kaplan Bauer," in Hans Oppelt, ed., *Würzburger Chronik des denkwürdigen Jahres 1945* (Würzburg, 1947), 35–36.
59. Quoted in Hans Dieter Schäfer, *Berlin im Zweiten Weltkrieg. Der Untergang der Reichshauptstadt in Augenzeugenberichten* (Munich, 1985), 295. The quotation is from Jacob Kronika, *Der Untergang Berlins* (Flensburg and Hamburg, 1946).
60. There were no official photographs of the corpses of German war dead (as opposed to those of enemy dead or of dead horses); German snapshots of German corpses were to be found only in private photo albums. See Bodo von Dewitz, "Zur Geschichte der Kriegsphotographie des Ersten Weltkrieges," in Rainer Rother, ed., *Die letzen Tage der Menschheit. Bilder des Ersten Welrkrieges* (Berlin, 1994), 174–175.

61. For description of one of the worst examples, that of the Mittelbau-Dora camp near Nordhausen, see Jens-Christian Wagner, *Produktion des Todes. Das KZ Mittelbau-Dora* (Göttingen, 2001), 267–86. The depth of the anger felt by the liberators may be gauged by the comments of one American corporal in a letter home: "I've just had the occasion to see one of the worst horrors of the war. I went to one of the crematories—this is where the Nazis burned people alive. Saw some of the half-cooked bodies. They were awful .... I saw rows and rows of bodies that these Germans had killed just before they retreated. After looking at the cremated bodies you just feel like killing every German alive." Quoted in Christof Strauß, *Kriegsgefangenschaft und Internierung. Die Lager in Heilbronn-Böckingen 1945–1946* (Heilbronn, 1998), 100: Headquarters ETOUSA, Office of the Assistant Chief of Staff, G-2: Censorship Report on Observance of Rules of Land Warfare for Period 1–15 May 45, in: NA, RG 338, ETOUSA, Historical Division, Administrative File; Box No. 9; Folder 58 (Censorship). A more sober but nevertheless deeply disturbing description of what was found at Dachau upon the camp's liberation may be seen in the report by Master Sergeant Jack Bessel, Sixth Army Group History, Section I, Narrative, 348–351; NA, RG 332, ETO, Historical Division Program Files, Sixth Army Group 1944-45.
62. See Harold Marcuse, *Legacies of Dachau. The Uses and Abuses of a Concentration Camp, 1933–2001* (Cambridge, 2001), 55–59; Dagmar Barnouw, *Germany 1945. Views of War and Violence* (Bloomington and Indianapolis, 1996), 1–87.
63. See, e.g., the discussion of the burial in Leipzig's *Südfriedhof* of some 300 prisoners who had been murdered in the camp at nearby Thekla, in Earl F. Ziemke, *The U.S. Army in the Occupation of Germany 1944–1946* (Washington, D.C., 1975), 244–245.
64. Barnouw, *Germany 1945*, 12–16; Marcuse, *Legacies of Dachau*, 56; Carina Baganz, "Wöbbelin: Das letzte Außenlager des KZ Neuengamme als Evakuierungs- und Sterbelager," *Dachauer Hefte*, no. 20 (Oct. 2004): 173. The burials in Ludwigslust took place on 7 May; on the following day reburials also took place in Schwerin and Hagenow. A photograph of the reburial in Ludwigslust is reproduced in Barnouw, *Germany 1945*, 15.
65. See Rainer Schulze, ed., *Unruhige Zeiten. Erlebnisberichte aus dem Landkreis Celle 1945–1949* (Munich, 1990), 83 (document 6: interview with Oskar Stillmark, Winsen, 25 July 1946)
66. Marcuse, *Legacies of Dachau*, 59–64; Barnouw, *Germany 1945*, 10.
67. Quoted in Marcuse, *Legacies of Dachau*, 61.
68. Marcuse, *Legacies of Dachau*, 57.
69. On the theme of how Germans emerged from the war with a sense of their victimhood generally, see Richard Bessel, *Nazism and War* (London, 2004), 150–82.
70. Klaus Scheel, "Veränderungen der Lebenslage," 32; Kurt Adamy and Kristina Hübener, "Provinz Mark Brandenburg - Gau Kurmark. Eine verwaltungsgeschichtliche Skizze," in Dietrich Eichholtz and Almuth Püschel, eds., *Brandenburg in der NS-Zeit. Studien und Dokumente* (Berlin, 1993), 27; Gerd Heinrich, *Berlin und Umgebung. Handbuch der historischen Stätten Deutschlands*, vol. 10 (Stuttgart, 1985), lxxxvii. Scheel gives the proportion killed as 38.9%, Adamy and Hübener as 39%, and Heinrich as 41.7%.
71. Some sense of the dimensions of the "missing" may be gauged by the numbers of war dead from Hamburg, which included over 44,000 soldiers who had fallen in battle and a further 27,000 who were missing; in addition, 41,000 inhabitants of the city had been killed in the bombings. See Frank Bajohr, "Hamburg—Der Zerfall der 'Volksgemeinschaft,'" in Ulrich Herbert and Axel Schildt, eds., *Kriegsende in Europa. Vom Beginn des deutschen Machtzerfalls bis zur Stabilisierung der Nachkriegsordnung 1944–1948* (Essen, 1998), 335.
72. Neil Gregor, "'Is he still alive, or long since dead?': Loss, Absence and Remembrance in Nuremberg, 1945–1956," *German History* 21, no. 2 (2003): 184–185.
73. In a survey conducted in 1952 by the Allensbach Institute for Opinion Research, of 535 young German men asked about their experiences during the war, 51 percent had lost family members. See Elisabeth Noelle and Erich Neumann, eds., *Jahrbuch der öffentlichen Meinung*

1947–1955, 2nd ed. (Allensbach, 1956), 23; quoted in Alice Förster and Birgit Beck, "Post-Traumatic Stress Disorder and World War II: Can a Psychiatric Concept Help Us Understand Postwar Society?" in Richard Bessel and Dirk Schumann, eds., *Life After Death: Approaches to a Cultural and Social History of Europe during the 1940s and 1950s* (Cambridge, 2003), 30.
74. John W. Dower, *Embracing Defeat: Japan in the Wake of World War II* (New York, 1999), 29, 119.
75. Hannah Arendt, "The Aftermath of Nazi Rule: Report from Germany," *Commentary* 10 (October 1950): 345.
76. See Sabine Behrenbeck, "Between Pain and Silence: Remembering the Victims of Violence in Germany after 1949," in Bessel and Schumann, eds., *Life After Death,* 37–64. Behrenbeck writes of the "tension between the wish to remember one's own pain and losses and the wish to forget what the Germans had done to other peoples during the war" (39).

Chapter 3

REBURYING AND REBUILDING
Reflecting on Proper Burial in Berlin after "Zero Hour"

Monica A. Black

In Berlin under Nazi rule, particularly during the Second World War, the notion of "proper burial" often took on racial overtones. In the context of the Allied bombing of the city—when hundreds and even thousands of people were sometimes killed in a matter of hours—the privilege of individual, as opposed to mass, burial was often reserved for members of the racial community. However, in the last months of the war, mounting casualties began gradually to overwhelm municipal officials' ability to see to the orderly and timely disposal of the city's dead. With the arrival of the ground war in April 1945, the municipal apparatus for the provision of burial services fell apart completely. During the resulting crisis, which lasted several weeks, thousands of Berliners came to be buried "irregularly"—in parks, squares, forests, and gardens—in what were referred to, in the contemporary vernacular, as *Notgräber* and *Notfriedhöfe* (emergency graves and cemeteries). Thousands more, on the orders of Soviet commanders, were unceremoniously dumped in mass graves as quickly as possible to avoid the spread of infectious disease.

For Berliners, who had long attached profound significance to the "pious" handling of the dead as evidence of Germans' status as a *Kulturvolk* ("people of culture"), the burial crisis of 1945 often represented a collapse in "civilization" writ large. But particularly in the aftermath of total defeat and the collapse of Nazism, "emergency" burial, the mass grave, and, indeed, the notion of "mass death" itself became imbued with a variety of new and ambiguous meanings. Looking at the sentiments Berliners attached to the experience and lingering evidence of mass death in their city after 1945, as I hope to demonstrate, can reveal both how traces of some of the values that had come to be associated with death

---

Notes for this chapter begin on page 87.

under Nazism continued to manifest themselves and how, at the same time, they began slowly to be reshaped in radically altered circumstances.

Mass Death and the Privilege of Individual Burial

As early as 4 March 1938—that is, just days before the *Anschluß*—secret protocols were issued to the Deutsche Gemeindetag indicating what municipalities were to do with corpses in the event of air raids.[1] With the beginning of hostilities, the chief of the Berlin city police produced further protocols. On 2 September 1939, "corpse collection sites" (*Leichensammelstellen*) were established in the districts of Wedding, Kreuzberg, and Prenzlauer Berg, and particular duties were assigned to various agents of the city administration, from identifying and transporting corpses to writing up death certificates to burying the dead. Regulations allotted a period of forty-eight hours in which family members were permitted to have their dead picked up for individual burial; thereafter, the city was responsible for providing "a solemn burial in mass graves."[2] These plans, when written, were largely theoretical. They envisioned an orderly war, whose consequences in human casualties would be handled in a tidy and methodical and purposeful fashion.

By April 1941, however, after initial air raids on the city had produced a few hundred deaths, the situation had changed. The leadership in the Deutsche Gemeindetag now concluded "after careful consideration" that burials of Berlin's air war dead could "only take place in individual graves," because the families demanded it.[3] By the time of the most intensive bombing of the city, between November 1943 and mid-March 1944—a period during which more than ten thousand people were killed in the city[4]—the commitment to individual graves was not only being insisted on by Berliners, but was indeed being affirmed at the highest levels of state. Adolf Hitler issued an order in February 1944 proscribing in no uncertain terms the compulsory use of mass graves for *Volksgenossen*.[5] Jörg Friedrich has suggested, quite plausibly, that in Hitler's mind mass graves were too suggestive of the methods of disposal used in the concentration camps.[6]

It is indeed revealing that even after the civilian death toll in Berlin had mounted very considerably, in June 1944, mass graves were not used anywhere in the city with the exception of an instance in which a group of 122 *Ostarbeiter* (a euphemism for slave laborers from Eastern Europe) had been buried en masse in a Wilmersdorf cemetery.[7] This suggests that the mass grave was associated with ignominy, that it was a patently unacceptable breach of custom, and that it was therefore spared only for racial subordinates and outsiders, despite the increasingly extreme circumstances. Burial in the Third Reich, in other words, both enacted and conflated moral, cultural, and racial distinctions. Thus, it is hardly surprising that it was also racial outsiders—concentration camp inmates, POWs, and forced laborers—who were given the task of recovering and burying corpses after air raids.[8]

The racialization of the culture of burial in Berlin had indeed been underway since the first days of the Third Reich, as a variety of supporters of the new regime had sponsored efforts, early on, to propagate cremation as a putatively *ur*-German practice, to reform the appearance of cemeteries and rid them of the aesthetic influence of "foreign races and worldviews,"[9] to find a "more truly German" ritual for commemorating death in the Third Reich,[10] and to ban Jewish Berliners from "German" cemeteries.[11] What linked many of these projects together was the assumption that Germans' meticulous traditions of handling and caring for their dead elevated Germany to the rarified status of *Kulturvolk*. How a people treated its dead, in other words, was the coin of cultural and racial distinction.

It is, nevertheless, particularly striking that racial divisions were maintained in the practices of burial—individual graves for Berliners, mass graves for "others"—even as the problem of disposing of the dead grew steadily worse over time. In the face of official proscriptions against mass graves, municipal authorities soon began to contemplate other avenues for creating more burial space. They discussed reducing the *Ruhefrist* (or the time one essentially "leased" a grave) to twenty years from the established twenty-five.[12] Where possible, officials licensed the construction of new cemeteries.[13] It bears noting in this connection that the majority of Berliners did not incline toward cremation; according to the comprehensive statistics of Lucian Hölscher, only around 14 percent of deceased Protestant Berliners—the overwhelming majority of the city's inhabitants—were being cremated circa 1939.[14]

As the wartime situation continued to worsen, however, the city's infrastructure for caring for the dead was ever more dramatically compromised. Burial space, indeed, was only one issue. Particularly after the massive attacks of 3 February 1945, which killed thousands,[15] city authorities had found private undertakers unable "to bury the fallen on such a large scale in an orderly fashion."[16] Berlin's mayor, Ludwig Steeg, thus announced the creation of a Central Burial Office (Hauptbestattungsamt)[17]—with suboffices in each of the city's districts, whose aim was to streamline the provision of burial services through central planning. These offices were made accountable for collecting and transporting the bodies of the dead, identifying them, and, quite often, seeing to their burial.

Despite such measures and the stated intention of the Central Burial Office to maintain "piety" by keeping corpses from public view,[18] the city government's ability to provide for burials that conformed to contemporary standards of decency deteriorated as conditions became more desperate over time. Bodies began to pile up in *Leichensammelstellen* in the inner districts and to overwhelm the municipality's ability to bury them in a timely way.[19] On 28 February, the local Gau propaganda office protested that a group of passers-by had seen corpses and body parts wrapped in rags being pulled from a truck at a Berlin cemetery in Baruther Straße, and "the remains of four or five people being buried in one coffin."[20] Even transporting bodies to cemeteries at all was now becoming more difficult, as vehicles and fuel were often lacking.

Coffins, too, which formed a powerful symbolic element in the ideal of "proper" burial as it had developed in Germany, were now becoming more and more difficult to come by. Their distribution, for one, much like individual burial, was conditioned by racial prerogative and hierarchy: in March 1945, in order to ensure the supply of coffins for *Volksgenossen,* the Central Burial Office decreed that only members of "friendly foreign nations" were to receive proper coffins; the coffins of Poles and *Ostarbeiter,* by contrast, were to be only of "the lowest quality," while POWs were to be buried without coffins altogether. As coffins became increasingly precious, their symbolic currency went up, too. Carpenters were even pulled out of Volkssturm duty and mobilized to build them,[21] surely some index of their significance: even the defense of the city, on some level, was less important. Many a postwar memoir attests to the extraordinary lengths Berliners went to build or otherwise to secure coffins for dead loved ones when they could not obtain them through ordinary channels. Those who were forced to bury their dead without them sometimes later, having now secured one, appealed to the Central Burial Office to dig up their dead so that they could be reburied "properly."[22] City officials would indeed discover after the war that some of those Berliners who had not been able to locate or build coffins in the last weeks of the war placed heavy doors, boards, and crates over their dead as they lay in the grave, in order to simulate a coffin before filling the grave in with earth.[23]

With the late April arrival in Berlin of the ground war—and the Red Army—what remained of the expected and routine provision of burial services entirely fell apart. The Central Burial Office ceased to function.[24] As a result, as journalist Curt Riess described, "Everywhere one ran into handcarts or wheelbarrows with corpses in them wrapped in paper, and the carts were being pushed or pulled by the grieving families themselves. ... [T]he streets were impassable, and so sometimes it was completely impossible to get the cart to the cemetery. So one went back home, having accomplished nothing, and had to reckon that if he came back too late he would be shot at by the Russians."[25] During the last days of the war and for weeks after, a great many of Berlin's dead came to be buried "irregularly," often outside cemeteries, or in parks or squares, by friends, family, colleagues, or complete strangers. Berliners sometimes hid the dead in their apartments or hallways while they waited for an opportune lull in the fighting to venture out and, armed with some improvised form of transportation, find a space to bury them—no mean feat in a city of apartment dwellers. With no coffins available, they wrapped the bodies of the dead in newspapers or sheets for burial, and marked their makeshift graves with whatever was to hand.

The burial crisis of 1945 did not end with Germany's surrender, however. "My first impression after the liberation," one woman later recalled, was of "the haggard women who went out with stretchers to find husbands or sons who had been drafted in the Volkssturm at the last minute or fell in the street fighting, and to carry them home and bury them in their garden."[26] The result of such improvisations was an urban landscape dotted from one end to the other with homemade crosses and makeshift cemeteries.[27] The graves of 1945 in the war's aftermath were simultaneously so ubiquitous and yet so remarkable that no standard account of the immediate postwar period in Berlin fails to mention them.[28]

Yet the piecemeal efforts of individuals in those days were hardly sufficient to cope with mass death. When the guns fell silent, corpses had accumulated in every conceivable place—streets, parks, railway stations, air raid shelters, canals, and cellars. So prevalent were they, in fact, that a new term now emerged for them: *herumliegende Leichen,* or "corpses lying around." Berliner Hertha von Gebhardt described the scene in early May: "[T]here are corpses in the streets, Russians, Germans, whom no one buries. In the gardens and the parks, here and there, everywhere, are graves, with crosses: 'unknown Volkssturm man, fell on this and that date.'"[29] Nor did the end of the fighting put an end to mass death. The death rate remained exceedingly high from disease,[30] hunger,[31] and suicide[32] for months afterward. Whereas in Berlin from 1937 to 1939, the death rate had been 13.5 per 1,000 persons, and from 1940 to 1944 14.8 per 1,000, in the second half of 1945 the death rate was 53.5 per 1,000. For small children the numbers were higher: in July 1945, for example, 66 of 100 newborns died.[33]

Confronting this disaster and the massive public health threat it implied for all the inhabitants of the city, Red Army commanders, as they took district after district of Berlin, ordered the burial of accumulated corpses. After the military defeat of the Wehrmacht, one of the most immediate demonstrations of the new Soviet hegemony in the city was the effort to place Berlin's "hygienic infrastructure"[34]—above all, the systematic provision of burial services—back on an orderly footing. While the aim of bringing order back to the disposal of the dead certainly had its practical and hygienic aspects, it was also fraught with symbolism, reinforcing the radical transfer of power that had taken place in the former "lair of the fascist beast." Every order, gesticulation, sign, and decree issued to the population of Berlin by the Soviets expressed the new terms of political life there in one way or another, but to the same end: to demonstrate that occupier was now occupied, subjugator had been subjugated. Even the time of day was now set by Moscow,[35] implying that in "the new Berlin," even the sun rose and set according to the rules of Soviet power.

But controlling the disposition of the dead in the aftermath of a lost war, in a society in which the proper burial of the dead had become, over the preceding twelve years, implicitly a demonstration of racial privilege, was especially loaded with meaning. Only months before, Hitler had personally forbidden the burial of members of the racial community in mass graves; now, thousands were buried en masse in sand pits, mostly anonymously, and in the greatest haste. What is more, the recovery and transportation and burial of the dead, jobs formerly done only by racial outsiders, were now accomplished by Germans pressed into service by the Soviets;[36] some were used as *Leichenkutscher* ("corpse drivers"), whose job it was to deliver the dead to cemeteries and find places to bury them.[37] Coffins, set aside in the last months of the Third Reich exclusively for members of the racial community, were now reserved only for burying those who died of infectious diseases and for the dead of the occupiers.[38] This was truly a reversal of fortunes.

If burying the dead in a particular way had been a symbolic instrument for marking racial, cultural, and moral distinctions during the Third Reich, the last had now truly become first.

Since Nazi propaganda had sought to dehumanize the Soviet enemy during the war by implying that he mishandled his dead, some Berliners now expressed frank amazement to find that the Soviets, too, had their own standards of "proper" burial. A Herr Schmidt described Russian burials with interest, noting, "Earlier I always read … that the Bolsheviks leave their dead lying around like cattle."[39] Matthias Menzel, too, was surprised to see, looking at a field of Russian graves near the barracks that had housed Hitler's bodyguard in Finckensteinallee, that each was decorated with red flags and "flowers upon flowers." During his time in the East while serving in the Wehrmacht, he had "always looked for the graves of [the Soviets'] fallen soldiers, [but] found only meager piles of earth."[40] A diarist described her amazement that the Soviets, too, had a funerary cult (*Gräberkult*). "In our newspapers it was reported again and again that the Russians hide their war dead as though they were dishonorable, that they bury them in mass graves and then flatten out the spot, so that it cannot be identified."[41]

If the handling and mishandling of the dead in the days and weeks just following the war now became emblematic of a reversal of fortunes, the Soviets and their German communist allies now sought to capitalize on that fact, and dealing with the dead was soon implicated in an explicit project of moral reeducation. Just a few weeks after the war's end, for example, Walter Seitz, a doctor at Charité Hospital, witnessed Hilde Benjamin (future Minister for Justice of East Germany), overseeing an exhumation from the grounds of the Markus School in Steglitz. During the last days of the war, "a group of people had been shot [by Nazis] and buried only superficially … . Former Nazis had to dig the corpses up. It was the end of May and already very hot. … Many of the Nazis became nauseated from the smell of the corpses. 'Red Hilde' screamed at them: 'You put them there, you can get them out again!'"[42] Disposing of the dead thus became a form of expiating political (and other) sins. The "former Nazis" hauled before Benjamin were made to bury the dead as a means of atonement.

In the earliest postwar days and weeks, Berliners responded to the horrors and humiliations of the burial crisis by taking sometimes extraordinary efforts to avoid, for their own dead, the anonymity of the mass grave and the dread they associated with burials without coffins. One woman, Marie H., simply refused to see her mother buried without a coffin. Instead, she tucked her mother in on a cot in her parlor, where she subsequently lay for a full fourteen days while Marie H. searched for one. When she was ultimately able to secure a coffin, she was offered five times what she paid for it by people on the street. Nevertheless, Marie H. recalled, "that coffin was for my mother."[43] A Weddinger named Maria M. helped the father of a four-week-old baby who died of hunger in her building to build a coffin out of two doors and to sew the child a burial shroud in August 1945. Despite the potential dangers of navigating the occupied city, she then assisted him in delivering the "tiny coffin, wrapped in a blanket, to the cemetery at

Nordend with the streetcar." When the driver balked at transporting the coffin into the Russian zone, Maria M. and her neighbor gave him their bread ration cards.[44] Still other Berliners enlisted the aid of family friends and relatives to disinter their dead from provisional and mass graves—often secretly, under cover of night—and to rebury them "properly," in coffins, in cemeteries, in individual graves. A man named Willy Henning was asked by a friend's wife to dig up the body of her husband, buried near Gotzkowsky Bridge, transport it to a cemetery by handcart, and rebury it with a pastor presiding.[45] In other words, with whatever limited means available to them, Berliners continued, in extreme conditions, to approximate as best they could the rituals of "proper" burial.

Mass Death and Sorting Through the Past

By autumn 1945, most "*herumliegende Leichen*" had been at least temporarily buried. Yet for years to come, remnants of the burial catastrophe of 1945, like emergency graves and cemeteries, continued to feature in Berlin's landscape. That autumn, alongside the massive effort begun to rebuild the city, brick by brick, the reburial of the tens of thousands of dead provisionally interred during the emergency period began. Both individual and mass graves alike were opened, and their contents disinterred and reburied in one or another of the city's graveyards. In Schöneberg, in Berlin's west, the hastily organized new district administration found when it took up its work that its "terribly battered cemeteries" consisted largely of "one bomb crater on top of the next. Between these craters families had buried their dead—some who died in the bombings, some who died naturally—randomly, all over the place." Some 1,300 corpses were found to have been so buried in Schöneberg's cemeteries alone, which was to say nothing of the more than 1,500 other provisionally interred corpses located in the district's gardens, squares, and parks, all of which had to be individually disinterred and reburied "properly" (*ordnungsgemäß*).[46]

The task before us now is to understand what the phenomena associated with mass death and the burial crisis meant to Berliners in the immediate postwar years. To begin, it is important to note, as the example of Schöneberg suggests, that perceived transgressions against the dead did not cease with the fighting in May or even with the end of emergency burial. A Berliner named Friedrich Löchner lodged a complaint with the mayor's office in November 1945. His wife, Käthe, it seems, had died in the hospital in the district of Friedrichshain after fainting and falling out a window in September. Löchner was informed that he would have to wait two or three weeks after her cremation to bury her ashes because there were no urns available in which to do so. Indignant, he demanded, "Has no one any understanding for the feelings of the bereaved … ? Hasn't anyone a sense of piety any more? … It is no wonder [one] loses his patience and his nerves fail, and he lets himself get carried away saying not very nice things about crematorium workers. … [I must insist] that my dead wife's urn be delivered at once, so that after the many worries that preceded her death, I (and the dead woman too!) can finally be at peace."[47] One wonders to which pious and empathetic past Löchner alluded. Did he perhaps refer to the Nazi past, when one had "real" sympathies for the dead? Or had the Nazis brought impiety in their wake? Or was it indeed the Soviets who had done so? Whoever bore responsibility, Löchner seemed to perceive the restoration of "piety" as crucial to bringing an end to the conditions of the war and to "being at peace."

Indeed, for occupier and occupied alike, the restoration of the routine provision of burial services after the catastrophe of 1945 now often became a symbol of the manifestation of a new order, even if its ultimate shape remained unknown. One Berliner, Rudolf Diesing, saw in Soviet power the chance to place life (and death) in Berlin back on its former (pre-Nazi era) moral footing. Diesing, a private undertaker and coffin seller, was appointed as a professional expert to help advise the newly constituted city government, or Magistrat, on burial matters in 1945. With his help, the Central Burial Office—the late wartime institution responsible for burial in the city—was reorganized, and it remained in place through most of 1946, while private undertakers struggled to get back on their feet.[48] As far as Diesing was concerned, the shortages and other problems facing the Magistrat where burial was concerned, including the lack of coffins and wood to build them, the destroyed cemeteries and damaged crematoria, the lack of transportation, and the persisting lack of space to bury the dead, were also moral issues. They were the result of Nazi policies, not least of which was the defense of Berlin, which Diesing regarded as "the maddest of all madnesses." Returning "piety" to the burial regime would necessarily entail rooting Nazis, or what he called "*Nazioten*" (an epithet combining the words "Nazis" and "idiots") out of the various burial professions. Thus, the disreputable coffin maker who had tried to ruin a competitor in 1935 by announcing in the anti-Semitic Julius Streicher publication *Der Stürmer* that his rival had "bought from Jews"; the unlicensed undertaker who had removed bodies awaiting burial from their coffins and stolen those coffins in order to resell them; the undertakers charging "unjustified" prices for their services: these had been phenomena of the depravity of Nazi rule, and formed a "cruel situation" that would, with the "generous help of the Red Army," be set right.[49]

It is safe enough to say, however, that Diesing's support for the Soviet occupiers placed him in a minority among his fellow Berliners, and that for many of the city's residents in 1945, the mistreatment of the dead in the immediate aftermath of the war was largely attributable not to the Nazis, but to the Soviets themselves. In this context, it is noteworthy that the abuse of the dead—as specific evidence of fascist degeneracy—became a prominent feature of the communist press early in the occupation. A story called "The Gravedigger," which appeared in June in the German Communist Party (KPD) daily, the *Deutsche Volkszeitung*, depicted a man who, until he defected to the Red Army, had been working for the Wehrmacht burying the dead. To the Russian commander who captures him, he explains:

It wasn't a pleasant job, I can tell you that, sir. ... Day after day, burying corpses ... the frozen ones were OK, [but a lot of them] weren't really corpses: here's a torso, there a head, here's a leg, there an arm ... . Earlier I made crosses with the names on them; not anymore, wood is scarce. ... Individual graves, couldn't do that anymore. Only the officers get a grave for themselves and usually a cross too. But it doesn't matter. You don't think the ones whose names are on the crosses are the ones in the grave! I know better. Mostly it's a bunch of arms and legs.[50]

After the great idealization of soldierly and heroic death in Nazi Germany,[51] where the soldier's sacrifice was glorified and his grave depicted as a sacred expression of collective duty and communal feeling, such stories were clearly meant to vilify the Nazi regime in a very particular and, to many Berliners, personal way. Revelations of soldiers lying unburied and unidentified in foreign fields, mass burials, dismembered corpses, burials without coffins: these did not square with the image the regime had projected for twelve years, nor did it speak to the values Berliners took so seriously when handling their dead. Moreover, in a context in which one in four Germans was searching for a lost family member,[52] and in which untold scores of Berliners still lay nameless in mass graves and more were believed to molder beneath millions of cubic meters of the city's rubble, the communist emphasis on the Nazis' role in the erasure of the identity of the dead—abandoned somewhere on the steppes of Russia—was meant quite intentionally to touch a nerve and to provoke Berliners into some kind of reckoning with the Nazi past.

Thus, the *Deutsche Volkszeitung* returned again to this theme in July, in an article concerning a mass burial in Spandau, in Berlin's west:

> What one has always known, that the Nazi regime was the embodiment of impiety and bestiality, was revealed here too. Numberless dead were thrown into holes in the ground ... many having had their clothing partially or totally stolen! As such, their identification papers were mostly lost. ... Who is to blame [that the dead cannot be identified]? Again and again one can give but one answer: Hitler and the beasts in human form whom he mastered. ... Out of pure fiendishness, in the last hours of fighting, the SS threw the grave register to the four winds.

Here, "the Nazis"—portrayed as beasts, devils, fiends—were charged with, of all things, corpse desecration, having chucked the dead in the ground after relieving them, apparently, of their clothes. "The Nazis," in this story, were cast as utterly depraved, only masquerading as human; only "devils," after all, would have so little respect for the "aura" attaching to the dead human body and "the grave."[53]

Accusations of Nazi mistreatment of the dead, however, were not a feature of the communist press alone. At the end of October 1945 the Christian Democratic Union (CDU) newspaper *Neue Zeit* carried a story that is representative of a number of contemporary reports. It concerned a large municipal cemetery in Marzahn, in the far eastern reaches of the city. There lay the graves of "foreign civilian workers of all nations, who died without experiencing liberation, [and] simple wooden crosses without names, where lie the unknown victims of the final battles in Berlin, reburied from [provisional] graves in Friedrichshain." In addition there were "Two long graves without gravestones—the final place of rest for 120 victims of the last air raids," who had not received "an orderly burial, … of grave decoration there is no trace." It was here, in Marzahn, moreover, that an unnamed "party member" (*Parteigenosse*) was said to have dumped the ashes of "the executed victims of Adolf Hitler"—ostensibly those implicated in the 20 July 1944 plot on Hitler's life.[54] Such stories clearly lumped all manner of victims "of the war" together, but at the same time implied that the final humiliation of the dead—mass, anonymous burial—had perhaps been greatest of all.

In this way, both the western and the communist press sought to discredit the Nazi regime in a very specific way for its mishandling of the dead and for having erased their individual identities. And indeed, whomever Berliners determined to have been to blame for it, postwar images of depersonalized death, mass burials, and neglected, unidentified corpses left to rot somewhere in the open presented an especially fearsome prospect to many. Ulrich Torrel, writing for the *Neue Zeit* in September 1945, described the recent death of his neighbor: "[The] comfort of [it] [was that] this man had been given the gift of finding his own death, and had remained protected from perishing en masse throughout all the preceding years."[55] An individual death was a "gift," a "comfort"; to die "en masse" was to die badly.

Such manifestations of anxiety concerning depersonalized death must be considered alongside the ongoing revelations of the methods of mass murder associated with the Holocaust. "The Berlin station is broadcasting on the radio, mostly there are news reports and disclosures stinking of blood, corpses, horror," wrote a woman diarist in late May 1945. "Millions of people—mostly Jews—are said to have been burned in huge camps in the east and that their ashes were used for fertilizer."[56] Reports of this type emerged simultaneously with a new visual culture associated with the genocide. Images of mass, often anonymous death—piles of naked corpses, sometimes being bulldozed into open pits—were widely disseminated in the American zone in such films as *Die Todesmühlen* (Death Mills), which was based on footage shot by the Allies as they liberated Nazi camps.[57] In the Soviet sector as well, as Jeffrey Herf explains, the "German public was presented with the horrible details of the Nazi death camps. The *Deutsche Volkszeitung* … prominently featured stories on Nazi … crimes against humanity … and details about Auschwitz and other 'factories of death.'"[58] As Habbo Knoch has pointed out, however, the pictures from the camps looked to many Germans like their own corpses at the front and during the bombing war. Rather than seeing those pictures as evidence of collective guilt for Nazi crimes, some Germans indeed drew from them a sense of equivalence between the victims of the Nazis and themselves.[59]

Germans' postwar claims to victimhood are only part of the story, however. It is sometimes easy to forget, because they were not openly voiced after 1945, that the values of the Third Reich had not vanished along with the Nazi state. Berliners, like other Germans, were necessarily circumspect about expressing any form of loyalty to the former regime. Knowing this, however, does not make it any easier for historians to discern what happened to Nazi values over time: of what did they consist in 1945? How did they begin to change thereafter? What influences reshaped them and how? Looking at the culture of death in postwar Berlin offers us an insight into the postwar Berlin mentality in its complexity.

To begin with, we might note that Jewish cemeteries, which had often been damaged during the Third Reich and then in the war and had thereafter fallen into a state of neglect, often remained derelict years after the war ended, despite protests from international Jewish organizations.[60] More pointedly, there were instances of Jewish grave desecration in the early postwar years.[61] Equally striking is the following example: when the British military government began hearing various proposals in early 1946 for creating a new cemetery space in their sector, one proposal—to create a graveyard on land south of the notorious Plötzensee prison, where thousands of those deemed enemies of the Nazi state had been executed—met with very specific objections. "The [proposed] cemetery would necessarily incorporate the prison cemetery," concluded a Magistrat Parks Department report drawn up in June 1946. "We can imagine that the majority of the population would find burying their dead beside executed prisoners abhorrent."[62] Clearly the dishonor many Berliners perceived to cling to the very graves of those executed at Plötzensee long outlasted Nazism and the attempts of the Allies to discredit it. Such sentiments were strong enough that plans for the cemetery near Plötzensee were shelved.

At the same time, though, there were also ways in which ideas about the treatment of the dead and views of the recent past were now in flux. In Friedrichshain in mid 1946, the Magistrat resolved to disinter an emergency cemetery located on the grounds of the Samaritan Church.[63] In April–May 1945, along with his wife and neighbors, a Dr. Harnisch, pastor of the Samaritan Church, had brought the bodies of hundreds of dead into the church sacristy, and then hunted for a place to bury them. Realizing that getting the bodies to a cemetery would involve "crossing the front lines," he and his wife and neighbors had buried the bodies they had collected in the churchyard.[64] By his own reckoning, Pastor Harnisch and his helpers buried hundreds of people on the grounds of the church during those days.[65]

These graves, however, were located on a very small plot of land in a densely populated area. The Magistrat claimed on that basis that the proposed disinterment of the dead was necessary to maintain public health but also insisted that the graves stood in the way of "city planning issues." More significantly, they questioned whether the churchyard burials had been undertaken "respectfully" (*in einer pietätsvollen Weise*), noting that "it had been determined" that the corpses had been laid in their grave "one on top of the other."[66] Harnisch's response to these allegations was swift and minced no words. "I don't know if [you] were in Berlin during the fighting," he wrote: "Corpses lay in their dozens in the streets. No one would bury them, because they were afraid of being shot, and because no one dared touch a German soldier for fear of the Russians. ... Still today people are trying to find out what happened to their dead—because so many were chucked in a hole [*verscharrt*] namelessly, then exhumed namelessly, and then buried again namelessly. I laid the bodies of the dead in the earth with my own hands, after I had carefully looked for their identity papers."[67] Suggesting that the representatives of the Magistrat had possibly not "been in Berlin" during the fighting implied that the people intent on digging up the Samaritan cemetery were outsiders who had not shared in the experience of the war, the burial catastrophe, and its aftermath. Indeed, some Magistrat representatives—Deputy Mayor Karl Maron and Otto Winzer, who headed the Magistrat office for education (*Volksbildung*), for example—had *not* been in Berlin during the war. They had been in exile in Moscow, a fact possibly not lost on Harnisch. Thus he implied a moral distance between himself and his interlocutors in the city government.

Treating the dead "piously," to Harnisch's mind, had to do—above all—with securing their identities and rescuing them from the oblivion of "namelessness." He emphasized how he had defied death by going into the streets during the fighting to collect the dead. He had then carefully gathered their identity papers, so that they would not end up, like so many others, anonymously and ignominiously "chucked in a hole"—surely a reference to the fundamental transgression implied by the mass burials ordered and overseen by Soviet commanders in the earliest postwar days. Harnisch's defense of the graves of the German dead in the Samaritan churchyard, thus, was an assertion of "proper" burial and, in that sense, of German values. Unlike so many thousands of others, Harnisch's letters suggested, the dead in the Samaritan churchyard had *not* been dishonored in death. They had been buried individually, and their identities had been secured. They would not slip, as so many had, into the void of depersonalized death. Moreover, Harnisch claimed to have honored the dead as fellow Germans—having "dared" to lay hands on them and demonstrate his connection to them when no one else would. Harnisch, in other words, made a particular claim to having rescued the dead from the awfulness of personal and collective obscurity. Having buried the dead "properly," he could not countenance disturbing them now.

Coming only months after the collapse of Nazi rule—during which proper burial, *individual* burial, had been elevated to a racial privilege—Harnisch's claims offer a vantage point from which to speculate on how some Berliners remembered Nazism and their experiences of war in the years immediately after the collapse of the Third Reich. The Magistrat proposed to dismantle the emergency cemetery at the Samaritan Church in order to get on with the project of building what was by now so often being referred to as "the new Berlin"; by doing so, it hoped to foreclose, in some sense, a disturbing past. For other Berliners, however, this implied sacrificing their memories of the war experience, memories inextricably connected to identity in the present. Berliners could not, after all, protest when the Allies ordered the dismantling of Nazi memorial culture,[68] imbued as it was with the glories of war and tacitly bound up with genocide, nor when they scratched swastikas out of building facades, or smashed Nazi statuary.

Nor were they in a position to protest when memorials to their dead heroes were promptly replaced with memorials honoring the occupation armies—particularly the Soviets.[69] But they could and did oppose attempts to remove graves that amounted to personal memorials, or that were in some way linked to the recent past and to individual memories of the war experience—particularly when doing so seemed likely to obliterate identities so painstakingly salvaged from the wreckage not only of the city but of history.

Indeed, Harnisch's hope that the cemetery could be "a small place of stillness removed from the hustle and bustle of the street, a soothing place for the bereaved, away from the curious eyes of the public,"[70] suggests that the Samaritan graveyard was to be somehow distinct from a world carrying on its business, separate from the creation of "the new Berlin." Moreover, the cemetery represented a place in which the bereaved could reflect on and remember the dead and the past in an atmosphere untouched by the perpetual activity that attended the reconstruction of the city, which tacitly urged setting aside such sentiments. Disputes over emergency graves in postwar Berlin, in other words, were a manifestation of the ambivalence involved in reconstructing not only the city, but Germany as well. On the one hand, Berliners were propelled in the postwar years toward "the future"—Joining the Free World or Building Socialism—but on the other, they wished to maintain their connections to the dead, which might imply lingering in the past, whatever it may have meant to them.

It might be argued, of course, that Harnisch's primary sense of obligation to the dead stemmed from his responsibilities as a minister, but the fact is that he never invoked this duty in his letters to the Magistrat. His commitment appears to have been rooted in a desire to defend the personal and collective identities of the dead (and indeed his own) against an "outsider" Magistrat that would erase all tangible evidence of the war experience—one that now, in the context of defeat and occupation, served as a new source of collective identity. Calling the graveyard, remarkably, "my cemetery for the fallen" in a letter of August 1946,[71] Harnisch described his plans to ring the area occupied by the graves with a wall, to plant it with wild grape vines, and to put in a small fountain. If anything, he hoped to make the cemetery's presence in the churchyard and neighborhood even more permanent. In a letter to an anxious relative of one of those buried in his cemetery, and in answer to the city's persistent claims that its presence was inauspicious, Harnisch asserted: "When I created the cemetery, I was driven to help by one desire only, that my work would aid the relatives; if my work has been a help to them, then I have reached my goal. None of the authorities has been able to convince me that this charming spot is disturbing the city landscape. And if it is the case that [the cemetery] is disturbing, then I am of the opinion that the wreckage of Berlin is far more disturbing. When it's removed, in 25 years, then they can take away the cemetery, if they are still of the opinion that it is disfiguring the landscape."[72]

Harnisch's palpably sarcastic remark about "25 years" suggests that while we tend to think of the rebuilding of Berlin after 1945 as the process of "getting back to normal," there was an experiential threshold between rubble and renewal, a period in which Berliners lived among the debris of Berlin as they had lived in the intact city. Ruins and the graves of the dead now comprised the city's new topography, became part of the new "way of seeing" that Rudy Koshar has described.[73] While from our perspective the rubble appears as an interim station on the way to somewhere else, to Berliners in the immediate postwar years, "somewhere else" was still beyond imagining. Standing in the midst of all that "disturbing" rubble, moreover, was Harnisch's cemetery, a symbol of the "proper" treatment of the dead having gone on despite it all, an assertion of German identity and even pride, a "charming spot." Even after Pastor Harnisch won preliminary battles regarding the continued existence of the cemetery,[74] he wrestled for years with the city on behalf of the families of those buried there. His commitment to his "cemetery for the fallen" was indeed great enough that several years later, in 1950, he petitioned the Magistrat to permit him and his wife to be buried there themselves.[75]

Communing with German dead in an environment that urged abandoning them was itself in some sense a political act, but it was one in which many Berliners, like Harnisch, engaged. The *Telegraf*, a newspaper linked to the Social Democratic Party (SPD) and licensed by the British, reported on Totensonntag 1946,[76] "the people do not forget their dead. Love, understanding, affection, and esteem, often unspoken or only hinted at in life, emerge" in the cemetery, to which they "make a pilgrimage. Never have the graves been kept so carefully, as they are now."[77] This commentator suggested that Berliners' connection to the dead had been made stronger, somehow, and that the cemetery was a site where emotions they otherwise felt the need to keep hidden could be expressed. As links to the past and anchors for the identities of individuals lost in the war—both those whose fates were known and those whose were not—the graves of 1945 served many functions in postwar Berlin.

Indeed, Pastor Walter Dress, later a professor of church history at Humboldt University, implied in a sermon for Totensonntag 1947 that something now bound Berliners particularly to the dead and their graves. But he also asked, "What are we seeking there?" Was it merely "the memory of what was gone?"[78] The answer to this question, it seems, was complex. Certainly for some Berliners, wartime graves were among the clearest remaining relics of the war itself, whose presence called to mind a discredited past and thus stood in the way of bringing "order" and "normalcy" back to Berlin. Particularly as time went on, emergency graves and other vestiges of the war appeared to block the path that led to Berlin's better, "cleaner" future, redeemed, above all, of its connections to Nazism, imperialist war, and genocide. Yet for others, to commune with the dead and to defend their wartime graves against the city's incursions was to make a claim to a shared past and to identity—particularly against the anxieties provoked by anonymous, depersonalized death.

These sensibilities—of hoping to distance oneself from the recent past on the one hand, and of attempting to salvage personal and collective identity from the wreckage on the other—came together in a particularly unsettling way in late winter 1947. In March, it was reported to officials in the Magistrat that dozens of corpses were lying unburied in a cemetery in Marzahn, many of them naked. It was here, in Marzahn, that *Sozialleichen*—those members of the urban poor whose burials were the responsibility of the city—were interred, particularly those who had resided in Friedrichshain and Kreuzberg. That winter, which was especially cold, the ground had frozen completely up to one meter deep, and for a time graves could not be dug. Nevertheless, bodies, perhaps as many as 120 of them, had continued to be transported to the cemetery and had collected there over a period of some weeks.[79]

A Protestant church official, Berlin General Superintendent Dr. Friedrich Wilhelm Krummacher,[80] described having himself seen "up to sixty corpses—young and old, men and women, some wrapped provisionally in rags or paper, some clothed in a piece of a shirt, others, in considerable numbers, totally unclothed" left lying on the floor of the cemetery chapel. "The view of these corpses," Krummacher wrote, "was unworthy of humanity, and reminded one in part of the notorious pictures of the concentration camps."[81] Krummacher's comments suggest ways in which images from the concentration camps had now become a new way of "seeing" the mishandling of the dead. Moreover, contemporary failings on the part of city workers to treat the dead in a way that conformed to local expectations of propriety and decency were now tacitly attributed to the Nazis, despite the regime having been history for more than two full years.

Something similar was at work when, only a few months later, in Reinickendorf, the Berlin Chief of Police lodged a complaint with the Magistrat's Office for Social Matters (Abteilung für Sozialwesen). From above-ground city trains, he noted, passengers could observe the burials of the poor taking place in the Old Reinickendorf Cemetery. This vision had "sparked the greatest indignation" among them. "For all to see," long boxes were being delivered to the cemetery, each of which contained "several completely naked corpses." Cemetery workers had tipped the dead into "so-called mass graves," from stretchers. "Even in the present difficulties," the chief went on, "we may not forget that we are dealing with the bodies of human beings who did their duty to the state ... as workers and taxpayers and have earned the right ... to be put under the earth decently." He concluded, "the sunken moral sensibilities of the majority during the Nazi years and through the brutalization of the war must be arrested."[82] Again, as in the Marzahn case, it was suggested that the contemporary mistreatment of the dead had less to do with present failings than with "sunken moral standards" associated with the Nazi era and the war. At the same time, however, and perhaps most disturbingly of all, the Marzahn and Reinickendorf dead seemed to call into question how past the past really was.

In her book on sexual morality and the reconstruction of postwar values, *Sex after Fascism,* Dagmar Herzog has argued that placing blame on the Nazis for diminished morals after the war was a way of distancing oneself from Nazism.[83] A related tendency, it seems, emerged in the discussions concerning the treatment of the dead in Marzahn and Reinickendorf in 1947. The dead, forlorn and forgotten in Berlin's cemeteries, looked to some Berliners like images from the concentration camps and like the work of the Nazis. It is noteworthy in this respect that those commenting on the two cases appear to have been particularly incensed by the nakedness of the dead—itself so suggestive of the images from the camps. At the same time, in his letter to the Office for Social Matters, the chief of police referred in practically the same breath to the dead having performed their "duty to the state," reminding us that the Nazi past lay not too far behind. Far from having been in any sense "forgotten" or "repressed," it would seem, Nazism served as a ready-to-hand reference not only for violations of the dead but for degraded moral, material, and social standards generally. In this sense, "the Nazis" could become, when needed, the transgressive other on to which the moral offenses of the present could be displaced and against which, simultaneously, moral life could be reenvisioned.

At the same time, it is striking that the Allies' efforts to propel Germans toward a sense of collective responsibility for the Holocaust through films like *Die Todesmühlen* may ironically have enabled some Berliners to see themselves as Nazi victims, by offering them a visual language through which to link their own experiences of the burial crisis—"*herumliegende Leichen*," mass, anonymous burials, provisional burials, burials without coffins, naked corpses, reburials—to the camps. What was more, the indignities one associated with the 1945 burial crisis seemed to continue without reprieve, years after the war was over, which only further encouraged some Berliners' sense of their victimhood—now not only at the hands of the occupiers, but also of "the Nazis."

This sense of victimhood was at least one reason why city authorities' efforts to remove and rebury occupants of emergency graves continued to be met with great disapproval by the Berlin public. In April 1949, municipal officials sought permission from the relatives to remove and rebury the remains of several dozen dead who had been buried on the grounds of the Matthäus Church in Steglitz just after the war. These plans were met with a storm of protest and a barrage of petitions. One of them, penned by a Professor L., read, in part: "[The Matthäus] dead were buried immediately after the collapse [*Zusammenbruch*]. These are either the graves of fallen soldiers or otherwise awake in the relatives particularly strong memories of a terrible time. They are therefore tended … in the most meticulous possible way, so in no sense are we speaking here of gravesites that are offensive to the public because of untidiness. … Some of the soldiers buried there have been already been disinterred and reburied once or twice, and we should grant them their peace at long last."[84] The bodies of these dead—already subjected to various reburials, mishandled time and again—had earned the right to be left in peace. Like Pastor Harnisch, Professor L. suggested that the dead had suffered enough, but also that their identities—and their connection to the wartime experiences of the families of the dead—had earned them the right to be at peace. Moreover, just as Harnisch had suggested of the Samaritan graves a few years previously, these dead, too, had been "properly" buried. The Matthäus graves were the very opposite of mass graves; they were "meticulously tended" and "tidy." Unlike the thousands of anonymous burials that had taken place during 1945, unlike the forlorn dead in Marzahn and Reinickendorf, these dead had had their identities secured, and their graves were well cared for. One petitioner indeed referred to the Matthäus graves as a "holy spot"[85] that should remain inviolate.

The soldiers buried on the grounds of the Matthäus Church, according to another letter protesting the reburials, were sons, husbands, and fathers who had "fallen so heroically in the final battle," whose "heroes' cemetery" (*Heldenfriedhof*) must continue to be maintained.[86] *Heldenfriedhof* was, significantly, the term used for soldiers' cemeteries in the Third Reich; neither time nor the Allies' reeducation and demilitarization initiatives had done much to change the popular attitudes toward German soldiers' wartime sacrifices. Another petitioner noted that the graves were from Steglitz's "most difficult days and have become a piece of our history," thus emphasizing again their connection to identity in the present.[87] Another bemoaned plans to "cut painfully through personal and local relationships" by disinterring the graves.[88]

One last petition to city authorities even recommended that rather than disinterring and reburying the dead in the Matthäus cemetery, their graves should instead be "leveled out."[89] Because in Germany individual graves are generally shaped into small, raised hills, the notion of "leveling" them implies obscuring their presence. This suggests an attempt to disguise the existence of the graves, which would then have become a private, perhaps even secret, place of reflection for the families of the dead. Metaphorically, at least, this was perhaps an acknowledgement that the graves of 1945 had indeed by 1949 become an incongruity in a city and a society struggling to rebuild from the catastrophes of Nazism and war. Still, it is quite clear that wartime graves remained an important *lieu de mémoire* for some Berliners many years after the war ended. Indeed, battles over the disinterment (and generally over the handling) of the "war dead"—soldiers and civilians—would continue in both postwar Berlins for years to come.[90]

Conclusion

Notions of "proper burial" may seem an odd place to have gone looking for vestiges of Nazi belief in the postwar years, let alone to see how these beliefs were reshaped over time. Yet perhaps it is in just such unobserved but ubiquitous aspects of life as the handling of the dead that these vestiges are likely to surface. Under the Nazis, but indeed well before then, Berliners had attached great moral value to the idea that they cared meticulously for the dead and that this was a central feature of belonging to a *Kulturvolk*. If we want to find evidence of beliefs and motivations, and of where the enthusiasm for Nazism came from and where it eventually went, this would seem precisely the sort of place to look. For it was in discussions of proper burial, during and after the war, that historical actors revealed some of their most profound convictions about the world and their place in it.

As I hope to have shown, "proper burial" was elevated to a racial privilege in the Third Reich: during the crisis engendered by the conditions of war, one received a coffin or was afforded the prerogative of individual burial based on his membership in the racial community. Racial outsiders, on the other hand, were ignominiously interred in mass graves. When the Nazi regime collapsed in 1945, however, Berliners were faced with a startling reversal of fate: they were compelled to bury their own dead, often without coffins; otherwise, they found their dead pitilessly dumped in mass graves. For the occupiers after 1945, restoring order to the processes of burial in the city was sometimes linked to a project of moral reform, as they strove to bring Berliners to some kind of acknowledgement of their responsibility for crimes committed in their name. Berliners, however, were not often inclined to see the images of the concentration camps as evidence of their own guilt. Instead, the pictures from the camps commingled with images of their own dead, and the methods by which corpses were disposed of in the camps, too, seemed to bear some resemblance to the experience of the burial crisis of 1945. Moreover, not a few Berliners continued to adhere to the attitudes that had informed the practices of burial under the Third Reich. Jewish cemeteries were not restored; Jewish graves were desecrated. No one would countenance placing a new cemetery in the proximity of the graves of those executed as "enemies of the people" and buried at Plötzensee.

At the same time, things did begin to change, as Berliners began trying to make sense of their recent past, often in contemplation of the treatment of the dead. However, postwar Berliners had a complex and often ambiguous relationship to Nazism and to the recent past in the aftermath of the Second World War. In the postwar years one might blame the Nazis for current predicaments, while at the same time continuing in some way to take the values of Nazism seriously. In the face of violations of the dead associated with the 1945 burial crisis, some Berliners, like Pastor Harnisch, defended proper burial and the right of the dead to remain "at peace" as evidence that all had not been lost in 1945. To defend the continued existence of wartime graves indeed became a way of asserting identity (both collective and individual), of laying a claim to the recent past, and of resisting the attempt to uproot every remnant of that past. Meanwhile, those who sought to defend the continued existence of emergency graves after the war also came to see their efforts, in some sense, as an attempt to rescue fellow Germans from the terrors of mass, anonymous burial—a horror to which Berliners had only recently subjected racial outsiders but could not sanction for themselves.

In other instances, defending proper burial became a way of disassociating oneself from the past, and of redeeming German cultural traditions from the experience of Nazism. Linking the mishandling of the dead to the former regime—as took place in Marzahn and Reinickendorf in 1947—enabled Berliners to displace their own offenses against the dead on to "the Nazis," who became the transgressive other against which German cultural values began now to be redefined. "The Nazis," in this sense, were not "real Germans" at all. To make this move, in turn, made it possible for Berliners to see German culture itself as having emerged essentially unharmed—not only from the burial crisis, but from the horrors of Nazism as well.

Notes

I am very pleased to have the chance to thank Lenard Berlanstein, Alon Confino, Matthew Gillis, Krishan Kumar, and Erik Midelfort, whose perceptive comments were invaluable to the development of this essay. I also thank the anonymous reader, whose insights greatly aided in the transformation of this article from an earlier iteration to its present form.

1. Bundesarchiv Berlin (hereafter BA) R 36/2735, Geschäftsführende Präsident des Deutschen Gemeindetags Heymann to Oberbürgermeister Erfurt, 21 April 1941.
2. Landesarchiv Berlin (hereafter LAB) A Rep 003-03/33, Der Polizeipräsident als örtlicher Luftschutzleiter, betr.: Beförderung von Leichen nach Luftangriffen, 2 September 1939.
3. BA R 36/2735, Geschäftsführende Präsident des Deutschen Gemeindetags Heymann to Oberbürgermeister Erfurt, 21 April 1941.
4. Olaf Groehler, *Bombenkrieg gegen Deutschland* (Berlin, 1990). See esp. "'Battle of Berlin' oder: Wie das britische strategische Luftkriegskonzept zerbrach," 172–194.
5. BA NS 6/346, p. 17, 9 February 1944.
6. Jörg Friedrich, *Der Brand: Deutschland im Bombenkrieg, 1940–1945* (Munich, 2002), 431.
7. LAB A Rep 009/31452, "Nachweisung der durch Feindeinwirkung getöteten Zivilpersonen," 1944–45.
8. See the recollections of Clemens Napieraj, whose father was the cemetery inspector of the St. Hedwig and St. Pius Cemetery in Hohenschönhausen, in Berlin's east. Thomas Friedrich and Monika Hansch, eds., *1945, Nun hat der Krieg ein Ende: Erinnerungen aus Hohenschönhausen* (Berlin, 1995), 155–159.
9. Klaus Konrad Weber, Peter Güttler, and Ditta Ahmadi, eds., *Berlin und seine Bauten, Teil X, Band A: Anlagen und Bauten für die Versorgung, Bestattungswesen* (Berlin and Munich, 1981), 8.
10. BA NS 18/832, p. 3, Dr. P. Danzer, "Totenkult oder Ahnenkult?" 10 April 1942.
11. The racialization of the culture of burial in Berlin after 1933 is discussed in Monica Black, "The Meaning of Death and the Making of Three Berlins: A History, 1933–1961," PhD thesis, University of Virginia, 2006.
12. LAB C Rep 110/1068, p. 81–82, 2 September 1944. See "Ruhefrist," in Reiner Sörries, ed., *Großes Lexikon der Bestattungs- und Friedhofskultur: Wörterbuch zur Sepulkralkultur* (Kassel, 2002), 260. The practice of reusing graves after a period of time for further burials in Germany was and is widespread.
13. LAB C Rep 110/168, Bezirksbürgermeister des Verwaltungsbezirks Charlottenburg, Friedhofs- und Bestattungsamt to Herrn Professor Scharoun, 14 February 1946.
14. Lucian Hölscher, ed., *Datenatlas zur religiösen Geographie im protestantischen Deutschland von der Mitte des 19. Jahrhunderts bis zum Zweiten Weltkrieg* Vol. 2: *Osten* (Berlin and New York, 2001), 472.
15. Great discrepancy characterizes the estimates of deaths associated with the 3 February 1945 attack on Berlin. Most plausible is Laurenz Demps's estimate of "at least" 2,541. See Demps, "Die Luftangriffe auf Berlin: Ein dokumentarischer Bericht, Teil II," in *Jahrbuch des Märkischen Museums* 4 (1978): 45.

16. LAB C Rep 110/1068, "Lenkung des Bestattungswesens," 23 February 1945.
17. LAB C Rep 110/1068, 17 February 1945.
18. LAB C Rep 110/1068, Niederschrift, 27 February 1945.
19. LAB C Rep 110/1069, Niederschrift, 6 March 1945.
20. LAB C Rep 110/1068, Gaupropagandaleiter der NSDAP Wernicke to Oberbürgermeister, 14 March 1945.
21. LAB C Rep 110/1068, Niederschrift, 6 March 1945.
22. LAB C Rep 110/1068, Hauptbestattungsamt to Bezirksbürgermeister, April 1945. No more precise date is given.
23. LAB C Rep 110/169, Bezirksbürgermeister Spandau to Magistrat Hauptamt für Grünplanung, 20 February 1946.
24. The wartime records of the Central Burial Office, housed today in the Berlin State Archives (LAB), end in April 1945.
25. Curt Riess, *Berlin Berlin 1945–1953* (Berlin, 2002), 23.
26. LAB F Rep 240, Acc. 2651/4, 1977 Senator für Arbeit und Soziales essay contest, entry by Erika Wollenburg. In 1977, (West) Berlin's Senator für Arbeit und Soziales (Senator for Labor and Social Issues) sponsored an essay contest called "Berlin nach dem Kriege—wie ich es erlebte" ("my experiences in Berlin after the war"). Some of the submissions, like this one, have been collected in the LAB; some appear as well in a booklet published under the title *Berlin nach dem Kriege—wie ich es erlebte* (Berlin, 1977).
27. The opening scene of Roberto Rossellini's 1948 neo-realist *Germania Anno Zero* depicts Berlin as a modern necropolis, where groups of Germans bury the dead among the ruins of their destroyed city.
28. See, for example: Anonyma, *Eine Frau in Berlin: Tagebuchaufzeichnungen vom 20. April bis 22. Juni 1945* (Frankfurt am Main, 2003); Margret Boveri, *Tage des Überlebens: Berlin 1945* (Munich, 1968); Wilfred Byford-Jones, *Berlin Twilight* (London and New York, 1947); Ingrid Hammer and Susanne zur Nieden, eds., *Sehr selten habe ich geweint: Briefe und Tagebücher aus dem Zweiten Weltkrieg von Menschen aus Berlin* (Zürich, 1992); Georg Holmsten, *Als keiner wußte, ob er überlebt: Zwischen den Sommern 1944/45* (Düsseldorf, 1995); Jochen Koehler, *Klettern in der Großstadt: Volkstümliche geschichten vom Überleben in Berlin 1933/45* (Berlin, 1979); Matthias Menzel, *Die Stadt ohne Tod: Berliner Tagebuch 1943/45* (Berlin, 1946); Kerrin Gräfin Schwerin, *Frauen im Krieg: Briefe, Dokumente, Aufzeichnungen* (Berlin, 1999); Ursula von Kardorff, *Berliner Aufzeichnungen 1942 bis 1945* (Munich, 1992).
29. LAB F Rep 280/10678, Tagebuch Hertha von Gebhardt, p. 2.
30. For details, see Andreas Dinter, *Seuchenalarm in Berlin: Seuchengeschehen und Seuchenbekämpfung in Berlin nach dem II. Weltkrieg* (Berlin, 1999).
31. Though he did not report on Berlin, the remarkable Victor Gollancz's account of social conditions in Germany (derived from an October-November 1946 visit to the British Zone) describes the food, housing, clothing, and public health situation in the immediate postwar years in Germany generally. See Gollancz, *In Darkest Germany* (Hinsdale, IL, 1947).
32. On the postwar "suicide wave" see Richard Bessel, "Hatred After War: Emotion and the Postwar History of East Germany," *History and Memory* 17 (special double issue, spring/summer 2005): 199-216, and Christian Goeschel, "Suicide at the End of the Third Reich," *Journal of Contemporary History* 41, no. 1 (2006): 153–173.
33. Joseph Orlopp, *Zusammenbruch und Aufbau Berlins 1945/1946* (Berlin, 1946), 25–28.
34. Dinter, *Seuchenalarm in Berlin,* 17.
35. Riess, *Berlin Berlin,* 23.
36. Friedrich and Hansch, *1945, Nun hat der Krieg ein Ende,* 159. Recollections of Clemens Napieraj. See also numerous entries in the 1977 "Berlin nach dem Kriege—wie ich es erelebte" essay contest collection, LAB F Rep 240, Acc. 2651.
37. Holmsten, *Als keiner wußte, ob er überlebt,* 165–167.
38. LAB C Rep 110/168/1, Vermerk, Abt. Grünplanung, 20 November 1945.

39. Michael Schütz, ed., *Das Tagebuch des Herrn Schmidt: Ein Zeitdokument aus Berlin vom 20. April bis 27. Juli* (Hamburg, 1999), 34–35.
40. Menzel, *Die Stadt ohne Tod,* 199–200.
41. Anonyma, *Eine Frau in Berlin,* 159–160.
42. Koehler, *Klettern in der Großstadt,* 243. Recollections of Walter Seitz.
43. LAB F Rep 240, Acc. 2651/4, contest entry of Marie Herweg.
44. LAB F Rep 240, Acc. 2651/4, contest entry of Maria M.
45. LAB F Rep 240, Acc. 2651/4, contest entry of Willy Henning.
46. LAB F Rep 280/10848, Amt für Grünplanung und Gartenbau, Berlin-Schöneberg, 15 May 1945.
47. LAB C Rep 110/168, Friedrich Löchner to Oberbürgermeister Berlins, 28 November 1945.
48. LAB C Rep 110/1068, Bezirksamt Köpenick, Garten- und Friedhofsverwaltung to Magistrat Amt für Grünplanung, 10 January 1946.
49. LAB C Rep 110/1068, "Das Bestattungswesen im neuen Berlin," n.d., and "Ergänzung zu meinen Ausführungen über 'Das Bestattungswesen im neuen Berlin,'" 2 July 1945.
50. Willi Bredel, "Der Totengräber," *Deutsche Volkszeitung,* 1. Jahrgang, 24 June 1945.
51. See Sabine Behrenbeck, *Die Kult um die toten Helden: Nationalsozialistische Mythen, Riten und Symbole 1923 bis 1945* (Vierow bei Greifswald, 1996), and Jay Baird, *To Die for Germany: Heroes in the Nazi Pantheon* (Bloomington, IN, 1990).
52. Deutsches Rotes Kreuz Generalsekretariat, ed., *20 Jahre DRK-Suchdienst* (Bonn, 1965), 2.
53. "Viel Tausend Gräber klagen an. Ein Friedhof von vielen. Die Totengräber unseres Volkes," *Deutsche Volkszeitung,* 1. Jahrgang, 18 July 1945.
54. R. Le., "Auf dem Friedhof von Marzahn: Hier liegen die Hingerichteten," *Neue Zeit,* 31 October 1945.
55. Ulrich Torrel, "Vom Sterben in dieser Zeit," *Neue Zeit,* 9 September 1945.
56. Anonyma, *Eine Frau in Berlin,* 244.
57. Dagmar Barnouw, *Germany 1945: Views of War and Violence* (Bloomington, IN, 1996), esp. chaps. 1 and 2, "To Make Them See," and "The Quality of Victory," 1–87.
58. Jeffrey Herf, *Divided Memory: The Nazi Past in the Two Germanys* (Cambridge, MA, 1997), 70.
59. Habbo Knoch, "Die Grenzen des Zeigbaren: Fotografien der NS-Verbrechen und die westdeutsche Gesellschaft, 1955–1965," in Sven Kramer, ed., *Die Shoah im Bild* (Munich, 2003), 93.
60. LAB C Rep 110/1078, London Office of the Jewish Committee for Relief Abroad to the Vorstand der Jüdischen Gemeinde, 21 April 1947.
61. Susanne Kerkhoff, *Berliner Briefe* (Berlin, 1947), 32.
62. LAB C Rep 110/168, report, Magistrat, Abteilung Grünplanung, 11 June 1946.
63. LAB C Rep 110/1058, Magistrat, Abteilung Grünplanung to Bezirksamt Friedrichshain, 15 May 1946.
64. LAB C Rep 110/1058, Dr. W. Harnisch to Bezirksamt Friedrichshain, 17 May 1946.
65. LAB C Rep 110/1058, Dr. W. Harnisch to Magistrat, Abteilung Grünplanung, 28 September 1950.
66. LAB C Rep 110/1058, Magistrat, Abteilung Grünplanung to Bezirksamt Friedrichshain, 15 May 1946.
67. LAB C Rep 110/1058, Dr. W. Harnisch to Bezirksamt Friedrichshain, 17 May 1946.
68. George Mosse, *Fallen Soldiers: Reshaping the Memory of the World Wars* (Oxford, 1990), 212.
69. The recollections of Dieter Noack in Helmut Engel, *"Es gab Schoten und Mohrrüben oder: Die Russen waren plötzlich da. Rahnsdorf am 21. April 1945* Beiheft 19 (Berlin, 1995), 35, recount an incident in Wilhelmshagen, in Berlin's east, in which a German WWI memorial was ripped out to make way for the construction of a Soviet memorial adorned with a red star. More dramatic are the memorials to the Red Army dead in Treptow Park and on Unter den Linden; the latter was completed even before the year 1945 was out.
70. LAB C Rep 110/1058, Harnisch to Frau Edith S., 27 May 1946.

71. LAB C Rep 110/1058, Harnisch to Evangelisches Konsistorium, 12 August 1946.
72. LAB C Rep 110/1058, Harnisch to Frau Edith S., 27 May 1946.
73. Rudy Koshar, *From Monuments to Traces: Artifacts of German Memory, 1870–1990* (Berkeley and Los Angeles, 2000), 81–83.
74. LAB C Rep 110/1058, Polizeipräsident to Samariterkirche, 21 May 1950. The police issued a permit for the cemetery to continue to exist for a time, as long as no one else was buried there and it was understood that it was not to be permanent.
75. LAB C Rep 110/1058, Bezirksamt Friedrichshain on the matter of Harnisch, 28 September 1950. The Magistrat refused to allow the couple's bodies to be buried among the Samaritan church graves. They were, however, ultimately permitted to have their ashes buried there, and a small memorial marks that spot today. After making a trip to the church to see Harnisch's cemetery and finding only a plaque, I inquired into the recent history of the graves with a representative of the Senatsverwaltung für Stadtentwicklung (the Berlin Senate's offices for city planning), which maintains war graves in Berlin. In the 1970s, it seems, the regular *Ruhefrist* on the Samaritan graves ran out. At this point the land was made into a playground. This was possible because war graves, except for those of foreign war dead, were not maintained in perpetuity in East Germany (as they were in the West). After the 1990 unification, the Senatsverwaltung, fearing that a child in the sandbox might by chance turn up bones there, made the decision to remove the remaining bones and to rebury them in the Gärtner Straße Cemetery in Hohenschönhausen. The parish still possessed a map—undoubtedly drawn by Harnisch—indicating where the dead had been buried.
76. The observance of Totensonntag (literally, "Sunday of the dead") began in Prussia in 1816, at the behest of Friedrich Wilhelm II, in response to the deaths associated with the Wars of Liberation. It was eventually taken on by the *Landeskirchen* (state churches) and became widespread. Totensonntag essentially reproduced some of the practices of All Souls' Day, the Catholic holiday for remembering and praying for the dead, including attending church services and making pilgrimages to cemeteries, and is observed on the last Sunday before the beginning of Advent. *Lexikon für Theologie und Kirche*, X. Band (Freiburg, 2001), 130–131.
77. Sonntags-Beilage zu Totensonntag, *Telegraf*, 24 November 1946.
78. Evangelisches Zentralarchiv (EZA) 604/4, Nachlaß Dress, sermon for Totensonntag 1947.
79. LAB C Rep 101-04/3, Letter from Propst Grüber, Beirat für kirchliche Angelegenheiten, 10 March 1947.
80. Krummacher had joined the National Committee for a Free Germany while an inmate in a Soviet POW camp. After the war, he was judged "an unimpeachable antifascist" by the leadership of the committee. See Gerhard Besier, *Der SED-Staat und die Kirche: Der Weg in der Anpassung* (Munich, 1993), 25.
81. LAB C Rep 101-04/3, p. 39-41, Superintendentur Berlin Land I Dr. Krummacher to Herrn Propst Grüber, 17 March 1947.
82. LAB C Rep 110/1070, Abschrift from Polizeipräsident to Magistrat Abt. für Sozialwesen, 4 June 1947.
83. Dagmar Herzog, *Sex After Fascism: Memory and Morality in Twentieth-Century Germany* (Princeton, 2005).
84. LAB B Rep 212/6134, Professor Dr. L. to Bezirksbürgermeister of Steglitz, 5 April 1949.
85. LAB B Rep 212/6134, petition, 28 March 1949.
86. LAB B Rep 212/6134, letter, 28 March 1949.
87. LAB B Rep 212/6134, petition to Magistrat Berlin-Steglitz, 31 March 1949.
88. LAB B Rep 212/6134, Frau Moldänke to Magistrat Berlin-Steglitz, 23 March 1949.
89. LAB B Rep 212/6134, petition, 28 March 1949.
90. A most insightful discussion of the meaning and role played by the war dead in the postwar Germanys is Alf Lüdtke, "Histories of Mourning: Flowers and Stones for the War Dead, Confusion for the Living—Vignettes from East and West Germany," in Gerald Sider and Gavin Smith, eds., *Between History and Histories: The Making of Silences and Commemorations* (Toronto, 1995).

Part II

DISPOSAL

Chapter 4

FANNING THE FLAMES
Cremation in Late Imperial and Weimar Germany

Simone Ameskamp

7:15 Incineration of the corpse begins, lying in a sturdy oak coffin,
7:25 coffin burned away, skull exposed,
7:30 chest bones exposed,
7:35 upper arm and shoulder blades completely exposed and crumbling,
7:40 abdomen burns. Muscles persist longest, all wooden parts disappear,
7:45 collarbone has loosened, rib cage is still standing completely free,
7:48 right lower jaw and right collarbone fall off,
7:50 some ribs collapse,
7:55 spine completely free,
8:00 thighs and lower legs separated from hips, skeleton quite disintegrated. Muscles around the spine burn,
8:05 wood of the supporting base mostly gone, head completely burned out,
8:10 liver burns. Legs completely burned. Bone ashes fall into the ash receptacle. Spine broken apart,
8:15 skull lies at the door maintaining its main shape. Hip bones lie square. Upper arm bones partly fell down,
8:20 skeleton completely burned and disintegrated. Only muscle parts on the right side of the back are still burning,
8:28 corpse burned. Some wooden pieces are still burning.
8:30 The fire is extinguishing. The incineration has come to an end.[1]

On one night in October 1874, flames consumed the portly woman's naked body, which was partly covered by her thick long hair, and within two hours, reduced it to less than two kilos of ashes.[2] Sir Charles Wentworth Dilke, British lower undersecretary and young widower, had brought his wife's corpse from

---

Notes for this chapter begin on page 110.

London to the glass factory of Friedrich Siemens in Dresden. Siemens had gained a reputation across Europe for maximizing the use of heat in his regenerative furnaces, which were used in heavy industry to melt glass and to remove impurities from iron ore. Subsequently he had discovered their use for burning organic material. Under the watch of Saxon health officials, Lady Dilke's corpse was incinerated at temperatures around 1000 degrees Celsius. The bone ashes were still glowing when Siemens removed them from the furnace and handed them over to the Englishman. Eyewitnesses described the first successful cremation on German soil as flawless, "extremely aesthetic," and the exact opposite of a "disgusting burial."[3] The natural decomposition of Lady Dilke's corpse would have taken decades.

The invention of regenerative furnaces removed the technological roadblock to modern cremation. Siemens had been asked by Carl Reclam, professor of medicine in Leipzig, on behalf of other cremationists to develop a method for burning bodies that did not offend the human senses or feelings. Other European engineers had failed to construct furnaces that were low-cost and energy-efficient, facilitated quick and complete incineration, produced pure and white ashes, and did not cause odors or smoke. Cremationist pioneers celebrated Siemens' technical breakthrough, which rekindled a reform movement to introduce and legalize cremation as an alternative to earth burial in Imperial Germany.

In the 1870s, bourgeois reformers like Reclam started campaigning for the reintroduction of optional cremation, which had been a legal and accepted funerary practice in the German lands until Charlemagne outlawed it as a pagan custom at the end of the eighth century. More than a millennium after Charlemagne's reign and attempts at Christianization, a small group of educated middle-class men formed associations, wrote pamphlets, gave speeches, published journals with illustrious names like *Die Flamme* or *Phoenix*, lobbied their political representatives, and raised money for the building of crematoria in order to be granted the opportunity to dispose of dead bodies through fire. Inspired by the public health movement and driven by concerns about a shortage of cemetery space in growing cities, they put forth hygienic and economic as well as aesthetic and ideological arguments for the introduction of cremation. The cremationist campaigns of the late nineteenth and early twentieth centuries met the opposition of lawmakers and governments in the bigger German states. Strong resistance by the Protestant and Catholic churches, along with what cremationists deemed "the forces of habit," delayed the takeoff of cremation until the interwar years, when the burning of the dead had at last become a legal, accepted, and affordable way of disposal for both members of the bourgeoisie and the working classes.

The rediscovery of cremation indicates a shift in attitudes toward mortality. The meaning that Germans gave to the experience of others' and the prospect of their own deaths changed at the turn of the twentieth century: the eighteenth-century conception of death as sleep slowly disappeared in the second half of the nineteenth century, making room for cyclical ideas of a return to the origins, which assumed an accelerated and unambiguous passage from life to death, which in turn required the ability to clearly identify and distinguish between the states of being alive and dead.[4] The debates surrounding the introduction of cremation provide insight into the treatment of dead and living bodies, relationships between the dead and the living, and changing concepts of self and time. Conflicts surrounding this reform movement pitted liberals and progressives against orthodox and conservatives, who disagreed on how to deal with change.

The study of cremation modifies the grand narratives of rationalization and secularization in Western European history, while it illuminates the complexities of individuation and the process of civilization as Norbert Elias conceived of it. The cremation movement testified to the ability of some modern Germans to overcome the dialectic of the Enlightenment. It also corroborates the power and resilience of unorganized religion by confirming that the declining influence of the Christian churches at the beginning of the twentieth century did not automatically entail the dechristianization of German society. When state authorities took over the tasks of providing education, performing marriages, and regulating burials, they relieved the Christian churches of some formal responsibilities and broke the religious monopoly on rites of passage, but secular institutions could not fulfill the spiritual need for giving meaning to the transitoriness of life, for example by promising the existence of a transcendent afterlife.

Even three decades after Philippe Ariès developed his typology and periodization of attitudes toward mortality,[5] for the lack of better models these still serve as a blueprint for writing and explaining the modern history of death. A closer look at the cremation movement cautions against the uncritical adaptation of Ariès' concept of forbidden death and the assumption that modern Western men and women have denied and suppressed their mortality. The clashes over and spread of cremation as an alternative form of disposal show that ordinary Germans cared deeply about their last journeys. In addition, these conflicts suggest that the grand caesurae of the twentieth century, above all mass death, destruction, and dying during the World Wars, had little impact on the way Germans conceived of their individual deaths. Rather, material conditions like family income or the effects of inflation and depression determined the choice of disposal more than mass murder and violence influenced attitudes toward everyday death, which changed at a slower pace than the tumultuous political events of the century.

Milestones and Markers

Four years had passed since the incineration of Lady Dilke in Siemens' glass factory, when Germany's first modern crematorium opened in the Thuringian city of Gotha in 1878. A second was dedicated in Heidelberg in 1891, followed by one in Hamburg in 1892, in the wake of a devastating cholera epidemic. By 1914 Imperial Germans had access to 43 crematoria; by 1939 Germany offered 131. Constructed in a hodgepodge of architectural styles, most early twentieth-century crematoria resembled churches, ancient temples, or national monuments.[6] Compared to the ancient custom, modern cremation added a unique twist to the practice of burning bodies: indoor furnaces replaced open pyres. Whole buildings were now exclusively dedicated to the purpose of bidding farewell to the deceased, of transforming their remnants into ashes, and of storing their cremains in the niches of adjacent columbaria. Such hybrids of practical and sacral functions challenged architects who, unable to find precedents, resorted to a strict separation of spheres: in most crematoria the funeral service and mourning took place upstairs, while the technology was banished to the basement, hidden from the public eye. With the help of hydraulic elevators the casket descended from the catafalque, imitating the lowering of the coffin into the grave during earth burials. Eager to avoid the cold industrial look of factories, which were devoid of metaphysical meaning, architects struggled to hide chimneys behind high facades and domes. The interior design posed a similar dilemma. On the one hand the demands of confessional and ideological neutrality forbade the use of concrete religious symbols, which on the other hand were best suited to convey the desired dignified and solemn atmosphere. Thus, if crucifixes were displayed they had to be removable. Where one might have expected Biblical quotations, neutral inscriptions appeared,[7] accompanied by evergreens and astronomical images or classical motifs like flames or the mythical bird Phoenix, an ancient symbol of renewal.

From the beginning in the 1870s, cremation was an urban phenomenon. The grassroots movement depended on local initiative and developed from the bottom up. Confessional and constitutional disparities led to striking regional differences in its expansion. In general, cremation spread from small, secular, and liberal states like the duchy of Saxony-Coburg-Gotha or the city-state of Bremen to bigger territories with a complex power structure. Prussia, with its strong alliance of throne and altar, and Catholic Bavaria were the last German states to allow cremation in 1911 and 1912. After cremationists had submitted numerous petitions, and several courts had decided that cremation did not violate the existing laws, individual states passed cremation bills and ended decades of legal limbo by introducing rules for the implementation of cremation.

To the dismay of cremationists, in some states these regulations added rather than removed practical obstacles to having one's body burned. Only the Imperial Law of 1934—concurrent with the National Socialist coordination of the cremation movement and its associations—standardized the official rules for all of Germany and put cremation on equal footing with earth burial. The Imperial Law, whose principal clauses are still in effect today, stipulated mandatory postmortems and last wills and testaments by the deceased. It also codified peculiarities of German cremation, which were geared toward the preservation of cemeteries and toward maintaining a resemblance to traditional earth burials: bodies had to be burned in coffins. Crematoria were forbidden to hand over cremains to relatives. Ashes could not be scattered but had to be stored above or under ground in individual and clearly identifiable containers. With the exception of confessional graveyards, all cemeteries were public; private enterprises were forbidden from operating burial grounds or crematoria.

The first crematoria were built with the private funds of bourgeois associations and handed over for operation to the cities, which then offered cremation as a municipal service at set fees. After the legalization of cremation in most German states in the 1910s, a building boom in crematoria set in, so that by the early 1930s more than one hundred crematoria were operating in Germany. The higher spatial concentration of crematoria shortened the distance that the deceased needed to be transported to the closest crematorium and thereby eased the financial burden for his or her family. The high cost of shipping corpses by rail had made cremation unaffordable for the lower classes in the nineteenth century.

Despite this built-in dynamic, the growth of the cremation movement was sluggish until the beginning of the twentieth century and remained slow until the interwar years. By the beginning of the First World War about 56,000 Germans had been cremated, on average less than 1 percent of the deceased. Few victims of the Great War were cremated, although engineers had developed mobile crematoria for use on battlefields and the fuel supply for municipal furnaces had been ensured. Only in the mid 1920s, aided by inflation, depression, lower prices, and a growing popularity among the working classes, the proportion of cremations increased to about 5 percent. In 1935 about 9 percent of the dead made their last journey to the crematorium, in 1949 a little over 10 percent.[8] Neither the Second World War nor the Holocaust influenced the long-term trend significantly. The share of cremations kept rising throughout the century: today on average one third of the German dead are cremated, while regional and confessional differences prevail. With a rate of over 50 percent, cremation was the preferred mode of disposal in East Germany.[9] In Sweden and Great Britain cremation surpassed burial in the late 1960s, when it accounted for merely 4 percent of disposals in the US. Since then, however, it has been catching on among American white middle-class professionals.[10]

The typical activist for cremation at the turn of the century was a highly educated, prosperous, and often self-employed Protestant male bourgeois. The first cremation associations counted among their ranks and board members many factory owners, lawyers, engineers, professors, publishers and editors, architects, officers, investors, higher civil servants, medical doctors, and some painters and writers. As pioneers, the linguist and folklorist Jacob Grimm, the writer and 1848er Gottfried Kinkel, and the doctor and political reformer Rudolf Virchow had the biggest name recognition for contemporaries. In the early twentieth century, they were joined by Albert Kalthoff, Bremen pastor, cofounder of the Protestant Reform Association, and leader of the League of German Monists, as well as Max Sievers, labor leader and socialist editor. About a quarter of association members were female, often the wives and daughters of male members. Few workers joined the first cremation associations but by 1913 their proportion had climbed to about 14 percent, by 1926 to about 46 percent. Working-class cremationists founded separate associations and burial insurances at the beginning of the twentieth century, like the Social Democratic Volksfeuerbestattungsverein and the predominantly atheist Verein der Freidenker für Feuerbestattung. All cremation associations pursued the same goals and similar agendas but could not bridge the class and ideological divides that separated their constituencies.

The cremated were distributed unevenly across the German population. With a share of more than 80 percent, Protestants predominated on the brink of the First World War; 8 percent were Catholic, 6 percent Jewish, and 3 percent dissidents, which meant they could have been atheists, monists, or freethinkers.[11] Cremation statistics provide strong evidence that the most common assumption about cremation was wrong: cremationists were not freethinkers or freemasons, as the Catholic church made them out to be in its defensive battle, but the majority belonged to the milieu of cultural Protestantism.[12] The number of cremated women fluctuated depending on geography and period, but in general it lagged behind the number of cremated men by about 30 percent.[13] Whereas gender and class differences gradually leveled out over the course of the century, confessional disparities persisted. In terms of political affiliation, cremationists were drawn toward the Liberals and National Liberals as well as the Social Democrats, while their opponents gravitated toward the Conservatives and the Center Party. However, even within political parties and confessions the main demarcation line ran between liberals and orthodox: progressives embraced change, while conservatives protected the status quo in burial customs.

Although Germans prided themselves on having the biggest number of crematoria on the continent in the early twentieth century, cremation was not a German peculiarity. International collaboration and exchange fostered at conventions and in publications spurred a European movement. German immigrants would export the rediscovered mode of disposal to the US, for example, dominating the Cremation Association of New York City, where fellow Europeans, in particular Italian engineers and scientists, had set the pace for their German neighbors. Whereas in Italy cremation symbolized anticlerical protest, in Germany the movement was much more moderate, with the exception of small radical circles of proletarian freethinkers during the interwar years who used cremation as a decoy to increase membership in their organizations. In Great Britain, functional and utilitarian views dominated the debates from the start. Economic and hygienic concerns drove the Queen's surgeon, Sir Henry Thompson, to found the Cremation Society of England in 1874, which thrived on the support of sanitarians.[14] The repertoire of German cremationist reasoning included hard facts as well as poetic reveries, cost estimates and quantitative data on bacteriological experiments as well as metaphysical speculations and sentimental appeals. In Germany cremationists combined arguments that were based on modern scientific knowledge with romantic images, which eluded calibration and calculation.

Against the Slow Rot

During the early years of the movement, cremationist speakers and writers focused on the shortcomings of traditional earth burial, criticized the status quo, and introduced cremation as the best remedy to solve the problems. The fear of being buried alive still plagued Europeans at the turn of the twentieth century although medical experts had discredited apparent death as a myth.[15] Burial reformers combined their campaigns for optional cremation with demands for the introduction of mandatory postmortems, which they advertised as effective protection against being buried alive as well as murder by poisoning, which equally frightened potential victims. Cremationists voiced two major grievances about burial and the state of cemeteries: they were hazardous and disgusting. Scientists complained that decomposing bodies in graves jeopardized the health and happiness of the living, while aesthetes debunked as an illusion the poetry of the grave, which had dampened the fear of death and consoled the mourning in previous centuries.

Twentieth-century reformers countered nineteenth-century fears of the returning dead. The dead were going to come back with a vengeance from perilous graveyards, Kinkel worried, "in the mist of the atmosphere and in the water of our wells in order to poison us. The tale of the vampire contains a terrible kernel of truth: It can happen that in this sense, the dead suck the blood out of the living."[16] Churchyards turned into Lucifer's playgrounds: "Cemeteries not only bring plague and infertility, but are almost factories of the devil, which fill the air with stench and pollute the water. The dead are virtually the murderers of the living!"[17] Fire promised to be the force that purified the other poisoned elements, as no contagion could resist its disinfecting powers.[18]

Furthermore, cremationists argued, earth burial harmed the senses and sentiments of the living as well as the dignity of the dead. The grave was traditionally romanticized as a cozy bed for peaceful slumber, but the restless activity of microorganisms as well as the frequent turnover of corpses placed in cemeteries prevented the dead from entering a state of eternal peace, which was usually interrupted when, after twenty or thirty years, the lease for a burial plot expired.[19] Thus a physician exclaimed, the "word *Friedhof* [courtyard of peace] is a conventional lie!"[20] The sight, smell, or simply the idea of a slowly rotting corpse, imprisoned in a cold, dark, and damp underground cell, offered as a dish to worms and vermin, horrified and repulsed cremationists.[21] Exposing a deceased loved one to the torture of slow decay was considered callous and cruel. Cremationists used a series of adjectives to describe earth burial: unaesthetic, gruesome, repulsive, disgusting, awful, revolting, slow, and unhealthy. By contrast, the advantages of cremation were captured in the designations: pure, fast, beautiful, elevating, sacred, dignified, simple, thorough, conscientious, universal, safe, gentle, economical, useful, efficient, sensible, natural, precise, clean, noble, majestic, cheap, hygienic, reverent, thrifty, rational, space-saving.

For Purification by Fire

In pamphlets, newspapers, talks, and parliamentary debates, cremationist reformers established four main lines of argument that centered on economics, hygiene, aesthetics, and piety. Economic reasons were cited least frequently. A few cremationists decried a short-sighted squandering of space and complained that the ground occupied by urban cemeteries was too valuable to be left unproductive. By the same token, cremationists criticized the wholesale transplantation of cemeteries beyond the city boundaries, because the increased distance raised the cost of funerals and made grave visits rarer and more burdensome.[22] Crematoria and columbaria, on the other hand, needed so little space that they could be constructed in densely populated cities.[23] In addition, they argued, cremation helped preserve communal funds. It offered an affordable alternative to mass graves for the less fortunate who died on the parish; cremating rather than burying the urban poor could halve the expenses borne by the local community.[24] Despite such pragmatic calculations and deliberations over using the waste heat from crematorium chimneys for general heating purposes, reformers stopped short of advocating that, like animal cadavers, human remains should be recycled for the production of grease, phosphorus, or fertilizer.[25] Cremationists lamented the wasting of resources by families as well as cities and national economies, but their desire for efficiency and the rational use of material assets ended where the dignity of the dead began.

More often than economic arguments, cremationists cited hygiene and aesthetics. They made use of the latest findings by bacteriologists like Robert Koch and Louis Pasteur, who were studying cholera, malaria, and other bacteria as well as the contaminating effects of decomposing matter on air and water. Sanitary reformers advocated the burning of victims of epidemics, just as victims of war had been incinerated on open pyres on battlefields of the nineteenth century.[26] Feeding on a belief in empirical science and disenchanted, physiological views of the human body, they conceived of burial as a problem of disposal rather than a rite of passage. "The purpose of burial is to foster the quick and complete decomposition of human bodies and the dissolution into their elementary components."[27] From this scientific standpoint, earth burial and cremation were manifestations of the same physiological process and resulted in identical chemical products but incineration accelerated the process of decay and eliminated the negative side effects that offended the senses.

While hygienists celebrated the destructive force of the flame, romantic spirits cherished its purifying, liberating, and enlightening powers. The longer the debates surrounding cremation lasted, the more arguments of hygiene and public health faded into the background and made room for considerations of aesthetics and piety. Respect for the dead, faithfulness to deceased loved ones, and the alleviation of fear of one's own death as well as concerns for beauty and taste made incineration a preferred mode of disposal. Often the aesthetic value of cremation[28] was simply asserted and illustrated with metaphors rather than discussed and argued about. Parliamentarians in the Prussian Diet remarked several times during their deliberation of the cremation bill that there is no accounting for taste.[29] Witnesses described feelings of awe and sensations of grandeur when in a modern furnace "the body consumes itself, untouched by a single flame from the fuel, in glowing air alone, in its own embers."[30] Incineration represented a process of purification, refinement, and elevation. Purity stood for innocence, which the male reformers saw embodied in their wives and children. Their loving memory had to be protected against gross images of decay. In the grave, "step by step the figure of the beloved woman who had rested in our arms, becomes more hideous down there, and even the darling angel of a child who delighted us so often in his or her little white crib, turns into a horrific monster."[31]

As a more poetic alternative to the grave, Max Pauly, president of the Berlin cremation association in the early 1900s, suggested laying the ashes to rest in the ground, mixing them with fertile soil, and planting pretty flowers in it.[32] Although the Prussian cremation bill of 1911 put an end to such visions, for the cremationists a small pile of snow-white ashes that had become one with nature symbolized the untainted innocence of the dead better than a worm-eaten decaying corpse and tombstones.[33] Modern furnaces reduced the mortal remains to a minimum, ensured the complete eradication of any traces of the sinful flesh, and thereby immortalized the organic remnants in an immutable shape. Fire destroyed a human individual and at the same time preserved its remnants and its memory.

At first sight the use of regenerative furnaces and fuel seems to indicate technical sobriety in dealing with the dead, a detached and mechanized form of disposal. For crementionists, however, crematoria and Romantic images of rising clouds or seas of flames did not constitute any contradiction. In their view cremation imitated the works of nature, except that modern technology accomplished the task more efficiently. "Quickly the body evaporates into the open free ether. Invisibly the elements, from which nature had created it, fall onto fields and meadows in order to be resurrected in leaves and blossoms—truly and in essence, and not only symbolically!"[34] To the reformers, cremation and its final product represented a peaceful state of unity and holistic integration: being one with nature and with lost loved ones. Thus burning the body of a family member appeared to be a mandatory last favor,[35] marking an affection between two people that outlasted physical demise. One author even designated the crematorium as a posthumous romantic destination for star-crossed lovers and wondered

> why the last wish of unhappy loving people, who do not see any other fulfillment of their love than voluntary death, has not been the crematorium. To be handed over to the licking flames in a coffin, the hearts that were cooled in death once again kindling red in the last fire, and finally both bodies falling into an inseparable small pile of ash, that is in fact the most intimate fusion and unification for all eternity. People who have fallen in love cannot wish for anything more beautiful. A new poetry of its own kind in our dreary time![36]

Cremation became a powerful symbol for the transcendence of temporal and spatial limits, which it seemed to dissolve into an eternal state. Eternity, in turn, was a quality at the heart of beauty and love. Cremation was regarded as the most beautiful way to dispose of the dead, therefore the most dignified way to remember them and to mitigate the horror many associated with their own death.

In Defense of Good Old Customs

Not only in the twentieth century, attitudes toward mortality were influenced by aesthetic sentiment, fears, and hopes, and depended on the subjective meaning people gave to their lives. Still, opponents of cremation shared several reservations against the disposal through fire; their objections focused on economics, social status, human dignity, and religious beliefs. At the core of such arguments lay the rejection of the enhanced, accelerated, and radical destruction of the corpse and the condemnation of change as such. Above all, the foes of cremation claimed that the new form of disposal violated the "good old custom" of earth burial, which had been sanctified by centuries of Christian practice. Rather than cultural progress, for them cremation symbolized a relapse into paganism. Orthodox Christians and representatives of the Catholic and Protestant churches considered it their duty to defend tradition against erosive novelties, while state authorities and legal experts were more concerned about practicalities like uncovering and preventing crimes. The distinct nomenclature used by the proponents and opponents of cremation indicated that the same physical process had different meanings for both camps. While reformers spoke of *Feuerbestattung,* which emphasized that as a rite of passage a burial in the flames had the same value as an interment in earth, their adversaries used the term *Leichenverbrennung,* which stressed the mere technical, allegedly callous process of incinerating human bodies.

Criminologists feared that the physical annihilation of bodies posed a problem for forensics, because cremation destroyed potential evidence of crimes. Some attorneys expected that the legalization of cremation would drive up homicide rates and incidents of poisoning; others worried that fatal injuries sustained in abortions, then illegal, could not be detected.[37] Pathologists were concerned about the lack of clear signs of death and the impossibility of properly identifying ashes, because the flames eradicated all physical markers of individuality. Life insurance companies had a special interest in keeping bodies available for autopsies, so that they could uncover attempts by dependents to conceal suicides.[38] Such legal uncertainties remained an object of parliamentary debate in particular, until state and federal laws stipulated postmortems and regulated the treatment of ashes in the first quarter of the twentieth century.[39]

Identifying the pro-cremation culprit in freemasonry and dissent, the Roman Catholic Church took up a defensive battle against the godless and prohibited its flock from participating in the new burial practice for almost eight decades. The Holy Office's decrees on 19 May and 15 December 1886 forbade Catholics to join cremation associations or to order the cremation of any human body. Bishops and parish priests cited these pronouncements until the last quarter of the twentieth century. On behalf of Pope Leo XIII, the Congregation of the Inquisition declared that cremationists had to expect the same punishment and repercussions as freemasons for fostering such a "pagan custom": excommunication. Rome feared a "weakening of respect for the lasting Christian practice to bury the corpses of believers, which the church honors in solemn rites."[40] Canonical law prohibited clerics and laypeople from complying with a testament that requested cremation and rescinded the obligation to honor this last wish. Can. 1203, §1 prescribed that amputated limbs, too, had to be buried. According to Can. 1240 and 1212, every Catholic who asked for cremation was denied the last rites and a church burial, so that he or she could only be laid to rest in unconsecrated ground. While some priests considered officiating at cremation ceremonies "a rape of our conscience,"[41] a few clergymen ignored the official prohibition and supported cremation. The papal ban remained in effect until 1963.

Protestant opposition to cremation was less resilient and subsided sooner than the stern Catholic resistance. The less centralized structure of the Protestant churches in Germany allowed for a wider variety of opinions and practices. Policies and regulations varied by regional church and affected the clergy rather than the laypeople. While, for example, the Saxon and the Bavarian leadership let the individual clergyman decide about his participation in cremation ceremonies, and in the small liberal city state of Bremen, Protestant clergy with leanings toward monism actually supported cremation, the biggest German state church refused to accept cremation and upheld a strong reactionary alliance between throne and altar until the 1920s. Although the Evangelical High Consistory of Berlin forbade pastors of the Evangelical Church of the Older Prussian Provinces to officiate in crematoria as early as 1885, many priests favored the need of the bereaved for spiritual consolation over obedience to their superiors. As one solution to their moral conflicts, they attended ceremonies and led prayers in plain clothes, leaving at home the cassocks that designated them as church officials. The discrepancy between official rejection and de facto tolerance grew stronger after the Church Conference of Eisenach decided in 1898 to uphold the stated policy to avoid any impression of endorsing the new burial practice.[42] When the Evangelical Church of the Old Prussian Union became the last regional church finally to repeal this decision in 1925, most Protestants had come to accept or consent tacitly to cremation.

The foes of cremation calculated and compared the cost of different burial practices. Until the 1920s, when the concentration of crematoria in Germany increased significantly, interment was cheaper than incineration. Catholic opponents of cremation pointed to socioeconomic differences and cast the conflict in the mold of class struggle. Before the depression and inflation of the interwar years, they noted that cremation was "a hobby of the rich," an elitist luxury, and "a sport of a few Enlightened spirits belonging to the propertied classes."[43] Opponents underscored that already during ancient times, pagan elites had used cremation to display their social status and noble heroism, whereas Christianity wanted to meet the needs of all ranks.[44] Not only did cremation stress social differences, it also threatened to corrupt the minds of simple churchgoing people; columbaria, for example, presumably had a strange and alienating effect on the masses.[45] An aberration in the first place, "too much education [*Überbildung*] and deformation [*Verbildung*] had led to the burning of corpses to begin with."[46] Opponents were convinced that cremation contradicted the healthy popular feeling of the masses who freely rejected the "views of hypermodern aesthetes" and whose "natural human intuition" urged them to preserve the cultural heritage of earth burial.[47]

Religious adversaries spoke in the name of a silent majority as well as the dead, who could not defend themselves against mistreatment. The dead enjoyed a special right to protection against abuse by the living, who had the moral duty to keep the form of the deceased intact and sacred.[48] In return, the dead were not to haunt the living. The foes of cremation did not accept the argument that dissolution in the flames was better suited to honor the dead and insisted instead that the allegedly more poetic manner of disposal would "really only end up in sentimental apotheosis or frivolous brutality!"[49] An innate sense of nature, they claimed, kept human beings from exposing corpses to such cruel violence. The dignified treatment that the human body demanded extended beyond death. Awe for the dead body guaranteed awe for the living body and reinforced respect for life, the opponents argued. Catholic opponents in particular saw themselves protecting human dignity, which seemed threatened by materialism and the idolization of man: "Once you permit the principle of denying God, once you transform the soul into phosphorus, establish our descent from chimpanzees, orangutans, and gorillas, you have kicked human dignity with your feet. What then is left of man but matter? Cremation is another consequence of this."[50]

The defenders of earth burial cited the Bible and referred to Jesus Christ as the example to be emulated in death. Although some worried about the repercussions of cremation for the belief in physical resurrection, life after death was not the crux of the matter. Only a few theologians raised dogmatic objections against cremation, arguing that it precluded the physical resurrection of the dead on the Day of Judgment.[51] They were more concerned about the threat of dechristianization in this life, based on the assumption that, as a pagan practice, cremation was irreconcilable with Christian rites and tradition. Church officials were anxious about the preservation of cemeteries and graves, which represented islands of calm and healing contemplation in a sea of change. These "sites of silence, meditation, and devotion" were to attract contemporaries who had grown tired of the "mad rush and chase of life."[52] In addition, the destruction of the corpse by industrial means would reinforce "the painful awareness of the transitoriness of human life to the extreme of absolute worthlessness and contempt."[53]

Friends and foes of cremation disagreed on the status and ownership of the human body. Like criminologists, orthodox believers objected to the radical destruction of the corpse, which implied the dethroning of the creator and the apotheosis of his creation. According to the Bible, they argued, the body was a seed and temple of the Holy Ghost.[54] Therefore it did not belong to man, but to God. Opponents complained that the violent and "unnatural destruction of the dead body becomes the deed of human despotism rather than that of relentless natural forces, yes, even the work of industry."[55] The foes of cremation denied humans the right to dispose of their bodies at will. Conservative politicians in Prussia claimed that the state had the right to restrict individual freedom in the interest of the common good or to preserve the integrity of the Christian people.[56]

Religious leaders warned against overcoming the fear of death because the "shiver of death and decay is a salutary medicine for human pride,"[57] whereas cremation was intended to transform death from a humbling experience into a display of haughtiness. It seemed like an attempt to push beyond the last frontier of human command: "[I]t is the Promethean defiance; the gods cannot rob us of fire or light. Everything is mustered up to demonstrate: we continue to be masters."[58]

Fiery Talk

Crematorist language reflected the crematorist creed. Metaphors and images employed in poems, songs, and declarations stemmed from the realm of nature, in particular the four elements and above all fire. The flames freed the spirit—*Geist*—from its mortal remains to return to its source. Like the mythical Phoenix, crematorists longed to "blaze heavenward, purified and annihilated by fire."[59] The upward movement signified release and progress. Images surrounding the flame could be charged with sexual overtones, when they captured sensations of burning passion, like descriptions of the beautiful flame coiling "itself around the human body to exterminate it,"[60] the body consuming itself in glowing air,[61] convulsing in its own heat,[62] and reaching an "ardor with a thousand peaks."[63] Fiery metaphors symbolized heat as well as light, catharsis as well as knowledge. Their connotations corresponded to such core values of the German bourgeoisie as purity, refinement, efficiency, moderation, and thoroughness: "The burning chamber is shining at us in perfect purity, comparable to the rising or setting sun, and each spectator is overwhelmed by the virtually immaculate cleanliness and reverent impression of this form of burial."[64]

Praise of cultural progress and embrace of technological advance did not prevent crematorists from being in close touch with nature. Wedding the legacies of the Enlightenment and Romanticism, they expressed their praise of progress and efficient means of disposal with metaphors from all four elements, as in the instruction: "when my ashes blow in the wind, imagine that they are merely flowering flakes of God's spring time."[65] "A short bath in the flames and all shudders of destruction are removed."[66] "The fire alone is life that circulates through the vessels. Thus, what descended wonderfully from it alone, ought to return to the fire."[67] Many images built on the tropes of returning to the origins and of life prescribing cycles. One speaker wished that his body would "quickly dissolve into its atoms and enter into the womb of the great nature, from which it sprang."[68] Cremation symbolized liberation, purification, and ennoblement as well as a sense of oceanic completeness.

Clashing Creeds

The heated tone of the debates, the complexity of arguments, and the length of the confrontation from the 1870s until the 1930s indicated that more than the practical disposal of corpses was at stake. Although the physical process of burning a body seems unambiguous, the meaning of this practice was in flux and subject to interpretation. Cremation served as a symbolic battleground for various agendas in orthodox and progressive camps and as a screen onto which the participants in the debates projected their metaphysical, political, and ideological beliefs. The conflict about cremation pitted reformers against defenders of the status quo who fundamentally disagreed on the necessity of change. Cremationists set out to fight the prejudices of simple minds that were "stuck in the dark Middle Ages and backward intolerance."[69] Progressive activists considered themselves the vanguard of cultural progress and went to battle for a metaphysical liberation of the mind or spirit (*Geist*) under the banner of reason and tolerance. They reiterated their religious and political neutrality and stressed that they only demanded the right for every individual to decide about the fate of his or her own life and corpse. The delegates at a cremationist convention in Vienna summed up the movement's credo in 1912:

1. Cremation is neither a matter of politics nor of religion. It is cultural progress in the field of burials and belongs to the duties of state or municipal organs.
2. The supporters of cremation make their demands for reasons of piety, hygiene, national economy, and aesthetics. They reject all other motives that are attributed to their endeavors.
3. The form of burial ought to be optional.

The argument that every person should be allowed to dispose freely of his or her body and the idea that minorities needed to be protected from state and church paternalism as well as what was often called rape by the majority, developed into cornerstones of more politicized debates as the twentieth century progressed. For enlightened spirits and liberals, optional cremation was a manifestation of inalienable rights of the individual and the responsible citizen, who should be able "to find happiness in his or her own fashion," as Frederick II had declared. The conflict between the preservation of "good old customs" and the freedom for Germans to choose among different forms of burial was settled only after the Nazi seizure of power in the Imperial Law of 1934, which put cremation and interment on equal footing in all of Germany and introduced uniform regulations for the entire country.

It took the so-called National Socialist revolution to tear down the final barriers to burial reform on the federal level. When the Nazi regime destroyed Weimar's multiparty system, stifled political opposition, and coordinated associational life, it also brought an end to partisan debate about cremation among the representatives of the people. Cremationists had used the means of parliamentary democracy to foster their agenda and to influence public opinion. Ironically, the end of the first German experiment in democracy brought the realization of their objectives. The complete legalization of cremation was paid for with the destruction of the civic reform movement that had fought for it. At the same time, several elements of the crematinist creed resonated with the Nazis. Cremationist and Nazi worldviews shared a few topoi that applied to dead individuals as well as the German nation: a preoccupation with monumental struggle, an emphasis on the ontological transition from mortal to eternal, a belief in the awakening and resurrection of a dormant entity, and hopes for a harmonious condition of being complete. The Nazis, for example, likened Germany to a murder victim and pledged to resurrect the humiliated nation.

For many Germans in the second half of the twentieth century, the word crematorium conjured up images and memories of concentration camps and the Holocaust. Few knew about the origins of cremation in Imperial Germany. What were the links between genocide and the cremation movement that had its roots in nineteenth-century burial reform? Some continuities are striking, like the effortless usurpation of bourgeois and proletarian cremation associations, their publications, and burial insurances in the course of the National Socialist coordination. The technical tools to dispose of a large number of corpses had been developed in the 1870s and perfected for everyday use by the 1930s. The furnaces in municipal crematoria and in extermination camps were produced by the same manufacturers: J.A. Topf und Söhne, Erfurt delivered the incineration equipment for Dachau, Auschwitz, and Flossenbürg, where many participants of the 20 July 1944 plot were executed. Heinrich Kori, Berlin supplied furnaces for Sachsenhausen.[70] In Munich, the municipal cemetery administration and the management of the Dachau concentration camp worked hand in hand. Complying with the Imperial Law of 1934, officials agreed in April 1941 to continue distributing the ashes of deceased prisoners evenly among Munich's cemeteries. Eventually, all urns were to be stored centrally in a large mass grave close to the city's crematorium.[71] The fact that about 10 percent of the German population embraced cremation enough to make it their choice of disposal facilitated the Nazis' employment and appropriation of this mode of disposal without causing a stir. As with other cultural practices, they used an established custom for their ideological purposes.

Major differences, however, distinguished the cremation movement from the use of crematoria in the extermination machinery of the Third Reich. Before the early 1930s, pamphlets and journals hardly ever celebrated incineration as an ur-Germanic tradition. With its coordination, cremationism became a movement to promote not only cultural progress but the advancement of German national culture. The *völkisch* movement welcomed this nationalist emphasis, which had been absent from the earlier cremationist ideology. The methods of disposal during the Third Reich and previous decades seemed identical only at first sight. Many rules established by cremationists to guarantee the dignified treatment of the human corpse and its ashes were disregarded in concentration camps: More than one body was introduced into the furnace at a time. Corpses were not burned in coffins, lacked inflammable tags with ID numbers, and were rarely completely reduced to white ashes. The cremains of prisoners were neither identifiable as belonging to a particular person nor buried in urns, but discarded, or even used as fertilizer for camp gardens, for instance in the satellite camp Neuengamme. The purpose of mechanized cremation in concentration camps was the removal of anonymous corpses, not the commemoration and laying to rest of deceased loved ones. This form of disposal was the consequence of mass murder. Billows of smoke rising from furnace barracks became a powerful symbol of the Holocaust because they epitomize the complete eradication of so-called undesired human lives and the dehumanizing treatment of dead bodies. A more accurate emblem for mass murder might be the gas chambers and shooting ranges where the killings took place. Although cremationists and perpetrators of the Holocaust favored the same means of disposal, they endowed it with different meanings.

In Imperial Germany and the Weimar Republic, progressive cremationists saw themselves climbing up the ladder of cultural progress and demanded tolerance from church and state authorities, while conservatives feared that the introduction of optional cremation would soon lead to mandatory incineration and in turn deprive them of their right to choose earth burial. They set out to defend Christian customs and a cultural legacy against irreligion, materialism, freemasonry, and a blind faith in science. Orthodox believers resisted the reduction of death to the simple question of "how one can move from one physical state to the next."[72] Incompatible creeds clashed and revealed divergent attitudes related to mortality: conflicting views of nature and the necessity of cultivating its force; incompatible concepts of progress, time, and eternity; contrasting notions of man as an autonomous subject and a dependent creation.

The friends and foes of cremation disagreed on three main issues: first, whether the forces of nature should be left to run their course or be domesticated by human ingenuity. At the beginning of the twentieth century cremation stood for expanding the realm of human agency. Determining the fate of dead bodies diminished the fear of death. Second, they argued over whether cremation constituted a relapse into pagan barbarism or cultural progression. It stood for the promotion and embrace of modernity. The burning of corpses accelerated the process of disintegration and thereby shortened the transition from life to death. Cremationists confronted the eschatological notion of time held by orthodox Christians with a cyclical concept of eternity. Third, they differed on what constituted the self. Both sides viewed human beings as compounds of lasting minds and mortal matter. Both sides relegated the body to the secondary status of a vessel, destined for destruction and to be liberated from its earthly prison through death.[73] Supporters and enemies of cremation disagreed, however, on who got to decide about the fate of this container: a transcendent power, the state, or the individual him- or herself. Cremationists asserted individual rights of property and disposal. What is remarkable about their demands for autonomy is that these rights did not end with physical demise. Although the subject ceased to exist as an historical agent, its will, power, and subjectivity continued.

A Master Narrative of Death in Germany

As an historical phenomenon, the movement to introduce cremation from the 1870s to the 1930s and the conflicts it sparked had implications for the history of death in modern Germany:

- Research on cremation cautions against the uncritical adoption of Philippe Ariès's models. He diagnosed a process of increasing unruliness; formerly tame and familiar, death became wild and terrifying in the eighteenth century. Ariès saw the origins of this development in the Enlightenment, which denied death because it confronted humans with the limits of their power over nature. Cremationists did not fit this pattern of denial or repression. They faced their mortality and reminded their contemporaries to prepare for their last journeys, which helps explain the lingering success of the movement, for which cremationists themselves held the force of habit responsible.
- Cremationists borrowed from Enlightened thought as well as Romantic images. Uniting the gospel of scientific progress with religious beliefs did not pose any problems for them. Simplifying theories of secularization and rationalization cannot sufficiently explain this historical phenomenon.[74] The decline of the power of the Christian churches was accompanied by a surge in less organized forms of religiousness. Although cremationists broke with the traditional Christian idea of death as sleep until resurrection, they resorted to religion and aesthetics to make sense of human mortality.
- Surprisingly, the World Wars had little impact on the cremation movement. Why man-made mass death and destruction did not more strongly affect the attitudes of ordinary individuals toward mortality, still begs a satisfactory explanation. Rituals surrounding dying and disposal have resisted change, remaining little affected by big political caesurae and only somewhat by economic trends.
- The history of the introduction of cremation can be read as a prologue to the history of the Third Reich, but it also stands as a chapter on its own in the history of everyday death in Germany. The Holocaust could have happened without the cremation movement, but the existence of incineration as a sepulchral practice made it easier for the Nazis to dispose of the victims of genocide.
- Concerns about the dignity of the dead and a treatment that does justice to their individuality, which is more threatened in times of mass destruction, emerge as a continuous theme for twentieth-century Germans.

Notes

1. Witnesses disagreed on the exact starting time of the incineration. This protocol, based on Richard Schneider's observations, was reprinted in [first name unknown] Nowak, *Zur Frage der Leichenverbrennung: Aus den Verhandlungen des n.ö. Sanitätsrathes* (Vienna, 1874), 10–11.
2. Siemens Archiv: 35/51/Lr 521 betr. Wärmetechnische Arbeiten, Leichenverbrennungsofen. Richard Schneider, "Aus meinen Lebenserinnerungen," *Deutsche Flamme* 3, no. 10 (1926): 234–236, 235.
3. Siemens Archiv: 3/Lr 505, vol 2, Friedrich to Wilhelm, Dresden 20 October 1874.
4. This important turning point still awaits adequate exploration. On relations between the living and the dead in French folk culture see Thomas A. Kselman, *Death and the Afterlife in Modern France* (Princeton, 1993). On fear of ghosts, *Wiedergänger*, and the persistence of the topos of the return of the dead until after WWI see the first chapter in Jay Winter, *Sites of Memory, Sites of Mourning: The Great War in European Cultural History* (Cambridge, 1995). On the corpse in modern British popular culture see Ruth Richardson, *Death, Dissection, and the Destitute*, 2nd ed. (Chicago and London, 2000).
5. Philippe Ariès, *Western Attitudes toward Death from the Middle Ages to the Present*, trans. Patricia Ranum (Baltimore, 1974), in French *Essais sur la mort en Occident du Moyen-Age à nos jours* (Paris, 1975), in German *Studien zur Geschichte des Todes im Abendland*, trans. Hans-Horst Henschen (Munich, 1976). Also Philippe Ariès, *L'Homme devant la Mort* (Paris, 1977), in German *Geschichte des Todes,* trans. Hans-Horst Henschen and Una Pfau (Munich and Vienna, 1980), in English *The Hour of Our Death*, trans. Helen Weaver (New York, 1981).
6. Henning Winter, *Die Architektur der Krematorien im Deutschen Reich: 1878–1918*, ed. Reiner Sörries (Dettelbach, 2001).
7. For example in Chemnitz, *"Friede!"* or in Coburg, *"Dir aber bleibet Glaube, Hoffnung, Liebe. Der Tod ist verschlungen in den Sieg."* For a more extensive list see *Die Volks-Feuerbestattung* 14, no. 8 (1931).
8. Martina Kaussen, "Die Feuerbestattung: Geschichtlich-statistische Entwicklung, forensische Problematik und ihre Bedeutung für Gesundheitspflege und Sepulkralkultur," PhD diss., University of Cologne, 1989, 64.
9. See the contribution of Felix Robin Schulz to this volume.
10. Stephen Prothero, *Purified by Fire: A History of Cremation in America* (Berkeley, 2001), 128.
11. Jochen-Christoph Kaiser, *Arbeiterbewegung und organisierte Religionskritik: Proletarische Freidenkerverbände in Kaiserreich und Weimarer Republik* (Stuttgart, 1981), 62; and Jochen-Christoph Kaiser, "Freireligiöse," in Diethart Kerbs and Jürgen Reulecke, eds., *Handbuch der deutschen Reformbewegungen 1880–1933* (Wuppertal, 1998), 532–549, 545.
12. As characterized by Gangolf Hübinger, *Kulturprotestantismus und Politik: Zum Verhältnis von Liberalismus und Protestantismus im Wilhelminischen Deutschland* (Tübingen, 1994).
13. Theodor Weinisch, *Die Feuerbestattung im Lichte der Statistik* (Zirndorf, 1929), 46f.
14. Jennifer Leaney, "Ashes to Ashes: Cremation and the Celebration of Death in Nineteenth-Century Britain," in Ralph Houlbrooke, ed., *Death, Ritual, and Bereavement* (London and New York, 1989), 118–135.
15. On apparent death see the dissertations by Kerstin Rehwinkel, University of the Bundeswehr, Hamburg and Gerlind Rüve, University of Bielefeld "Scheintod: Wandlungen der Sinnstiftung des Todes im Übergang vom 18. zum 19. Jahrhundert." Also Martina Kessel, "Sterben/Tod—Neuzeit," in Peter Dinzelbacher, ed., *Europäische Mentalitätsgeschichte: Hauptthemen in Einzeldarstellungen* (Stuttgart, 1993), 260–273.
16. Gottfried Kinkel, *Für die Feuerbestattung: Vortrag gehalten zur Eröffnung des Europäischen Congresses für Feuerbestattung, Dresden, 7. Juni 1876* (Berlin, 1877), 13; Prosper Müllendorff, *Feuerbestattung und Freiheit: Eine Rundschau im Auslande* (Cologne, 1911), 46.
17. Quote attributed to a Dr. Lieball in H. Bock, *Leichenverbrennung oder Leichenbestattung: Was ist Christenrecht und Christenpflicht?* (Königsberg Pr., 1911), 14.

18. M. Gerson, *Die medizinisch-hygienische Bedeutung der Feuerbestattung: Eine Preisarbeit* (Hamburg, 1896), 64.
19. Kaussen, "Die Feuerbestattung," 132. The so-called *Ruhezeiten* for corpses depended on local regulation as well as the conditions of the soil and the ground water. For adults they ranged between 15 and 40 years, for children between 6 and 20 years.
20. A. Kronfeld, *Die Leichenverbrennung in alter und neuer Zeit* (Vienna, 1890), 26.
21. S. Bernstein, *Über Pietät gegen die Todten* (Berlin, 1874), 61.
22. Max Pauly, *Die Feuerbestattung*, 3rd ed. (Berlin, 1902), 19.
23. Walter Huber, *Feuerbestattung: Vortrag im Einwohnerverein Aargau Samstag den 25. Februar 1905* (Aarau, 1905), 17.
24. Pauly, *Die Feuerbestattung*, 20.
25. Friedrich Goppelsroeder, *Über Feuerbestattung: Vortrag gehalten am 13. Februar 1890 im Naturwissenschaftlichen Vereine zu Mülhausen im Elsasse* (Mülhausen, 1890), 61.
26. Johann Peter Trusen, *Die Leichenverbrennung als die geeignetste Art der Todtenbestattung: oder Darstellung der verschiedenen Arten und Gebräuche der Todtenbestattung aus älterer und neuerer Zeit* (Breslau, 1855).
27. Gerson, *Die medizinisch-hygienische Bedeutung*, 23.
28. This line of argument built on ideas of the sublime, the beautiful, and the good, which the representatives of the German classic tradition had propagated, notably Lessing, Schiller, and Goethe, whose *Braut von Korinth* was often quoted. Huber, *Feuerbestattung*, 40, adds to this list of "most famous thinkers and poets" who presumably were enthusiastic about cremation: Jean Paul, Rückert, Hebbel, Lübke, Justinus Kerner, Platen, Detlev von Lilienkron, Emanuel Geibel, Gottfried Kinkel, and Gottfried Keller.
29. For example, see heckling during the twenty-sixth meeting of the Prussian House of Representatives, 16 February 1900, *Stenographic Protocols*, vol. 256, session 19, 2; or Representatives Schall and Barth during the fifty-seventh meeting of the Prussian House of Representatives, 1 March 1903; *Stenographic Protocols*, vol. 281, session 19, 5.
30. Pauly, *Die Feuerbestattung*, 26.
31. Kinkel, *Für die Feuerbestattung*, 13.
32. Pauly, *Die Feuerbestattung*, 24.
33. Hans Jakob Wegmann-Ercolani, *Über Leichenverbrennung als rationellste Bestattungsart* (Zurich, 1874), 36.
34. Kinkel, *Für die Feuerbestattung*, 15.
35. Georg Müller, *Empfiehlt sich für kleinere Stadtgemeinden die Errichtung von Krematorien?* (Bernburg, 1912), 8.
36. Josef Schmall, *Von der Wiege bis zum Crematorium: Ein Erziehungs- und Selbstveredlungs-Büchlein* (Vienna, 1901), 58.
37. Rolf Thalmann, *Urne oder Sarg? Auseinandersetzungen um die Einführung der Feuerbestattung im 19. Jahrhundert* (Berne, 1978), 38.
38. Albert Hellwig, *Feuerbestattung und Rechtspflege* (Leipzig, 1911), 67.
39. Ibid., 3.
40. Latin original in Archiv des Erzbistums München und Freising, *Amtsblatt für die Erzdiöcese München und Freising* 22 (3 August 1886), 113 "Ex S. Congr. Inquis. Feria IV. die 19 Maii 1886"; and ibid. 30 (15 December 1892), 159f. "Ex S. Congreg. R.U. Inquisitionis. Decretum quoad corporum cremationem, Feria IV. die. 15. Decembris 1886."
41. [Author unknown] *Leichenverbrennung oder Erdbestattung? Drei Vorträge: Was sagt dazu die Bibel? Was sagt dazu die Kirche? Was sagt dazu die Bürgerschaft?* (Barmen, 1912), 12.
42. For example, see the explanation by Wilhelm Bahnsen in Ursula Staiger, "Die Auseinandersetzung um die Feuerbestattung in Deutschland im 19. Jahrhundert," PhD diss., Johannes Gutenberg University Mainz, 1981, 47.
43. Bock, *Leichenverbrennung oder Leichenbestattung*, 19. Also see Representative Crüger during the 78th meeting of the Prussian House of Representatives, 4 June 1910; *Stenographic Protocols*, vol. 359, session 21, 3.

44. Georg Friedrich Fuchs, *Grab oder Urne. Eine Beleuchtung der Zeitfrage: Wie wollen und sollen wir unsere Todten bestatten?* (Heilbronn, 1886), 13f.
45. Staiger, "Die Auseinandersetzung," 32.
46. "Leichenverbrennung" in Heinrich Joseph Wetzer and Benedikt Welte, eds. *Wetzer und Welte's Kirchenlexikon*, 2nd ed., vol. 7 (Freiburg, 1891), 1680.
47. *Leichenverbrennung oder Erdbestattung?* 15.
48. Thalmann, *Urne oder Sarg?* 60.
49. *Leichenverbrennung oder Erdbestattung?* 6.
50. Franz von Berndorf, *Beerdigung oder Verbrennung der Leichen* (Berlin, 1892), 39.
51. Good discussion in Thalmann, *Urne oder Sarg?* 55–59.
52. *Leichenverbrennung oder Erdbestattung?* 21.
53. Eugen Anthes, "Leichenverbrennung und religiöse Sitte," *Westermann's illustrierte deutsche Monats-Hefte für das gesammte geistige Leben der Gegenwart* (April 1875): 105–110, 108.
54. Bock, *Leichenverbrennung oder Leichenbestattung*, 25, cites Paul's words in 1 Corinthians.
55. Thalmann, *Urne oder Sarg?* 51, referring to Eugen Anthes.
56. Representative von Heyking during the 73rd meeting of the Prussian House of Representatives, 13 May 1904, *Stenographic Protocols*, vol. 289, session 20, 1. Representative Schrock during the fifty-fifth meeting of the Prussian House of Representatives, 22 March 1911, *Stenographic Protocols*, vol. 370, session 21, 4.
57. *Leichenverbrennung oder Erdbestattung?* 7.
58. Fuchs, *Grab oder Urne*, 12.
59. Poem printed in Wegmann-Ercolani, *Über Leichenverbrennung*, 8.
60. Buddeus in Stadtvorstand Gotha, ed., *Gedenkschrift zum 50jährigen Bestehen des Krematoriums in Gotha* (Gotha, 1928), 44.
61. Friedrich Rücker, *Feuerhalle-Urnenhain in Reichenberg (Böhmen). Gedenkschrift zum zehnjährigen Betriebe* (Reichenberg, 1928), 30.
62. Pauly, *Die Feuerbestattung*, 26.
63. From Goethe's tragedy *"Die natürliche Tochter,"* quoted in Stadtvorstand Gotha, *Gedenkschrift*, 48.
64. Huber, *Feuerbestattung*, 12. See also Manuel Frey, *Der reinliche Bürger: Entstehung und Verbreitung bürgerlicher Tugenden in Deutschland, 1760–1860* (Göttingen, 1997).
65. Huber, *Feuerbestattung*, 40.
66. Kronfeld, *Die Leichenverbrennung*, 39.
67. Anonymous poem printed in *Phönix* 3, no. 5 (1890) and attributed to Reclam.
68. Oswald Marcuse, *Ein neuer Gegner der Feuerbestattung von ethnographischem Gesichtspunkt* (Vienna, 1915), 9.
69. [Author unknown] *Religion und Feuerbestattung* (Nuremberg, 1912), 15.
70. Jean-Claude Pressac, *Die Krematorien von Auschwitz: Die Technik des Massenmordes*, 2nd ed. (Munich, 1995). See also Stiftung Gedenkstätten Buchenwald und Mittelbau-Dora, ed., *Techniker der "Endlösung." Topf & Söhne: Die Ofenbauer von Auschwitz* (Weimar, 2005).
71. Stadtarchiv München Bestattungsamt Nr. 453.
72. Fuchs, *Grab oder Urne*, 39.
73. U. Zinck, *Soll ich mich verbrennen oder begraben lassen? Aufschlüsse über die aktuelle Frage der Feuerbestattung und Verwesung* (Leipzig, 1911), 17.
74. In the twentieth century death was less disenchanted than reenchanted. Labeling cremationists "conservative modernizers" is a mischaracterization. Norbert Fischer, *Vom Gottesacker zum Krematorium: Eine Sozialgeschichte der Friedhöfe in Deutschland seit dem 18. Jahrhundert* (Cologne, 1996), 107. For a brief but useful survey of the history of sepulchral culture in Germany see Norbert Fischer, *Geschichte des Todes in der Neuzeit* (Erfurt, 2001).

Chapter 5

Disposing of the Dead in East Germany, 1945–1990

Felix Robin Schulz

Near the entrance of the Potsdam cemetery there is an area of closely cropped grass where, separated from the footpath by a row of cobblestones, a small sign reads "Caution, Graves: Do not Enter!" Few areas in the cemeteries of this world require a sign to prevent the casual visitor from stumbling over the graves. Normally in modern German cemeteries the graves are clearly demarcated from their surroundings by gravestones or grave-mounds. In East Germany, however, dispensing with such markers and physical borders left that quintessential feature of East German sepulchral culture, the anonymous communal area for the internment of urns (*Urnengemeinschaftsanlagen* or *UGA*), in dire need of protective measures. This sign cannot be regarded as just another "keep-off-the-grass" warning; it is an attempt to make up for a lack of inherent sacrosanctity. An area of mown lawn surrounded by gray concrete slabs with only a single central feature, frequently of uncertain meaning (such as a concrete stele with a wrought iron sun painted in light blue), and a designated area for depositing flowers, is far removed from conventional ideas of a final resting place. This sign is, therefore, not merely a necessary warning; it is symbolic of the entire attempt to establish a socialist sepulchral culture in East Germany, and of what survives of this attempt to the present day.

In recent years, public discussion about East German sepulchral culture has mainly focused on the issue of political influence, ultimately centering on the issue of influence and the question of the *durchherrschte Gesellschaft* (pervasively ruled society).[1] The initial question, often posed, concerns whether there was a specifically East German cemetery culture. However, this approach barely scrapes the surface of the issues of death, dying, and corpse disposal. While the extent of political influence on cemetery design and sepulchral culture warrants analysis

---

Notes for this chapter begin on page 126.

and discussion, one cannot be sidetracked into giving it paramount consideration. By 1985 around 140 *UGAs* had been opened in cemeteries throughout the German Democratic Republic (GDR).[2] Given the number of *UGAs* that occupy prominent locations in many East German municipal cemeteries, there can be little doubt that certain aspects of a specific sepulchral culture were widely established. The real crux of the history of death, dying, and disposal in the GDR, however, lies in its complexity and, ultimately, in the juxtaposition of both fundamental change and continuity, which cannot easily be aligned. Additionally, it is questionable whether it is helpful to even refer to an East German sepulchral culture in the singular.

It is also necessary to examine the variations in the many responses to death, dying, and disposal and, where possible, to compare these with the changes in other countries. For example, anonymous communal urn graves and fields for scattering ashes were not confined to East Germany; after 1945 Czechoslovakia saw far more stringent socialist sepulchral reforms that were regarded as exemplary by members of the IfK (Institut für Kommunalwirtschaft)—the East German think tank concerned with the local service sector.[3] Hitherto there has been too great a focus on single aspects of sepulchral culture, such as the socialist transformation of cemeteries, their design, or even the *UGA*. In consequence, profound changes in more elusive dimensions, such as the formation of socialist or secular rituals, are overlooked, while changes in both design and ritual are overstated because regional variations are not considered. This chapter therefore addresses the changes in the practicalities of death and disposal in the GDR from a much wider perspective, tracing the tensions between the human, ideological, economic, and bureaucratic imperatives governing the system of disposal and revealing the complex history of the multifaceted East German sepulchral culture.

In the aftermath of the Second World War, the organization of disposal was chaotic, especially in towns and cities, where it often became utterly utilitarian.[4] Organizational chaos, alongside rising death rates, resulted in precarious hygienic conditions in urban areas in particular. Undignified storage and mass burials were the consequence of a lack of resources such as wood—leading on one occasion to the burial of a corpse in the case of a grandfather clock to avoid wrapping a beloved merely in paper or cloth for burial—as well as of the destruction of the cemeteries and mortuaries themselves.[5] Nevertheless, as in so many other areas of postwar life, "normality," when understood as a decent burial, was a high priority that returned with astonishing rapidity. While many rural areas were less affected by the devastation and disruption of the war, this rapid return to "normality" in the urban areas was astounding. In Berlin, for example, with its heavy bomb damage, its many refugees, and numerous exhumations of bombing victims buried in mass graves, the demand for coffins was completely covered from April 1946 onward.

A similar indication of returning normality is visible in the number of deaths. Mortality immediately after the war remained higher in the East than in the West of Germany, but in both mortality rates declined swiftly owing to the recovery of the social and medical services and improvements in public health and dietary standards. By 1951, the East German mortality rate had returned to its prewar level. With some minor exceptions, mortality patterns in East and West remained similar until the early 1970s. From then onward the two countries diverged. In the East, both female and male life expectancy rose, but much more slowly than in the West.[6] The economic constraints of the East German planned economy played a major role, as they curbed dietary changes as well as investment in medical equipment, pharmaceuticals, and nursing care. Old age care in East Germany was chronically underfunded, and traditional caregivers, females under the age of 65, were more likely to work outside of their homes. The stagnating life expectancy figures of the GDR mirror those elsewhere in Central and Eastern Europe, though other countries, like Poland, fared far worse. However, as was the case in Poland and Czechoslovakia, the GDR figures conceal an increasing mortality rate among the young and the middle-aged, counterbalanced only by a much-reduced infant mortality rate.[7] Unofficial internal statistics of the IfK record that the 1970 mortality rate, measured in deaths per 1,000, had climbed 13.2 percent above the 1956 rate. Due to the aging of the population the death rate kept on rising from 13.6 per 1,000 (1960) to 14.2 per 1,000 (1980); thereafter a slow decline until 2005 was projected, when a sharp rise (especially in East Berlin, Rostock, and Neubrandenburg) was predicted owing to the aging of the postwar (and refugee) generation.

Ignoring minor peaks and troughs, the GDR had to organize about 230,000 burials each year.[8] While on a personal level an encounter with a death is generally infrequent, on the national level it posed a vast organizational task. Moreover, one should not forget that in a planned economy 8,000 extra coffins and burials in a peak year constituted a significant challenge to the economic planning system. In these cases emergency manufacture was at best haphazard; coffin wood was not seasoned properly, resulting in coffins that were covered in white fungus or in lids that did not close.[9] This suggests the extent to which traditional values and the practicalities of disposal (e.g. the demand for a proper coffin) could clash with the realities of a planned economy.

In the GDR traditional values and attitudes to death were challenged even more sharply by the state ideology. East German state and society existed in a highly charged ideological setting of state-sponsored Marxist-Leninist materialism. Socialist thanatology gave death a very specific interpretation:

> As materialists we know: Nature does not make sense. Death and life "themselves" are senseless, like the sun or the snow. No God, no spirit is the creator of the world. But paradoxically, laws keep stars and atoms in motion.
> Not "God's unfathomable will," but the workings of objective laws govern creation and demise in nature, as well as life and death in humans.
> The knowledge of these related issues cannot in tragic situations—for example the death of a young person in a traffic accident or through a malignant illness—comfort us and help us overcome the painful death; death is and remains without sense. That knowledge, however, can do one thing: it can make even such a deeply nonsensical

death become philosophically comprehensible, understandable, and one can draw from this insight with composed earnestness strength, in order not to despair in the face of calamity, and let oneself drift, but with all the intensity of our tried and tested personality give life what is its due.[10]

If one accepts modern biological knowledge, then one also has to accept a rather technical interpretation of death: that dying is a process that terminates in the moment of death, resulting in the state of being dead. When the body ceases to function, the entire human organism is dead, and after its death the human being is, by definition, no more. Being dead is then the absolute, unequivocal, and permanent end of existence—one's utter annihilation. What remains is the corpse— like a shell—devoid of life and actual individuality, remaining without meaning and purpose, a mere agglomeration of organic material awaiting disposal. In the light of such stark socialist materialist views, together with comprehensive notions of the political and ideological importance of culture, one could easily expect an environment that not only demanded but also required change and reform of the organization of disposal, the conduct of rituals, and the public perception of death. In view of the evidence, however, this hypothesis has to be quickly abandoned. Change and reform with regard to these fields were gradual, patchy, always drawn out, and seldom drastic.

This nature of change is already adumbrated by the way in which the question of religion and the churches was dealt with in the GDR. The GDR was predominantly Protestant, with the exception of the Eichsfeld. The Protestant Church, however, was well organized and could rely on a strong legal position. When the Allies signed the Potsdam accords in August 1945, finalizing the framework for the postwar era, they succeeded in placing church property under special safeguards; later, in reference to Leninist doctrine, GDR constitutions always incorporated the right to religious freedom. Together with initial political attempts to win over progressive elements in the church—mainly forced upon the party by Moscow—the legal position of the church with regard to property issues was consolidated.[11] This ultimately created a politically insurmountable obstacle to the large-scale dispossession of church cemeteries. Since the disposal of the dead had traditionally been a local issue in Germany, governed by local regulations and only circumscribed by state legislation, this lack of actual centralization further aided the fact that the many idiosyncrasies and regional variations in sepulchral cultures remained largely intact.

While a standard set of regulations (*Musterfriedhofsordnung*) was issued in 1967, this did not amount to anything close to the wholesale municipalization (with the exception of Jewish cemeteries) that had been carried out in Czechoslovakia in 1958. But it was precisely that policy that had laid the successful foundation for the exemplary socialist sepulchral culture reform there.[12] With the direct route blocked, the SED decided to challenge the primacy of the church in the areas lightheartedly referred to as "hatch, match, and dispatch" (baptisms, marriages, and funerals). The minutes of a meeting of the committee concerned with church matters in the Central Committee (ZK) in December 1957 hint at the long-term objective:

> The church protects and covers up everything the criminals within her are doing. Now it is important that substitutes be created for church ceremonies, such as christenings, marriages, funerals, etc. This has been done by the state officials in the town of Stralsund by creating a socialist name-giving-ceremony. ... Every local Party organization, in conjunction with the state apparatus, should try to find a number of suitable individuals for this task (funeral speeches). Many people still fall back on the church because locally there are no suitable orators. ... If all this is not organized by us, then it will be done by the church. ... If we do organize this, then it means a serious constraint on the church.[13]

From 1956 onward secular alternatives to the Christian rites were widely introduced, and handbooks, pamphlets, and training materials were printed outlining how to conduct secular rituals such as naming ceremonies, socialist marriages, and secular funerals, as well as secular alternatives to confirmation (*Jugendweihe*). Most of these materials stress the importance of these ceremonies for ideology and propaganda.[14]

The typical secular and socialist funeral liturgy was not that far removed from that of a Protestant funeral. The first part of the ceremony took place in the ceremonial room of the cemetery (*Feierhalle*), which doubled as a chapel when a cross was mounted. The proceedings were opened with a piece of music, ideally a piece from the communist repertoire or appropriate classical music—most handbooks had a small appendix of suitable pieces by classical composers including Beethoven, Chopin, Bach, and Schumann. This was followed by an address from a secular funeral orator recounting the life of the deceased and celebrating his or her achievements with regard to work, society, and state; then a moment of silent commemoration preceded the removal of the coffin or the urn to the gravesite followed by the assembled crowd. There the orator (a party functionary, the director of the local factory of collective farm, or most likely a hired professional) delivered the final words of farewell, followed by a "meaningful" quotation. The coffin or urn was lowered into the ground, and the orator threw three handfuls of earth on top of it with words such as "For Peace, for unity of the fatherland, for socialism" and expressed his commiseration with the bereaved. A final music piece rounded off the procedure; a particular favorite, besides "The International," was "The Song of the Small Trumpeter."[15] The result was a fairly strict liturgy that all too often framed a host of standardized speeches, many of which ended in particularly common quotations. One of the most frequently quoted was by the Russian author Nicolai Ostrowski:

> The most precious [possession] that a man owns is his life. It is given to him only once, and he has to spend it in such a way that the pointlessly spent years do not plague him later, that the shame of an unworthy, insignificant past does not weigh upon him, so that dying he can say: "My whole life, my whole strength have I dedicated to the most

glorious thing in the world—to the struggle for the liberation of mankind." And he must grab life's chances. Since a stupid illness or some tragic coincidence can put an abrupt end to life.[16]

Indeed, as was the case with the nonreligious rite's predecessor, the ceremony conducted by freethinkers (*Freidenker*), there is a distinct similarity between secular and socialist funerals compared with religious ones; only certain elements were redefined, and references to God were removed.[17] However, there are key functional differences from religious ceremonies. As Ansgar Franz rightly argues, the secular ritual does not center on the issue of death but on the issue of life. The deceased has become the object (as opposed to the subject) of the ceremony; those addressed are explicitly the people attending the ceremony and the bereaved; death as a *conditio humana* is rarely mentioned; past deeds become the ultimate justification of the social worth of a life—a productive life therefore represents a source of solace; the spoken word in form of speech and condolence are the key elements, and as such the ritual is passive. Unlike the Christian funeral rite, it does not ask for participation, such as in prayers or singing, and the ceremony, like the eulogy, is delivered toward the audience, which only sits and absorbs.[18]

The introduction of secular funerals was in fact very gradual, hampered by a lack of speakers, and largely uncoordinated except on an individual local basis, despite the collection of statistics by the Ministry of the Interior.[19] These statistics also reveal the increasing fragmentation in the forms of private ceremonies that occurred in the GDR. By the 1980s one has to distinguish between socialist, secular, silent, collective (with and without a public ceremony), religious, and anonymous funerals, as well as the religious ceremonies for non-church members. Propagation (a term used to refer to popularizing through means of agitation, propaganda, regulations, and incentives) of the secular funeral and cremation through the municipal burial services remained a force, but other forces such as secularization, demographic change, the inert nature of rituals, and church policy also played important roles. Because cremation and the secular funeral were labeled as the "modern form of disposal," subtle pressure could be exercised via the funeral service provider.[20]

Yet even in "progressive" urban areas with a traditionally high rate of cremation, the rate of secular funerals remained low and had only reached a share of about 50 percent by the 1980s. In the region of Frankfurt (Oder), for example, the rate of secular and socialist rituals rose from 9.1 percent in 1959 to 41.8 percent in 1980 and finally reached 52.5 percent in 1988.[21] In East Berlin, with a rate of about 80 percent, the secular funeral was most successful.[22] However, the church as the traditional funeral purveyor accommodated change and falling numbers of active church members by allowing for religious funerals, even if the deceased individual had not been a member of the congregation as such:

> To an increasing degree Christians live together with others in a marriage, with family, relatives, in friendship, who are not, or who are no longer, members of the church, or whose church rights are no longer active. While on the one hand Christians are

no longer buried by the Church because the relatives reject this option, on the other hand, Christians specifically ask that their deceased, who do not have this right, be buried by the church. … The church takes such questions for answers drawn from the Christian message, as well as the sorrow and the appeals of its parishioners seriously. It offers the bereaved a "Church funeral in special circumstances" if, above and beyond the immediate context, a relationship can be identified between the bereaved and the Christian message.[23]

This reflects a fundamental change that had occurred with regard to religious ceremonies in the GDR, where the church accommodated (within reason) a change that was by no means limited to communist states. Nevertheless, when one compares the propagation of the secular funeral ceremony with the introduction of other secular alternatives, namely the *Jugendweihe*, the contrast is striking. This socialist ceremony was established within four years through intense political pressure and the threat of repercussions. Secular funerals, on the other hand, were still seen as a poor alternative to a proper Christian burial.[24] They were never made compulsory, despite the IfK observation that every year millions of people took part in funerals and thus represented an important target for the propagation of a secular ideology.[25]

Other reasons for the low popularity of secular funerals can be found in the nature of the topic as well as in the specific administrative structure of the GDR. Kay Blumenthal-Barby rightly argues that all issues related to the end of life are, to a degree, repressed, including public policy towards disposal.[26] Undertaking and the disposal of the dead is a highly specialized field that generally warrants little interest on the part of the general public. A society has to dispose of its dead, but in the modern world this has increasingly become a task delegated to specialists and professionals. Whatever the circumstances and however disrupted normal life is, the disposal of the dead cannot be delayed for long. This is especially the case in a modern urban environment where very little space is left for improvisation or self-help. Disposal of the dead is thus an essential service and as such is prone to evolutionary rather than revolutionary transformation by those in charge of its organization, with the possible exception of times of dire need. Any close examination of systems of disposal during times of great upheaval underlines this tendency to return to "normality" most emphatically: while radical measures may be acceptable for a short period of emergency, there is an inherent tendency to return to what constitutes the "normal" state—i.e., a return to the equilibrium between past principles, values, and customs, and the limitations dictated by current reality. In June 1945 normality for the individual with regard to burying a beloved one would have meant a solid wooden coffin, a properly dug grave on an official burial plot, a clergyman delivering a personalized funeral service, and possibly some greenery for a wreath. In many cases dictated by necessity this was far from a reality, that consisted of mass graves, lye, cremation, and rented coffins. However, for the whole of society, a return to normality meant simply the "decent" and hygienic organization of the disposal of the dead. Consequently, after the destruction of the Second World War had been overcome, radical change in the organization of burial services in the GDR was not and could not be precipitated. At the same time future changes were to be expected, not least because of the social, economic, cultural, and political realities of the GDR.

From 1948 onward municipal burial services extended their responsibilities, and privatized burial services were remunicipalized. The aim was to establish a uniform state-run system of burial services, reducing the cost of disposal for the individual as well as for the state. During the 1950s and 1960s many cities and towns municipalized their undertaking industry. However, all initiatives were local. The state had set out only the right to municipalize, so some cities such as Dresden had a highly integrated municipal burial service, while other cities either regulated the work of undertakers or, as in Leipzig, relied entirely on private businesses.[27] However, the greater obstacle to the aim of a unified organization of disposal was that no single ministry was in charge of coordinating the disposal of the dead overall and, more importantly, no ministry actually wanted to be responsible. Discussions could necessitate the involvement of a) the Ministry of the Interior (because of policing matters), b) the Ministry of Health (because of regulative issues), c) the Ministry of Finance, d) the Secretariat for Church Questions, and e) diverse ministries for industry, such as the Ministry for Regionally Administered Industries, Ministry for Light Industry, or the Ministry for the Wood Processing Industry. Any consultation on reform consequently necessitated tedious and time-consuming cross-ministerial dialogue that needed to be coordinated by often unwilling civil servants. This task was fulfilled, more or less reluctantly, by the Ministry of the Interior (which repeatedly tried to shift this responsibility to the Ministry of Health). Ultimately, this meant that fundamental, all-encompassing central governmental reforms were not and could not be carried out. The many changes that did occur were conceived and implemented by the technocratic specialist.

These impediments to reform were somewhat alleviated when the IfK was set up in 1962. The organization provided the ideal platform for the existing specialists in burial service organization and cemetery design to work together to effect wider reforms. The IfK and its specialists became de facto the only force that persistently pressed for reform and change. It is striking that, in the political and organizational environment of the GDR, change driven by the IfK was brought about not by decree but by the application of direct influence, by consultation and interaction with the management of individual cities' burial services and cemeteries. Informal communication with the regional *Leitbetrieb* (leading concern) became the pivotal tool of coordination. These *Leitbetriebe* served as models within the region and beyond, as well as coordinating institutions for collecting the necessary data to plan the economy. The resulting changes could be sweeping, but they took place step by step and, more importantly, place by place. This necessarily resulted in a slow process of perpetuating general organizational reform by constant reference to those prototypical burial services in which certain elements of the proposed concepts had been implemented successfully.

Burial services, like those in Dresden—praised for economic efficiency and a high cremation rate—were used to advocate institutions that would conduct the whole process of disposal, from the collection of the corpse to the organization of all aspects of the funeral ceremony. From the early 1970s onward, this concept envisaged not merely an undertaking service; it looked forward to a fully fledged socialist funeral directing service. The word "service" became pivotal and extended from the transport, laying-out, and decoration of the celebration hall to the organization of the funeral service and help with the formalities and paperwork such as applications for pensions. In short, it offered a package program for socialist burial, as had been envisaged in a 1958 proposal for the reform of cemeteries and burial services in Berlin:

> In the further development of the cemetery- and burial system in Berlin a people's-own corporation is to be formed, analogous to the organizational form of the cemetery- and burial systems in the larger cities of the Republic and in Moscow. This corporation will conduct all services that are required in the case of a death. This includes, besides dealing with formalities, the delivery of coffins, transportation, the selling of grave plots, the planning of burial ceremonies with vocal and instrumental performers, the decoration, the closing of the grave and planting, the production of floral wreaths, and the selling of plants to decorate the grave plots. We are also of the opinion that, in addition, the manufacture of gravestones must be conducted within such a corporation.[28]

The coordination of the different elements of the ceremony and the funeral meant that the municipal burial services would offer the same level of services as provided by funeral directors in the capitalist West. Thus the rise of large municipal burial services, at least in the cities and larger towns, mirrored the development of undertaking in the capitalist West. However, the role of the funeral services as a vehicle for ideology was also apparent. As in many other fields of socialist public policy and services, the idea of leading by setting positive precedents was adopted, but by the very nature of the model provided by the *Leitbetrieb* was limited to the specific location and its sphere of influence. The intention is evident: to demonstrate that only a good burial service is capable of organizing attractive secular funerals and, more importantly, to advocate that most socialist of burials—interment of the ashes in *UGA*. The ultimate goal for the socialist sepulchral culture was to propagate the scattering of the ashes on a designated field, a process that was entirely in line with a materialist concept of death and disposal, both in conduct and in character, as well as the desire for efficiency.[29]

Examining the evidence, one has to acknowledge that, as in Britain but unlike Sweden (both countries had state-sponsored attempts to advocate cremation), these policies were predominately driven by an economic and planning rationale.[30] In East German publications and sources there are numerous references to the practicalities of increasing efficiency in order ultimately to achieve the economic sustainability of the municipal cemeteries within the troubled GDR economy. Ideological coherence played an important role in making cremation attractive as a socialist form of disposal, serving as an ideological justification for a more economic means of disposal. However, day-to-day operation was governed by a more mundane concern for efficiency. A comprehensive prognosis for the entire sepulchral culture from 1968 onward noted: "Difficulties arise with regard to inhumations to an ever larger extent through the lack of personnel, spaces, and the decreasing willingness to aid neighbours in excavating graves in smaller villages. The form of disposal 'inhumation,' must therefore, be widely replaced by the form of disposal 'cremation.' For the period of the prognosis, it is thus essential actively to exert influence on the population through explanation, stimulation, and, amongst other means, through prices and the fostering of farewell ceremonies of a high cultural standard. In 1980 an average cremation rate of 65 percent should be achieved in the GDR, and consequently the rate of inhumation should be reduced to 35 percent."[31]

With regard to cemetery design the issue of economic efficiency is not as clear-cut as in the case of cremation. One cannot, however, overlook the fact that the principles and aesthetics advocated did not cut across the ideal of efficiency. The IfK to a large extent propagated ideals reminiscent of the earlier cemetery reform movement, ideals that themselves already contained a significant element of utility. While purely aesthetic considerations initially played a more prominent role in cemetery design than in cremation, the focus in both areas shifted toward practical concerns. An excerpt from a 1963 brochure entitled "Our Cemeteries" vividly demonstrates that transition: "It should not be the case that there are only a few forms and materials as well as methods of sculpting left that are then endlessly repeated. That would constitute torturous monotony and a leveling that would contravene the justified wishes of the bereaved for an individual treatment of their deceased. The personal relationship (to the gravestone and grave plot) should certainly be retained. ... Basic types must be used, in which new findings combine with well-established forms and sizes. If these standard forms, with their appropriate variations, accommodate the specific nature of the raw materials, they will guarantee an economic and efficient application."[32]

In 1969 the IfK named its three key targets for all its measures: a) the reduction of investment in new cemeteries and the extension of existing ones by increasing the rate of cremation; b) the concentration of investment in cemeteries in areas with dense settlement and the closure of small (rural) cemeteries; and c) the introduction of new forms of burial such as *Urnengemeinschaftsanlagen* and *Aschestreuwiesen* (ash scattering fields).[33] The concern for efficiency and socioeconomic factors had by this time clearly surpassed primarily ideological considerations as the chief motivation. In particular, the introduction and propagation of the new forms of burial were seen as very efficient ways to economize. For planning purposes, in cities with a low rate of cremation and a high rate of normal burials, three to five square meters of cemetery space had to be set aside for each projected denizen, while in cities with a high rate of cremation that figure was reduced to 1.8 to 2.5 square meter. Considering that in an *Urnengemeinschaftsanlage* that could be cut to a mere 0.25–0.50 square meter, and combined with the fact that a number of cemeteries were no longer able to offer anything except cremation—as there was neither anybody to dig a grave except family members, nor any mechanical gravediggers--there was an overwhelming case for such measures. Moreover, the large-scale introduction of ash-scattering fields would have allowed for repeated use of the same space and thus further reduction of cost and cemetery space. While these three key policies conformed to a socialist ideal of a uniform and communal organization of the cemetery, by the 1980s the task of uniting both economic and ideological aspects in the socialist reconstruction of cemeteries was proving increasingly difficult to achieve within the increasing economic constraints of the GDR's planned economy and the chronic lack of manpower in areas such as burial services and cemeteries.

Nevertheless, these policies once more focused only on the ideal case: the large urban municipal cemetery. The reality in the countryside was very different. An analysis of sepulchral culture undertaken in 1976 on behalf of the SED and conducted by the Ministry of the Interior noted that, when offered, such wide-ranging services were taken up to varying degrees, mainly dependent on the location: "It is clearly apparent that the services are conducted to a large extent on the premises of the burial institutions, but that the organizations providing the other services are predominately concerned with the transportation of corpses and urns. The performance of burials in smaller towns and municipalities without burial institutions is largely organized by citizens themselves. This ultimately leads to many citizens turning to the church authorities in this matter."[34] As in the West, urban areas were in the vanguard of sepulchral change while the small and rural communities lagged behind—not surprisingly, given demographic change and the localized nature of disposal.

Until fairly recently in the East as well as the West, the organization of funerals remained largely in the hands of the bereaved family. In the GDR this inertia with regard to changes in fashions and traditions was further accentuated by the role the church played within rural areas of the GDR. Even in 1989 roughly 70 percent of the cemeteries and 60 percent of the overall cemetery space of the GDR were owned by the Protestant Church. However, most of these cemeteries were small or medium-sized rural cemeteries; urban cemeteries, with the exception of some larger ones in Berlin, were exclusively municipally owned. That left the burial service with the problem of advancing a socialist agenda in rural areas without the support of a resident organizational framework. Furthermore, in rural areas the church cemeteries were better able than urban cemeteries to cope with the lack of personnel and financial constraints. East German sepulchral reform was, therefore, predominantly urban. The 1975 *Waldfriedhof* (a woodland cemetery) in Schwerin is a good example of a reform limited to some large-scale projects. This quintessential socialist cemetery was built as a prototype, with a concrete celebration hall, socialist statues and murals, and a park-like design. A wide and long open space along a natural dell divides the two parts of the cemetery, while the fields on both sides are arranged in the typical GDR grid-system of rows of 1.30m × 2.80m burial plots that included an 80 cm path at the bottom of each plot, avoiding the head-to-head system of earlier periods (and leading to the impression of a sea of stones). The individual fields are separated physically but visually linked to form a unity. Schwerin demonstrates that the socialist administration favored the grand gesture, whereas the other cemeteries in the region received hardly any governmental investment.

The example of Schwerin also reveals that most of the uniform feel of GDR cemeteries was created by the limited supply of gravestones, the reliance on a number of machine-cut standard patterns, and the specific usage of plants, not deliberate policy but rather industrial and economic imperatives. The outcome of this is still evident in the vast numbers of red or gray upright format gravestones that still dominate many cemeteries, thus lending themselves to the perception of what is quintessentially East German—uniformity by default, rather than coherence by decree. This lack of general coherence with regard to policy was even officially recognized and rightly deemed to be the result of the hitherto sporadic legislative and administrative interest.[35] However, it took a further four years to tackle the lack of a single coherent national legal framework. Furthermore, the new legal framework that finally emerged in 1980 singularly lacked any radical social or political agenda and, notably, most regulations resembled those passed in West Germany.[36]

Nevertheless, it is precisely with this comparison that a tricky balancing act begins. Changes in the disposal of the dead were brought about despite a formidable number of obstacles. Regardless of intense disorganization, local idiosyncrasies, ministerial apathy, church resistance and compromise, inherent traditionalism, political deliberations, economic constraints, and very different regional preconditions (the south traditionally had a high rate of cremation while the north was more staunchly conservative), East German sepulchral cultures did change fundamentally. That change was much more diverse and complex than has often been assumed. It is essential to understand that many aspects of death, dying, and disposal in East Germany after 1945 went through a step by step change constrained by what was economically viable, politically possible, aesthetically de-sirable, or ideologically feasible, and in every individual case the bottom line was simple practicability. The example of East Berlin amplifies this point. Despite numerous plans, not least the sweeping reform proposed in 1958, very few things changed. In 1971 private undertakers still operated alongside the municipalized burial service, but both worked in a decentralized and often highly disorganized system unsuitable for a city of that size. Further plans for the restructuring of the Berlin burial services written in 1971 stress this contradiction and reveal the distance between ambition and reality:

> In order to stabilize the situation of the cemetery- and burial system in Berlin and for a future development according to plan, centralization, concentration, specialization, and combination are indispensable. This process can only be realized step by step and requires uniform management of the cemetery system. The effect of these measures consists in particular of fulfilling the main tasks of the cemetery and burial system, to

guarantee in the long term a hygienically impeccable, dignified, and timely burial of the deceased in conjuncture with a reduction in societal expenditure and an increase of cemetery and burial culture. The existing and deteriorating precarious situation regarding the realization of burial duties does not allow for any alternative to the immediate concentration of existing funds and capacities under an uniform administration of the whole process by the capital.[37]

This describes the ambition of the GDR: to combine the propagation of a political ideology, e.g., of a "dignified" secular funeral, within tight economic constraints. One might argue that such an ambition can only be described as a paradox, but it is exactly this paradox that defined the socialist sepulchral cultures of the GDR: the attempt to achieve an ideological ideal and the optimal provision of services on a very tight budget. On the one hand, it was politically impossible to increase the price of funerals, and there was little inclination to spend more than necessary on this sector of the economy. On the other hand, burial services were expected to fulfill their role in advocating and advancing socialist culture as well as to provide a vital local service. As one might expect, the reality of this approach often looked different:

> For the farewell we were led into a room; there the flowers were taken from me, against my will. I wanted to throw them on the coffin [before it was transported to the cremation oven]—that was not possible! The coffin stood undecorated in front of a dirty tiled wall. Visible numbers had been scrawled in chalk on the coffin. At that time—five minutes before the ceremony—a "Herr" appeared, and tried to explain to my father that he was the speaker. … How can such a speaker [without prior discussion] understand the deep pain of the bereaved and in his speech pay the deceased the last respect? Is this only about being paid—or better still—the receiving of 25.00 Marks? We declined his speech…. When the coffin was brought into the ceremony hall, we were all overwhelmed by great indignation despite our deep grief. The coffin and the pedestal were basically naked. Not even 10 percent of the flowers were there. Where are the beautiful orchids and chrysanthemums? There are no technical reasons nor is there a lack of space![38]

Drawing a clear dividing line between exceptions and the general rule in this regard is extremely difficult, considering that about 230,000 funerals were conducted per year—and had to be conducted. Moreover, distressed and bereaved individuals had to seek professional help to organize the disposal of their dead. Nevertheless, complaints about the quality of the burials, the cleanliness of cemeteries, and air pollution by crematoria increased in the 1970s and 1980s. This reflected the general lack of investment, personnel, and equipment. In spite of these constraints, and despite the many *UGAs*, the existence of the only operational ash-scattering field in Germany, the introduction of the biodegradable plastic urn, and a very high rate of secular funerals in East Berlin, it is essential to stress that the sepulchral cultures of East Germany were not unlike those anywhere else.[39] One has to resist the notion of peculiarity, which too easily is used to explain the obvious differences.[40]

In conclusion, from the 1960s onward in the GDR as well as in Western Europe, both cemeteries and burial services became part of an integrated service economy. However, there were differences: one fundamental difference was that in Western Europe this led to the commercialization of funeral direction and, to a lesser degree, of cemetery operation. In the GDR with its planned economy, this led to ever more strained conditions and subsequently visions of more efficient means of disposal. In this light it is not surprising that an incensed visitor to the *Heidefriedhof* in Dresden wrote in June 1979:

> You certainly have not yet looked at the appearance of the resting place of our loved ones! It resembles a dumping site for rubble! Yesterday we once again had to observe that the last burial area [of the *UGA*] for May is covered only in weeds, and it is intended for humans, who have dedicated all their energy to the construction of our Republic![41]

The reality of many cemeteries in the GDR confirms the initial observation made that the socialist sepulchral culture of the GDR lacked in sacrosanctity. The political and ideological tone of the source material stands in stark contrast to the overall reality of disposal within the GDR. We must question to what extent one can speak of the GDR as a *durchherrschte Gesellschaft*, at least with regard to the organization of disposal and the creation of an idealized socialist sepulchral culture. The inability to sustain overall reform and the complexity of the ensuing picture—for example, the many differences between urban areas and the countryside; between the north and the south; and the similarities of certain policies and developments to those of West Germany, the United Kingdom, or Sweden—contradict fundamentally the concept of a monolithic culture and state. This leaves us with the challenging, complex, and contradictory understanding of the sepulchral cultures of the GDR, cultures that, as in the West, were very much dependent on and shaped by local and regional idiosyncrasies.

Notes

1. Reiner Sörries, "Kontroverse um Sozialistische Friedhofskultur," *Friedhof und Denkmal* 41, no. 1(1996): 11; R. Schelenz and S. Meinel, "'Sozialistische' Friedhofskultur in der DDR," *Friedhof und Denkmal* 41, no. 1 (1996):12–15; Gerti Maria Hoffjan, "Existierte eine spezifische realsozialistische Friedhofgestaltung in der DDR und was waren ihre Charakteristika?," in Barbara Leisner, ed., *Vom Reichsausschuss zur Arbeitsgemeinschaft Friedhof und Denkmal* (Kassel, 2002), 179–180; Jürgen Kocka, "Eine durchherrschte Gesellschaft," in Hartmut Kaeble, Jürgen Kocka, and Hartmut Zwahr, eds., *Sozialgeschichte der DDR* (Stuttgart, 1994), 547–553.
2. M. Kramer, ed., *Planung, Gestaltung und Pflege von Urnengemeinschaftsanlagen* (Dresden, 1985), 7. Some of these *UGAs* were capable of holding 20,000 to 50,000 urns.
3. Bundesarchiv Berlin, DO4, Nr. 891. The Arbeitsgemeinschaft Friedhof und Denkmal was founded in 1951 and continued the function of the Reichsausschuss für Friedhof und Denkmal (1921) as a platform for those interested in sepulchral issues.

4. Jörg Friedrich, *Der Brand* (Berlin, 2002), 431; Rainer Behring, "Das Kriegsende 1945," in C. Christian Vollnhals, ed., *Sachsen in der NS-Zeit* (Leipzig, 2002), 227.
5. Brandenburgisches Landeshauptarchiv Potsdam, Rep. 211 MfG, Nr. 1126, f. 3 VS.
6. Allgemeine Sterbetafeln der Jahrbücher der DDR; Siegfried Grundmann, *Bevölkerungsentwicklung in Ostdeutschland—Demographische Strukturen uns räumliche Wandlungsprozesse auf dem Gebiet der neuen Bundesländer (1945 bis zur Gegenwart)* (Opladen, 1998); C. Höhn and J. Pollard, "Mortality in the two Germanies in 1986 and Trends 1976–1986," *European Journal of Population* 7, no.1 (1991): 1–29.
7. Ellen Nolte, Vladimir Shkolnikov, and Martin McKee, "Changing Mortality Patterns in East and West Germany and Poland—1: Long Term Trends (1960–1997)," *Journal for Epidemiological Community Health* 54, no. 12 (2000): 890–898.
8. Brandenburgisches Landeshauptarchiv Potsdam, Rep. 60, Nr. 34043.
9. Stadtarchiv Dresden, Rep. 9.1.14, Nr. 131.
10. G. Freidank, *Alles hat am Ende sich gelohnt. Material für weltliche Trauerfeiern*, 5–6, in Bibliothek des Zentralinstitutes und Museum für Sepulkralkultur, Kassel, BES Box 176.
11. Stefan Creuzberger, *Die sowjetische Besatzungsmacht und das politische System der SBZ* (Weimar, 1996), 80.
12. Stadtarchiv Dresden, Rep. 9.1.14, Nr. 205.
13. Thüringisches Hauptstaatsarchiv Weimar, BPA Erfurt, B II / 2 / 14 – 001.
14. "The funeral eulogy is a potent form of ideological influence and education." Sächsisches Staatsarchiv Leipzig, BT/RdB Leipzig, Nr. 21195. Moreover, Czech material was translated into German to serve as a guideline: Bundesarchiv Berlin, DO1, Nr. 7800.
15. Mecklenburgisches Staatsarchiv Schwerin, RdB Schwerin, 7.1-1, 1. Überlieferungschicht, 3995 b.
16. Sächsisches Staatsarchiv Chemnitz, RdB Karl-Marx-Stadt, Abt. Inneres, Nr. 47109.
17. Klemens Richter, "Toten – Liturgie – Der Umgang mit Tot und Trauer in den Bestattungsriten der DDR," in Hansjakob Becker, Bernhard Einig. Peter-Otto Ullrich, eds., *Im Angesicht des Todes: Ein interdisziplinäres Kompendium*, Vol. 1 (St. Ottilien, 1987), 242–255.
18. Ansgar Franz, "Alles hat am Ende sich Gelohnt? Christliche Begräbnisliturgie zwischen Tradition und säkularen Riten," *Liturgisches Jahrbuch* 51 (2001): 204–205. Most speeches by professional speakers were based on initial questionnaires that recorded the main points to be woven into the speech. A questionnaire from Dresden asks for names of all the relatives, the career of the deceased, and graciously leaves a single line for his character and his interests, but two for medals and titles, as well as four for a description of who is attending the ceremony.
19. For example, in March 1977 there were 46 professional secular speakers registered in the region of Leipzig, compared with 485 pastors. Moreover, 50 percent of all secular funerals in the region of Leipzig were actually conducted by pastors rather than secular speakers. Sächsisches Staatsarchiv Leipzig, RdB Leipzig, Nr. 21195; Bundesarchiv Berlin, DO1 34.0, Nr. 26207.
20. Stadtarchiv Rostock, Rep. 2.2.8, Nr. 12, Befragungsschema, Anlage F/B 2-77. IfK, ed., *Dienstleistungen im Bestattungswesen* (Dresden, 1979), 51.
21. Brandenburgisches Landeshauptarchiv Potsdam, Rep. 601, Nr. 34043; Bundesarchiv Berlin, DO1 34.0, Nr. 26207.
22. Horst Groschopp, "Weltliche Trauerkultur in der DDR: Toten- und Bestattungsrituale in der politischen Symbolik des DDR-Systems," *Zeitschrift für Sozialwissenschaften* 29, no. 2 (2000): 109.
23. Evangelisches Zentralarchiv Berlin, ZA 5109/02, Nr. 101/3377.
24. Bundesarchiv Berlin, DO 4, Nr. 2162.
25. Brandenburgisches Landeshauptarchiv Potsdam, Rep. 601, Nr. 34044.
26. Kay Blumenthal-Barby, *Betreuung Sterbender: Tendenzen, Fakten, Probleme* (Berlin-Ost, 1982).
27. Bundesarchiv Berlin, DO4, Nr. 2162.
28. Landesarchiv Berlin, C Rep. 115, Nr. 220.
29. "The task of the cemetery reform is perhaps only fulfilled if we once more have a cemetery without graves as a 'death grove' (*Totenhain*) in midst of our settlement." H. Keller, "Möglich-

keiten zur Ermittlung des Friedhofsflächenbedarf," Belegarbeit Humboldt Universität Berlin, Sektion Pflanzenproduktion, Abteilung Freiflächengestaltung Dessau, 40, as quoted in Barbara Happe, "Sozialistische Reform der Friedhofs- und Bestattungskultur der DDR," in Leisner, *Vom Reichsausschuss zur Arbeitsgemeinschaft Friedhof und Denkmal,* 185.

30. Nils Grufman and Sten Ingemark, *Feuerbestattung und Friedhofswesen in der DDR—Schwedische Feuerbestatter berichten* (Berlin, 1972), 3–4, 8.
31. Bundesarchiv Berlin, DO4, Nr. 892.
32. IfK, ed., *Gestaltung unserer Friedhöfe* (Berlin, 1963), 40.
33. One ash scattering field was operational in Rostock, one remained unopened in Zittau. IfK Archiv beim AFD Kassel, Sig. 20 A, 20B; 12/69.
34. Bundesarchiv Berlin, DO1 34.0, Nr. 48678.
35. Bundesarchiv Berlin, DO1 34.0, Nr. 48678.
36. Jürgen Gaedke, "Friedhofs- und Bestattungsrecht in der DDR," *Deutsche Friedhofskultur— Zeitschrift für das gesamte Friedhofswesen* 71 (1981): 274.
37. LAB, C Rep. 104, Nr. 607.
38. StA Dresden, Rep. 9.1.14, Nr. 288, Eingabe, 6. September 1979.
39. Cornelia Geißler, "Unter der Erde der DDR," in Karl Marcus Michel and Tilman Spengler, eds., *Todesbilder, Kursbuch* 114 (Berlin, 1993), 79–81.
40. According to the 1985 figures, the last complete set available: a) The southern regions had a much higher rate of cremation (78.8 percent) than the northern regions (33.1 percent), and both were close to the level they were supposed to have reached by 1980; b) Berlin's cremation rate remains uncertain, as the crematorium (*Baumschulenweg*) did not compile statistics of who was from Berlin and who was transported from outside to be cremated in Berlin; furthermore, Potsdam and Teltow took some of Berlin's dead. A conservative estimate is that the cremation rate in Berlin was somewhere around 80 percent, with a likelihood that it might have been even higher. For 1991 the cremation rate for unified Berlin was 71.7 percent, and in 2002 it was 75.8 percent. *Pressemitteilung 210/03 vom 18.9.2003,* Statistisches Landesamt Berlin.
41. Stadtarchiv Dresden, Rep. 9.1.14, Nr. 288.

Chapter 6

DEATH AT THE MUNICH OLYMPICS

Kay Schiller

Introduction

Rather than for their sports, the Munich Olympic Games are known around the world for the terrorist attack that disrupted them on 5 September 1972. This is because the hostage-taking and massacre of eleven members of the Israeli team at the hands of a PLO commando was the first globally televised act of terrorism. Almost three decades before the planes hit the World Trade Center, an estimated 800 million television viewers watched the crisis unfold in the Olympic Village. In fact, were it not for an older generation of historians and politicians for whom "Munich" is still synonymous with the 1938 appeasement agreement, the name of the host city of the 1972 Olympics would probably already be the normal shorthand for this first global media event of terrorism.

Steven Spielberg and his scriptwriter Tony Kushner certainly felt entitled to use it in this way for their 2006 thriller on the terrorist attack and the Israeli retribution measures in its aftermath. During Operations "Wrath of God" and "Spring of Youth," Mossad and Israeli Defense Force squads hunted down and killed a number of Palestinian officials and operatives, often wrongly believed to have been involved.[1] Spielberg's *Munich* liberally mixes fact and fiction, using these events only as props for a discussion of the legitimacy of the use of violence for political ends on both sides of the Israeli-Palestinian divide.

Accordingly, in the atmosphere of the so-called "war on terror," the reception of the film has revolved around the question of whether the director establishes a moral equivalence between state and terrorist political violence—a charge that Spielberg, a liberal Jewish American, has vigorously denied.[2] The German share of responsibility for the death of Jews in turn was of little concern to him on this occasion. Neither does *Munich* emphasize that the taking of Israeli hostages

---

Notes for this chapter begin on page 146.

was only made possible by German security failures, nor that nine of the eleven victims were killed as a result of a botched liberation attempt by the German authorities.

This is rather different from the treatment the Munich events and their aftermath received in Kevin MacDonald's 1999 documentary *One Day in September* and Simon Reeve's book by the same title, which accompanied it.[3] Relying on stylistic devices and techniques more familiar from blockbuster movies than from documentaries, MacDonald's film makes for gripping and suspenseful viewing. Perhaps not surprisingly, despite a number of unsubstantiated but all the more suggestive claims, such as that the terrorists were helped by members of the GDR team, it won the 2000 Academy Award for best documentary.

Reeve's companion volume, which avoids such errors, is largely based on the extensive interviews conducted for the film. He interweaves the vivid accounts of Israeli athletes unharmed by sheer luck with the emotional memories of the relatives of the Israeli victims of both Palestinian violence and the blatant incompetence of the West German police. The reader listens to the largely self-exculpatory statements of politicians and officials, the emotional observations of representatives of the media who followed the events from close by, and the sober explanations provided by the one Palestinian terrorist who survived Israeli retribution in the aftermath of the drama and is still in hiding.

Whereas Spielberg's film is a moral indictment of both Palestinian and Israeli practitioners of "eye-for-an-eye" politics, the fall guys in *One Day in September* are the Germans. In essence, the message of MacDonald and (to a lesser extent) Reeve is that during the 1972 Olympics "ordinary Germans" once again did either not try hard enough to prevent the murder of Jews or merely stood by when it happened.[4] The positive reception both the film and the book received in the Federal Republic and the US has to be seen in the wider context of German and American "politics of the past" since the 1990s, in particular concerning the memory of the Holocaust. It is rather obvious that in this context, the combination of Jewish victims and German bystanders, if not perpetrators, exerts a potent attraction.

However, rather than looking at the politics of the past in the present, this essay will focus on how the events of 5 September 1972 were interpreted in West Germany at the time. By examining the reactions of the organizers and the wider public, speeches by politicians, and items in the contemporary press, it will show how the reception of the terrorist attack and the failed rescue attempt fit into Germany's "second history of national socialism," that is, the complex history of trauma, evasion, and commemoration of the Nazi past in the West German public sphere in the postwar era.[5]

How were these deaths of the eleven Israelis disposed of in the context of the German "politics of the past" (*Vergangenheitspolitik*)? My main argument is that the ways in which these events were perceived and interpreted at the time mark a transitional stage in German attempts at "coming to terms with the past" (*Vergangenheitsbewältigung*) between the evasion of the past in the first decade of the Federal Republic and the current obsession with it.[6] This is simply because the violent death of Jews during a mega-event that was central to the self-understanding of the Federal Republic, and to the image it wanted to project to the world, could not but bring back the memory of Jewish suffering at the hands of Germans during the Nazi period to the forefront of public consciousness. While the 1972 Games were meant to symbolically uncouple the Federal Republic from the historical legacy that Nazi Germany had left to it, the death of the Israeli athletes, for which the local security forces bore a large share of responsibility, provoked the opposite, albeit only for a short time.

Even though the attack on the Olympics as such had nothing to do with the Holocaust, the reactions in the immediate aftermath prove that politicians, the media, and the wider public were well aware of the existence of a link between the past and the present. Indicative of this is, for instance, that while in public and private utterances the victims were primarily addressed as Israelis, the fact that they were also Jews and thus particularly deserving of German sympathies was never far from the surface and, if not explicitly mentioned, could always be read between the lines.

This return of the past, which paradoxically occurred against the backdrop of an event that was meant to blanket over the memory of Nazism in the minds of the world, became obvious through a discourse that stressed the identification with Israel and condemned terrorism and the Arab states that supported it. This discourse of identification with the victims and their state was facilitated by the fact that it allowed for the conflation between real and symbolic victims, that is, the eleven athletes and their hosts—hosts whose "mega show" had been spoiled by the conflicts from another area of the world.

This chapter is divided into three parts. First I will explain the broader West German "past-political" contexts in which the 1972 Games were situated. Next I will concentrate on the planning and staging of the Munich Olympics in relation to the 1936 Olympics in Berlin. Then I will focus on the terrorist attack of 5 September 1972 and the reactions it provoked in West Germany.

Past-Political Contexts

As a rule the International Olympic Committee (IOC) awards the Games to a city. There can be no doubt that they were the central event in the history of Munich in the 1960s and 1970s. A city whose postwar population expanded rapidly from barely a half-million in 1945 to surpass the figure of one million in 1957 and reach 1.4 million in 1972, Munich needed the Games not least for the financing of the modernization of its urban infrastructure and transport systems.[7] The Games also played an important role in raising the profile of Munich and Bavaria as important locations for business and industry, culture and the arts, and tourism.

Additionally however, the 1972 Games were a showcase for West Germany. They were instrumental in terms of the image of the country that its political elite wanted to project to the world. Both the success of the West German contribution to détente, that is, normalization of relations with Poland and the other Warsaw Pact countries, including the GDR, and the fact that the former resistance fighter Willy Brandt had replaced Kurt Georg Kiesinger, a former civil servant in Goebbels's propaganda ministry, as chancellor pointed to the increased international status of the Federal Republic. The Games in turn were meant to reflect this, consolidating and extending what had already been achieved in this respect. They were intended to be "cheerful Games," that is, to present an easy-going and relaxed yet self-confident Germany to the world.

In relation to the legacy of Nazism, the 1972 Games fell into a period that was characterized by two contradictory trends. On the one hand, efforts at coming to terms with the past intensified during the 1960s and, as a result of "1968," particularly between 1966 and 1969.[8] This was a general development which continued into the 1970s. At the same time, an opposing trend can be observed from the mid 1960s onwards—"technocracy without memory."[9] An important element of the optimistic discourse of a modern Germany that informed contemporary politics, including the reform projects of the social-liberal coalitions in the 1970s, this trend also significantly affected the planning and staging of the Games from the IOC's decision to award them to Munich in April 1966 to the event itself in August and September 1972. In (mis-)quoting the title of a famous book of the period by H. M. Enzensberger on the Spanish Civil War, the years from 1963 to 1973 have been ironically called a "short summer of concrete utopia" between the difficulties of the postwar period and the crisis management from the first oil price shock onward.[10] Seen in this light, the Olympics were symptomatic of the euphoric implementation of a technocratic optimism that meant to make permanent the achievements of the West German welfare state and consumer society through technocratic planning.

To a large extent this optimism reflected a belief widespread among conservative as well as social-liberal elites that the postwar era had come to an end and a new period of German history had begun.[11] This planning optimism reached its apex under the first Brandt government from 1969 to 1972, where it met with a belief by both government and larger sections of civil society that long-overdue reforms would be implemented and West Germany become a more liberal and democratic state. The first change of the main party of government in the history of the Federal Republic, which passed in an entirely unproblematic fashion, despite fears—arising from, among other factors, the civil unrest of the late 1960s—that the Federal Republic might go down the route of the Weimar Republic, was accompanied by Brandt's promise "to dare more democracy." As he put it in his government declaration of 28 October 1969: "We do not stand at the end of our democracy, we are only just beginning."[12]

Brandt, like most of the SPD leadership—including Hans-Jochen Vogel (born 1926), Munich's lord mayor from 1960 to the eve of the Games, who with Willi Daume (1913–1996), the president of the West German National Olympic Committee (NOC),[13] was instrumental in bringing them to the city—was convinced that in the context of a deepening of democracy the silence and "selective memories" concerning the Nazi past of the first decade of the republic had had their day.[14] Instead, in order to come to terms with the past the German people had to be capable of acknowledging that history and reflecting upon it in a sober and rational fashion. Only this way would they be able to understand the present and plan for the future. This was Brandt's main message to the Germans during the Bundestag's first-ever commemoration of the end of the war on 8 May 1970.[15] Consequently, he advocated that 8 May 1945 should not be seen as the date that marked German military defeat, but rather as the day of its liberation from the Nazi dictatorship.

This important shift in the politics of the past, however, somewhat paradoxically left only relatively little space for the legacy of Nazi crimes to be perceived as a burden. This is to say that the figure of the charismatic chancellor, the first Social Democrat in this office since 1930, who, having resisted Nazi Germany in Norwegian emigration, was beyond reproach in terms of his own past, arguably served as a surrogate for a deeper soul-searching for many West Germans.

Ostpolitik is a case in point. While it reminded Germans of the postwar order's roots in the crimes of the Nazi regime and the lost war, at the same time détente and reconciliation with Eastern Europe seemed to offer a chance of letting bygones be bygones by acknowledging the realities of the present, including borders and cohabitation. This was also the implicit message of Brandt's famous symbolic act in Warsaw in December 1970. Contrary to what Robert Moeller argues in a recent article,[16] it did not inevitably lead to an intensified soul-searching. Rather, it is likely that Brandt's famous gesture allowed many West Germans to perceive the past as less of a burden. Arguably, it was admiration for the figure of Brandt and his willingness to apologize for German crimes against the Jews, for which he himself bore no responsibility whatsoever, that united the 41 percent questioned on the occasion in an Emnid opinion poll who thought that the gesture was appropriate versus the 48 percent who, in line with the traditional denial of German "collective guilt" of the first years of the Federal Republic, felt that it was exaggerated and the 54 percent of the 30- to 59-year-olds who rejected it outright.[17] By honoring the victims of the 1943 Warsaw ghetto uprising on his knees, the unblemished Brandt, in their perception, took on all of German guilt in relation to the Holocaust—"for all those, who should kneel but do not—because they dare not or cannot or cannot dare it," as *Der Spiegel* put it at the time.[18]

Thus, one can argue that even though efforts at preserving the admonitory value of the memory of Nazism intensified further during Brandt's two periods in office, their impact on the population at large should not be overestimated. Rather, the figure of an antifascist whose reputation was skyrocketing internationally—in 1971 he was awarded the Nobel Peace Prize, not least because of Warsaw—and who represented the hopes of a younger generation of West Germans, along with the general pervasive atmosphere of a technocratic optimism, hindered rather than fostered progress in coming to terms with the past.[19]

The 1972 Olympics

While it would be unfair to claim that the Games were symptomatic of attempts to let bygones be bygones and dispose of the Nazi past once and for all, the aim of their organizers was without doubt to use them as a propaganda tool to show how much Germany had changed since the end of the war. In short, the Games were meant to demonstrate that the Western part of the country had become a modern democracy. At the same time, the organizers attempted to keep the business of day-to-day politics as far away as possible from this festive occasion. It is telling in this respect that Brandt, who was planning to run for reelection after the Olympics, suggested to Daume that before and during the Games advertising pillars in Munich should preferably be kept free of all political propaganda from both his own campaign and that of his challenger, Rainer Barzel, the leader of the conservative opposition in the Bundestag.[20] Living for most of the time in the vicinity of Munich and meeting with foreign heads of state and government during the Games, Brandt generally kept a low profile and was rarely seen at sporting events.

This coincided with the ban in the IOC statutes on all types of political activities in the host city during the Games (part VI of IOC statutes). Accordingly, the IOC's rule could be used not only to diffuse attempts by radical youth to use the Games as a platform to make political statements in the aftermath of "1968"—the previous Olympics in Mexico City had been blighted by mass unrest that claimed hundreds of lives before the Games, and by the Black Power fists of 200-meter race medalists Tommie Smith and John Carlos[21]—but also to keep the past from intruding too much upon the present.

Of course, despite declarations to the contrary both national and international politics had always played an important role in modern Olympic history. The 1966 decision to give the Games to Munich was itself a highly political act. In essence, it was the consolation prize for the IOC Madrid Session's decision of the previous year to allow the GDR to enter a separate team from the 1968 Olympics onward, though with the qualification that in Mexico City both German teams had to fly the Olympic flag and to share the choral theme from Beethoven's Ninth Symphony as their victory anthem.[22] The decision by the IOC Executive Committee came about under pressure from its Soviet member, Konstantin Andrianov, and made a mockery of the West German government's Hallstein doctrine.[23] In return, the American IOC President Avery Brundage, himself a staunch anticommunist, confidentially let Daume know "that he and a number of IOC members would welcome it, if the Olympic Games in 1972 would not be held in a communist state, but preferably in the Federal Republic and in Munich."[24] However, at the same time the IOC under Brundage insisted that in the tradition of Pierre de Coubertin, partisan politics (as well as professional sports) had no role to play during the quadrennial competition between the "youth of the world." This by and large suited the majority of the Munich organizers well.

One particular episode in relation to the Games is indicative of this. When faced with a request to support an exhibit on German antifascism that had previously been shown successfully in West German museums, including, under the patronage of Vogel, in Munich's Stadtmuseum in April 1971, the Organizing Committee (OC) refused to sponsor it in Munich during the Games.[25] This was because the OC, in which the Federal Republic, the State of Bavaria, and the City of Munich were represented on equal terms, felt bound to behave "politically completely abstinent and neutral." Thus, although Vogel, himself one of its three vice-presidents, highlighted the importance of the initiative by pointing out to OC President Daume that its presentation was historically balanced and objective, the latter felt the OC could under no circumstance offer its official endorsement. Likewise, it was out of the question that this initiative, as its curator had demanded, be included in the official cultural program for the Games.[26] The exhibit must have seemed particularly problematic for Daume, as it included images of German antifascists during the Spanish Civil War. In 1972, Spain was still ruled by Franco and was represented on the IOC Executive Committee by Juan Antonio Samaranch, the dictator's minister for sports, who later became the IOC president himself. While Daume expressed his sympathy in principle for the venture to its curator,[27] he obviously felt that he had to take such sensibilities into account.

Moreover, the exhibit was tricky for Daume because its title, *Antifascist Resistance 1933–1945*, had to remind whoever heard it at the time of the New Left agitation against "capitalist imperialism." Furthermore, "antifascism" was central to the other Germany's self-definition as a state. Accordingly, GDR propaganda in the runup to the Olympics ceaselessly pointed out that Munich had been the "capital of the movement" and still was a "hotbed of fascist and revanchist agitators."[28] Munich, after all, was where the headquarters of ninety-two organizations of refugees and émigrés from Eastern Europe and the Soviet Union were located.[29] It was also the place from where radio stations like Radio Free Europe and Radio Liberty broadcast anticommunist propaganda across the Iron Curtain. The organizers eventually decided to move the exhibit to the concentration camp memorial site in Dachau whose establishment in May 1965 was itself part of the intensification of attempts at coming to terms with the past in West Germany.[30] In return the OC decided not to try to stop them but, despite Vogel's warning that this might create negative public relations, also decided not to support the venture financially after receiving a modest request for DM 15,000.[31] This indeed seems a paltry sum compared to the cost of the most prestigious exhibit of the Games' cultural program, *World Cultures and Modern Art*, which had a budget of five million DM, or to the overall expenditure that the planning and staging of the Olympic Games involved—a sum shouldered by two thirds by the Federal Republic that came close to two billion DM.[32]

While the OC had problems with the legacy of antifascism, this did not mean that there were no references to the Nazi past in the way these second Games on German soil were organized. On the contrary, one can find them in abundance.

This was inevitable because the shadow of the 1936 Games in Berlin loomed large over the 1972 Games. Tellingly, the most infamous piece of agitation emanating from East Berlin in relation to the Games was the arithmetic exercise: "2 × 36 = 72!"[33] While the OC was well aware that it was impossible to make the world forget that precedent, its main effort was to at least weaken the world's memory of the Nazi Olympics.

Accordingly, the official commemoration of the victims of Nazism on the occasion of the Olympics was deliberately held before the Games even began and outside Munich, that is, also in Dachau on the morning of 25 August 1972. Its organization was left in the hands of the Catholic and Protestant churches, the Munich Jewish community and the Central Council of Jews in Germany (Zentralrat der Juden in Deutschland), as well as the International Committee Dachau. While this was a high-profile event, "packed with VIPs and extensively reported by the media,"[34] the OC did not have to assume responsibility for it and thus the Games could not be too directly associated with the Nazi past. Tellingly, among the five hundred people present on the occasion there were hardly any athletes.[35]

This fitted well with the OC's attempt to use the Games as a showcase for West Germany, as Brandt had demanded in his 1969 declaration of government. The organizers took seriously his exhortation to use "the opportunity to show the modern Germany to the world."[36] However, for the organizers Berlin 1936 represented a major stumbling block on the way toward the image of a modern Germany. The best way of overcoming this problem, or so it seemed, was to put on Games at least as stage-managed as the ones in Berlin—pretending, however, that they were not. That such a feat was considered possible in the first place is evidence of the optimism that was one of the characteristics of the period. Since the 1936 Games were considered a "triumph of bluff and propaganda"[37] that seduced the world into believing that news of the racist nature of the Nazi regime was exaggerated and that Germany was harboring no aggressive intentions toward her neighbors,[38] the Munich organizers felt they had to stress even more strongly that after 1945 Germans had become peace-loving, tolerant, and cosmopolitan.

Moreover, as the Berlin Games and those in Tokyo in 1964 had displayed a tendency towards gigantism, the Munich application to the IOC emphasized that these would not be Games of superlatives in scale—the comparatively small Olympic stadium for only 80,000 spectators was evidence of this. And, whilst ultramodern and comprehensively organized like Berlin 1936, as this was "what the world expected of Germany," Munich 1972 would lack the machine-like, military precision of that precedent. Rather, these Olympics would present a relaxed and easy-going yet self-confident Germany to the world. Precisely, because the 1936 Games had been blighted by their abuse through politics, the Munich OC put the accent on the Games as an expression of Germany as a modern leisure society. They were meant to become a synthesis of sport, culture, and play, taking place in a "green" park environment (*Spiele im Grünen*) four kilometers from the

Munich city centre with only short distances to cover on foot by both athletes and spectators (*Spiele der kurzen Wege*)—the latter also a reflection of the long distances which had had to be overcome in Mexico City.[39]

In order to consistently convey these basic messages, Daume made sure that from the beginning of the planning process the Games would have a design commissioner (*Gestaltungsbeauftragter*) in Otl Aicher from the Ulm College of Design (*Hochschule für Gestaltung*). Aicher was an industrial designer of world repute and an important representative of the West German contribution to international modernism, having, among others, created designs for consumer durables by Max Braun and modernized the Lufthansa logo. In the eyes of Daume and the OC, his was an entirely unproblematic, if not the ideal choice due to his political credentials and aesthetic vision. Aicher had been close friends with the Scholl twins, both of whom were killed as members of the Munich university resistance group "White Rose" in 1943, and was married to Inge Scholl, their surviving sister.[40]

Moreover, the Ulm College, founded by Aicher and Scholl in 1955 and conceived in the tradition of Bauhaus modernism was, as Paul Betts has put it, like its predecessor "infused with a grand vision of social reform, based on the reconciliation of art and life, morality and material culture."[41] In terms of an overarching vision for postwar architecture, photography, and design products, the aesthetics developed there meant to negate what the school's founders "viewed as the Nazi legacy of emotional manipulation and irrationalism."[42] This was based on a perhaps naïvely idealist belief in the educational powers of reason and rationality, as expressed in a purely functionalist aesthetic, as opposed to the monumentalizing proclivities of Nazi art and architecture.[43] The sober appearance of postwar industrial products and architecture presumably permitted that this problematic past could be erased, that memories, myths, and history could be expunged by visual means. Accordingly, the Ulm aesthetic was "cool, functional, rational, without pathos."[44]

It is in the spirit of a technocratic optimism that trusted in the powers of persuasion of its own aesthetic that one ought to see Aicher's 1967 memorandum on the design for the Munich Olympics and its relation to that of the 1936 Games. Under the heading "Reversal of Berlin," he wrote: "Will the world believe us, if we point out that today's Germany is different from the Germany of then? Trust will not be won through words but through visible testimonies and gained sympathy. It matters less to declare that a different Germany exists than to demonstrate it. … The world expects a correction of Berlin not least because it largely succumbed to its influence."[45] And under the heading "What does Munich want?": "There will be no displays of nationalism and no gigantism. Sport will not be seen in relation to military discipline or as preparation for it. Pathos will be avoided.... Depth is not always expressed in seriousness. Lightness and nonconformity are also indicators of a respectable subjectivity. The Munich Olympic Games shall have the character of informality, openness, lightness, and cheerfulness."[46]

These planning premises for the Games served as a basis for Aicher's designs. Perhaps the most significant example of this was his choice of colors for the

Olympics' visual markers "from letterheads to the festive decoration of the city."[47] The primary color used for posters, pictograms, and personnel uniforms was a light blue, which was also the color of the official West German team attire. This was complemented by a light green; additionally white and silver were used as well as orange. The "imperial color" red, which had figured prominently in Berlin, was avoided altogether. Light blue was chosen not only because, with white, it reflected the colors of the Bavarian sky and state flag, but also because according to opinion polls it was considered an "apolitical" color.[48] Likewise, *Univers*, a sans-serif script rooted in pen-and-ink writing that was used for all Olympic publications and signposts, was meant to signal "ease and agility."[49] According to Aicher, this combination of color and script allowed for "a graphic image for the Games that was both well-defined and evocative."[50]

The same premises applied for the Olympic architecture on the Munich Oberwiesenfeld, itself previously the location of the airport where Édouard Daladier and Neville Chamberlain had landed to sign the agreement that handed the Sudetenland to Nazi Germany and, after the war, the disposal site for ten million cubic meters of debris left by the Allied bombing of Munich. On the main Olympic site, 2.8 square kilometers of wasteland with the so-called *Schuttberg*, rubble mountain, were artificially turned into an undulating landscape into which the main Olympic sites were integrated. The most expensive part and centerpiece of Olympic architecture, the transparent bat-winged roof of nearly 75,000 square meters that covered half of the stadium as well as the adjoining multipurpose gym and swimming hall, replicated and magnified Frei Otto's design for the German pavilion at Expo '67 in Montreal, a prominent official aesthetic manifestation of the "modern Germany" on the international stage.[51] By using Plexiglas covers affixed to steel-cable netting, which was held up by fifty-eight pylons, some up to eighty meters high, the Stuttgart architects Behnisch & Partners intended the roof to create "an atmosphere of openness, transparency, and clarity."[52] For Aicher, this "super roof" was "truly a reversal of Berlin": "The tent is light, full of movement, almost a symbol of the leisure civilization."[53]

Following the same aesthetic principles, the remaining Olympic architecture avoided buildings of colossal dimensions as well as the axes and monumental squares that had characterized Werner March's Berlin *Reichssportfeld*, in favor of "embedding the buildings in the landscape, so that their visually perceptible magnitude [was] reduced."[54] As Fritz Auer, one of the architects, put it: "This way you don't walk up to a wall that frightens or haunts you. The main stadium suddenly opens in front of you like a huge bowl instead of something you have to climb up to."[55]

Likewise, the opening ceremony on 26 August 1972 was conceived with the idea in mind to erase the memory of Berlin. This implied the elimination of as many nationalistic and militaristic rituals as possible under IOC statutes.[56] For example, the majority of athletes had used the Hitler salute to greet the German head of state in 1936, whereas in 1972 no ritual for the greeting of Federal President Gustav Heinemann was prescribed for the day. This was, strictly speaking, in contravention of section 57 of the IOC statutes. Nevertheless, it was left to the international teams' decision whether to wave small banners and scarves "in all directions" or toward the VIP lounge. The West German team on the occasion, it was suggested, should engage in the former "with light-blue scarves."[57] As opposed to previous Olympics, the national anthem of the host country was played only once rather than twice, and only after IOC President Brundage, OC President Daume, and Heinemann had taken their seats: "The national anthem of the Federal Republic of Germany is played. It cannot be avoided at this point because with it the organizer (IOC) honors the host (FRG)."[58]

5 September 1972

The desire to make the world forget the 1936 precedent—and it would be easy to list a myriad of additional examples—also significantly contributed to the lax security measures that allowed the attack by a Palestinian terrorist commando on the Israeli quarters in the Olympic Village during the morning of 5 September 1972. Arguably, the main aim of the so-called Ordnungsdienst, responsible for security at the Games, was paradoxically not so much to provide security but to avoid at all costs the impression that the host country of the 1972 Olympics was a "police state." The propaganda message the so-called "Olys" were meant to convey was reflected both in their "safari-look" attire—trousers and jackets in the "apolitical" color light blue—and in that the 2,106 state police and federal border guard officers on leave of absence from their normal posts were usually unarmed.[59]

This, it must be admitted, coincided with the IOC's intention to correct the negative impression left by the 1968 Games in Mexico City, where the Olympic venues had been guarded by more than forty thousand often heavily armed Mexican soldiers. However, the question whether to give priority to security or to the image the Federal Republic wanted to project was thus clearly answered in favor of the latter. As Manfred Schreiber, the Munich police chief and security commissioner (*Ordnungsbeauftragter*) of the Games, put it in his official report: "[It] must not be forgotten, that very often sport-political perspectives and architectural facts ... were decisive for the planning of measures of security and order and that even the idea of 'cheerful Games' carried certain security risks with it. ... If 'difficulties' occurred in practice, these factors must be taken into consideration. ... Absolute security could not be provided [by the security service]; not even the regular police could have provided it."[60]

Accordingly, the Ordnungsdienst was unable to prevent eight members of the PLO faction Black September from invading the accommodations of the male members of the Israeli team in the early hours of 5 September, shooting the wrestling coach Moshe Weinberg and the weightlifter Yossef Romano and taking a further nine team members hostage.[61] Taking advantage of the free publicity the Games offered to their cause, the Palestinians demanded that two hundred of their comrades held in Israeli prisons be released. According to Schreiber, the hostages' fate was essentially sealed when Israeli Prime Minister Golda Meir told Bonn "no deal."[62] Moreover, negotiations conducted between the leader of the Black September commando and a "crisis committee" (*Krisenstab*) remained unsuccessful. The strategy of the "crisis committee," which included Schreiber as well as Hans-Dietrich Genscher and Bruno Merk, the federal and Bavarian interior ministers, was to buy time, de-escalate the situation and physically and psychologically wear down the hostage takers.[63] While the German negotiators succeeded in getting various deadlines extended throughout the day, they could not convince the Palestinians to consider alternative solutions to the crisis. Neither were they willing to accept an "unspecified sum of money" in return for the hostages, nor did they contemplate the offer by committee members to take the Israelis' place.[64] In the evening the Palestinians demanded to be flown out with their hostages to an Arab country of their choice, despite the fact that they had been unable to secure the release of their comrades in Israeli jails. In view of the German past, it was out of the question that Jews be "deported to the desert to a certain death."[65] This meant in effect that the liberation of the hostages by force had to be attempted. And for this the local police forces were ill-prepared.

The botched rescue operation in the late hours of 5 September at the military airport Fürstenfeldbruck near Munich, during which all nine Israelis were killed, along with five of the eight members of the Palestinian commando and the Munich Police Brigadier Anton Fliegerbauer, was amateurish to say the least. A lot of mistakes were made on the occasion. To mention just the most obvious: only five marksmen, who had not been trained for such occasions, took on eight terrorists, and they did so with an inadequate type of rifle.[66] This led to a gun battle during which not all of the Palestinians were disabled. This gave the remaining ones the opportunity to murder the hostages, which they duly did.

Grief and Anger

Although the German past already determined the hostage crisis both by making it possible in the first place and by bringing it to a tragic conclusion, in the context of my argument it is more relevant to look at the response of officials, politicians, and the press in the aftermath. As was to be expected, the first reactions by officials and politicians were statements that stressed the shock and horror the attack had caused them. Then, and particularly in the context of the memorial ceremony on 6 September, there followed expressions of grief for the victims, accompanied by angry recriminations against the terrorists and the Arab states that supported them.

Before the crisis had run its course, the IOC had given in to mounting public pressure and interrupted the Games on the afternoon of 5 September. The OC scheduled a memorial ceremony to commemorate the victims for the morning of the following day. The speakers in the Olympic stadium on 6 September included Federal President Heinemann, Daume, Brundage, Shmuel Lalkin, the Israeli chef de mission, and Eliashiv Ben-Horin, the Israeli ambassador to Bonn. The strongest words came from Heinemann: "Who are guilty of this misdeed? In the forefront is a criminal organization which believes that hate and death can be weapons of political struggles. But those nations who do not hinder the acts of these men also bear responsibility."[67]

This expression of anger by the West German head of state was met with the sadness and anger of an entirely full stadium. Initially many were seen crying, but when Heinemann spoke he was interrupted eight times with rapturous applause, which became loudest when he condemned the sponsors of terrorism among Arab states.[68] Rather than a commemoration, over time the event became more and more a mass political demonstration against terror and violence and for the state of Israel.[69] On the evening of 6 September, there followed a rally in the same spirit with seven thousand participants on the Munich Königsplatz. The speakers, which included Vogel and Hans Lamm, the leader of the local Jewish community, expressed their sincere sympathy for the relatives of the victims and solidarity with Israel.[70] Smaller demonstrations and marches also took place in other German cities, for instance in Bonn.[71]

Once the decision was taken that the Games would continue—Brundage's famous credo during the memorial ceremony being "The Games must go on!"[72]—because stopping them would presumably have set a dangerous precedent for future political extremism, it was criticized by only a minority. In some press reactions, one can also observe a critical questioning of the illusion that politics could be kept away from the Olympics.[73] However, much more ink was spilled in reporting on the police errors in the aftermath of the attack. On the last day of the Games, for instance, *Der Spiegel*'s extensive cover story "The Massacre of Munich: Could it have been avoided?" provided a detailed analysis of the mistakes.[74] Yet, despite extensive criticism in the media, those politically responsible did not resign. Neither Schreiber nor his immediate superior Merk felt compelled even to offer to give up their posts. Federal Interior Minister Genscher offered his resignation, but it was not accepted by Chancellor Brandt.[75] An official documentation by the Federal Republic and the State of Bavaria that was being published still in September also affirmed that the "crisis committee" had done "everything possible" to save the Israeli athletes and "had acted adequately and made the right decisions" to the best of its knowledge.[76] Likewise, a judicial enquiry conducted in early 1973 into the decisions of Schreiber and Georg Wolf, his deputy who had led the operation in Fürstenfeldbruck, could find no fault with their actions.[77]

After the terrorist attack, the common ground of the discourse by politicians and commentators was that a moral equivalence was established between the Israeli victims on the one hand, and the population of the host country whose Olympic mega-show had been spoiled by the terrorist attack on the other. To a large extent this conflation of real and symbolic victims happened via identification with the dead Israeli hostages and their country of origin. Expressions of sympathy with the athletes and declarations of solidarity with Israel abounded, both in the media and among the public. These included, for instance, a telegram of condolence to Golda Meir by Axel Springer, West Germany's conservative newspaper tycoon and a well-known friend of Israel, which was reprinted in the papers of his press empire on 7 September. Another example was the suggestion by one member of the public that the Olympic stadium be renamed after Moshe Weinberg, the first Israeli team member to die.[78] Another citizen of the Federal Republic proposed that memorial coins be minted, the sale of which would benefit the victims' dependants.[79] A medium-sized business from Reutlingen went so far as to volunteer to cover the salaries of ten of its employees who wanted to work in Israel free of charge for two to four weeks. In a letter to the Israeli ambassador in Bonn, its management explained that "this way we want to make a small and modest contribution in order to make better known in the Federal Republic of Germany your idea, your struggle for life (*Lebenskampf*) and your problems in general."[80] Heinemann received around 400 letters from both abroad and home, most of which congratulated him for speaking out against violence and terrorism and on behalf of Israel.[81]

Some journalists and politicians even saw the chance of overcoming the legacy of the past through common mourning. As one editorial in the mass-circulation Munich paper *Abendzeitung* stated: "Historians will note that here in Munich, only a few kilometers from Dachau, at the location of a horrible crime, Germans have cried next to Israelis. From the perspective of history, the image of the Germans who mourn the dead of Israel will be a marker—a marker at the beginning of a road which one day leads two nations away from bitterness."[82] This was, by and large, also the tenor of a speech that Georg Kronawitter, Vogel's successor as lord mayor of Munich, gave at a memorial ceremony of the Munich City Council on 7 September: "We know and we understand that this [act of violence] is likely to reawaken memories of an unhappy past. But the common loathing of this crime and the hope that worldwide disgust may finally contribute to breaking the terror, brings us close together."[83]

A further integral part of this discourse was the condemnation of Palestinian terrorism and all Arab states that were enemies of Israel. Heinemann had set the stage for it with his speech at the memorial ceremony. It was taken up both by the public and by the media. Popular reactions ranged from demands for an immediate extradition of the three surviving Palestinians to Israel, to calls for an end of all aid to Arab states and the breaking off of diplomatic relations with them.[84] To be sure, the terrorist commando had conducted the attack on West German soil and the anger of the host country was certainly justified, but to interpret the hostage crisis as a declaration of war by Palestinians and their Arab allies against the Federal Republic, as Henri Nannen for example did, can only be classified as an overreaction. The founder and editor-in-chief of the left-liberal magazine *Der Stern* went so far as to demand the immediate expulsion of all citizens of Arab states from German soil, regardless of whether they had any links to extremist groups or not.[85]

A populist call like this was unnecessary, as the shock went deep for those politically responsible for law and order and their response was swift. State governments and the federal government alike immediately stepped up the "policy of inner security" (*Politik der inneren Sicherheit*) by several gears. After the arrest of the entire leadership of the Red Army Faction before the Games between 1 June and 7 July, there was a misleading sense of increased security from terrorism. After they had been proven wrong, the authorities' countermeasures included the banning of Palestinian political organizations close to the PLO,[86] the expulsion of Palestinian students, some of whom were suspected of having provided logistical assistance to the Black September commando,[87] and the foundation of GSG 9, an elite antiterrorism unit of the Bundesgrenzschutz.[88] Moreover, the federal government latched on to the public mood and made *Ausländerpolitik* a topic in its reelection campaign. After the SPD-FDP coalition was confirmed in November, life became much harder not only for the 70,000 Arabs but, with the 1973 "recruitment stop," also for the 3.4 million "guest workers" and citizens of non-EC countries living in West Germany at the time.[89]

The commemoration of the death of Police Brigadier Anton Fliegerbauer, the one German victim, also played an important role in handling the aftermath of the attack. That a German had died as well made it certainly easier to cope with the death of the Israelis. On 8 September he was given an honorary funeral by the city of Munich in the presence of more than a thousand of his colleagues and hundreds of citizens. Both Kronawitter and Alfons Goppel, the minister president of Bavaria, attended, and Brandt and Heinemann had wreaths laid on behalf of the Federal Republic. On the occasion Fliegerbauer was celebrated as a hero who had paid the ultimate price in his attempt to liberate innocent hostages from the hands of "fanatics blind with rage" (*blindwütige Fanatiker*). At the end of the ceremony, a representative of the Israeli government expressed the condolences and gratitude of the Israeli people.[90]

The conflation of real and symbolic victims was fostered by Israeli reactions like this one. Yes, initially there were angry outbursts like that of the German-born Israeli Interior Minister Yossef Burg, who remarked that from now on one would have to get used to the notion that Munich lay in the vicinity of Dachau rather than the other way round, but these were one-offs.[91] In general, however, rather than attacking the German authorities, the Israeli government heaped praise on their conduct in the media in order to both influence domestic public opinion and preserve good relations with the Federal Republic.

Jesko von Puttkamer, the German ambassador to Israel, reported to Bonn on the generally positive and restrained reaction of the local authorities. On the occasion of the return of ten of the eleven victims to Tel Aviv's Lod Airport on 7 September, Foreign Minister Abbas Eban remarked to him that in a radio address the day before he had emphasized that the German authorities had done everything in their power and that the Federal Republic had suffered a casualty itself. Moreover, Eban stressed that what mattered most was that this was the first time a Western government had reacted "in the Israeli way," that is, the German government had not succumbed to blackmail but attempted, if unsuccessfully, to liberate the Israeli citizens by force. Simon Peres in turn had thanked Puttkamer for Heinemann's speech, in particular in Golda Meir's name.[92]

Vogel, who accompanied the coffins of the murdered athletes and the Israeli team home, found similar words in a regular column he wrote for *Sportinformationsdienst* on occasion of the Games: "[N]obody blamed Munich or the Federal Republic. Nobody invoked the past. Many inquired about the dead police officer and his dependents. Nowhere did I hear the ugly word repeated that in the future Munich was in the vicinity of Dachau again."[93]

After this period of grief and anger during the first few days after the attack, people in general returned to enjoying the remainder of the sporting events.[94] Other than the Israelis, only a handful of teams and individual athletes had quit the Games, and they had done so without much fanfare. For the majority, however, it seemed unfair to both athletes and spectators to cancel the rest of the events. As the commentator for the German television evening news put it only a couple of days after the attack: "Today Munich showed itself again completely cheerful. The cityscape, the atmosphere on the sporting venues—it was as if nothing at all had happened. People in Munich but also in front of the television screens were much more interested in the speed with which Renate Stecher [a GDR athlete] ran the 200 meters than in the names of the dead Israelis—names which had hardly entered people's minds."[95]

Conclusion

So was all well and in order then? Of course, as many of the immediate reactions and statements in the aftermath of the crisis show, both the West German public and the political class were all too aware of the past-political dimension of what had happened. Brandt, for instance, initially thought that the memories the terrorist attack had reawoken were a major setback that turned back the clock for German foreign policy by many years.[96] His pessimism turned out to be largely unwarranted, as in June 1973 he became the first ever chancellor to visit Israel.[97] The importance of the Federal Republic as a friend of Israel can be seen in that the invitation was not even withdrawn when, less than two months after the terrorist attack, the three surviving members of the Black September commando were released in exchange for the hostages of a Lufthansa Boeing hijacked by Palestinians on 29 October.

In the aftermath of the Olympics the Federal Republic made one million dollars available to the families of the victims. Although this was explicitly declared to be no more than a gesture of generosity, it could also be read as admission of culpability.[98] This at least went through the mind of Daume, when he refused to make additional payments on behalf of the OC. He wrote to Vogel: "As a result of the generous donation by the Federal Government a new situation has arisen. This makes the expenditure of budgetary means by the OC no longer necessary. Too much could naturally easily create the impression of a confession of responsibility."⁹⁹

The desire to tread carefully in relation to legal claims for compensation by the dependents of the murdered Israelis, which is expressed here and which has characterized the German authorities' attitude up to the present, should not obscure the fact that in Germany it was those who had brought the Olympics to Munich, namely, Daume and Vogel, whom the events initially hit hardest. During the memorial ceremony a visibly shaken Daume stressed that "a celebration that … so clearly expressed the yearning of mankind for understanding, joy and peace, ha[d] been called into question" by the actions of Black September.¹⁰⁰ While he agreed with the continuation of the Games, he had, against the majority of the IOC Executive Committee including President Brundage, insisted that they at least be interrupted for more than just a minute of silence.¹⁰¹

Vogel, in turn, had accompanied the dead athletes home not only as the politician who had gotten Munich the Games and who saw it as his personal responsibility to honor the victims in this manner, but also because he was known in Israel for his efforts to preserve the memory of the past and promote reconciliation between Germans and Jews via regular contacts and visits between local politicians, members of the public, and youth exchanges between Munich and Israeli communes since the early 1960s.¹⁰² He had even invited a number of Israeli mayors to the Olympics at the expense of the host city.¹⁰³

While in the immediate aftermath both Daume and Vogel did little to keep alive the memory of the events of 5 September, with the passing of time their attitude changed. In 1973 the OC donated the Olympic Village building in which the hostages had been held to the Max Planck Society which still uses it as a guesthouse for its international fellows.¹⁰⁴ Had it not been for a modest plaque with the names of the murdered Israelis, installed in front of Connolly Street 31 by the Munich Jewish community and the Central Council of Jews as early as December 1972, there would have been no memorial for the victims of the attack in Germany whatsoever. Likewise, the commemorative ceremonies on the first and tenth anniversaries of the terrorist attack in the Olympic Village were low-profile events.¹⁰⁵

This changed in the 1990s. On the twentieth anniversary, Daume himself, by then almost eighty years old, participated in a memorial ceremony in the Olympic Village. This was organized by the German NOC and conducted in the presence of some of the relatives of the murdered athletes, flown in from Israel for the occasion. Three years later a representative memorial for the victims of the terrorist attack, at the cost of half a million DM, the Wailing Beam (*Klagebalken*) by sculptor Fritz König, with the names of all victims including that of Fliegerbauer, was unveiled on the Munich Olympic site.¹⁰⁶ A further memorial was inaugurated in 1999, upon the suggestion of Vogel, at Fürstenfeldbruck military airport. In his speech on the occasion, he emphasized the permanence of Jewish suffering from the Holocaust to the Olympics to late twentieth-century German anti-Semitism, as evidenced by, for instance, as many as forty-seven desecrations of Jewish gravestones in German cemeteries in 1998.[107] The continuity of Jewish suffering had also been the theme of Daume's speech during the 1992 ceremony.[108]

While this latest proliferation of memorials and commemorative ceremonies for 5 September 1972 is indicative of a shift in the cultures of memory concerning the Nazi past since the end of the Cold War and, some may say, typical for an "obsession with history," the roots of this shift lie among others in the events of the 1972 Olympics.

Notes

1. See Aaron J. Klein, *Striking Back: The 1972 Munich Olympics Massacre and Israel's Deadly Response* (New York, 2005).
2. See Fritz Göttler, "Hamlets Frieden: Die Diskussion um Steven Spielbergs 'Munich' hält an," *Süddeutsche Zeitung*, 5 January, 2006.
3. Simon Reeve, *One Day in September: The Story of the 1972 Munich Olympics Massacre* (London, 2000).
4. See Kay Schiller, "Bad but not as bad as Dachau," *Times Literary Supplement*, 22 September 2000.
5. See Alon Confino and Peter Fritzsche, "Introduction: Noises of the Past," in Confino and Fritzsche, eds., *The Work of Memory: New Directions in the Study of German Society and Culture* (Champaign, IL, 2002), 1–21.
6. See Kay Schiller, "The Presence of the Nazi Past in the Early Decades of the Bonn Republic," *Journal of Contemporary History* 39 (2004): 285–294.
7. See Robert Geipel, Ilse Helbrecht, and Jürgen Pohl, "Die Münchner Olympischen Spiele von 1972 als Instrument der Stadtentwicklungspolitik," in Hartmut Häußermann and Walter Siebel, eds., *Festivalisierung der Stadtpolitik: Stadtentwicklung durch große Projekte, Leviathan. Zeitschrift für Sozialwissenschaft,* Sonderheft 13 (1993): 278–304.
8. Peter Reichel, *Vergangenheitsbewältigung: Die Auseinandersetzung mit der NS-Diktatur von 1945 bis heute* (Munich, 2001), 110; Detlef Siegfried, "Zwischen Aufarbeitung und Schlußstrich: Der Umgang mit der NS-Vergangenheit in den beiden deutschen Staaten, 1958–1969," in Axel Schildt, Detlef Siegfried, and Karl Christian Lammers, eds., *Dynamische Zeiten: die 60er Jahre in den beiden deutschen Gesellschaften* (Hamburg, 2000), 114–146, 99–108.
9. Aleida Assmann and Ute Frevert, *Geschichtsvergessenheit / Geschichtsversessenheit: Vom Umgang mit deutschen Vergangenheiten nach 1945* (Stuttgart, 1999), 232, 245.
10. Michael Ruck, "Ein kurzer Sommer der konkreten Utopie: Zur westdeutschen Planungsgeschichte der langen 60er Jahre," in Schildt, Siegfried, and Lammers, *Dynamische Zeiten,* 362–401.
11. Helmut Dubiel, *Niemand ist frei von der Geschichte: Die nationalsozialistische Herrschaft in den Debatten des Deutschen Bundestages* (Munich, 1999), 98; Edgar Wolfrum, "Die Suche nach dem 'Ende der Nachkriegszeit': Krieg und Diktatur in öffentlichen Geschichtsbildern der 'alten' Bundesrepublik Deutschland," in Christoph Cornelissen, Lutz Klinkhammer, and Wolfgang Schwentker, eds., *Erinnerungskulturen: Deutschland, Italien und Japan seit 1945* (Frankfurt am Main, 2003), 183–197, 185.
12. Stenographische Berichte, Deutscher Bundestag, 6. Wahlperiode, 5. Sitzung, 28 October 1969.
13. On Vogel's time as Munich's lord mayor see his memoir *Die Amtskette. Meine 12 Münchner Jahre. Ein Erlebnisbericht* (Munich, 1972); on Daume see the contributions in Bundesinstitut

für Sportwissenschaft and Deutsches Olympisches Institut, eds., *Willi Daume: Olympische Dimensionen. Ein Symposion* (Bonn, 2004).

14. Hermann Lübbe, "Der Nationalsozialismus im deutschen Nachkriegsbewußtsein," *Historische Zeitschrift* 236 (1983): 579–599; Robert G. Moeller, *War Stories: The Search for a Usable Past in the Federal Republic of Germany* (Berkeley and Los Angeles, 2001).
15. Dubiel, *Niemand ist frei von der Geschichte*, 133.
16. Robert G. Moeller, "What Has 'Coming to Terms with the Past' Meant in Post-World War II Germany? From History to Memory to the 'History of Memory,'" *Central European History* 35 (2002): 223–256, 227–228.
17. Figures according to Adam Krzemiński, "Der Kniefall," in Etienne François and Hagen Schulze, eds., *Deutsche Erinnerungsorte: Eine Auswahl* (Munich, 2005), 431–446, 444.
18. Quoted in Peter Merseburger, *Willy Brandt 1913–1992: Visionär und Realist* (Munich, 2002), 615.
19. Ibid., 639.
20. Willi Daume to Hans-Jochen Vogel, 13 August 1972, Depositum Hans-Jochen Vogel, Archiv der sozialen Demokratie der Friedrich-Ebert-Stiftung Bonn (hereafter FES), 1/HJVA400099.
21. Claire and Keith Brewster, "Mexico City 1968: Sombreros and Skyscrapers," in Alan Tomlinson and Christopher Young, eds., *National Identity and Global Sports Events: Culture, Politics, and Spectacle in the Olympics and the Football World Cup* (Albany, 2006), 99–116, 99; Arif Dirlik, "The Third World," in Carole Fink, Philipp Gassert, and Detlef Junker, eds., *1968: The World Transformed* (Cambridge, 1998), 295–317, 311.
22. German Embassy Madrid to Bundeskanzleramt, 10 October 1965 (telex), Bundesarchiv Koblenz (hereafter BAK), B136/5555 (Bundeskanzleramt). On the background see Martin H. Geyer, "Der Kampf um nationale Repräsentation. Deutsch-deutsche Sportsbeziehungen und die 'Hallstein-Doktrin,'" *Vierteljahrshefte für Zeitgeschichte* 44 (1996): 55–86 and Tobias Blasius, *Olympische Bewegung, Kalter Krieg und Deutschlandpolitik 1949–1972* (Frankfurt am Main, 2001).
23. Allen Guttman, *The Games Must Go On: Avery Brundage and the Olympic Movement* (New York, 1983), 156.
24. Cornelius v. Hovora (Abt. Sport, Bundesministerium des Innern), Sprechzettel für Kabinettssitzung am Donnerstag, den 2. Dezember 1965, außerhalb der Tagesordnung. Betr.: Bewerbung der Landeshauptstadt München um die Ausrichtung der Olympischen Sommerspiele 1972, BAK/B136/5566.
25. See Hans-Jochen Vogel, Ansprache zur Eröffnung der Ausstellung "Antifaschistischer Widerstand" am 14. April 1971, FES Hans-Jochen Vogel, Reden 1971, Jan.–Juni.
26. Willi Daume to Hans-Jochen Vogel, 17 August 1972, FES 1/HJVA 400100.
27. Quoted in Heinz-Joachim Heydorn (Studienkreis zur Erforschung und Vermittlung des deutschen Widerstandes 1933–1945 e.V.) to Hans-Jochen Vogel, 21 July 1972, FES 1/HJVA 400100.
28. See, e.g., Heinz Koch et al., *München 1972: Schicksalsspiele. Eine Dokumentation über den Mißbrauch der olympischen Bewegung und ihrer Spiele durch den deutschen Imperialismus* (East Berlin, 1969); the GDR-sponsored German Communist Party (DKP) publication by Erhard Hexelschneider, Gusti Heine, and Siegfried Zeimer, *München: Stadt im Blickpunkt. Eine dokumentarische Analyse* (Frankfurt am Main, 1972); and regular defamatory commentaries and articles in *Theorie und Praxis der Körperkultur*, the GDR's main journal of sports studies from 1967 to 1972.
29. Georg Wolf, Der Polizeieinsatz im Raum München anläßlich der Olympischen Spiele 1972 (July 1971), Bayerisches Hauptstaatsarchiv München (hereafter BayHStA), MInn 88578 (Bayerisches Staatsministerium des Innern).
30. Harold Marcuse, *Legacies of Dachau: The Uses and Abuses of a Concentration Camp, 1933–2001* (Cambridge, 2001), chaps. 9 and 12.
31. Hans-Jochen Vogel to Willi Daume, 1 and 17 August 1972, FES 1/HJVA 400100 and Niederschrift über die 25. Sitzung des Vorstandes des Organisationskomitees für die Spiele der XX.

Olympiade München 1972 e.V. am 25. Mai 1972, BAK/B185/2604 (Organisationskomitee für die Spiele der XX. Olympiade München 1972 e.V.).
32. *The Official Report of the Organizing Committee for the Games of the XXth Olympiad Munich 1972, Volume 1: The Organization* (Munich, 1972), 52.
33. "Editorial," *Theorie und Praxis der Körperkultur* 18 (1969): 290–291.
34. Marcuse, *Legacies of Dachau*, 272.
35. Landespolizeidirektion Oberbayern, Erfahrungsbericht: Polizeilicher Einsatz anläßlich der Olympischen Spiele 1972, 9 January 1973, 49, BayHStA/MInn 88581.
36. Stenographische Berichte, Deutscher Bundestag, 6. Wahlperiode, 5. Sitzung, 28 October 1968. See also Niederschrift über die 2. Sitzung des Beirats des Organisationskomitees für die Spiele der XX. Olympiade München 1972 am 23. März 1970 in Munich, BAK/B185/2632.
37. Duff Hart-Davis, *Hitler's Games: The 1936 Olympics* (New York, 1986), 9.
38. Christiane Eisenberg has provided a revisionist interpretation of the 1936 Olympics that convincingly stresses the Games' relative autonomy from their later abuse by Nazi propaganda. See Eisenberg, *"English Sports" und deutsche Bürger: Eine Gesellschaftsgeschichte 1800–1939* (Paderborn, 1999), 409–429.
39. Kurzfassung der Bewerbung der Landeshauptstadt München um die Austragung der Olympischen Spiele 1972 and Address of the Lord Mayor of Munich, Dr. Hans-Jochen Vogel to the International Olympic Committee in Rome on 26 April 1966, BayHStA/StK 14030 (Staatskanzlei).
40. Barbara Schüler, *"Im Geiste der Gemordeten...": Die "Weiße Rose" und ihre Wirkung in der Nachkriegszeit* (Paderborn, 2000), 13.
41. Paul Betts, *The Authority of Everyday Objects: A Cultural History of West German Industrial Design* (Berkeley and Los Angeles, 2004), 151.
42. Ibid., 145. See also René Spitz, *The View Behind the Foreground: The Political History of the Ulm School of Design 1953–1968* (Stuttgart and London, 2002).
43. See, e.g., Otl Aicher, *Die Welt als Entwurf* (Berlin, 1991), 87–95.
44. Betts, *The Authority of Everyday Objects*, 166.
45. Otl Aicher, Das Erscheinungsbild der Olympischen Spiele München 1972 (November 1967), BAK/B185/2791 (my translation).
46. Ibid.
47. Organisationskomitee für die Spiele der XX. Olympiade München 1972, Richtlinien und Normen für die visuelle Gestaltung (June 1969), BAK/B185/3197.
48. Aicher, Das Erscheinungsbild.
49. Organisationskomitee, Richtlinien und Normen für die visuelle Gestaltung.
50. Otl Aicher, *Typographie* (Berlin, 1988), 175.
51. See Winfried Nerdinger, ed., *Frei Otto. Das Gesamtwerk: Leicht bauen natürlich gestalten* (Basle, Boston and Berlin, 2005), 227–236, 260–269.
52. Quoted in Gavriel D. Rosenfeld, *Munich and Memory: Architecture, Monuments, and the Legacy of the Third Reich* (Berkeley and Los Angeles, 2000), 155.
53. Aicher, Das Erscheinungsbild.
54. Rosenfeld, *Munich and Memory,* 155.
55. Quoted in David Butwin, "It Isn't Whether You Win or Lose But How You Stage the Games," *The Arts Saturday Review,* 25 March 1972.
56. See also Uta Andrea Balbier, "Die Eröffnungsfeier der Olympischen Spiele in München," in Johannes Paulmann, ed., *Auswärtige Repräsentationen: Deutsche Kulturdiplomatie nach 1945* (Vienna, 2005), 105–119.
57. Niederschrift über die 21. Sitzung des Vorstandes des Organisationskomitees für die Spiele der XX. Olympiade München 1972 e.V. am 8.–9. Januar 1971, BAK/B185/2604.
58. Ibid.
59. Merkblatt: Aufgaben, Ausbildung, Organisation und Arbeitsweise des Ordnungsdienstes und seine Abgrenzung zur Polizei (November 1971), BayHStA/MInn 88620.

60. Manfred Schreiber, Tätigkeitsbericht der Abt. XIII (Der Ordnungsbeauftragte) (1972), BAK/B185/3230 (my translation).
61. These were David Berger, weightlifter; Ze'ev Friedman, weightlifter; Yossef Gutfreund, wrestling referee; Eliezer Halfin, wrestler; Amitzur Shapira, track and field coach; Kehat Shorr, marksmanship coach; Mark Slavin, wrestler; Andrei Spitzer, fencing coach; and Yaakov Springer, weightlifting referee.
62. "'Mal der eine Falke, mal der andere Taube.' Spiegel-Interview mit dem Münchner Polizeipräsidenten Manfred Schreiber," *Der Spiegel*, 11 September 1972.
63. Otto Heindl (Staatsanwaltschaft bei dem Landgericht München), Einstellungsverfügung des Ermittlungsverfahrens gegen Dr. Manfred Schreiber und Dr. Georg Wolf wegen des Vorwurfs der fahrlässigen Tötung, 5 February 1973, BAK/B106/146541.
64. "'Hätte man doch Moshe Dajan geschickt.' Spiegel-Analyse der Polizeiaktion in München," *Der Spiegel*, 18 September 1972; Hans-Dietrich Genscher, *Erinnerungen* (Berlin, 1995), 155–156; and Reeve, *One Day in September*, 81.
65. Hannes Burger, "Terror und Tod: Trauer und Trotz," in Harry Valérien, *Olympia 1972: München – Kiel – Sapporo* (Munich, 1972), 28–29, 29.
66. "Hätte man doch Moshe Dajan geschickt."
67. Reproduced in *Official Report, Volume 1: The Organization*, 38.
68. Persönliches Büro (des Bundespräsidenten), Betreff: Teilnahme der Bundespräsidenten an der Trauerfeier für die Opfer des Terroranschlags während der XX. Olympiade in München, 6.9.1972, 7 September 1972, BAK/B122/15033 (Bundespräsidialamt).
69. "Weiter, weiter, weiter!—Das neue olympische Gebot," *Die Presse* (Vienna), 7 September 1972.
70. Angelika Fox, *Olympia-Attentat 1972: Begleitheft zur Errichtung der Gedenkstätte für die ermordeten israelischen Sportler und den deutschen Polizeibeamten am 5. September 1999* (Fürstenfeldbruck, 1999), 37.
71. "Trauerzug der Jugend," *Bonner Rundschau*, 8 September 1972.
72. *Official Report, Volume 1: The Organization*, 38. See Allen Guttmann, "The Games Must Go On: On the Origins of Avery Brundage's Life-Credo," *Stadion. International Journal for the History of Sport* 5 (1979): 253–262.
73. See, e.g., Fritz Wirth, "Tage des Jubels und der Tränen: Heiterkeit als Vorsatz—der Irrtum der Münchner Olympiade," *Die Welt*, 12 September 1972.
74. "Das Massaker von München: War es zu vermeiden?," *Der Spiegel*, 11 September 1972.
75. Genscher, *Erinnerungen*, 159–160.
76. Presse- und Informationsamt der Bundesregierung und Bayerische Staatskanzlei, Pressestelle der Staatsregierung, *Dokumentation über die Vorfälle in München* (Bonn and Munich, 1972), 70.
77. Heindl, Einstellungsverfügung des Ermittlungsverfahrens.
78. Otto Bammel to Hans-Jochen Vogel, 8 September 1972 (telegram), FES 1/HJVA 400099.
79. Hans-Jochen Vogel to Helmut Schulz, 12 September 1972, FES 1/HJVA 400099.
80. Wolfgang Oechßler to Eliashiv Ben-Horin, 7 September 1972, FES 1/HJVA 400099.
81. See, e.g., Bergbau AG Westfalen, Heesen, to Gustav Heinemann, with a list of signatures, 6 September 1972, BAK/B122/15033.
82. Horst Vetten, "Was bleibt von diesen Spielen?" *Abendzeitung München*, 11 September 1972 (my translation).
83. Quoted in Otto Fischer, "Gemeinsame Abscheu – gemeinsame Hoffnung," *Süddeutsche Zeitung*, 8 September 1972 (my translation).
84. See the examples in BAK/B141/30902 (Bundesjustizministerium) and B122/15033 and 15034.
85. Henri Nannen, "Wir sind im Krieg," *Der Stern*, 14 September 1972.
86. See, e.g., Der Bundesminister des Innern an die Generalunion Palästinensischer Studenten—Konföderation in der Bundesrepublik Deutschland, Verbotsverfügung, 3 October 1972, BAK/B106/146541.

87. Günther Nollau (Präsident des Bundesamts für Verfassungsschutz) to "Bild"-Chefredaktion z. Hd. Graf von Brockdorff-Ahlefeldt (answering 11 questions posed in writing), 13 September 1972 and (answers to) Weitere Fragen der "Bild"-Redakteure, no date, BAK/B106/146540.
88. Beschlüsse der Sitzung der Ständigen Konferenz der Innenminister der Länder am 13. September 1972 in Bonn, BayHStA/StK 12107.
89. See Karen Schönwälder, *Einwanderung und ethnische Pluralität: Politische Entscheidungen und öffentliche Debatten in Großbritannien und der Bundesrepublik von den 1950er bis zu den 1970er Jahren* (Essen, 2001), 595–601.
90. Heiner Müller, "Ein Opfer im Kampf gegen Gewalt," *Süddeutsche Zeitung*, 9–10 September 1972.
91. Quoted in *Die Zeit*, 15 September 1972.
92. Deutsche Botschaft Tel Aviv to Auswärtiges Amt, 8 September 1972 (telex), BAK/B141/30899.
93. Hans-Jochen Vogel, 12. Kolumne (7 September 1972): Die Botschaft von Lod, in *Olympia in München* (private reprint, no date), FES 1/HJVA400150 (my translation).
94. Thomas Meyer, "Das Publikum bekommt, was es will," *Frankfurter Allgemeine Zeitung*, 8 September 1972.
95. Thilo Koch, "Nach dem Sturm" (ARD-Tagesschau-Kommentar vom Bayerischen Rundfunk), 7 September 1972, BayHStA/StK 14041 (my translation).
96. Quoted in "Worte der Woche," *Die Zeit*, 15 September 1972.
97. Merseburger, *Willy Brandt 1913–1992*, 682–684.
98. See, e.g., Niederschrift über die 27. Sitzung des Vorstandes des Organisationskomitees für die Spiele der XX. Olympiade München 1972 am 14. September 1973, BAK/B185/2604.
99. Willi Daume to Hans-Jochen Vogel, 27 September 1972, FES 1/HJVA400100 (my translation).
100. *Official Report, Volume 1: The Organization*, 38.
101. "Spiele ohne Staat—das geht nicht mehr," Spiegel-Gespräch mit dem Olympia-Organisator Willi Daume über das Massaker in München, *Der Spiegel*, 11 September 1972.
102. See, e.g., Hans-Jochen Vogel, Bericht über die Israel-Reise in der Zeit vom 19.3.1964 bis 31.3.1964 (April 1964), FES Hans-Jochen Vogel, Reden 1963–1964 and Anthony D. Kauders, *Democratization and the Jews: Munich 1945–1965* (Lincoln, NE, 2004), 212–214, 216.
103. Hans Steinkohl to Dr. Kessler, 27 June 1972, BayHStA/StK 14033.
104. Direktorium-Verwaltungsamt (der Stadt München), Betreff: Olympisches Dorf; Verwendung des Hauses Connollystr. 31, 11 December 1973, Stadtarchiv München, Olympiade 1972/601.
105. See Martin Rehm, "Hört auf mit diesem sinnlosen Morden!" *Süddeutsche Zeitung*, 6 September 1973 and Walter Maria Skarba, "Kampf dem politischen Verbrechen," *Süddeutsche Zeitung*, 6 September 1982.
106. Fox, *Olympia-Attentat 1972*, 44–45.
107. Hans-Jochen Vogel, "Stichworte für eine Ansprache anläßlich der Übergabe einer Gedenkstätte für die Opfer des Anschlags vom 5. September 1972 in Fürstenfeldbruck," in Fox, *Olympia-Attentat 1972*, 73–75, 74–75.
108. Commemorative Address by the President of the National Olympic Committee, Mr. Willi Daume, Willi Daume Archiv, Deutsche Olympische Akademie Willi Daume, 5, 40 Sportpolitik, 1992 Sportausschuß/MBI, Ablage zur deutsch-israelischen Gedenkfeier in München, A Allgemein.

Chapter 7

WHEN COLD WARRIORS DIE
The State Funerals of Konrad Adenauer and Walter Ulbricht

Paul Betts

It has long been commonplace to associate twentieth century Germany with the specter of mass death that so dramatically disfigured the so-called Age of Extremes. Over the decades Paul Celan's famous line that "death is a master from Germany" has become a favorite mantra for invoking Germany's preeminent place at the slaughter bench of twentieth century history. Such attitudes certainly colored the judgments at Versailles and Nuremberg, and have continued to inform academic and popular perceptions of the country ever since. But despite the twentieth century German experience of mass destruction, recurrent political upheaval, and radical social engineering, it may be a little surprising to recall that German state leaders rarely met bloody fates themselves. Although a good many of them were either the architects or direct beneficiaries of mass violence, all remained remarkably untouched by the waves of assassination, public execution, and/or post-regime change trials that marred political life in much of Europe since the end of the First World War. In Germany's case, by contrast, the Kaiser abdicated and went into exile, while the Weimar Republic's chancellors—however threatened—all died of natural causes. Peaceful ends also punctuated the lives of post-1945 leaders, ranging from Adenauer, Erhard, Kiesinger and Brandt in the Federal Republic on the one hand, to Ulbricht and Honecker in the GDR on the other. Of course, the newly established League of Nations energetically pressed to extradite the Kaiser as a war criminal; Honecker too, if it weren't for his ill-health, was to stand trial for "crimes against the people." Hitler most obviously would surely have faced summary justice from the Allies, whether in the form of instant execution by the Soviets or a post-Nuremberg Trial hanging by the Western Allies. The point, though, is that none of it came to pass. The Kaiser

---

Notes for this chapter begin on page 173.

died peacefully in Holland; Honecker expired in Chile; and Hitler took his own life. The unlikely result was that no twentieth century German head of state was either assassinated or tried for past misdeeds.

This is plainly not to suggest that key twentieth century German leaders did not meet tragic ends. The killing of Walter Rathenau, Rosa Luxemburg, Karl Liebknecht, and Ernst Röhm are only the most famous in an unsavory roster of twentieth century German political assassinations. Furthermore, the political martyrdom of those who died for supposedly greater causes, be they Horst Wessel, Stauffenberg, the Scholl-Siblings, Ernst Thälmann, Benno Ohnesorg, and perhaps even the "unknown soldier," underline the extent to which the fallen have loomed large in Germany's twentieth century social imagination. Little scholarly attention, however, has been paid to state funerals, with the exception of Volker Ackermann's 1990 *Nationale Totenfeiern in Deutschland: Von Wilhelm I bis Franz Josef Strauss*. This is quite unfortunate, not least because the country underwent such dizzying political transformation over the century. After all, Germany was the only country that experienced the full spectrum of twentieth century political forms—from constitutional monarchy to democratic socialism, fascism to Soviet-style socialism to Western-style liberalism. With each new government came the need to announce the end of the old regime and in turn mint new and necessary traditions, broadcasting founding narratives of both change and continuity to an uncertain and at times hostile public. That many of these new German regimes were born of revolution, extreme violence, and "cultures of defeat" made these new state self-representations all the more urgent for political stability and legitimacy.

This was especially the case after 1945, as each rival German republic desperately set out to distance itself from both the Third Reich and its Cold War counterpart. How the great and the good of each German state were to be memorialized in funeral ceremonies took on special symbolic importance at the time. But here again, little scholarship has been devoted to the topic. Ackermann's book focuses primarily on the period 1871–1945, with only passing references to Cold War era state funerals. In this essay, I compare the state funerals of Konrad Adenauer and Walter Ulbricht as a means of exploring each state's political culture. While they remained bitter ideological enemies, each leader was hailed as the father of his respective German republic. What made both of these particular funerals so interesting is the fact that both countries expressed a discernible uncertainty about how to bury their first post-fascist political patriarchs. What values and messages were to be imparted? Should the past be invoked as a means of placing the leaders into a well-established pantheon of great leaders, or should the occasion serve as a means of constructing a new postwar canon of German national heroes? If these leaders were to be buried as citizen-leaders, then how were the ceremonies to bridge the gap between leader and led?

"The Greatest German Statesman since Bismarck"

Let us begin with Adenauer. The West German chancellor died on 19 April 1967. The week before he had suffered his fourth heart attack, and he lay in a coma for days before finally passing away. Given Adenauer's old age and deteriorating health, funeral arrangements had been prepared well in advance by Adenauer's long-time friend and then-serving Bundespräsident, Heinrich Luebke. For Luebke, the great "architect of the Federal Republic" deserved a special ceremony, one that went beyond the more subdued recent state burials for Theodor Heuss and Erich Ollenhauer.[1] The problem, however, was the absence of any useful precedent on which to draw. Bismarck's funeral—following his specific instructions—was emphatically low-key, largely because the Iron Chancellor did not wish his wake to be exploited by the grandstanding Kaiser Wilhelm II. The kaiser himself died with modest fanfare in Dutch exile in 1941, while Ebert and Stresemann's funerals were relatively low-profile state affairs.[2] In fact, Germany's most elaborate modern state funeral up to this point had been Hindenburg's send-off in 1934.[3] But reproducing such goosestepping pageantry and Prussian pomp was anathema to Luebke, who wanted to bury Adenauer in a manner befitting Golo Mann's remark that Adenauer ruled not as a Junker, but as a "hard-working burgher."[4] And if Churchill was right that Adenauer was the "greatest German statesman since Bismarck," then how best to honor him accordingly?

Significantly, Luebke looked abroad to commemorate West Germany's first chancellor. The clear model was the state funeral held two years before for Churchill, whose state interment was the first for an English commoner since Gladstone in 1898. Churchill's funeral ceremony was divided into two parts: it began with a lying-in-state in Westminster Hall for four days, as some 300,000 people queued to pay their tributes; his coffin was then drawn to St. Paul's Cathedral, passing Whitehall, the Strand, and Fleet Street along the way, a spectacle that was watched by some 350 million television viewers worldwide.[5] Reportedly Luebke spent weeks studying the film footage of the Englishman's funeral and labored to fashion Adenauer's in a similar manner. Luebke was particularly enamored by the idea of staging part of the funeral in a traditional cathedral as well as a "ceremonial passage along a great river and the final burial in a modest country cemetery."[6] On Luebke's explicit instructions, there would be little military pageantry, and no undue pomp or death-mask memorial.

So what happened? On the morning of 22 April, six officers of the Federal Frontier Guard carried the coffin out of Adenauer's private residence in Rhöndorf and escorted it across the Rhine to Bonn, where it was put on display in the cabinet room of the Palais Schaumburg until the next evening (Figs 7.1 and 7.2). Journalists reported that many "tens of thousands" of citizens filed by in great solemnity to bid farewell. A valedictory speech was delivered that evening, and again at every stage of the nearly week-long funeral proceedings. The second evening's ceremony concluded with the orchestra playing "Poco Adagio Cantabile"

Figure 7.1. Border Guard Officers escorting Adenauer's coffin from his private residence in Rhöndorf, Germany. Source: *Der Spiegel*, 19/1967, p. 42. Courtesy of Bildarchiv, Preussischer Kulturbesitz, Berlin

Figure 7.2. Konrad Adenauer Lying-in-State in the Great Cabinet Hall, Cologne, Germany, 1967. Source: *Abschied von Konrad Adenauer* (Bonn, 1967), 25. Courtesy of Bildarchiv, Preussischer Kulturbesitz, Berlin

from Haydn's *Kaiserquartet,* which forms the basis of the *Deutschlandlied.* The next day the coffin was taken to Cologne Cathedral, where it remained for another full day to allow residents of Adenauer's hometown to pay their last respects. During the day numerous international dignitaries arrived, among them French President Charles De Gaulle, US President Lyndon B. Johnson, British Prime Minister Harold Wilson, and former Israeli Prime Minister Ben-Gurion. That evening the Pontifical Requiem was celebrated in the Cologne Cathedral, with Adenauer's old friend Cardinal Frings presiding (Figs. 7.3 and 7.4). The requiem

Figure 7.3. Adenauer Lying-in-State, Cologne Dome, Cologne, Germany, 1967. Source: *Der Spiegel,* 19/1967, p. 46. Courtesy of Bildarchiv, Preussischer Kulturbesitz, Berlin

Figure 7.4. Adenauer Lying-in-State, Cologne Dome, Cologne, Germany, 1967.
Source: *Abschied*, 41. Courtesy of Bildarchiv, Preussischer Kulturbesitz, Berlin

was explicitly designed to invoke the German-French amity celebration at Reims Cathedral five years earlier, which culminated in the 1963 Treaty of Friendship between the two countries. On this occasion no fewer than twenty-five heads of state were on hand, accompanied by a throng of one hundred ambassadors and a large assortment of politicians, generals, civic notables, and cardinals. Once the mass was finished, the coffin was carried down to the banks of the Rhine. It was then draped with the Bundeswehr flag, loaded on to a motorboat, and ferried back upstream to Rhöndorf "past thousands who stood in silence on both banks of the river." By the time the coffin was transported back from Bad Honnef to Rhönsdorf, many more thousands had gathered; as the coffin reached the small cemetery, a town choir sang farewell and Adenauer's son, Monsignore Paul Adenauer, read a few intimate prayers for Adenauer's kin and closest friends.[7]

What are we to make of all this? First of all, never before had a German funeral featured so many foreign heads of state; not since Bismarck's Congress of Berlin in 1878 had so many foreign leaders gathered on German soil. (Even the Soviet Embassy in Bonn flew its flag at half-mast for the occasion.) To be sure, such massive funerals had become a distinctive feature of Cold War politics across the Iron Curtain. The 1963 Kennedy funeral was laden with political pomp and circumstance, and featured representatives from ninety-two countries; Churchill's burial in 1965 departed from English understatement in its grandeur, with delegates from no less than one hundred and ten countries in attendance. Stalin's death in 1953 was of course a huge Soviet spectacle in its own right, as was Mao's Chinese send-off a generation later. While these twentieth century mega-funerals had their roots in Queen Victoria's lavish funeral in 1901, they took on a new dimension during the Cold War in the battle to stage historical pathos, national heroism and political accomplishment.[8]

Adenauer's funeral was distinctive in this regard. For one thing, it departed from the twentieth century German trend toward the secularization of state burials. Whereas an Imperial Court Lutheran minister presided over every Wilhelmine-era state funeral, for example, the Reichskanzler assumed this function during the Weimar Republic. Such a shift was very much in keeping with the Weimar Republic's social democratic thrust, and in particular the desire to honor its constitutional separation of church and state.[9] The combination of state and religious elements in Adenauer's commemoration thus reflected a key element of West German political culture, as the country's first chancellor was expressly buried as a "Christian and democrat."[10] The military presence was also quite delicate given the Nazi legacy. Of the 134 state funerals that took place in Germany between 1871 and 1989, over half of them (70) were celebrated during the Third Reich as part of the regime's broader death cult and "commemoration culture" honoring fallen Party leaders and loyalists. A great deal of military pageantry surrounded these burials, usually with Goebbels or Hitler delivering the funeral oration personally. But the "democratization" of state funerals was hardly an invention of the Third Reich; in fact, the Weimar Republic had organized a state funeral for the thirteen workers killed by French occupying forces in the 1923 Ruhr strikes as martyrs to the republic. Yet it was really under the Third Reich that state funerals became regular events to reaffirm political solidarity, national heroism, and military mission, often extended to remember young Nazi activists (such as Horst Wessel) who died for the cause.[11]

Unsurprisingly, the Federal Republic took great pains to distance itself from this legacy.[12] Not only were state funerals now strictly limited to established political leaders, but the country's two most celebrated state funerals before Adenauer's (for Heuss and Ollenhauer) consciously refrained from having any military presence whatsoever.[13] At other state ceremonies, too, the West German military kept a very low profile. In a 1951 speech, Bundestag President Hermann Ehlers identified this as one of the new republic's great virtues, citing the Federal Republic's lack of a cult of fallen soldiers as proof of the German people's healthy antipathy toward the Nazi-era worship of violence.[14] Adenauer nonetheless wished to have a small military presence on hand, though he made it clear that this was to be the Federal Frontier Guard (*Bundesgrenzschutz*), and not the *Bundeswehr*, since it was the protection of West German borders and sovereignty that was for him the main issue at stake.

Adenauer's funeral was unique in other ways as well. On the one hand, it was clearly conceived as a kind of last journey through the main stations of Adenauer's life: from his hometown of Cologne, where he eventually became mayor, to Petersberg Mountain, where he concluded the pact with the occupying forces, to Bonn, from where he ruled half of Germany, and then finally back home. On the other, the ceremony was calculated to showcase Adenauer's prized policy successes. In particular the cumulative effect was to demonstrate his work in achieving West German sovereignty and rearmament, Western European integration, reconciliation with the French, close alliance with America, good relations with Israel, as well as affirming the CDU's strong belief in "Christian social order" as the bedrock of postwar peace and recovery. With it the long-standing images of the "hated German" and pariah-like status of the country had apparently been overcome, what one journalist called the postwar's true "political miracle" to go alongside the country's more famous economic wonder.[15] The funeral thus served to underscore the point that relations with Germany's former enemies in the West had been repaired, in effect healing the political wounds of the Second World War.[16]

The presence of Ben-Gurion was crucial in this respect. In this case, Ben-Gurion was repaying his old friend the favor of a state visit. Here it is worth recalling that in May 1966 Adenauer journeyed to Israel on Ben-Gurion's invitation. The visit was the first by a (in this instance, former) German head of state since the founding of Israel, and it unleashed vociferous anti-German demonstrations. There was even a "deliberate act of discourtesy" from Ben-Gurion's successor, Levi Eschkol, who failed to show up for a party thrown in honor of the former West German chancellor after a disagreement about Eschkol's speech the evening before, when the Israeli prime minister intoned that Adenauer's so-called "policy of making good on the past" (*Wiedergutmachung*) "only represents a symbolic restitution of the bloody robbery [of our people]. There is no expiation for the atrocity and no consolation for our mourning."[17] But even this was smoothed over in the press, as Adenauer's visit was widely seen as a crowning episode in his long-desired reconciliation with Israel.[18] Ben-Gurion's journey to Germany to honor Adenauer was thus another big symbolic step in the reconciliation between West Germany and Israel, even if its significance—as Ben-Gurion complained—found little echo in the more general reflections of Adenauer's achievements in West German speeches and the mainstream press.[19] As Ben-Gurion put it to one reporter: "If I were German, I would be very proud."[20] And on this occasion, Eshkol sent his condolences, praising Adenauer that among his "most noble personal ambitions" had been to own up to Germany's responsibility for Nazi crimes against the Jews.[21]

But the politicking did not stop there. In fact, the funeral itself was also crafted to help repair fraying Western solidarity. To this end, Luebke exploited the opportunity to have Johnson and De Gaulle, who had not met since Kennedy's funeral, shake hands in front of journalists so as to affirm that the Western alliance was alive and well. The event also brought Johnson and Chancellor Kiesinger together for the first time and gave them a chance to discuss their growing differences over Europe and Vietnam. Like Bismarck at the Congress of Berlin, Adenauer was still brokering European politics—even at his own funeral. As one reporter noted with discernible exacerbation, Adenauer the eternal politician was still engaging in politics even from "beyond the grave."[22] Willy Brandt, too, mocked the CDU politicking at Adenauer's gravesite as a "working funeral."[23]

No less significant was the celebration of the fallen German leader as above all a civilian. In fact, *Der Spiegel*'s lead article on Adenauer's death was entitled "Der Zivilist." However much Adenauer had been criticized for West Germany's NATO policies and rearmament, the *Spiegel* reporter made no bones about Adenauer's greatest contribution having been to "lead the Germans with energy and dignity to a consciousness of national modesty (*nationale Kleinheit*)," all the while showing "Germans, of all people, that a civilian can also possess a straight spine."[24] Chancellor Kiesinger made a similar point in his funeral oration, lauding Adenauer for proving to Germans that "decisive political leadership and respect for democratic-parliamentary order can be and are united."[25] American historian Gordon Craig perhaps put it most starkly in saying that Adenauer "was the first German statesman who was able to overcome the unconscious tendency of his countrymen to believe that leaders could only be taken seriously when they wore uniforms."[26]

For this reason, there was little looking back to the past during the commemoration. Typically Adenauer was praised for representing "the continuity of democratic, lawful [*rechtsstaatlichen*] thinking and European sensibilities, which had been disrupted by the Nazis."[27] Historical references to past German leaders were noticeably muted. Rather, Adenauer was stylized as a kind of Great Redeemer of the unnamed crises of the first half of the century.[28] Bundestag President Eugen Gerstenmaier summed it up by saying that "over his predecessors from this century hang the shadows of tragedy and failure. From this he brought Germany fortune and honor."[29] Fortune and honor, however, played second fiddle to the most frequent terms used to describe the Adenauer era: restored trust and self-confidence.[30] Virtually every politician from Erhard to Brandt stressed Adenauer's success in making "Germany respectable again" his signal accomplishment.[31] One

English biographer went even further, describing his legacy mainly in terms of restoring "the self-respect of over 50 million Germans after an era of unparalleled self-deception and degradation, culminating in total defeat ... He broke away from the long-established traditions of hysteria and hate, of gods and demons dominating the German scene. He gave the German people a long overdue dose of commonsense, as well as *das kleine Habe*—a decent competence in material well-being."[32] As such Adenauer's accomplishments were repeatedly painted in terms that went far beyond the workings of Metternich and Talleyrand,[33] to the extent that his legacy combined political regeneration, diplomatic trust, and moral regeneration in the shadow of Nazism and the war.

Yet this event was not simply limited to shrewd statecraft. After all, it triggered enormous public interest and press coverage. True, the mass media were no strangers to German state funerals. Stresemann's funeral, for example, was broadcast over the radio and received worldwide coverage; Nazi-era state funerals were also given lavish media attention and even featured in the "Wochenschauen" programs in cinema houses.[34] Still, this was a unique event in West German history. On this occasion, the newspapers *Die Zeit* and *Die Welt* sold record numbers for their special edition on Adenauer's death; *Der Stern* printed no fewer than 2 million copies of its illustrated special issue. Radio stations played only funeral or classical music on the day that the death was announced, since pop music and comedy programs were judged inappropriate.[35] What is more, never before had a German funeral been so widely televised; thanks in part to the great number of television crews hailing from as far as the United States and Japan, the procession was reportedly viewed by some 400 million people around the world. Hastily prepared biographies, souvenirs, and sundry memorabilia were rife. Virtually every West German city renamed a major street or square in his honor; Adenauerdamm and Adenauer Platz became new fixtures across the country. Everywhere it was reported that the "nation was in sorrow," indicating that the country had some "ability to mourn" after all. How deep or widespread these feelings were is of course impossible to say for sure. Yet it was widely reported that over 180,000 citizens filed past Adenauer's coffin in Bonn and Cologne, while many more waited for hours along the banks of the Rhine to watch the funeral entourage sail by.[36] Poll results show that Adenauer's popular reputation as a great leader increased over his tenure. In response to the question "In your opinion, which German has done the most for Germany?" Adenauer lagged way behind Bismarck and even Hitler in a 1952 poll; by 1958 he had surpassed Bismarck as Germany's most accomplished German leader ever. Over fifty percent of those polled in 1958 even placed Adenauer "among the really great men of our century."[37]

But not everyone extolled Adenauer's glory. The follow-up *Der Spiegel* issue, for example, was filled with disgruntled letters to the editor taking issue with the embarrassing "emotional outpouring of our people." Some criticized the press for overlooking Adenauer's failure to bring about reunification; others objected to the way that commentators downplayed Adenauer's legacy of "economic chaos and the diplomatic isolation of the Bundesrepublik." Still others condemned the *Spiegel* itself for having abandoned its usual critical edge by "participating in the 'excesses' of Adenauer's funeral coverage."[38] It certainly was true that the news magazine's usual biting commentary on Adenauer and his policies, to say nothing of the hard assessment of the chancellor in Rudolf Augstein's edited 1962 book, *Konrad Adenauer,* had gone missing this time.[39] Popular protests also erupted in Berlin over decisions to change Kaiserdamm to Adenauerdamm; over a thousand citizens took to the street to make clear that they would rather "live with the Prussian emperor than with the Rhenish chancellor"[40] (Fig. 7.5).

If nothing else, such actions dramatized that there was no universal adulation, and that there were still strong regional differences of memory and loyalty. But even so, the funeral on the whole was a great success as a spectacle of West German achievement and long-sought self-respect. This was even more evident in the foreign coverage, which was invariably laudatory. For all of these reasons, one West German journalist was certainly justified in claiming that "it was probably the most ostentatious interment of modern German history, certainly—by virtue of Johnson's presence—the politically most important on German soil."[41]

Figure 7.5. Demonstrators on Adenauerdamm, Berlin, 1967. Source: *Der Spiegel,* 19/1967, p. 50. Courtesy of Bildarchiv, Preussischer Kulturbesitz, Berlin

"Ein Professor Unrat der Revolution"

Ulbricht's funeral was of course a different matter. Before his death on 1 August 1973, his health had deteriorated noticeably since handing over the reins of power to Erich Honecker in 1971 so his final collapse caught no one by surprise. How then did the state greet the death of its founding father? For if it was true, as Sebastian Haffner famously said, that Ulbricht was actually the "most successful German ruler since Bismarck" by virtue of his nearly twenty-six years in power, then how did the GDR send him off? With as little fanfare as possible, was the SED's initial answer. As it happened, East Berlin was hosting the World Youth Festival that week, and no effort was made—allegedly following Ulbricht's personal request—to cancel or delay the festivities on account of his death. Yet even the news of his death was barely publicized: announcements were delayed for hours, and radio and television stations did not even interrupt their programs until later that night. When they did, there was scant reporting beyond simply noting his passing.[42] One West German reporter covering the festival was amazed that no one seemed to care in East Berlin or anywhere else in the country: "The youth of the GDR and from other socialist countries simply go on as before."[43] Even if the next day's *Neues Deutschland* ran Ulbricht's death as its lead story, the language was remarkably reserved and formulaic.[44] Honecker's GDR hardly seemed in mourning, official or otherwise.

On one level, this comes as no great surprise. It is well known that Ulbricht had become a kind of *Unperson* after leaving office. He had fallen out with the Soviet Union over *Ostpolitik* and economic policies, and was seen as out of touch with contemporary concerns. Like so many other fallen Eastern Bloc leaders, Ulbricht was subject to a reversed cult of personality and airbrushed marginalization. The once-ubiquitous label of the GDR as the "Ulbricht-State," or even Honecker's 1961 remark that "Walter Ulbricht is all of us" ("Walter Ulbricht, das sind wir alle") had become distant memories. Already before leaving office, Ulbricht's long-familiar quotations were expunged from official publications, Party literature, and school textbooks; his published work on the history of the German communist movement were removed from all public libraries and dropped from citation; factories, schools, and public buildings bearing his name were now renamed; and stamps featuring his face were discontinued and destroyed. His presence was explicitly ignored by the cameras in Central Committee proceedings,[45] and his face and name—which enjoyed daily presence in East German mass media over the years—summarily vanished from national newspapers and television screens.[46] Even the stadium used to host the World Youth Festival—formerly known as Walter-Ulbricht-Stadium—was rechristened for the occasion as the World Youth Stadium.

Much of this was naturally the result of Honecker's campaign to isolate and undermine Ulbricht after taking power. In part this was due to Ulbricht's unwillingness to surrender his hold on GDR politics. Despite increasing health problems, for example, Ulbricht insisted on staying on as part of the Politburo Steering

Committee and retaining his post as head of the National Defense Committee. With increasing intensity Honecker worked to discredit his predecessor, at one point passing around Ulbricht's medical file at a Central Committee conference in September 1971 so as to expose Ulbricht's physical incapacity to continue to serve. Such strategies to cut him down to size were even broadcast to the nation, when Honecker used unflattering footage of his predecessor accepting an award on the occasion of his seventy-eighth birthday to drive home the point of Ulbricht's physical frailty and political powerlessness (Fig. 7.6). While he made sure to wear more appropriate garments for his eightieth birthday celebration, the official photograph of the event conveyed the same message of the sitting broken leader.

Figure 7.6. Erich Honecker Congratulating Walter Ulbricht on the Occasion of his 78th Birthday, 30 June 1971, Berlin. Source: Mario Frank, *Walter Ulbricht: Eine deutsche Biographie* (Berlin: Berlin Taschenbuch, 2003), 455. Courtesy of Bildarchiv, Preussischer Kulturbesitz, Berlin

Ulbricht, for his part, fought hard against the Party's new tendency to blame him for everything and to exclude the SED's former First Secretary from politics altogether. He was especially angered at not being invited to the fifty-fifth anniversary festivities of the Great Socialist October Revolution in 1972, writing first to Honecker about this affront and then to Brezhnev about the injustices inherent in the now-common belief that "Everything's Ulbricht's fault."[47] Ulbricht even stormed aboard the GDR's state yacht in 1972 with the aim of making his case to state guest Fidel Castro about his poor treatment at the hands of his successors. So bothersome was Ulbricht by the end that Honecker felt obliged to encharge Stasi Chief Erich Mielke with assigning Ulbricht a personal guard to make sure that such indelicacies never happened again. Officially in the name of health and safety, Ulbricht was essentially quarantined at Wandlitz for the last year of his life.[48]

But Ulbricht's political death was more than just a power struggle at the top. Alone the terms used by Honecker to isolate Ulbricht were quite revealing. In one special October 1971 Central Committee session devoted to resolving this embarrassing *primus inter pares* dispute, high-ranking party members openly took issue with Ulbricht's excessive regard for his own power. Kurt Hager, for instance, criticized the perceived "infallibility of Comrade Ulbricht," while Werner Krolikowski was quick to add that "[i]n our Party there are neither saints nor popes, Comrade Ulbricht." In another party conference speech a few months earlier, Honecker had argued that there were "certain comrades, who have forgotten the value of criticism and self-criticism. They think of themselves as wiser than the collective. They can't countenance any constructive contradictions, and see themselves as infallible and untouchable."[49] Underlying all of these statements was the desire to break from the Stalin era's cult of personality, and to return power back to the Party in a post-Stalinist spirit. Yet they were also designed to shore up Honecker's political legitimacy. Newspaper coverage of Ulbricht's death downplayed his former centrality and once-invincible authority. Repeatedly Ulbricht was represented "on the side of" and "aligned with" other founding figures such as Grotewahl and Pieck. The first sentence in the cover story on Ulbricht's death in *Neues Deutschland* said it all in describing the founder of the republic as above all "an outstanding functionary."[50] This was an image that perfectly accorded with Honecker's preferred image of his predecessor, one conveying Ulbricht's lack of power and importance.[51]

Such politicking was in part intended as a gesture of solidarity with the Soviet Union, in that a muted funeral ceremony would help distance Honecker's GDR from the politics of autonomy that Ulbricht championed at the end of his career.[52] What was so interesting, however, was the Soviet reaction. Brezhnev was reportedly shocked by the SED's disrespectful coverage of Ulbricht's death, and wanted a proper state ceremony honoring his central political role and loyalty over the years. Such sentiment was already apparent in the Soviet recommendations for celebrating Ulbricht's eightieth birthday, which ended up being his last public appearance.[53] In full regalia at the state government building on Marx-Engels Platz, Ulbricht was decorated with the GDR's "Great Star of International

Friendship" (*Grosser Stern der Volkerfreundschaft*) and the Soviet Union's "Medal of International Friendship." *Pravda* honored him with a front-page story and elaborate congratulations from Brezhnev. Again, GDR coverage was much more muted. While *Neues Deutschland* dedicated a front-page laudatory story to the event, television coverage conveyed the image of a broken old man, whose soft words of gratitude were rendered inaudible to viewers.[54]

For his death, however, Moscow made sure that Ulbricht was given a proper state funeral. Now Ulbricht's singularity and achievements took center stage. All GDR public buildings were instructed to fly their flags at half-mast. Condolences from governments and leaders all over the world were reprinted in *Neues Deutschland*,[55] along with reprinted extracts from Honecker's speech, in which the fallen former leader was now hailed as "one of the great proletariat revolutionaries, as well as a distinguished leader of our Party and working class."[56] Delegates (though notably no heads of state) from all of the Warsaw Pact countries, along with the USSR's Präsidium Chairman Podgorny, flew out to East Berlin to pay their respects, while a delegation of Soviet leaders—including Brezhnev—made a high-profile visit to the East German embassy in Moscow to pay their respects.

The funeral procession was also instructive. Ulbricht's casket was draped with a GDR flag, and his numerous commemorative honors and medals were displayed alongside his coffin. The front side of the SED's Great Hall of Parliament was adorned with a huge portrait of Ulbricht, while ten huge wreaths were hung behind the coffin. SED leaders—Honecker, Willi Stolph, and Friedrich Ebert—served as pallbearers (Fig. 7.7). The national hymn was played, followed

Figure 7.7. Erich Honecker, Friedrich Ebert and Willi Stoph Accompanying Ulbricht's Coffin, Berlin, 1973. Source: *Neues Deutschland,* 8 August 1973, p. 1. Courtesy of Bildarchiv, Preussischer Kulturbesitz, Berlin

by the second verse of Beethoven's Third Symphony. A short speech by Honecker was followed by the International. An honorary formation of the People's Army, together with eight generals, hoisted the coffin onto a military transport truck, and drove it through the streets of East Berlin toward the crematorium (Figs. 7.8 and 7.9). His widow Lotte led the procession, as members of the People's Army played "Undying Victim" (*Unsterbliche Opfer*), long the standard funeral march of the worker movement. Once the train had reached the crematorium, the band replayed the International amid the sounds of the twenty-one gun salute. Six weeks later his cremated remains were interred at Berlin's Friedrichfelde cemetery for socialist notables alongside Wilhelm Pieck, Otto Grotewahl, Rosa Luxembourg, Karl Liebknecht, Ernst Thälmann, and Franz Mehring. Unlike Khrushchev or many other Eastern Bloc leaders who fell out of favor along the way, Ulbricht's name was not forgotten, even if his place in public life was systematically erased. In fact, he was the only Eastern Bloc leader to survive both the Stalinist purges of the 1950s and de-stalinization reform waves of the 1960s.[57] That Ulbricht's ashes were buried at Berlin's Friedrichfelde cemetery amid such communist luminaries attests to his unusual fortune. The efforts in the 1950s and 1960s by Johannes Becher's Culture Ministry to place Ulbricht in the pantheon of German communist figures—as Becher once put it, "Karl Liebknecht's will emanates from you, while Thälmann's eyes shine out from your face"[58]—seem to have succeeded against all odds.

Even so, the funeral proceedings were hardly a great emotional affair. As Western observers noted, Ulbricht's funeral looked more like duty than devotion. After all, Ulbricht was never a greatly loved figure. He was most admired for his Prussian diligence, work habits, and remarkable memory for names and administrative details. So colorless was he that Carola Stern opened her 1965 biography with the words: "Is Walter Ulbricht worth a biography? His life is devoid of great passions or petty vices. He is dull, compared to other dictators; he lacks Stalin's demonism, Hitler's hysteria, or Khrushchev's earthiness. Most of the time, he did not even originate the policies he carried out. For many years, I have read his speeches and articles, discussed his politics with others, and always come to the same conclusion: as that merciless Viennese critic, Karl Kraus, would have written, 'I can't think of a thing to say about him.'"[59] Contemporaries too expressed great misgivings about Ulbricht over the decades. In the early 1920s, Clara Zetkin supposedly remarked: "May destiny prevent this man from climbing to the top of the Party. One look into his eyes is enough to tell how suspicious and dishonest he is." Older communist comrades liked to mock him as "Professor Unrat der Revolution." Even Thälmann himself once quipped that "Ulbricht is and will always remain a bureaucrat."[60] Other more contemporary Eastern Bloc leaders such as Novotny constantly mocked the East German as a "Red Prussian" completely out of touch with reform needs across the satellite states.[61]

But what about the people? Events at the funeral certainly indicate that Ulbricht had more popular support than the SED either expected or desired. While Ulbricht was never the object of great popular affection, a good many

Figure 7.8. Ulbricht's Funeral Procession, Berlin, 1973. Source: *Neues Deutschland,* 8 August 1973, p. 1. Courtesy of Bildarchiv, Preussischer Kulturbesitz, Berlin

citizens voiced their dissatisfaction with his rude banishment after Honecker's takeover. Many people reacted very angrily to the photograph depicting Ulbricht on his seventy-eighth birthday in bathrobe and house slippers, calling their local television stations as well as the Central Committee headquarters about the wholly inappropriate nature of the image.[62] As one Ulbricht biographer put it, the reaction was "one of the few instances that evoked sympathy for Ulbricht." But this was nothing compared to the outpouring at the funeral itself. By eight o'clock that morning a line of people "a kilometer long" stretched from Karl-Marx Platz to the Lustgarden. The ceremony had to be delayed several times because so many people were on hand to bid farewell to their former leader.[63] A good number of people also laid private wreaths next to official ones at the beginning of the ceremony.[64] One West German reporter noted that many East Berlin shops had pasted clipped-out newspaper pictures of Ulbricht in shopwindows, since pictures of the former leader—once ubiquitous and everywhere available—were no longer in supply.[65] Why? As Western journalists on hand rightly sensed, this outpouring of support was revealing. What they were forced to conclude was that over the years GDR citizens did warm to Ulbricht, as the declining hopes for reunification gave rise to a renewed loyalty to the state and its leadership. In this way, Ulbricht seemed to be the beneficiary of this 1960s boom in "East German self-consciousness," a kind of East German version of the West German "Wir sind wieder wer" restored pride born of relative economic affluence, political partnership with the USSR, and growing worldwide recognition of the GDR as a serious political entity.[66]

What can we say about these comparative funeral events? For one thing, they were quite unusual in that unlike other state funerals, there was little linkage between death, nationalism, and ancestor worship. While both figures were clearly seen as founders of the country, scarcely any effort was spent situating them in longer elective lineages. This was particularly true in Adenauer's case: scant mention was made of any other German leader, with the exception of Bismarck as a negative counterfoil. Hitler's spirit was clearly ever-present in both cases, but remained all but unnamed. That Adenauer began and ended his funeral journey at his home residence was indicative; in the end, the former chancellor was buried in a small cemetery alongside family members, not in a state cemetery surrounded by past political notables. A remarkable amount of funeral coverage was devoted to recalling Adenauer's role as father and family man,[67] replete with images of him playing boccia, tending his rose garden, or flanked by his grandchildren.[68] The high-profile funeral of the Federal Republic's founding father ended with his interment as simply a private citizen hailed for his public service

Figure 7.9. Ulbricht's Funeral Procession, Berlin, 1973. Source: Frank, 467. Courtesy of Bildarchiv, Preussischer Kulturbesitz, Berlin

and Christian devotion. While it is true that Ulbricht was ultimately buried in the GDR's state cemetery alongside the great German communist leaders of the twentieth century, this was clearly not the way the GDR media commemorated the event. Instead, he was remembered first and foremost as an "outstanding functionary" and "worker son," with little reference to great communists past. Both leaders were therefore hailed for their public service, but were oddly cut off from any public past. Admittedly, Adenauer was raised as an "exemplar whose legacy served to encourage and warn."[69] But his link to the present was more one of a witness from the past than shaper of the future. Ulbricht, by contrast, was not figured as part of the present or future at all. His biographer Manfred Frank may ultimately be correct in asserting that his name is "inseparable from history of communism in Germany. His legacy was the GDR. The end of this legacy occurred sixteen years later after his death, on November 9, 1989, with the fall of the Wall."[70] But no one put his life in any larger context at the time; in this sense, both Cold War German patriarchs were buried as singular figures distinguished by their great public service to the state, not the nation.

It is tempting to say at this point that such treatment was the typical result of two cultures little versed in hero worship. But that of course is not quite right. Political festivals and hero worship were common features of socialist culture in general from the 1930s on,[71] and the GDR clearly created its own version of it.[72] To be sure, the prototype of the GDR hero had changed over the decades from antifascists to everyday "heroes of labor" and then to sports figures.[73] Such shifts found corresponding expression in GDR state funerals, which—unlike their West German state counterpart—honored both political (Pieck and Grotewahl) and cultural (Brecht, Arnold Zweig, and Anna Seghers) figures.[74]

By the early 1960s, Ulbricht also benefited from the changing official ideal of the socialist hero. The new GDR hero, as articulated in a week-long 1964 debate in *Neues Deutschland,* was no longer the transcendent figure of special blessings and extraordinary qualities, but rather an "ordinary person" distinguished by hard work and achievement. In this spirit, the 1960s image of Ulbricht was restylized as more human and humble, as less a fear-inspiring state leader than the "son and father of the people."[75] His vocational training as a furniture maker was repeatedly emphasized as further evidence of his worker roots, proximity to the people, and practical spirit. His image took on an especially avuncular tone after the death of Ulbricht's rival socialist patriarch, Wilhelm "Papa" Pieck. The country's popular first (and last) president, Pieck was affectionately regarded as the people's "most important *Ansprechspartner,*" in large measure because he oversaw the GDR's famed "citizen complaint" system (*Eingaben-System*). When he died, Ulbricht quickly created a new State Council (*Staatsrat*) as a go-between institution, whose main brief included processing the thousands upon thousands of citizen petitions as quickly and fairly as possible. As a consequence, Ulbricht's popular image as a guardian of the people and champion of their concerns was strengthened.[76] Little wonder that at his seventy-fifth birthday celebration in 1968, when Ulbricht was arguably at the peak of his power, he was hailed more earthily as "the state's supreme furniture maker" (*erster Tischler seines Staates*) and "confidence man of the people."[77]

As for Adenauer, there was virtually no hero worship. While West German hero worship was all but reserved for select heroes such as the 20 July 1944 group, the Scholl-Siblings (though of course this was always more official than popular), and the members of the 1954 World Cup Champion soccer team, the press's relentless efforts to cut Adenauer down to size through political criticism were taken as proof of West Germany's healthy democratic culture. With this one might say that the cult of personality took on different forms on each side of the Berlin Wall. Over most of his career Ulbricht was hailed as the embodiment of Marxist progress, the Party's will and the agent of History writ large. This was certainly the case with his ubiquitous media and cultural presence in the 50s and 60s; however, his funeral underlined his ultimate status as an *Unperson,* a symbolic figure with no bearing on the present. The wheels of history were grinding on without him; more precisely, he was in the way. Adenauer, by comparison, enjoyed no saintly status while living—yet in death his stature was elevated as "the architect of the Federal Republic," a "republican patriarch" of Germany, Europe, and the Christian West.[78] This even found expression beyond West Germany. Two months before his death, Adenauer journeyed to Franco's Spain, where he was regally feted as the "Grand Old Man of Europe," something all the more touching to him given his lifelong fascination with Charles V of Spain as the last ruler of Catholic Europe.[79] But this kind of adulation was not something he enjoyed back home. Such popular appreciation came only after his death, as the funeral made clear. This too inadvertently underlined the Federal Republic's decidedly democratic credentials and liberal political culture. As Sidney Hook observed in his 1940 *The Hero in History*: "If we were to list as heroes the event-making men of the past, we should find few of them in the histories of democratic societies. It is in conformity with the genius of democratic society that this should be so. There is great wisdom in the notorious political ingratitude of democratic communities. They usually refuse to glorify their leaders until they are dead."[80]

Put differently, one might say that both funerals marked the normalization of politics in each country. There was neither any succession intrigue, nor any real political turmoil at either ceremony. In each case, the successor was firmly in place and the political system stable. While both had been out of power a few years before expiring, each man's party remained ascendant. So unlike in 1945, the "death of the father" did not signal the end of political authority.[81] That both ruled for so long meant that neither funeral was suffused with the pathos of broken dreams. In contrast to interwar political funerals, there was a noticeable absence of narratives of victimhood and danger, aggrieved nationalism, and unfinished business. Whatever one thinks of "chancellor democracy" or SED consolidation, political stability and legitimacy had been achieved. As a result, their deaths did not—and did not need to—serve as occasions of political nation-building in the face of imagined dangers; each state was already well-established, with no great political threat in sight. For this reason their deaths were not construed as tragic, nor were they transposed into metaphors of the nation. Granted, they were both buried as emblems of a "better Germany" that had re-emerged from the ashes of fascism. But they were not buried as heroes in the traditional sense, not least because hero worship feeds on collective feelings of insecurity and crisis.[82] They were honored above all as public servants dedicated to peace and reconstruction, political stability, and material well-being. This was a far cry from Wilhelmine triumphalism or Nazi-era chauvinism; on the contrary, each funeral was designed to underscore each Germany's secure place within a larger international order. The amount of coverage devoted to reporting the conspicuous presence of international guests and superpower patrons—above all, Johnson and the Western allies for West Germany, the Soviet and Eastern Bloc delegations for East Germany—perfectly illustrated this point.

No less significant were the effects of the Cold War. What is most striking about each state funeral is the complete lack of hostile Cold War rhetoric about the other Germany at each funeral. To be sure, Ulbricht's death was an occasion for hostile criticism by West German journalists. One *Die Welt* reporter probably went furthest in saying that "[b]oth were murderers, Ulbricht and Hitler, the one on a small scale, the other on a grand. Both destroyed their Fatherlands, the one from hubris, the other on assignment [from Moscow]."[83] The Berlin Wall was often mocked as Ulbricht's true "place of honor" (*Ehrenplatz*) in West German political cartoons (Fig. 7.10). Adenauer's death, by contrast, went largely unreported in the East German media. Instead, the main reporting of the day was given over to the opening of the SED's Seventh Party Congress and the death of Russian cosmonaut Vladimir Komarov in the Sojus 1 air disaster. Still, a short

Figure 7.10. Newspaper Cartoon, "Ehrenplatz," or "Square of Honor" (Artist: Hicks). Source: *Die Welt*, 3 August 1973. Courtesy of Bildarchiv, Preussischer Kulturbesitz, Berlin

statement was issued by the GDR newsagent AGN, stating that Adenauer's "life work was against the interests of the German nation" by "cementing German division" through the Federal Republic's NATO membership.[84] There was no mention of the GDR at Adenauer's funeral, nor any words about the FRG at Ulbricht's either. In part this was because each funeral was designed to reaffirm divided Germany's divided place within a larger international order, as the early Cold War idea of a shared German nation transcending geopolitical division had been abandoned by both sides. These were first and foremost state funerals, scripted to celebrate state achievements. On display was precious little ancestor worship or mystical nationalism associated with the fallen patriarchs.[85] The link to the nation had been fully severed, and it is perhaps this that accounts for the funerals' oddly officious tone, lack of "will to metaphor," and paucity of historical allusion. The "pre-political values" of Volk, *demos*, and sacred community played virtually no role here—this was the apotheosis of the postnational state. In the end, the two German politicians most responsible for divorcing state and nation got the funerals they desired and deserved.

Notes

I would like to thank Jeannine Fiedler for her research assistance on this article.

1. The phrase "Baumeister der Bundesrepublik Deutschland" was often used in the newspaper coverage of the funeral. See for example the headlines above Carlo Schmid, "Ein Denkmal seiner Zeit," *Die Zeit* 21 April 1967. Willy Brandt also referred to Adenauer as the "Architekten der Bundesrepublik Deutschlands" in a radio broadcast in honor of the former chancellor's life and career. See *Abschied von Konrad Adenauer, 19. April 1967,* special issue of the *Bulletin der Presse- und Informationsamtes der Bundesregierung,* Nr. 41 bis 44 (Bonn, 1967), 11.
2. See for example, Felix Hirsch, *Stresemann: Ein Lebensbild* (Göttingen, 1978), 252–268.
3. John W. Wheeler-Bennett, *Hindenburg: The Wooden Titan* (London, 1967), 468–470 and Volker Ackermann, *Nationale Totenfeiern in Deutschland: Von Wilhelm I. bis Franz-Josef Strauss* (Stuttgart, 1990), 67–73.
4. Golo Mann, "Der Staatsmann und sein Werk: Auszüge aus einem Artikel zum Rücktritt des Bundeskanzlers Adenauer im Oktober 1963," *Die Zeit,* 21 July 1967.
5. Geoffrey Best, *Churchill: A Study in Greatness* (London, 2001), 226–227.
6. Charles Williams, *Adenauer: The Father of the New Germany* (New York, 2000), 537.
7. Williams, *Adenauer,* 538.
8. Queen Victoria's funeral is discussed in Christopher Hibbert, *Queen Victoria: A Personal History* (London, 2000), chaps. 65–66. More generally, John Plunkett, *Queen Victoria: First Media Monarch* (Oxford, 2003).
9. Ackermann, *Nationale Totenfeiern,* 19, 40.
10. "Konrad Adenauer gestorben," *Frankfurter Allgemeine Zeitung,* 20 April 1967, 1.
11. Sabine Behrenbeck, *Der Kult um die toten Helden: Nationalsozialistische Mythen, Riten und Symbole 1923 bis 1945* (Vierow bei Greifswald, 1996).
12. Peter Reichel, *Politik der Erinnerung: Gedächtnisorte im Streit um die nationalsozialistische Vergangenheit* (Munich, 1995).
13. Ackermann, *Nationale Totenfeiern,* 19–93, 292.

14. Sabine Behrenbeck, "Between Pain and Silence: Remembering the Victims of Violence in Germany after 1949," in Richard Bessel and Dirk Schumann, eds., *Life After Death: Approaches to a Cultural and Social History of Europe during the 1940s and 1950s* (New York, 2003), 49, 58.
15. "Als Freund geachtet—als Gegner gefürchtet," *Der Tagesspiegel,* 21 April 1967, 3.
16. Luebke's funeral speech is reprinted in *Abschied von Konrad Adenauer,* 5–7.
17. To which Adanauer shot back: "Wenn guter Wille nicht anerkannt wird, kann daraus nicht Gutes entstehen." The whole incident is recapitulated in Hans-Peter Schwarz, *Adenauer: Der Staatsmann, 1952–1967* (Stuttgart, 1991), 968.
18. Williams, *Adenauer,* 534.
19. This omission was noted by Josef Mueller-Marein, "Die Woche des Abschieds: Am Sarge Adenauers vereint: Staatsmänner und Bürger, Freunde und Gegner," *Die Zeit,* 28 April 1967, 2. An exception can be found in "Gedenksitzung im Abgeordnetenhaus," *Der Tagesspiegel,* 20 April 1967, 2.
20. "Wenn ich Deutscher wäre…" *Der Spiegel* 19 (1967), 36.
21. *Abschied von Konrad Adenauer,* 52.
22. Hans Gresmann, "Aus gegebendem Anlass…: Die weltpolitischen Begegnungen in Bonn und Köln," *Die Zeit,* 28 April 1967, 1.
23. Ackermann, *Nationale Totenfeiern,* 73.
24. "Der Zivilist," *Der Spiegel* 18 (1967): 26.
25. Kiesinger's speech is reprinted in *Abschied von Konrad Adenauer,* 25.
26. Gordon Craig, *The Germans* (New York, 1982), 44.
27. "Konrad Adenauer gestorben," 1.
28. Notably, it was not the Angel of Death who was embossed on the gravestone, but rather the Figure of the Resurrection. A bright bench and flowers were added as well, giving the whole scene a feeling of "transcendent optimism." Hermann Schreiber, "Konrad Adenauers letzte Worte: 'Kein Grund zum Weinen,'" *Der Spiegel* 18 (1967): 34.
29. Quoted in *Abschied von Konrad Adenauer,* 8.
30. On this theme see Karl Christian Führer, "'Aufmerksamkeit' und 'Vertrauen' als Kategorien der Mediengeschichte," in Bernd Weisbrod, ed., *Die Politik der Öffentlichkeit—Die Öffentlichkeit der Politik: Politische Medialisierung in der Geschichte der Bundesrepublik* (Göttingen, 2003), 151–174 and Ute Frevert, ed., *Vertrauen: Historische Annäherungen* (Göttingen, 2003).
31. Gresmann, "Aus gegebendem Anlass," 1.
32. Terence Prittie, *Konrad Adenauer, 1867–1967* (London, 1972), 312, 315–316.
33. Gösta von Uexküll, *Konrad Adenauer im Selbstzeugnis und Bilddokumenten* (Reinbek bei Hamburg, 1976), 120.
34. Ackermann, *Nationale Totenfeiern,* 59, 17.
35. "Musik in Moll," *Der Spiegel* 18 (1967): 49.
36. "Hunderttausend an Adenauers Sarg," *Süddeutsche Zeitung,* 25 April 1967, 3.
37. Erich Peter Neumann and Elisabeth Noelle, *Statistics on Adenauer: Portrait of a Statesman* (Allensbach, 1962), 137–150.
38. These excerpts are culled from "Briefe," *Der Spiegel* 19 (1967), 5. For a general discussion of the relationship between Adenauer and the media, see Karl-Günther von Hase, ed., *Konrad Adenauer und die Presse* (Bonn, 1988).
39. Rudolf Augstein, *Konrad Adenauer* (London, 1964 [1962]).
40. "Adenauer-Strassen," *Der Spiegel* 19 (1967): 50.
41. "Ein Stück von Haydn," *Der Spiegel* 19 (1967): 27.
42. Mario Frank, *Walter Ulbricht: Eine deutsche Biographie* (Berlin, 2003), 464.
43. "Lesen Sie mal Marx, Herr Dutschke: Peter Brügge über die Deutschen beim Weltjugendfestival in Ost-Berlin," *Der Spiegel* 32 (1973): 47.
44. "Das Kämpferleben des Genossen Walter Ulbricht hat sich vollendet: Nachruf," *Neues Deutschland,* 2 August 1973, 1.

45. Norbert Podewin, *Walter Ulbricht: Eine neue Biographie* (Berlin, 1995), 485.
46. "Ulbricht: Am Ende ein Hauch von Tragik," *Der Spiegel* 32 (1973): 32–33.
47. Ulbricht's letter to Honecker is reproduced in Jochen Staadt and Monika Deutz-Schroeder, eds., *Teurer Genosse: Briefe an Erich Honecker* (Berlin, 1994), 12; the letter to Brezhnev is quoted in Podewin, *Ulbricht*, 486–487.
48. Podewin, *Ulbricht*, 477.
49. Frank, *Walter Ulbricht*, 456–457, 452.
50. "Das Kämpferleben," *Neues Deutschland*, 1.
51. Frank, *Walter Ulbricht*, 465.
52. Frank, *Walter Ulbricht*, 462.
53. "Zentralkomitee der SED gratuliert Genosse Walter Ulbricht: Herzliche Glückwunsch zum 80. Geburtstag," *Neues Deutschland*, 30 June 1973.
54. Frank, *Walter Ulbricht*, 464.
55. "Kondolenzen zum Ableben Walter Ulbrichts," *Neues Deutschland*, 7 August 1973, 1–4.
56. "Ehrung und letztes Geleit für Genossen Walter Ulbricht," *Neues Deutschland*, 8 August 1973, 1.
57. Wolfgang Leonhard, "Walter Ulbrichts langer Marsch," *Die Zeit*, 10 August 1973.
58. The original ran: "Karl Liebknechts 'Trotzdem' aus dir weiterspricht, das Auge Thälmanns blickt durch dein Gesicht." Quoted in "Ulbricht: Am Ende," 34.
59. Carola Stern, *Ulbricht: A Political Biography*, trans. Abe Farbstein (London, 1965), v.
60. All of these quotations are taken from "'Ein Professor Unrat der Revolution'; Zeitgenossen über Walter Ulbricht," *Der Spiegel* 32 (1973): 34.
61. Carola Stern, "'Wenn nötig, unter Druck setzen': Ulbricht und der Ostblock," *Der Spiegel* 32 (1973): 38.
62. Podewin, *Ulbricht*, 474.
63. Frank, *Walter Ulbricht*, 466.
64. Frank, *Walter Ulbricht*, 468.
65. "Ulbricht mit militärischem Gepränge beigesetzt," *Frankfurter Allgemeine Zeitung*, 8 August 1973.
66. "Ulbricht: Am Ende," 39.
67. See for example the comments by CDU Leader Barzel, as reprinted in "Konrad Adenauer gestorben," 1, and Hans-Werner Graf Finck von Finckelstein, "Deutschlands grosser alter Mann," *Die Welt*, 20 April 1967, 2.
68. "Konrad Adenauer," *Der Tagesspiegel*, 20 April 1967, 1, and Claus Heinrich Meyer, "Mensch und Mythos, Politiker und Patriarch," *Süddeutsche Zeitung*, 20 April 1967, 3.
69. Quoted in *Abschied von Konrad Adenauer*, 17.
70. Frank, *Walter Ulbricht*, 468.
71. The practice of decorating new "heroes of labor," for example, first began in the Soviet Union in 1934. Silke Satjukow and Rainer Gries, "Zur Konstruktion des 'sozialistischen Helden': Geschichte und Bedeutung," in their edited *Sozialistische Helden: Eine Kulturgeschichte von Propagandafiguren in Osteuropa und der DDR* (Berlin, 2002), 15.
72. Monika Gibas, "'Auferstanden aus Ruinen und die Zukunft zugewandt!' Politische Feier und Gedenkstage der DDR," in Sabine Behrenbeck and Alexander Nützenadel, eds., *Inszenierung des Nationalstaats: Politische Feier in Italien und Deutschland seit 1861/1871* (Vierow bei Greifswald, 2000), 191–220.
73. Maoz Azayahu, *Von Wilhelmplatz zu Thälmannplatz: Politische Symbole im öffentlichen Leben in der DDR* (Gerlingen, l991).
74. Ackermann, *Nationale Totenfeiern*, 28.
75. Rainer Gries, "Die Heldenbühne der DDR: Zur Einführung," in Satjukow and Gries, *Sozialistische Helden*, 84.
76. Ina Merkel, ed., *Wir sind doch nicht die Meckerecke der Nation! Briefe an das Fernsehen der DDR* (Berlin, 2000), 21.

77. "Ulbricht: Am Ende," 41. The phrase "Vertrauensmann des Volkes" was first used to describe to Ulbricht by Otto Grotewahl in his lead article celebrating Ulbricht's seventieth birthday in 1963. Grotewahl, "Vertrauensmann des Volkes," *Neues Deutschland*, 20 June 1963, 1–2.
78. Schwarz, *Adenauer,* 980.
79. "Der Zivilist," 29; Williams, *Adenauer,* 535; and Schwarz, *Adenauer,* 972–973.
80. Sidney Hook, *The Hero in History: A Study in Limitation and Possibility* (London, 1945), 161.
81. John Borneman, "*Gottvater, Landesvater, Familienvater*: Identification and Authority in Germany," in his edited *Death of the Father: An Anthropology of the End in Political Authority* (New York and Oxford, 2004), 63–95. See too Sergio Luzzatto, *The Body of Il Duce: Mussolini's Corpse and the Fortunes of Italy,* trans. Frederika Randall (New York, 2005).
82. The classic discussion is Thomas Carlyle, *On Heroes, Hero-Worship and the Heroic in History* (London, 1872). See too Peter Berghoff, *Der Tod des politischen Kollektivs: Politische Religion und das Sterben und Töten für Volk, Nation und Rasse* (Frankfurt am Main, 1997).
83. Herbert Kremp, "Das Erbe Ulbrichts," *Die Welt,* 3 August 1973. See too "DDR-Staatsratsvorsitzender Walter Ulbricht gestorben," *Die Welt,* 2 August 1973.
84. "Der Anteilnahme am Tod Konrad Adenauers," *Frankfurter Allegemeine Zeitung,* 20 April 1967, 4.
85. Compare Katherine Verdery, *The Political Lives of Dead Bodies: Reburial and Postsocialist Change* (New York, 1999).

Part III

SUBJECTIVITY

Chapter 8

A COMMON EXPERIENCE OF DEATH
Commemorating the German-Jewish Soldiers of the First World War, 1914–1923

Tim Grady

Some four weeks after the Nuremberg Laws had irreparably altered the lives of Germany's Jewish population, the Nazi regime turned its attention to the Jewish dead. In October 1935, Joseph Goebbels's Ministry for Enlightenment and Propaganda issued a decree targeting the public commemoration of the Jewish soldiers killed fighting for Germany in the First World War. According to the ministry's statement, the names of the Jewish war dead should no longer be displayed alongside those of non-Jews on German war memorials.[1] In some areas, but by no means all, the decree was rigorously applied and the names of the Jewish soldiers were carefully chiseled out of public remembrance sites.[2] After 1945, the effects of this officially sanctioned attack on the Jewish war dead were gradually reversed. Only in the early 1960s, however, were the first concerted efforts to restore the Jewish war dead to non-Jewish memorial sites undertaken in the Federal Republic.[3]

The Jewish war dead may have been reintegrated into Germany's memorial culture, but they still remain largely absent from the historiography of the war. A boom in remembrance studies from the early 1980s onward has paid almost no attention to the commemoration of Germany's Jewish soldiers of the First World War. The first historical studies to focus on the remembrance of the war, as opposed to the history of war itself, mainly explored the politics of war memory.[4] Where these studies have considered the German-Jewish war dead, they have viewed them mainly as objects of German anti-Semitism.[5] George Mosse's pathbreaking study of the myths of the war experience exemplifies this approach. Wartime accusations of Jewish shirking, argued Mosse, led to the exclusion of

---

Notes for this chapter begin on page 192.

German Jews from veterans' organizations and commemorative activity after the conflict. For Mosse, this agitation reached "its logical … conclusion" when the Nazi regime removed Jewish names from public war memorials in 1935.[6]

In the mid to late 1990s, a second wave of historiography began to view the remembrance process as being driven less by the political machinations of different interest groups and more by a fundamental need to mourn the war dead.[7] Influenced largely by the work of Jay Winter, a number of these studies highlighted the centrality of personal grief to memorial practices.[8] This conceptual shift, however, did little to alter perceptions of the Jewish war dead. They remained a separate, marginalized group. Winter, for example, suggests that during the interwar years, German veterans obscured the sacrifice of their Jewish comrades.[9] It seemed that German Jews had no need to mourn their loved ones killed in the war. Even in the most recent historiography, which has sought to bridge the gap between political and psychological approaches to war memory, the German-Jewish servicemen of the First World War still remain separated from the non-Jewish soldiers killed in German uniform.[10]

Yet to ignore the German-Jewish soldiers killed in the conflict is to disregard the war's very real impact on ordinary German Jews. This article argues, firstly, that the sheer scale of wartime death had a deep emotional impact on all sections of German-Jewish life. From a prewar population of 550,000 almost 100,000 Jewish servicemen fought for Germany, and some 12,000 of them were killed.[11] The death of every single Jewish soldier had a profound effect on a great number of people. Each soldier left behind friends and family who had to cope without a father, husband, son, or brother. German Jews, as with Germany's non-Jewish population, were forced to try to transcend their horrific losses. They attended remembrance services, prayed for their war dead, and dedicated permanent war memorials. In many German cities, First World War memorials for the Jewish war dead can still be observed in Jewish burial grounds and communal buildings.[12]

By refocusing the history of the conflict onto the Jewish war dead, this article also provides an alternative narrative of the war's impact on Germany's Jewish communities.[13] Its second and most significant contention is that in commemorating the war dead, relations between Jews and non-Jews initially remained close. Ironically, this becomes clear from the Nazi regime's attempt to "Aryanize" non-Jewish remembrance sites in 1935. As Rudy Koshar rightly argues, the desecration of these memorials was a part of the regime's policy of racial purification.[14] Yet this is only half of the picture. For the regime to have taken this action, it must also imply that up until this point the Jewish and non-Jewish war dead had been commemorated together in the same remembrance sites. This argument runs counter to a set of historiographical approaches that suggest that the war marked a negative turning point in German Jewish/non-Jewish relations.[15] As Paul Mendes Flohr maintains, for many Jews the conflict marked a "critical moment in the crystallisation of a new direction to their Jewish identity."[16] In the existing historiography, then, the turmoil of the First World War effectively led many German Jews to return to a separate Jewish subculture.[17]

Without dismissing the obvious social, cultural, and political changes that followed the First World War, this article challenges the notion that the conflict led to an immediate and complete turning point in Jewish/non-Jewish relations. Focusing primarily on the cities of Hamburg and Würzburg, it argues instead that in many areas Jews also crossed religious and ethnic divides to remember the war dead together with non-Jewish Germans. Although these two local case studies cannot possibly capture all facets of the German remembrance process, they do, nonetheless, reflect some of Germany's regional, religious, and socioeconomic diversity. Besides the underlying structural differences of the cities—rural Würzburg was mainly Catholic, while industrial Hamburg had a predominantly Protestant population—there were also clear variances between the Jewish communities. For example, Würzburg's Jewish population, at just over 2,000, was much smaller and far less influential than the 19,000 German Jews living in Hamburg.[18]

The mass mobilization of men that followed the outbreak of hostilities in August 1914 laid the foundation for this entangled remembrance process. Although there were, of course, a multitude of Jewish and non-Jewish war experiences, many aspects of the conflict affected all sections of German society equally. In particular, as the war took an increasingly bloody course, almost all Germans, whether Jew or non-Jew, had to confront mass death. The process of transcendence brought people together into small communities of mourning. As these communities tended to be formed from small preexisting groups, such as schools, workplaces, or sports clubs, Jews and non-Jews often mourned their war dead together. After the war, this overlapping remembrance process continued. In many places, war memorials commemorated both the Jewish and non-Jewish soldiers killed in the war. It was only in the early to mid 1920s, as newly formed veterans' organizations began to dominate remembrance activity, that this entangled commemorative process began to break down.

From the *Burgfrieden* to the *Judenzählung*

Recent studies into the outbreak of hostilities in August 1914 have highlighted the diversity of German public opinion.[19] Although some people gathered in Berlin, sang patriotic songs, and cheered the onset of war, not all Germans shared this initial euphoria. Support for the conflict differed between town and city, men and women, and age groups.[20] Understandably, for many people the outbreak of war brought with it fears of change, as well as uncertainty about the future. Nonetheless, as a total war, the conflict could not simply be ignored.[21] From the start, it intruded into the everyday lives of all sections of Germany's Jewish and non-Jewish populations: daily routines changed, men were mobilized for the front, and people died in battle.

On 4 August 1914, speaking before an assembled group of parliamentarians, Kaiser Wilhelm II sought to gain the support of the entire German population for the war. To great applause, he proclaimed that from then on he would no longer recognize parties, he knew only Germans.[22] For many German Jews, the Kaiser's famous *Burgfrieden* (civil truce) speech appeared to assure them of their position within a nation unified in defense against an external enemy. Cologne's *Israelitisches Gemeindeblatt* declared optimistically that the dangers that had led to discrimination against Jews during the years of peace were now forgotten.[23] Convinced of the benefits that could be accrued from the war, and of course fearing the repercussions of not supporting it, the main Jewish organizations called on their members to fight for Germany. The largest of Germany's Jewish associations, the Centralverein deutscher Staatsbürger jüdischen Glaubens (CV) pledged its wholehearted support for the conflict, while even the main Zionist organization, the Zionistische Vereinigung für Deutschland (ZVfD), printed a call to arms.[24]

A number of prominent Jewish intellectuals also added their own voices to this clamor of support for the war. The theologian and Zionist Martin Buber declared that in the conflict all soldiers would fight together for their Judaism, while in Berlin the philosopher Hermann Cohen argued that the war revealed the strength of a long-standing cultural symbiosis between Germans and Jews.[25] As with wider German society, however, a small minority of intellectuals openly expressed their reservations to the conflict. Albert Einstein became a committed pacifist, while the young Gershom Scholem argued that the Jews should not be concerned with Germany's war.[26] Interspersed among German Jewry's support of the conflict, then, were also a few prominent voices of dissent.

Nonetheless, as a total war, even those German Jews who opposed the onset of hostilities had to live with the conflict in their midst. As Scholem later recalled, the war profoundly affected everyone, including those like himself "who had an entirely negative attitude towards its events."[27] The war intruded into even the most mundane aspects of daily life in various and unexpected ways. At Hamburg's Talmud-Tora school, the directors proudly reported that its "pupils live and mingle with the daily events." The classroom walls were festooned with maps of the main battlefields so that the pupils could follow the course of the conflict.[28] Jewish associational life was also disrupted by the outbreak of fighting. In Cologne, the city's Jewish reading room was used as a temporary home for Belgian refugees, while the hall belonging to the Jewish gymnastics association was requisitioned for military training.[29]

The mass military mobilization of men, of course, had a much greater effect on people's everyday lives. The size of the army increased steadily until there were on average 6.3 million men serving in German uniform, a figure that included almost 100,000 German Jews.[30] With such large numbers at the front, almost all Germans had a personal interest in the course of the war. The fear that loved ones could be killed or injured dominated many people's lives.[31] Many newspapers, including the main Jewish weeklies, attempted to address these concerns by printing soldiers' letters from the front (*Feldpostbriefe*).[32] The first letters published generally presented the war in bellicose terms. The Zionist *Jüdische*

Rundschau printed a letter from a lightly wounded soldier who hoped to return to action as quickly as possible: "It is ghastly to sit here idly, when my comrades have to fight hard" at the front.[33] By late 1914, however, many of these letters had become increasingly ambivalent in their discussion of the war. A small selection in the newsletter of a Berlin Zionist youth group, the Herzl-Bund, even replaced mention of Germany's heroic struggle with a discussion of anti-Semitism in the trenches.[34]

As the fighting dragged on, cracks in the *Burgfrieden,* which had been visible from the very start of hostilities, also became more acute. Growing food shortages, rationing, and the centralization of economic controls all served to drain the population's morale.[35] At the same time, many right-wing groups and individuals increasingly began to accuse German Jews of shirking their patriotic duty.[36] What in late 1914 had started as minor criticisms of German Jewry had by 1916 developed into a sustained anti-Semitic campaign against the Jewish communities' contribution to the war effort. German Jews were labeled war profiteers, accused of taking easy jobs behind the lines and of being poor soldiers.[37] The Prussian war ministry also received a stream of letters that attacked Germany's Jewish population for supposedly securing themselves cozy jobs behind the lines.[38] In October 1916, the ministry finally succumbed to the pressure of these growing complaints. It ordered a census of Jewish soldiers (*Judenzählung*) to ascertain how many were actually serving at the front. The commanders of all German army units were instructed to complete a questionnaire listing how many Jews were currently on active military service.[39]

The results of the count were never released. Nonetheless, for many German Jews the census understandably caused much consternation. In the Reichstag, Ludwig Haas (Deutsche Demokratische Partei) argued that the war ministry's actions demeaned the Jewish soldiers at the front, while the main Jewish press strongly condemned the count.[40] Most fervently, the Zionist *Jüdische Rundschau* called it "a flagrant abuse of the honour and of the civic equality of German Jewry."[41] Many historical accounts of the German-Jewish experience have come to place even greater significance on the census, as signifying the prevalence of wartime anti-Semitism and marking the growing estrangement of German Jews from mainstream German society.[42] This was the moment, as Christhard Hoffmann suggests, when the "rift between Christians and Jews … was opened up again."[43]

While these accounts are correct to stress the inflammatory nature of the census, it is important to recognize that it did not suddenly end German Jews' involvement in the conflict. With the war ongoing, Jewish soldiers, of course, continued to fight in large numbers at the front. The month after the census, Emil Heilbronner, a 24-year-old German Jew from Munich, could report to his family that he had been hailed a hero for saving the lives of several members of his regiment.[44] After more than two years of grim fighting, though, many Jewish and non-Jewish soldiers had far less enthusiasm for the war. When the Berliner Georg Luft was transferred from barracks duty to the Eastern Front in December

1916, he complained bitterly about the move. "I would especially like to return to Bojanowo," wrote Luft, "as I really don't enjoy the life etc here."[45]

More significantly, as Jewish soldiers remained at the front, they continued to face the very real prospect of death, injury, or mutilation on a daily basis. Indeed, the number of German soldiers killed in the fighting, whether Jew or non-Jew, continued to rise steadily. In 1918, almost two years after the army's census of Jewish combatants, both Heilbronner and Luft were dead. Heilbronner was killed in July 1915 in France, and Luft died from wounds sustained in the field in October of the same year.[46] Although the Jewish census finally ended the supposed internal unity of the *Burgfrieden,* German Jews and non-Jews alike lost their lives in the fighting for the remainder of the conflict. The war, which had started with such an upsurge in patriotism, had rapidly descended into a theater of mass death.

Wartime Communities of Mourning

During the war, grief was an all too common experience. Every soldier killed at the front had loved ones at home who somehow had to overcome their loss. Even Gershom Scholem, who had rejected the war from the start, had to cope with the experience of irreplaceable loss: his brother Werner was wounded on the Eastern Front in 1916, while one of his closest non-Jewish school friends was killed on the frontline.[47] Although much of the grieving process took place in the private sphere and as such is hard to uncover, forms of public mourning were also widespread. Crucially, in many areas of public life Jews and non-Jews came together to mourn their loved ones.

In Germany, the idea of a heroic and glorious death underpinned the dominant wartime discourse on military death. Relatives were to be proud of their loved ones for "having taken part and sacrificed in a noble cause."[48] A standard letter of condolence from the Prussian war ministry asked families to take comfort from the knowledge that in "the defence of the German fatherland" their loved one had suffered a "hero's death" fighting "on the field of honour."[49] During the war, notions of a dutiful and gentle death also permeated common modes of mourning. Black-framed obituaries, for example, which filled the pages of Jewish and non-Jewish newspapers alike, tended to reflect death as a sacred event. These short entries recorded the heroic sacrifice of soldiers at the front who had "fallen on the field of honour" or suffered "a hero's death for the fatherland."[50]

For many people, though, the thought that their loved ones had died a dutiful death in the service of their country did little to allay their personal sense of grief. Some families were never able to recover. The parents of one German Jew from Hamburg killed in the war died "from grief and sorrow" themselves soon after their only son's death.[51] Others were simply overwhelmed by their loss. When Julius Hirsch, a Jewish soldier from the Hamburg suburb of Wandsbek, was killed on the Eastern Front in August 1915, his family clearly took little comfort from his heroic sacrifice. In marked contrast to the many euphemistic death notices, the obituary Hirsch's relatives placed in the *Hamburger Fremdenblatt* mourned his death in the "cruel war." The notice, which was signed by his children and siblings, as well as his "inconsolable wife," highlighted the pain that his death had caused.[52]

The mourning process often extended far beyond the private sphere. Social networks, for example, also provided people with an opportunity to articulate their private grief. During the war, as Jay Winter suggests, many of the bereaved began to come together on a local level to form small communities of mourning. In these groups people could seek consolation and draw support from those suffering similar losses.[53] The primary focus of Winter's research has been on the communities of mourning that emerged as a result of the conflict, such as French associations of wounded veterans, *mutilés de guerre,* or the local activities of the Red Cross.[54] However, by examining the form of remembrance activity undertaken within Germany, it becomes clear that communities of mourning were also typically formed from preexisting social structures, such as religious groups, schools, and workplaces. It was within these that the bereaved began to form a collective remembrance of the war, both as Jews and as members of a wider community simultaneously.

Religious communities offer the clearest example of how individuals came together in small groups to mourn their loved ones. Conventional forms of religious worship in Jewish synagogues and Christian churches provided both Jews and Christians with a familiar structure in which to seek comfort for their losses. On the first anniversary of the war's outbreak, for example, the Protestant *Kreuzkirche* in Hamburg-Barmbeck staged a service to remember the wounded, missing, and dead soldiers from the local community.[55] In Hamburg's synagogues special memorial services for those killed and wounded in the war were held throughout the conflict. In September 1914, the community's leaders ordered that all the *Yahrzeit* candles in the city's main *Bornplatz* synagogue be lit in remembrance of the fallen, while on the last day of Passover in 1915 members of the Jewish communities remembered their war dead in the city's synagogues.[56] This activity, which was staged in memory of the Jewish war dead, provided the bereaved with a public space in which they could reflect upon their losses.

Jewish clubs and associations also acted as communities of mourning for the bereaved. The *Herzl-Bund,* for example, published short obituaries for each of its members killed in the war, in which it described the individuals' lives, their achievements for the group, and the void left by their death.[57] In Würzburg, the predominantly Jewish Salia student fraternity formed a close community of mourning too. Besides publishing short tributes to their war dead, members of the Salia also provided surviving family members with help and support.[58] When the parents of one member killed at the front sought to repatriate their son's remains, members of the Salia managed to secure the necessary permits from the authorities in Würzburg. They also accompanied the family during the funeral ceremony.[59]

Significantly, these Jewish groups were just one small part of a much wider process of mourning in wartime Germany. The University of Würzburg, for example, provided the friends and relatives of all of its students killed in the war, whether Jewish or non-Jewish, with comfort and support. Besides large public remembrance services held in the institution, the university community also offered a place for the bereaved to express their personal sorrow. Many relatives wrote to the university authorities informing them of the death of their loved one at the front.[60] This, though, was more than simply an administrative courtesy, for the university authorities replied to these letters, sending their own condolences to the relatives. They even asked the parents of one fallen Jewish student to send them information about "everything that appears intrinsic and significant from the life of your dear son," as they intended to create a book detailing all of the institution's war dead.[61] In this way, the university came together to form a community of the bereaved that included both its Jewish and non-Jewish members.

This situation in which Jews and non-Jews participated in the same communities of mourning was repeated in a wide variety of non-Jewish organizations. The Deutsche Bank group in Hamburg, for example, was one of many businesses that published long obituaries for both Jewish and non-Jewish employees killed in the war.[62] Small communities of mourning for Jewish and non-Jewish war dead were also common in Hamburg's schools. During the war, the city's Wilhelm-Gymnasium reported on the deaths of its former pupils and staff in its newsletter and held regular remembrance services.[63] The director of the Wilhelm-Gymnasium also expressed his sorrow to a wider audience. When Joseph Koch, a senior teacher and member of Hamburg's Jewish community, was killed at the front in 1915, the school submitted an obituary to a local newspaper: "In the departed, we mourn a genial colleague," declared the school's director, "who through his friendly manner and his loyal fulfilment of duty had earned … the respect of his fellow staff and the love of his pupils."[64]

As the communities of mourning that emerged in Hamburg and Würzburg demonstrate, the mourning process did not divide Jew from non-Jew. In many areas, Jews and other Germans belonged to several different communities of mourning. The bereaved sought comfort from individuals who were either already familiar to them or who shared a similar set of beliefs. While this was often in specific religious communities, whether Christian or Jewish, people also returned to the groups and associations of civil society to which their loved one had once belonged. As a result workplaces, social groups, sports clubs, and schools found themselves at the center of the wartime mourning process.

The long-standing nature of many of these associations proved crucial for ensuring that Jews and non-Jews mourned their losses together. Because Jews in Imperial Germany had often played a significant role in German society, whether through shared schooling, membership in clubs, or participation in political associations, these non-Jewish groups also mourned their Jewish members killed in the war.[65] Hamburg's Wilhelm-Gymnasium, for example, which was located in the traditionally Jewish Rothenbaum district of the city, enjoyed high levels of Jewish enrollment before the war. Accordingly, it helped both the Jewish and non-Jewish relatives of the war dead to transcend their losses during the conflict. During the war, then, German Jews continued to maintain some sense of multiple belonging that enabled them to cross the boundaries between Jewish and non-Jewish associational life.

Overlapping Remembrance after the Armistice

The turmoil of defeat and revolution in November 1918 had a dramatic impact on Germany's Jewish communities. Leaflets and pamphlets blaming Jews for Germany's collapse and asserting that German Jews had avoided the worst of the fighting circulated widely.[66] The ferocity of this anti-Semitic wave led some German Jews to place greater emphasis on their Jewishness. For Ernst Simon, the disillusionment of the conflict drew him into the Zionist movement. "We soon learnt that the only path leading our people from their wretched spiritual, mental and material duality is the path to Zion," he pronounced in 1919.[67] Reflecting such assertions, many historical accounts suggest that the unrest of the immediate postwar years forced Jewish and non-Jewish society further apart.[68] Even Till van Rahden, who explores the strength of intergroup relations in nineteenth century Breslau, maintains that the relationship between Jews and non-Jews deteriorated dramatically after the conflict.[69]

Yet the immediate postwar years were also dominated by a different history. Loss, grief, and the need to remember the soldiers killed in the conflict continued to intrude into many people's everyday lives. The process of mourning the war dead initially took place in the multiple and various communities of mourning that had been formed during the war. A focus on the continuity of remembrance structures reveals a far more complex relationship between German Jews and non-Jews than the existing historiography suggests. First, it is important to recognize that all sections of Jewish society continued to remember their war dead after the armistice. Although some Jews may have turned inward, a fundamental need to mourn the soldiers killed in the conflict remained. Second, in many places Jews and non-Jews, far from being irreparably divided by the postwar turmoil, actually continued to remember the war dead together.

After the armistice, the German authorities eased restrictions on the erection of permanent remembrance sites, which had been imposed during the war years as a means to conserve raw materials.[70] The relaxation of these constraints triggered a massive wave of memorialization as the different communities of mourning began to construct memorials for their war dead. By November 1921 in Hamburg, for example, 112 permanent sites of remembrance had already been built or were in the planning stage.[71] This figure included several different Jewish sites of mourning. In 1919, the Israelitische Tempel-Verband placed a memorial in its synagogue.[72] The Mekor Chajim study society dedicated its own memorial the following year, and in March 1921 Hamburg's Talmud-Tora school dedicated a plaque to the teachers and pupils killed in the war.[73]

Irrespective of German Jews' personal stance toward the war, almost all sections of Jewish life were involved in the initial remembrance of the war dead. Each Jewish community of mourning, however, tended to stress particular aspects of the war that were closest to the concerns of its own members. For Berlin's reform community this meant continuing to frame the war dead within an existing language of heroic sacrifice for the fatherland. When the community dedicated a bronze memorial plaque in September 1919, it opened the religious service with a rendition of Beethoven's Funeral March (Trauermarsch). The patriotic tones of Beethoven's music were followed by a series of speeches that stressed the soldiers' heroic sacrifice for Germany.[74] "Filled with love of the fatherland, glowing with enthusiasm, carried by pure idealism," declared one speaker, "they moved out in the struggle for Germany's greatness."[75]

In orthodox communities, permanent expressions of remembrance often espoused a more traditional vocabulary. Rather than emphasizing the ideals of a heroic death, they sought to discourage what they considered to be inappropriate displays of remembrance. When the Jewish community in Halle planned to erect a memorial plaque in its synagogue, it received religious instruction from several orthodox communities.[76] Berlin's Adaß Jisroel community, for example, advised Halle's Jewish community against placing its plaque above the synagogue's Holy Ark. "This most sacred place ... is dedicated solely to the honour of God," declared the Adaß Jisroel group. It added that the Holy Ark should not "be weakened by any distracting thoughts."[77]

Zionist groups also created permanent sites of remembrance for their members who had been killed in the war. The Herzl-Bund produced a large remembrance book containing a long list of its war dead with their place of birth and date of death. Examples of their final letters sent from the front constituted the book's concluding section. In contrast to other Jewish groups, the Herzl-Bund openly interpreted the war as a negative event for German Jewry. It regretted that its members had died for Germany rather than Zion. "There was ... no camaraderie and we Jews had to suffer the most from this," it complained.[78]

In commemorating the war dead, however, these Jewish communities of mourning were not isolated associations. Reflecting German Jews' multiple sense of belonging, many non-Jewish communities of mourning also commemorated Jewish soldiers who had lost their lives at the front. Where an individual soldier killed in the war had belonged to an organization before the outbreak of hostilities, this same group tended to remember its lost member after the war. Several different groups could, therefore, potentially remember the same Jewish soldier. In this way, the commemoration of Jewish soldiers interacted and intersected with non-Jewish communities of mourning to create a form of overlapping remembrance.

When Hamburg's Wilhelm-Gymnasium constructed a permanent war memorial plaque for the school's war dead, it remembered all of its members killed in the conflict together. The names of nineteen Jewish pupils and teachers, including the senior teacher Joseph Koch, were inscribed alongside the school's other 142 war dead.[79] During the memorial's dedication in September 1921, Dr. Uetzmann, a senior teacher at the school, bemoaned Germany's capitulation in the war. "Today, on the day of our memorial plaque's unveiling, we are a defeated, slain, impotent people," complained Uetzmann.[80] Although this was a bitter, vengeful speech, Uetzmann did not seek to blame elements within Germany, such as the Jews or the socialists, for the country's defeat. Instead he stressed the sacrifice of all of the school's war dead.[81] The school had hoped that many of the "relatives, friends and former pupils" of the war dead "would be united at the service."[82] Clearly, this wish was fulfilled, as all of the Wilhelm-Gymnasium's former pupils and teachers were remembered together, in a single site of mourning for both the Jewish and non-Jewish war dead.

The practice of overlapping remembrance was not restricted to the Wilhelm-Gymnasium. In the immediate postwar years, it occurred elsewhere in Hamburg as well as in large urban centers throughout Germany. In 1919, for instance, the Association of Senior Teachers at Hamburg's State Schools (Verein der Oberlehrer an den höheren Staatsschulen Hamburgs) published a book of remembrance for its fallen members. In this, Joseph Koch and the three other teachers from the Wilhelm-Gymnasium killed in the war were remembered in a further Hamburg community of mourning.[83] Elsewhere, all of the University of Breslau's war dead were mourned in a single remembrance service held in the city's Centennial Hall (Jahrhunderthalle), which was followed by religious ceremonies in the Catholic and Protestant churches and in the city's main synagogue.[84] Similarly, in March 1919 the University of Bonn held remembrance services in the religious houses of all three confessions, which were attended by the chancellor and Senate members.[85]

What is most striking about this process is the continuity in relations from prewar to postwar German society. Because the remembrance process was grounded in small, local groups that had existed before the outbreak of hostilities, prewar social structures were often maintained. These groups, therefore, tended to remember all people killed in the war, whether Jewish or non-Jewish, who had once been members of their particular organization. Although the turmoil of Germany's collapse led to a rise in anti-Semitism and growing divisions in German society, in some areas a close relationship between Jews and non-Jews was initially maintained.

The Decline of Overlapping Remembrance Activity

The process of overlapping remembrance was extremely short-lived. By the mid 1920s, the small-scale commemorative activities of the communities of mourning had begun to be replaced by much larger schemes of remembrance. In 1924, the state staged the Weimar Republic's first official Day of National Mourning (Volkstrauertag) and at the same time announced plans for a national memorial for all of Germany's war dead.[86] There was also a growing politicization of the remembrance process during the mid 1920s as veterans' organizations, in particular, started to shape the memory of the war.[87] These changes weakened German Jews' position in the commemoration of the war and increasingly marginalized the Jewish soldiers' wartime sacrifice.

In the immediate postwar years, some divisions in the overlapping process were already visible, particularly in areas where Jewish/non-Jewish relations had been historically poor. Indeed, this proved to be the case with many German student fraternities. Anti-Semitism, which had been rife among some sections of the student population, intensified after the war, and in 1920 the main dueling fraternities banned Jewish membership.[88] In Würzburg, these tensions were reflected in the university's postwar remembrance activity, which overlooked the Jewish Salia fraternity's eighteen fallen members. When the university held a ceremony in November 1920 to remember all of the institution's fallen, it excluded representatives from the Salia. Such omissions forced the fraternity to use statistics to emphasize its wartime sacrifice. "We deeply regret now having to exploit the memory of our fallen as a statistic," noted Salia's newsletter, "but believe we owe this step to all of our living and dead fraternity brothers."[89]

By 1923, the process of small-scale overlapping remembrance had come to almost a complete halt. This was visible in a dramatic slump in the number of war memorials constructed by local groups and societies. In Upper Bavaria, for example, some 200 memorials were constructed in 1922; by 1924 this figure had dropped to only 39.[90] While the postwar inflationary crisis was the principal reason for this slump in memorial construction, this decline also reflected a change in the agencies of remembrance. In many areas, the small communities of mourning that had dominated the memorial boom of the immediate postwar years gradually began to withdraw from the remembrance process. Because most of these communities were formed from preexisting groups, such as schools or clubs, other activities inevitably began to dominate. After Hamburg's Wilhelm-Gymnasium had completed its memorial plaque, for example, education again took precedence and the committee that had originally been formed to organize its construction dissolved.[91]

As the influence of the wartime communities of mourning began to decline, veterans' organizations increasingly began to dominate the remembrance process. By 1923 in Ulm, for example, the city's ex-servicemen and regimental associations had erected eight different war memorials.[92] The rise of the veterans' organizations contributed to a more divided remembrance process. In contrast to the communities of mourning, which had their origins in prewar organizational life, membership of the ex-servicemen's organizations was based on postwar politics. Although the large groups for war-wounded soldiers were often open to all eligible veterans, most associations attracted former soldiers from a particular political direction. On the political left, the Reichsbanner Schwarz-Rot-Gold had a membership base that overlapped with the SPD, while on the political right the Stahlhelm mainly appealed to conservative, middle-class citizens. These divisions were particularly evident during memorial dedication ceremonies and remembrance services. When a memorial for Munich's war dead was to be dedicated in front of the Bavarian Army Museum (Bayerische Armeemuseum) in 1924, for example, conservative veterans' groups ensured that the left-wing group Reichsbanner was banned from attending.[93] On the annual Day of National Mourning, veterans' organizations even staged different ceremonies to reflect their diverse political allegiances.[94]

The growing dominance of the ex-servicemen's associations also challenged the involvement of Germany's Jewish population in the wider remembrance process. Although veterans' organizations on the political left, such as the Reichsbanner, generally accepted Jewish members, German Jews' position in right-wing associations was far more ambiguous. The large Stahlhelm organization initially accepted Jews as members, but by 1924, its stance had changed.[95] The group's constitution now stated that "only those of German stock" could become members.[96] Confirming the deep disunity of the veterans, German-Jewish ex-servicemen also formed their own organization. Some six years after its formation in 1919, the national membership of the Reichsbund jüdischer Frontsoldaten (RjF) had risen to almost 40,000 in some 360 local branches.[97] By the mid 1920s, as the Weimar Republic was beginning to achieve some level of political stability, the previous unity of the commemorative process was gone. And German Jews' position in the wider remembrance of the war was now threatened.

Conclusion

In much recent writing on German history, the First World War marks a crucial turning point in the dissolution of Jewish/non-Jewish relations. The war, as Peter Pulzer declares, "brought about a dramatic change in the relationships between Jews and their governments in both the German and the Austro-Hungarian-Empires."[98] The implication is that the turmoil of the conflict brought about the permanent separation of Jews from mainstream German society. Disappointed by the war, Jews began to recreate their own distinct subculture during the Weimar Republic. There is much evidence to support this view. As the German army's census of Jewish soldiers in November 1916 emphasized, anti-Semitism remained a feature of German-Jewish life.

Yet this widely held narrative captures only one important aspect of the war. It overlooks those people who actually fought and died at the front. By the war's end, some two million German servicemen, including almost 12,000 German Jews, had been killed in the conflict. Death, grief, and loss must also be a part of any consideration of the war's impact on Germany's Jewish population. For Jews as well as non-Jews, the death of close friends or family in the First World War permanently altered communities. While the war may have led some Jews to turn away from mainstream society, many others could not simply forget the war's devastating impact on their lives.

Because almost all Germans experienced the loss of a loved one in the war, all sections of German society also faced the difficult task of attempting to transcend the death of a close friend or relative. Many people came together in small communities of mourning to seek comfort from those suffering similar losses. In established groups, such as schools, workplaces, or clubs, Jews and non-Jews often mourned the war dead together. When Karl August Regensburger, a Jewish teacher from Hamburg, was killed in August 1915, for example, the staff and pupils of the St Pauli Realschule, where he had worked, commemorated him in a special memorial service.[99]

The preexisting nature of communities like the St Pauli Realschule ensured that their membership was shared. German Jews did not mourn their war dead alone; rather, they had a multiple sense of belonging that crossed ethnic, cultural, and religious boundaries. During the immediate postwar years, this continued. When the wartime communities of mourning constructed permanent sites of remembrance, they generally dedicated their memorials to all of their members killed in the war. In Hamburg, for example, Regensburger's name was inscribed on war memorials in the Jewish community's war cemetery, in the St Pauli Realschule, and in the Oberrealschule auf der Uhlenhorst, where he had once been a pupil.[100]

If Jews often remembered their war dead together with other Germans in the immediate postwar years, then it would be hard to contend that the war led to the sudden and complete separation of Jewish society. It was only during the early to mid 1920s, as the newly formed veterans' organizations began to dominate the remembrance process, that German Jews' position in the commemoration of the war was seriously threatened. It is important, therefore, to recognize that the First World War brought with it continuity as well as dramatic change. In many areas of German society, Jewish and non-Jewish life was deeply entangled. While the turmoil of the conflict disrupted this relationship, Jewish/non-Jewish relations did not suddenly collapse.

Notes

I am grateful to the AHRC for funding this research. I would also like to thank Neil Gregor, Gavin Schaffer, and Catherine Edgecombe for commenting on earlier drafts of this article.

1. Letter, Landesstelle Brandenburg des Reichsministerium für Volksaufklärung und Propaganda, 17 October 1935, Brandenburgisches Landeshauptarchiv Potsdam, Rep. 61A, Nr. 312.
2. Saul Friedländer, *Nazi Germany and the Jews: Volume I, The Years of Persecution, 1933–39* (London, 1998), 292–293.
3. "Späte Wiedergutmachung," *Allgemeine Wochenzeitung der Juden in Deutschland,* 9 December 1960, 1.
4. Reinhart Koselleck, "Kriegerdenkmale als Identitätsstiftungen der Überlebenden," in Odo Marquard and Karlheinz Stierle, eds., *Identität* (Munich, 1979), 255–276; George Mosse,

"National Cemeteries and National Revival: The Cult of the Fallen Soldiers in Germany," *Journal of Contemporary History* 14, no. 1 (1979): 1–20.

5. For regional exceptions, see Ingrid Kirsch, "80 Jahre Denkmal zu Ehren der im Ersten Weltkrieg gefallenen Mitglieder der Dresdener jüdischen Gemeinde auf dem Friedhof Dresden-Johannstadt," *Sächsische Heimatblätter* 42, no. 6 (1996): 363–368; Judith Prokasky, "Treue zu Deutschland und Treue zum Judentum—das Gedenken an die deutschen jüdischen Gefallenen des Ersten Weltkrieges," *Aschkenas: Zeitschrift für Geschichte und Kultur der Juden* 9, no. 2 (1999): 503–516.

6. George Mosse, *Fallen Soldiers: Reshaping the Memory of the World Wars* (Oxford, 1990), 175–176.

7. David Cannadine, "War and Death, Grief and Mourning in Modern Britain," in Joachim Whaley, ed., *Mirrors of Mortality: Studies in the Social History of Death* (London, 1981), 187–242; David Lloyd, *Battlefield Tourism: Pilgrimage and the Commemoration of the Great War in Britain, Australia and Canada, 1919–1939* (Oxford, 1998).

8. Jay Winter, *Sites of Memory Sites of Mourning: The Great War in European Cultural History* (Cambridge, 1995); Alex King, *Memorials of the Great War in Britain: The Symbolism and Politics of Remembrance* (Oxford, 1998); Adrian Gregory, *The Silence of Memory: Armistice Day, 1919–1946* (Oxford, 1994).

9. Jay Winter and Emmanuel Sivan, "Setting the Framework," in Jay Winter and Emmanuel Sivan eds., *War and Remembrance in the Twentieth Century* (Cambridge, 1999), 6–39, 33.

10. T. G. Ashplant, Graham Dawson, and Michael Roper, eds., *The Politics of War Memory and Commemoration* (London, 2000); Stefan Goebel, "Re-membered and Re-mobilized: The 'Sleeping Dead' in Interwar Germany and Britain," *Journal of Contemporary History* 39, no. 4 (2004): 487–501.

11. Reichsbund jüdischer Frontsoldaten, ed., *Die jüdischen Gefallenen des deutschen Heeres, der deutschen Marine und der deutschen Schutztruppen 1914–1918: Ein Gedenkbuch* (Berlin, 1932), 421.

12. On Berlin: Sabine Hank and Hermann Simon, eds., *"Bis der Krieg uns lehrt, was der Friede bedeutet" Das Ehrenfeld für die jüdischen Gefallenen des Weltkrieges auf dem Friedhof der Berliner jüdischen Gemeinde* (Berlin, 2004). On Hamburg: Roland Jaeger, *Block & Hochfeld, die Architekten des Deutschlandhauses: Bauten und Projekte in Hamburg 1921–1938, Exil in Los Angeles* (Berlin, 1996).

13. For recent studies on death in German history see Richard Bessel and Dirk Schumann, eds., *Life After Death: Approaches to a Cultural and Social History of Europe During the 1940s and 1950s* (Cambridge, 2003); Neil Gregor, "'Is he Alive or Long Since Dead?': Loss, Absence and Remembrance in Nuremberg, 1945–1956," *German History* 21, no. 2 (2003): 183–203.

14. Rudy Koshar, *From Monuments to Traces—Artifacts of German Memory, 1870–1990* (Berkeley, 2000), 125.

15. Eva Reichmann, "Der Bewusstseinwandel der deutschen Juden," in Werner Mosse, ed., *Deutsches Judentum in Krieg und Revolution, 1916–1923* (Tübingen, 1971), 511–612; Peter Pulzer, *Jews and the German State: The Political History of a Minority 1848–1933* (Oxford, 1992), 207; Cornelia Hecht, *Deutsche Juden und Antisemitismus in der Weimarer Republik* (Bonn, 2003), 71; Matthias Thorns, "Britisches und deutsches Judentum in der Krise (1918–1921)," *Zeitschrift für Geschichtswissenschaft* 53, no. 11 (2005), 1000–1018.

16. Paul Mendes-Flohr, "The 'Kriegserlebnis' and Jewish Consciousness," in Wolfgang Benz, Arnold Paucker, and Peter Pulzer, eds., *Jüdisches Leben in der Weimarer Republik / Jews in the Weimar Republic* (Tübingen, 1998), 225–237, 232. See also Christhard Hoffmann, "Between Integration and Rejection: The Jewish Community in Germany 1914–1918," in John Horne, ed., *State, Society and Mobilization in Europe during the First World War* (Cambridge, 1997), 89–104; Michael Brenner, *The Renaissance of Jewish Culture in Weimar Germany* (New Haven, 1996), 6.

17. On German-Jewish subcultures see David Sorkin, *The Transformation of German Jewry, 1780–1840* (Oxford, 1987); Jacob Borut, "'Verjudung des Judentums': Was there a Zionist Subcul-

ture in Weimar Germany?," in Michael Brenner and Derek Penslar, eds., *In Search of Jewish Community: Jewish Identities in Germany and Austria, 1918–1933* (Bloomington, 1998), 92–114.
18. Baruch Ophir und Falk Wiesemann, *Die jüdischen Gemeinden in Bayern, 1918–1945: Geschichte und Zerstörung* (Munich, 1979), 433; Avraham Barkai, "Jewish Life in its German Milieu," in Michael Meyer, ed., *German-Jewish History in Modern Times: Volume 4, Renewal and Destruction 1918–1945* (New York, 1998), 45–71, 56.
19. Benjamin Ziemann, *Front und Heimat. Ländliche Kriegserfahrungen im südlichen Bayern 1914–1923* (Essen, 1997); Thomas Raithel, *Das 'Wunder' der inneren Einheit: Studien zur deutschen und französischen Öffentlichkeit bei Beginn des Ersten Weltkrieges* (Bonn, 1996).
20. Jeffrey Verhey, *The Spirit of 1914: Militarism, Myth and Mobilization in Germany* (Cambridge, 2000), 112.
21. On the use of the term "total war," see John Horne, "Introduction: Mobilizing for 'Total War,'" in John Horne, ed., *State, Society and Mobilization in Europe during the First World War* (Cambridge, 1997), 1–17.
22. Verhey, *The Spirit of 1914*, 158–159.
23. "Der Weltkrieg," *Israelitisches Gemeindeblatt*, 7 August 1914, 879–881.
24. "An die deutschen Juden," *Im deutschen Reich*, September 1914, 339; "Deutsche Juden!," *Jüdische Rundschau*, 7 August 1914, 343.
25. Hermann Cohen, *Deutschtum und Judentum* (Gießen, 1915).
26. Rivka Horwitz, "Voices of Opposition to the First World War among Jewish Thinkers," *Leo Baeck Institute Year Book* 33 (1988): 233–259.
27. Gershom Scholem, *From Berlin to Jerusalem: Memories of My Youth* (New York, 1980), 51.
28. "Talmud Tora Realschule. Bericht über das Schuljahr 1914–1915," Staatsarchiv Hamburg (hereafter StAHH), 522-1, Nr. 534d.
29. "Mitteilungen," *Israelitisches Gemeindeblatt*, 4 September 1914, 364–365.
30. Richard Bessel, *Germany After the First World War* (Oxford, 1993), 5.
31. On this point, see Jay Winter, "Paris, London, Berlin 1914–1919: Capital Cities at War," in Jay Winter and Jean-Louis Robert, eds., *Capital Cities at War: Paris, London, Berlin 1914–1919* (Cambridge, 1997), 3–24, 14.
32. Bernd Ulrich, *Die Augenzeugen: Deutsche Feldpostbriefe in Kriegs- und Nachkriegszeit 1914–1933* (Essen, 1997), 28.
33. "Zwei Feldpostbriefe," *Jüdische Rundschau*, 2 October 1914, 383.
34. "Aus Feldpostbriefen," *Herzl-Bund-Blätter*, November–December 1914, 159–161.
35. Belinda Davis, *Home Fires Burning: Food, Politics, and Everyday Life in World War I Berlin* (Chapel Hill, 2000).
36. "Burgfrieden," *Israelitisches Gemeindeblatt*, 4 September 1914, 362–363.
37. Werner Jochmann, "Die Ausbreitung des Antisemitismus," in Werner Mosse, *Deutsches Judentum in Krieg und Revolution*, 409–510, 422–423.
38. Werner Angress, "The German Army's 'Judenzählung' of 1916: Genesis – Consequences – Significance," *Leo Baeck Institute Year Book* 23 (1978): 117–135, 121.
39. On the *Judenzählung*, see also Werner Angress, "Das deutsche Militär und die Juden im Ersten Weltkrieg," *Militärgeschichtliche Mitteilungen* 19, no. 1 (1976): 77–146.
40. "Die Rede des Reichstagsabgeordneten Dr. Haas," *Im deutschen Reich*, November-December 1916, 258–264.
41. "Jüdenzählung," *Jüdische Rundschau*, 27 October 1916, 351.
42. Mosse, *Fallen Soldiers*, 176–77; Jochmann, "Die Ausbreitung des Antisemitismus," 426.
43. Hoffmann, "Between Integration and Rejection," 98.
44. Letter, Emil Heilbronner, 7 November 1916, in Ortsgruppe München des Reichsbundes jüdischer Frontsoldaten, ed., *Unseren Gefallenen Kameraden: Gedenkbuch für die im Weltkrieg Gefallenen Münchener Juden* (Munich, 1929), 209.
45. Letter, Georg Luft to Sigmund Feist, 8 December 1916, in Sabine Hank and Hermann Simon, eds., *Feldpostbriefe jüdischer Soldaten 1914–1918* (Teetz, 2002), 473.

46. Reichsbund jüdischer Frontsoldaten, *Die jüdischen Gefallenen*, 291, 152.
47. Scholem, *Berlin to Jerusalem*, 63–64, 83.
48. Mosse, *Fallen Soldiers*, 6.
49. "Gedenkblatt" from War Minister von Stein, 8 August 1918, Bundesarchiv Freiburg, BW 1/21633.
50. See, for example, obituaries in *Hamburger Fremdenblatt*, 19 August 1915, 4; *Hamburger Fremdenblatt*, 23 August 1915, 4.
51. Letter, Gebrüder Alsberg to Gemeindeblatt der Deutsch-Israelitischen Gemeinde zu Hamburg, 13 July 1925, StAHH, 522-1, Nr. 628a.
52. *Hamburger Fremdenblatt*, 24 August 1915, 4.
53. Winter, *Sites of Memory*, 30; Jay Winter, "Forms of Kinship and Remembrance in the Aftermath of the Great War," in Winter and Sivan, *War and Remembrance in the Twentieth Century*, 40–60, 40–41.
54. Winter, *Sites of Memory*, 36–46.
55. "Kreuzkirche im Barmbeck," *Hamburger Fremdenblatt*, 28 July 1915, 5.
56. "Zum Gedächtnis der Gefallenen," *Hamburger Familienblatt*, 29 September 1914, 3.
57. See for example "Martin Daniel," *Herzl-Bund-Blätter*, December 1915, 282.
58. "Sterns letzte Grüße," *Kriegsbericht der Salia*, 1 April 1915, 4–7.
59. "Wie wir Rolf Stern in heimatlicher Erde borgen," *Kriegsbericht der Salia*, 1 May 1915, 4.
60. Letter, M. Rotschild to Rectorat Universität Würzburg, 5 July 1915, Universitätsarchiv Würzburg (hereafter UAW), ARS, Nr. 1457.
61. Letter, Rektorat der Julius-Maximilians-Universität Würzburg to Aron Goldschmidt, 21 February 1917, UAW, ARS, Nr. 1457.
62. Obituaries in *Hamburger Fremdenblatt*, 30 August 1916, 4.
63. "Wilhelm-Gymnasium zu Hamburg: Bericht über das 35. Schuljahr 1915/16," Wilhelm Gymnasium Archiv Hamburg (hereafter WGA) (uncatalogued).
64. Joseph Koch Obituary, StAHH, 362-2/20, Nr.216.
65. On Jewish participation in wider German society, see Till van Rahden, *Juden und andere Breslauer: Die Beziehungen zwischen Juden, Protestanten und Katholiken in einer deutschen Großstadt von 1860 bis 1925* (Göttingen, 2000).
66. See, for example, Kurt Sabatzky, "Meine Erinnerungen an den Nationalsozialismus," Leo Baeck Institute Jewish Museum Berlin, MM65; Otto Armin, *Die Juden im Heere: Eine statische Untersuchung nach amtlichen Quellen* (Munich, 1919).
67. Ernst Simon, "Unser Kriegserlebnis," in Ernst Simon, ed., *Brücken: Gesammelte Aufsätze* (Heidelberg, 1965), 17–23, 22.
68. David Brenner, *Marketing Identities: The Invention of Jewish Ethnicity in "Ost und West"* (Detroit, 1998), 144; Marion Kaplan, "As Germans and as Jews in Imperial Germany," in Marion Kaplan, ed., *Jewish Daily Life in Germany, 1618–1945* (Oxford, 2004), 173–269.
69. Van Rahden, *Juden und andere Breslauer*, 317.
70. On the wartime ban on memorials, see Letter, Minister des Innern to Regierungspräsidenten, 12 December 1916, Bundesarchiv Berlin, R1501 / 113066.
71. "Statistik Kriegerehrung," StAHH, 324-4, Nr. 183.
72. "Lokale Nachrichten," *Hamburger Familienblatt*, 3 March 1919, 1.
73. Letter, Verein Mekor Chajim to Vorstand der Deutsch-Israelitischen Gemeinde Hamburg, 11 December 1921, StAHH, 522-1, Nr. 628b; "Die Enthüllung der Gedenktafel," *Hamburger Familienblatt*, 4 April 1921, 2.
74. On the nationalist use of Beethoven's music during the war, see David Dennis, *Beethoven in German Politics, 1870–1989* (New Haven, 1996), 66–72.
75. "Ehrentafel für die Gefallenen," *Mitteilungen der jüdischen Reformgemeinde zu Berlin*, 1 October 1919, 15.
76. Letter, Rabbinat Halle, 5 March 1920, Centrum Judaicum Archiv Berlin (hereafter CJA), 2A2, Nr. 1214.

77. Letter, Adaß Jisroel Berlin to Rabbiner Dr. Kahlberg Halle, 9 March 1920, CJA, 2A2, Nr. 1214.
78. Der Herzl-Bund, ed., *Den gefallenen Brüdern* (Berlin, 1919[?]), 9.
79. Hermann Lüssenhop, "Das Wilhelm-Gymnasium 1881–1931," in Franz Bömer, ed., *Wilhelm Gymnasium Hamburg 1881–1956* (Hamburg, 1956), 9–16, 13.
80. Dr. Uetzmann, Memorial Dedication Speech, 25 September 1921, WGA (uncatalogued).
81. Ibid.
82. *Hamburger Familienblatt,* 11 September 1921, StAHH, 324-4, Nr. 180.
83. Der Verein der Oberlehrer an den höheren Statatsschulen Hamburgs, ed., *Unsern für das Vaterland 1914–1918 gefallenen Brüdern zum Gedächtnis!* (Hamburg, 1919).
84. Letter, Rektor Schlesischen Friedrich-Wilhelms-Universität Breslau to Rektor Universität Würzburg, 20 August 1919, UAW, ARS Nr. 265.
85. Letter, Rektor Rheinsche-Friedrich-Wilhelms-Universität to Rektor Universität Würzburg, 26 August 1919, UAW, ARS Nr. 265.
86. Meinhold Lurz, *Kriegerdenkmäler in Deutschland: Band 4, Weimarer Republik* (Heidelberg, 1985), 49.
87. Bessel, *Germany After the First World War,* 265.
88. Donald Niewyk, *The Jews in Weimar Germany* (Manchester, 1981), 61–62. On student anti-Semitism, see Keith Pickus, *Constructing Modern Identities: Jewish University Students in Germany, 1815–1914* (Detroit, 1999), 65–73.
89. "Unsere Kriegsverluste," *Bericht der Salia,* March 1921, 11.
90. Ziemann, *Front und Heimat,* 440.
91. See Lehrkollegium des Wilhelm-Gymnasiums, ed., *Festschrift zum 50jährigen Jubiläum des Wilhelm-Gymnasiums zu Hamburg 1881–1931* (Hamburg, 1931).
92. "Übersicht über die hiesigen Kriegerdenkmäler und sonstigen Kriegerehrungen," 1928, Stadtarchiv Ulm, B362/10, Nr. 7.
93. Benjamin Ziemann, "Republikanische Kriegserinnerung in einer polarisierten Öffentlichkeit: Das Reichsbanner Schwarz-Rot-Gold als Veteranenverband der sozialistischen Arbeiterschaft," *Historische Zeitschrift* 267, no. 2 (1998): 357–398, 385–386.
94. Peter Fritzsche, *Rehearsals for Fascism: Populism and Political Mobilization in Weimar Germany* (Oxford, 1990), 81.
95. Letter, Stahlhelm to Stahlhelm Brandenburg, 28 March 1927, Bundesarchiv Berlin, R72/71.
96. Stahlhelm, "Rundschreiben Nr. 87," 18 September 1928, Bundesarchiv Berlin, R72/273.
97. Ruth Pierson, "Embattled Veterans: The Reichsbund jüdischer Frontsoldaten," *Leo Baeck Institute Year Book,* 19 (1974): 139–154, 141.
98. Peter Pulzer, "The First World War," in Michael Meyer, ed., *German-Jewish History in Modern Times: Volume 3, Integration in Dispute 1871–1918* (New York, 1997) 360–384, 360.
99. "Trauerfeier," *Hamburger Fremdenblatt,* 25 August 1915, 5.
100. Karl Hahn, *Die Geschichte der Oberrealschule auf der Uhlenhorst* (Hamburg, 1921).

Chapter 9

LAUGHING ABOUT DEATH?
"GERMAN HUMOR" IN THE TWO WORLD WARS

Martina Kessel

In 1915, the journalist Peter Scher published a collection entitled *Kampf und Lachen* (Fighting and Laughter).[1] Scher worked for *Simplicissimus,* one of the best-known satirical journals in Wilhelmine Germany.[2] He did not explain and did not need to explain the connection he evoked between fighting and laughter. During the First World War, every print medium carried jokes that dealt with the hardships of war and rendered the Allies ridiculous:[3] countless joke collections, ranging from just a few to several hundred pages, periodicals like *Simplicissimus* or *Die lustigen Blätter,* well-established newspapers like the *Vossische Zeitung,* which included an additional "funny page" in its Sunday edition, postcards with humorous motifs, and trench journals with a "humor corner." These media presented the figure of the humorous German soldier, a jocular fighter who laughingly went into battle and single-handedly defeated every enemy in sight in a mixture of heroic patriotism, Protestant seriousness, and honest worthiness. This militaristic "Michel," whose individualistic and traditional method of fighting had become hopelessly anachronistic within mere months of the start of the First World War, did not disappear with defeat in 1918. Although the aesthetically conventional representation of the courageous and yet always subaltern soldier changed its appearance, the connection between "German humor" and fighting war was revived by both the party and the army during World War II.

This essay investigates some of the meanings the notion of "German humor" acquired during the wars. It certainly does not argue that there *is* a distinctly German national form of humor. Rather, a discourse developed from the early nineteenth century onward among German intellectuals and writers who claimed that their culture's humor was particular and different from other nations' humor. This notion has since acquired, in the words of Hermann Bausinger, "an inglori-

---

Notes for this chapter begin on page 213.

ous history."⁴ It became particularly intense during the wars, with the figure of the humorous German soldier as its major icon. This chapter focuses on the question of how death was articulated in joke collections gathered under the heading of "humor." Such volumes circled repetitively around certain basic topics. During the First World War, the editors—publishers, writers, and other intellectuals—collected reverential stories about great German military heroes like Frederick the Great or "Papa Wrangel," recounted supposedly funny jokes about military hierarchies, depicted the heroic qualities of the true German soldier and the steadfastness of the population at home despite bad living conditions, and poured scorn on the Allies. Violence was ever present, albeit veiled. During the Second World War, when propaganda was controlled to an even greater extent, the topics changed somewhat. Many collections ignored the war completely, either praising German literary traditions or assembling harmless stories in dialect. When they did touch on the war, only the *Blitzkriege* were referred to in timeless soldiers' jokes that reflected the style of earlier wars. Concerning the war in Russia, however, the tone changed. Whenever stories dealt with current war events, their tone became immediate and urgent, either calling for an iron will to hold out or implying danger and fear between the lines.

This essay does not deal with jokes that were told by soldiers themselves.[5] Rather, it analyzes what producers of humorous collections in both wars, in a mixture of willingness, desire to make a living, and working under conditions of censorship, presented as soldiers' humor.[6] The chapter also excludes the question of reception and can only point to the immense number of publications, literally hundreds in both wars, that indicates their success. In both wars, despite the differences in censorship, supposedly humorous narratives told soldiers and civilians how to understand the war, how to cope with its darker sides, and also how to tell others about it. Such stories cannot be reduced to sheer propaganda, however, even if most of them had a strong normative character. Instead, they were a part of the many media trying to give meaning to the war. These stories were one means of talking about the war in an everyday fashion, and they were vividly recalled by contemporaries as such. In his memoirs, Klaus Mann remembers the funny, kitschy postcards he saw everywhere as a young boy during the war that denigrated the Allies in caricatures: the drunken Russian, the Scotsman in flying skirts, the sly Frenchman, and the lying Briton,[7] whereas the complacent and victorious German soldier kissed his bride. Together with the constant news of victory, they led Mann to see the war as a great game without understanding its tragedies and hardship.[8]

However authentic or funny these representations may have been to contemporaries (they rarely are for today's readers), they are understood here as part of a process of communication that gave meaning to war and warfare and continuously (re)created notions of community and subjectivity. Caricatures and jokes could serve to incite emotions against the enemy. At the same time, they could be read as semantic and pictorial routines in a disintegrating world that offered the German soldiers spatial, temporal, and gendered ordering concepts to help them live in a world of death. In this sense, they could, on the one hand, be understood as one of those seemingly marginal elements that helped individuals to understand their own world, allowing people to hold fast to the world they knew in an unobtrusive way.[9] On the other hand, they might be understood as a means to help reorganize social knowledge, integrating new experiences into perceptions of masculinity, warfare, and social order. The question asked here is whether and how deadly violence, both experienced and perpetrated, was articulated in such collections and thereby introduced into widely distributed, everyday social knowledge about the war. The argument advanced is that during the First World War, these collections tried to make violence not only bearable but also acceptable. During the Second World War, however, they helped to create the realm of silence around the mass murder that was an integral part of that war.

Creating Unity: The Notion of "German Humor"

Using caricature as a weapon and attempting to cheer up soldiers with funny magazines were by no means only German phenomena during the wars.[10] But only the Germans claimed to have a supposedly superior humor as an expression of their superior culture. The concept of a peculiarly "German humor" can be traced back to intellectual elites around 1800. Fichte, Schiller, and company established what Karl Heinz Bohrer has called a "serious mode of reflection,"[11] a representation of history and society that—in all seriousness—contrasted "German humor" with "un-German" satire or irony. Over the course of the nineteenth and early twentieth centuries, "un-German" came to mean a variety of things, most notably French, Jewish, or feminine. Intellectuals aggressively excluded the ironic or satiric mode from the aesthetically and politically accepted canon of speech by criticizing it as superficial and tendentious. By the same token, they connected humor with seriousness, depth, and truthfulness. Whoever used "German humor" as a term of difference could thus imply that irony and satire lacked depth and were simply not true.

Formally speaking, German humor as a term of difference thus organized the "un-serious" perception of society in polarized ways and stigmatized any serious criticism. In terms of its own content, however, it tolerated no difference in the sense that it ruled out the critical articulation of social and political problems and delegitimized satire as a means of social and political improvement. Instead, in bourgeois philosophy and aesthetics, German humor translated into not criticizing social differences but accepting them in an overarching "humorous" understanding.[12] The notion therefore developed into a concept that privileged conservative social behavior and unquestioning descriptions of social relations. Humor constituted a divergence from norm or expectation that lasted only temporarily, without implying any fundamental critique of society, and that was resolved in the end into a harmonious picture of social bonding. In grotesque and satire, conversely, the difference between ideal and reality remained. Throughout the nineteenth and early twentieth centuries, members of the (mostly Protestant) elites used this differentiation to draw boundaries, first between German culture and other national entities, and secondly within their own culture, by labeling witty social critics like Heinrich Heine un-German and denouncing ironic sociopolitical criticism as unjustified.[13] In the "arena of wit," as one might call this debate about the legitimate place of irony, satire, and humor, the humor authors claimed that only their script spoke the truth about reality.

In the wars of unification, the figure of the humorous German soldier appeared on the scene. He represented the ideal carrier of "true" humor, a man bent on establishing German unity by fighting, willing to sacrifice his life for the nation, heroic, chivalrous, and yet always gladly tolerant of his subaltern position.[14] In collections, which always mixed jokes with serious descriptions of heroic feats, the semantics of exclusion and inclusion went hand in hand. The difference toward France supposedly constructed internal cohesion. At the same time, stories about how the Germans developed into one nation through fighting implied that the sense of being one nation, forged by war, remained fragile. At least, a number of stories repeatedly reworked a particular hierarchy. Thus, repetitive and very Prussian jokes held that Bavarian soldiers had become true Germans by realizing that the Protestant Prussians turned out to be the most reliable, truthful allies while the French, although Catholic, were full of falsehood.[15]

Throughout the German empire, as the media revolution and the proliferation of satiric journals got under way, traditional elites continued to perceive satire and irony as forms of representation that could subvert social relations. They had to be tamed in order to undermine their message that society could always be imagined differently.[16] Elites polemically charged that social satire, as it pointed out flaws in German society, supposedly undercut the development of a common sense of national unity and therefore betrayed the national endeavor. These charges never disappeared completely.[17] As an alternative, writers like Artur Moeller van den Bruck established a canon of politically correct texts in his volume *Lachende Deutsche,* published in 1910,[18] while authors of popular fiction like Thilo von Trotha connected the militarization of society with social harmony and equated the acceptance of such a perspective with the promise of social success.[19] The outbreak of war, however, found all editors and writers of satirical journals on the side of the *Burgfrieden;* as in 1870, all of them supported the war effort wholeheartedly, even the editors of the Social Democratic magazine *Der Wahre Jakob.*[20]

These extremely short remarks have to suffice to show that the notion of "German humor" was established during the nineteenth century as a term prescribing a holistic, unquestioned picture of a (militarized) society. Its history can explain to some extent why joke collections would become so important in 1914. As of 1870, "German humor on the battlefield" became an established cultural mode of representation, and it carried a very particular semantic arsenal. It served to establish "Germanness" as opposed to "non-Germanness" without needing to elaborate those concepts further, and it claimed to offer the only truthful account of events.

Therefore, one could read these repetitive stories as well-known forms of storytelling, and thereby history-telling, addressed primarily to the German soldiers and the home front, that established again and again conceptions of the "imagined community" (Benedict Anderson), of the ideal soldier, and of ways to cope.

Turning Atrocities into Jokes: Humor in World War I

Beyond the endless series of drawings and stories that were supposed to render the Allies ridiculous, with an often ambivalent distance toward the French and an unmitigated assertion of superiority over the enemies in the East, many instances of humor production during the First World War simply wrote violence and death out of the picture. Heinrich Zille's 1916 drawings of *Vadding und Korl* were typical in excluding any destruction. This picture series showed two gray-haired militiamen from Berlin who, with irrepressible composure and placidness, "cleaned up" in the East and West.[21] It depicted the two characters as good-willed visitors, happily greeted by the inhabitants of a cozy and peaceful French village draped with flags, pursuing the business of a normal day, where shells, death, or tears were unthinkable.

At the same time, most collections somehow circled around the great void of death, either telling soldiers how to meet their deaths or explaining why they had happened or had to happen. Recent research has shown that the much-quoted "spirit of 1914" was largely an affair of intellectuals.[22] Reacting to the lack of enthusiasm in letters and on the home front, propaganda increased, and censorship became sharper.[23] The normative character of the humorous soldier was particularly evident in prominent genres like fictitious *Feldpostbriefe* in local dialect or conversations between soldiers. Concerning the threat of death German soldiers had to face, these prescriptive narratives tried to uphold a vision of individualized action and personal courage that could still seem to have an impact on the outcome of battle—a vision mostly negated by the actual fighting, at least on the Western Front. Calls for voluntary enlistment were, however, often immediately coupled with a not so hidden warning. In 1914, the journalist Gustav Hochstetter urged young men to enlist with the slogan: "I don't want any pension from you, Father State!" insisting that soldiers would experience a "happy death at the age of 33."[24] He not only invoked the religious dimensions of martyrdom in this analogy with Jesus in a representative manner but also made a statement about politics and individuality. Telling soldiers not to ask for any rewards for their sacrifice, he constructed an autonomous, soldierly masculinity that never asked for support from the new welfare state and implicitly threatened sanctions if soldiers should attempt to mix war and social policy.

Correspondingly, humor producers brought the notion of a *Siegfrieden* (victorious peace only) to bear on the characterisitics of the ideal soldier. They presented perseverance and, implicitly, honorable death as the only possible courses of action and rejected any form of compromise or negotiation, the more so after the scenes of comradeship of Christmas 1914. Fritz Mielert explained that (war) aims, once defined, had to be strictly followed and never changed; only such unshakeable conviction, he argued, could be considered truly "manly."[25] His colleague Hanns Floerke, editor of numerous "humorous" publications about the German fleet, ruled out surrender as inconceivable.[26]

This aspect continued to structure joke collections well into the later war years. At the same time, the character of the war forbade the continuation of some topics. For example, it quickly ruled out the easy jokes of the early war months,[27] while more and more publications appearing in the Reich denied neither the hardships of war nor the danger of death. Collections like *Vom "Kammrad": Feldgraue Kostproben aus meiner Soldatenzeit,* by Albert Brinitzer, appealed to exactly that mental structure that Klaus Latzel has shown to have been so effective in the First World War,[28] the sense of duty, which pushed older men, too, if not into voluntary service as Brinitzer suggested, then at least into dutiful continuation of the fight once drafted.[29] Most jokes in this 64-page edition were typical in the sense that they were soldiers' jokes with no relation to this particular war. (An example: playing on hierarchies in the military, Sergeant says to Lehmann, explaining soldiers' rights of complaint, "If I hit you on the head with a shaft, what could you do?" Lehmann: "Have myself entered in the list of casualties."[30]) Only the first poem, entitled "Comrade reports for duty" ('Kammrad' rückt ein) supposedly was composed and sung by militiamen on the Eastern Front. It emphasized, first of all, the lack of war enthusiasm and, secondly, the hunger soldiers experienced:

Nobody knew—nobody suspected,
When we went to the district's recruiting office,
early in the morning,
but the sad civilian hearts felt flat and poorly.
Because there is no place like home,
and no food like mother's cooking.
Nobody knew—nobody suspected
That a warrior was hiding inside him.[31]

Another verse explained their first experience: they learned that a recruit could live off plain air for thirty hours straight. The final lines, however, underscored the same message Zille offered in his drawings. Jovially, the poem was signed "brr," indicating the discomfort the soldiers experienced. Willingly and happily these gray-haired militiamen answered the call to duty and sacrificed comfort and safety in order to join the fight against the rest of the world, thriving less on good nourishment than on the praise Hindenburg lavished on them.[32] Throughout the war, numerous booklets, particularly the series *Tornister-Humor* (Humor in the Knapsack), edited mostly by the publisher and writer Artur Lokesch, drastically articulated the horrible living conditions, both at home and on the front, and urged people to overcome them as they encouraged resistance and a fighting spirit.[33]

How the soldiers themselves might have coped with the fear of death was not necessarily conveyed in stories about death but, rather, in comments about the destruction of the very normal assumptions about everyday life that people had before the war. Cast in between affable reminiscences of peaceful maneuver days and exhortations to hold out, one punch line related the experience of broken time that the mass death of young men meant. Only in modern times had it become "normal" to assume that death was something primarily to be expected in older age. At the same time, looking toward and planning a future that stretched out in a linear way had become an ever more important element of masculinity during the nineteenth century; to be futureoriented had become an essential requirement for a man in order to construct his own life and his nation's history.[34] One soldier quipped that it would be utterly presumptuous to plan anything beyond a period of eight days,[35] implying that death smashed the illusory certainty of time stretching out endlessly. Soldiers might try to cope by imagining a safe life after the war yet always had to come to terms with the utter fragility of time. The horror of receiving the bad news of a future cut short, in turn, hid in the story of the little village that fell completely silent while the postman made his tour. People despaired when a letter with unknown handwriting arrived, and others felt deep but secret relief when they had been spared.[36] The promise of time was broken, and yet hope for the future again and again offered the only comfort for those still alive.

Concerning the violence and the death Germans themselves suffered, the humorous narratives thus drew on the traditional meaning of "German humor" to accept social relations and historical development as they were. They offered the average "Michel," who fought off fear, anger, and resentment and good-naturedly went about his task, as a norm. Even when such collections acknowledged the fear of death, they offered no alternative but a traditional understanding of honor and soldierly masculinity. In relation to the violence German soldiers perpetrated themselves, however, such humor not only served to make it bearable but also acceptable. In his famous essay about laughter, Henri Bergson argued that laughing about somebody else's misfortune required a lack of compassion; in his opinion, any form of commiseration would prevent derision and scorn.[37] Some stories conveyed and produced the very kind of scorn that could prevent compassion for the enemy. They tried to instill a laughter that could relieve a soldier's conscience from human compassion for the other side, whose experiences so often resembled their own.[38] The Berlin playwright Paul Oskar Höcker, the main editor of the *Liller Kriegszeitung* and one of the most notorious in this field of cultural production, in May 1916 urged soldiers never to forget that laughing soldiers remained invincible because laughter expressed their superiority and hardened them against others and themselves: "Keep laughing! [...] You know: A laughing soldier remains invincible!"[39] A year later, at Easter 1917, in the introduction to *Arnolds Kriegsflugblättern* he praised the cartoonist for having warded off for three years any emotion that could endanger the war effort. Höcker further praised his colleague Arnold for having been able, "in quiet and in hard times [...] with his compelling mockery and his funny ideas to keep awake the true German aggressiveness" and to awaken everywhere "the holy laughter [...], which protects us against all sorrows of war."⁴⁰ On the one hand, Höcker cemented the conception of laughter as a protective shield for the soldiers' aggressiveness; on the other hand, he tried to prevent laughter from becoming a bond between soldiers from all sides regarding the danger of death they all experienced alike.

Particularly when it came to violence that transgressed the rules of (European) war, the derisive turn in jokes marked the connection between handing out death and laughing away the violence used. Soldierly masculinity was not only destabilized by the industrialized forms of modern warfare or the evident shift in gender roles during the war, another common theme. The almost endemic violence perpetrated by the German soldiers against civilians also impinged on the soldiers' representation and self-representation as not only heroic, but also chivalrous and honorable men. The most important topic of Allied propaganda during the war, at least in the first years, was indeed the "German atrocities" committed in Belgium and France.⁴¹ The Germans broke most of the laws in war adopted by the Hague Land Warfare Convention of 1907 by violating Belgian neutrality, killing civilians labeled franc-tireurs, and destroying unguarded villages and civilian monuments.⁴² A huge amount of German propaganda, in turn, tried to refute this charge of barbarism. Eberhard Demm is certainly right to argue that Germans could not answer these allegations with similar charges against the Allies because the Allies were not occupying German territory. In his eyes, they rather pathetically opposed this critique with the recurring image of a generous victor who handed out bread to the civilians.⁴³ Exactly such pictures, however, rewrote the violence the Germans used.

On the one hand, some "jokes" vividly described the violence perpetrated and the spirit in which it was justified. In his 1915 collection *Kriegs-Humor*, Richard Merker offered a story of a batallion moving through a Belgian town that took along "everything male and also all ham and bacon," because "one had to live and also did not like being shot from behind." At one doorstep, they found a wounded "francireur" and a fat pig. When the commander said, "Take the swine along!" one soldier asked, "Which one, Herr Major?"⁴⁴ Such condescending contempt could help to diminish fears. But it could also block out the realization that both wounded civilians and wounded soldiers needed to be treated with soldierly respect, according to binding laws. Other stories were even more explicit about German violence. They fed into what John Horne and Alan Kramer have analyzed as one of the most powerful narratives of the first war months, i.e., the continuously recycled myth of the franc-tireur as a self-fulfilling explanation of why Germans attacked civilians.⁴⁵ Fritz Mielert noted how, during the entrance into Liège, three "francireurs" had been hanged quickly and another, who had supposedly used his gun against the Germans, had been "stuck on a spear." As a result, Mielert bragged, the German soldiers had slept peacefully.⁴⁶ Whereas the French and British published an endless series of cartoons showing the German Hun torturing women and children, Mielert cold-bloodedly praised a "magnanimous officer" who had a couple shot and then sent their four-year-old child home to his wife, with whom he had no children.⁴⁷ Nonlegitimate violence, seriously recounted under the heading of humor, was turned into acceptable and praiseworthy behavior in war.

On the other hand, the humor producers used various narrative strategies to redefine events. Two of them in particular touched upon death perpetrated. Some authors, for example, transported the killing that took place beyond the immediate military action back onto the battlefield. Thus, they explicitly made fun of international efforts to establish laws in war that were binding for all sides and ridiculed such rules as a bureaucratic element that only losers would cling to as a last resort with no place in real war. The collection *Trara, - die Feldpost* reported the "news" that the French now wanted the Germans to announce every attack, with a timetable, weapons deployed, and so on.⁴⁸ Shifting the alleged context of action to an arena where deadly violence had its traditional place also turned this death of the other into a legitimate form of killing. Soldiers who might feel less manly—first because women were taking over their jobs at home, and second because the Allies accused them of not acting like honorable soldiers but like plain murderers—could be reassured by such readings.

The second strategy went even further. It denied the acts as such and associated them with the discourse of hygienization. So far this discourse has been discussed primarily in relation to the German perception of the Eastern landscape and peoples.⁴⁹ Vejas Liulevicius has described the conception of Eastern Europe by the command *Ober-Ost* in the First World War as one of its most durable and disastrous legacies. It was a "mindscape" in which the description of a dirty, bottomless swamp melded with the prescription of a tough cleaning up, the mixture leading to a utopian vision of military and eternal possession.⁵⁰ Hundreds of caricatures about Russians and Serbs fashioned this vision.⁵¹ Regarding the Western Front, these hygienic notions were less apparent. Some pictures, however, in a more or less subtle way converted the charge of barbarism into an insistence on the virtue of cleanliness. One postcard reprinted several times showed a huge, dirty German soldier with a wild beard wielding a knife and racing toward a French or Belgian washerwoman with soap in her hand. She screams, expecting to be violated or killed, but he only cuts off a piece of soap and races back to his comrades so that the German soldiers can start the big wash they had done without for five days.⁵² Such narratives integrated the reaffirmation of one's own sense of subjectivity with the knowledge of the death of the other. In the breakdown of civilization, (re)writing violence as the fulfillment of everyday virtues could comfort the soldiers by assuring them that they were completing a necessary cleaning and ordering task in the occupied territories, staying true to the classical picture of a soldier and citizen. Caricatures and jokes were supposed to stir and soothe emotions at the same time. They could also turn violence into a shared element of social knowledge.

However, the meaning of humor could never be entirely fixed. Reinhard Olt has shown that soldiers could turn war songs into a biting and satirical critique of the war;[53] this was also true of humor. It is harder to find such evidence, but in rare instances, soldiers exploded into a bitter critique of their forced confrontation with death in some trench journals that used "humor" in their title. These examples either escaped the censors' eyes or were tolerated because the criticism was directed against the home front and not against the war leaders or the war as such. In March 1918, a contributor to the trench journal *Papatacci: Südöstlicher Feld- und Etappenhumor* harshly pointed out the different experience of sex and death at home and on the front phrased as the typical complaint about war-profiteers and faithless women. In a style that had nothing in common with the stereotyped jocularity of the humor collections but rather resembled the critical war literature of the 1920s, the soldier ruminated about men at home who won the women while the soldiers, in their fourth year of war, had seen "all the horrors," had heard "the sound when a man's skull bursts," and had seen "intestines draped like ivy on trees."[54]

Casual Presence: Death and Humor in World War II

At the end of the Weimar Republic, such drastic expressions of terrifying experiences were written out of collective memory. The fight about the meaning of death was one of the most important legacies of the Great War,[55] deeply influencing the politics and culture of the Weimar Republic in particular and framing its path to National Socialism and the Second World War.[56] Right-wing authors and politicians won this fight to define the memory of the war at the end of the 1920s, which also meant, in the words of Bernd Hüppauf, a massive regression regarding the representation of death. The violent and often agonizing death of millions of men was transformed once again into a mythical death for greater ideals, becoming even more aggressive than the images of collective honor through individual death in the propaganda before 1914.[57] This transformation was not an immediate result of the experiences during the war itself but depended on the way these experiences were dealt with during the Weimar Republic. Whereas in the earlier years of the republic the dead were represented as dead, the nationalistic literature around 1930 refused to acknowledge the finality of death and revived instead the mythical identity of the dead and the living, proclaiming that the duty of the living was to fulfill the legacy of the dead.[58]

Texts about soldiers' humor shared in this redefinition of death. The major icon of "German humor" by no means disappeared with defeat in 1918, even if it was rarely used in the first years of the republic. But the history of the comical in the 1920s definitely consisted of more than just Tucholskys.[59] The interwar years cannot be treated here at length. Suffice it to say that in the intensive fight in the late 1920s about what the Great War meant, several nostalgic remembrances that were published under the heading of humor contributed to narrowing the meaning of humor itself. After the late Weimar Republic days, the dominant definition of death in war allowed no alternative to stoic heroism, and similarly, the notion of humor narrowed to either a description of heroic death that had to be avenged or a plain cover for violence. On the one hand, authors who celebrated the supposed comradeship of the First World War picked up the humorous vein. They subscribed to the stab-in-the-back legend, gathering the typical jokes about heroic joviality in the midst of terror but finishing on the note that the huge sacrifices had to be avenged because there had been no final German victory.[60] On the other hand, storm troopers celebrated physical violence against political opponents as sheer fun in their publications. Members of the Sturmabteilung (SA), bound together by their cult of violence, went beyond singing songs to render their opponents ridiculous; only physical fights and beaten-up "enemies" guaranteed a truly humorous evening.[61] The connection was also evident in their publications: to mention humor was to talk about violence. Manfred Freiherr von Killinger, a member of the free corps Ehrhardt and ministerpresident of Saxony between 1933 and 1935, was only one of the more notorious authors who connected humor and violence.[62] Members of the SA polemically conceptualized democracy as a form of politics that brought war into peacetime; accordingly, in their texts, they turned humor into a key notion that served to legitimize violence as a normal means of resolving disputes also in peacetime.

After 1933, a great number of joke collections talked exclusively about an "Aryan" society, in opposition to media like the *Stürmer* that aggressively attacked Jewish Germans and used satire to do so. Collections presenting "German humor" increasingly excluded the open celebration of violence, at least during the war, and picked up the glorification of comradeship instead. While National Socialist ideology cultivated the death of the fallen soldier as a binding legacy for the next generations, "German humor" in the sense of creating the "cheerful person" (den heiteren Menschen) became a duty for the *Volk* and a task for the media.[63]

This idea of humor was thus obviously not conceptualized during the Third Reich. Rather, it was one of those integral parts of German culture that had been "naturally" present and particularly defined for a long time, which the regime could activate in the sense it desired. Its central meanings did not change. What changed was the regime's intolerance toward alternatives, evident in its exiling, silencing, or killing of truly critical satirists.[64] "Cheerfulness" prescribed unreserved and unquestioning acceptance of the National Socialist *Volksgemeinschaft*. To be sure, the regime did not come down hard on all jokes. Meike Wöhlert has demonstrated convincingly that underground jokes, so-called *Flüsterwitze,* on the one hand by no means always signaled an oppositional attitude, while on the other hand they received very differentiated treatment, depending on the person who told them.[65] Still, the publication policy of the Third Reich took no chances and defined humor as the expression of the "trustingly believing attitude of the smiling person" that contrasted with intellectual, ironic modernism and targeted anybody who might cling to a different opinion.[66]

All important media participated in a real humor campaign. Gerd Fricke, who was responsible for light entertainment on radio's *Deutschlandsender,* argued in 1935 that "German cheerfulness" would in due time overcome all "un-German criticism" (*undeutschen Kritikastergeist*).⁶⁷ While the *Black Corps,* the journal of the SS, used scorn and derision to exclude Jews from the *Volksgemeinschaft,*⁶⁸ it called for "more humor" and insisted that only "doubters never laugh."⁶⁹ Both print media and the radio swamped their audiences with examples of how to be cheerful in the right way. The motto of the well-known radio show the "Happy Saturday Afternoon" (Der frohe Samstagnachmittag) was exemplary: "Laughingly to hold one's one, laughingly to go one's own way, laughingly to make one's way, laughingly to give joy—Laughter conquers life!"⁷⁰ Alfred Schröter published the results of the radio program "Soldiers, comrades" (*Soldaten, Kameraden*), which had asked soldiers to present their most humorous experience.⁷¹ Evidently, sending in a story did not mean that the sender was a fervent National Socialist. But the high number of participants showed the desire for light entertainment, and this kind of light entertainment praised exactly that form of subjectivity that was propagated at the time. It came as no surprise that Goebbels, while congratulating the popular radio show "Wunschkonzert" in December 1940 on its fiftieth broadcast, called humor and music the best allies for strengthening body and soul for the continuation of the fight.⁷²

Despite paper shortages and a drastic reduction of the number of publishing houses over the course of the war,⁷³ the rate of publications seems to have remained at least stable until 1943 or even 1944. Humorous stories were some of the best-selling titles until 1944, when most publishers had to quit due to paper shortages. This does not mean, however, that readers rejected National Socialist literature.⁷⁴ Rather, the regime was very much aware of the need for light entertainment, particularly when it came to supplying soldiers with reading material.⁷⁵ The joke collections also conveyed the demand to support the *Volksgemeinschaft,* sometimes in crude fashion. The fusion of propaganda with entertainment was here as evident as in film, cabaret, or other media,⁷⁶ and the intention similar: to block out the war and to create normalcy, but also to bolster aggressiveness through the fusion of militaristic wording with the semantics of humor: "A battle of cheerfulness has been fought and won" (Eine Schlacht des Frohsinns ist geschlagen und gewonnen).⁷⁷

Broadly speaking, the publications during the Second World War differed in two respects from those during the first. On the one hand, a large proportion did not mention the war at all but tried to divert attention away from the present. For example, they gathered texts from the German literary tradition to establish a canon of cultural heroes, excluding distinctly National Socialist authors but including all those who had celebrated *Volk* and *Heimat* in centuries past.⁷⁸ A second group of collections presented regional jokes, often in dialect, and sometimes from regions now claimed for Greater Germany.⁷⁹ When they did mention current events, the editors called for endurance and applauded the Germans as a people who supposedly had never lost their humor "amidst all the terror the so-called benefactors of mankind from the other side of the canal" would force them to live through.⁸⁰

Some regional publications, however, went further in their propaganda. In their collection of humor from the Rhineland, Laurenz Kiesgen and Wilhelm

Spael not only tried to whip up support for the Third Reich but also explicitly targeted so-called internal enemies with the reminder that those critics who considered only their own individuality ("ihr eigenes Ich") instead of the interests of the community would never be able to feel honest joy.[81] The message was clear: those who lacked "German humor" allegedly placed themselves outside of the community. So, "humorous stories" were intended to mark and then to exclude internal critics much more rigorously than during the First World War. To be sure, their exclusion was not achieved by racially defining enemies; racial dichotomies rarely appeared in these collections.[82] Rather, the average "Aryan" citizen was warned not to behave like "Herr Bramsig und Frau Knöterich," figures created, if rather unsuccessfully, by the propaganda ministry in 1941 to delegitimize people who produced rumors, listened to foreign radio stations, and passed on unwelcome news.[83] Here it became particularly evident that "humor" no longer derived from a split between expectation and behavior but that it immediately required an ideal picture of unquestioned *völkisch* unity. Inscribed into the notion of humor, cheerful acceptance of the present constituted a central feature of the ideal National Socialist personality: active, joyful, dutiful, and intolerant of second thoughts and hesitation. The inverse (of the ideal personality) was just as clearly outlined: anybody displaying "foolishness" (Dummheit), "half-heartedness" (Lauheit) or a "listless attitude" (schlappes Wesen) betrayed a lack of "correct" conviction.[84]

Utz Jeggle has shown how the regime dealt with letters from Stalingrad describing real death and soldiers' disillusionment, pain, and despair. It altered such letters both on the level of language and in terms of the memory it wanted to create before delivering them to families.[85] The representation of death in joke collections accordingly tied in with the public ideal. Descriptions of fallen soldiers' funerals on the battlefield offered the ideologically preferred meaning for the suvivors' fear and suffering, pointing beyond death toward an (undefined) future promised by the regime. Bernhard Poiess, in his booklet *Soldaten-Geschichten* published in a series for the troops (*Schriftenreihe zur Truppenbetreuung*), outlined the correct form of consolation and of memory. As always, he mixed supposedly funny incidents with serious events. Poiess described a soldier burying a friend who had just become a father. The survivor therefore felt rather depressed. But Poiess had him conjure up memories of another man in Bohemia who had survived and who, with his little son on his arm (who represented their future), hailed the Führer as liberator of the region.[86] Other stories, often published in numerous editions until 1944, celebrated the heroes of World War I who supposedly had preferred death to captivity, thus reminding soldiers of their obligation to redeem them.[87]

Still, publications after 1941 sometimes subtly changed, now paying tribute to the costs and the development of the war. *Der Völkische Beobachter* published several collections for the forces' postal service during the later war years. The editors of the 1944 number, *Privates are Laughing: Humor from the Front* (*Landser lachen: Fronthumor dieses Krieges*), plainly stated that the soldiers on the Eastern Front had to make do without "women, wine, and song" (Wein, Weib und Gesang). They admitted that the soldiers' humor had become "bitter," but, so they claimed, the fighting in the Russian swamps, which could only be endured with humor, had brought out its deepest and truest forms at the same time.[88] At this point humor meant nothing but hardened aggressiveness. Being tough and hard had become key to soldierly masculinity during National Socialism. Increasingly, this meant that soldiers had to be willing to hold out against all odds, an ideal they clung to despite their disillusionment in the final years.[89] Oberbereichsleiter Werner Lass and Lieutenant Hans-Adolf Weber appealed to exactly this hardness when they insisted that humor was particularly present in the most difficult situations: "Then the hard laughter of the 'Nevertheless' can be heard, and comradeship will only become more solid!"[90]

Whenever the stories did mention the actual fighting, however—which happened rarely enough—, they never promised easy victory. Feelings of superiority are hard to detect in descriptions of the fighting in Russia. Instead, self-irony appeared, or at least ironic commentaries on the surrender of the renowned German machinery to the Russian winter. According to Omer Bartov, the combination of man and machine characterized the cult of the hero after 1918, a hero who subjugated territories and peoples.[91] Now, anecdotes turned in by soldiers or officers used the classical cultural heroes to make fun of German cars and trucks getting stuck in the snow:

After Goethe:
Above all hoods silence reigns.
From most engines
you do not hear a sound.
They traveled some distance.
Wait only a little while,
and the last ones
will also come to a standstill. [92]

Sometimes the vastness and silence of the Russian territory and the invisibility and ferocious fighting quality of the Russian soldiers appeared beyond the punch line. In 1943, Wilhelm Utermann, editor of *Der Völkische Beobachter*, issued a collection gathering the results of a competition the newspaper had arranged that asked soldiers to recount the funniest story that happened to them during the war. Such competitions seemed quite successful as entertainment and diversion. At the same time, they allowed contemporary readers short glimpses into the experiences of impending death. Under the heading "Such irresponsible behavior" (So was Unvernünftiges), SS member Rudi Dziadek described how his unit had besieged a small Russian village. Humor appeared in the figure of a "true" SS member who brightened up the depressed atmosphere with his exclamation among heavy shooting: "These guys shoot and shoot until something actually happens!" But not only this sentence in fact betrayed the Russians' determination. The longer part of the joke had already described how they had fought so hard that the Germans sometimes did not know how to save themselves: "Sometimes it really looked bad for us. Often we hardly knew where to take cover."[93] This story ended with the quote from the SS man. Any reader from the front might have sympathized and come up with his own conclusions regarding the development of the war, as one soldier-cartoonist did in a picture story with just a few strokes: A lieutenant of an engineering unit (a German *Pioniereinheit*) is ordered to draw a bridge his unit has to build across a river. At first, two men appear fishing on the bridge in the drawing, and their producer is reprimanded; next, the two appear beside the river, and the reprimand again follows quickly. In the final scene, two wooden crosses crown the bridge; it seems unlikely that they cover Russian graves.[94]

It was obviously permissible to vent fear about death in normal fighting situations, when both sides risked death. The utterly asymmetric situation of mass murder, however, was covered over with silence.[95] Joke collections of the First World War spread knowledge of occupation policy, but those of the Second almost completely blocked out such information. This void paralleled another absence: while Hitler, Göring, and Goebbels figured prominently in underground jokes, Himmler was missing. His black angels of death defied both irony and humor. When the violence that the Germans exerted did appear, however, it was referred to in remarks that were strikingly casual. In their collection *Lachendes Feldgrau* from 1942, Hans Riebau and Hans Reimann mentioned a British newspaper clipping from 1939 that criticized German violence toward civilians in Lublin at that time. They assured their readers that the Germans had only carried an almost deaf old man with bad eyesight out of a park, teasing readers with the possible implication that he simply had not moved quickly enough out of their way.[96]

Other anecdotes emphasized just as laboriously the German ordering task in the occupied territories and explicitly wrote violence out of the picture. The political situation there was likened to the "*Systemzeit*," the "untidy" Weimar Republic, in order to present the German occupiers as peacekeepers and carriers not only of a superior civilization but also of a superior political system. One short story explained that German soldiers had to deal with very intricate situations in the occupied territories (the place was called Belgium), for example, when civilians "gathered for a demonstration" or "were fighting among themselves." The reference to Weimar could evoke memories of the violence used before and after 1933 to install National Socialism, but the upshot of such stories was always that the Germans solved each difficult situation without resorting to violence—for example, by starting a money collection for some purpose that immediately, so the argument went, helped to disperse any group.[97] Money collections were always going on in the Reich, and they were the butt of many jokes, so these narratives could both provoke winking among those who knew better and invoke familiar ways of making sense of National Socialism at home.

Thus, when the violence Germans perpetrated was mentioned, it came in a mixed bag. Further evidence is needed, but it appears that joke collections allowed insight into both the terrible experiences of German soldiers and their feelings of superiority, which were spawned by at least the early war years and German occupation policy in general. Humorous stories therefore indicate a shared space of knowledge concerning both aspects. In a collection that presented "the funniest stories from the war," Oberwachtmeister Röhl talked about his anti-aircraft unit on its way through Poland in 1939/40. They had entered a little village that appeared deserted when suddenly many Jews showed up. Jewish population as such was nothing extraordinary at all, as Röhl noted, but it seemed "very strange" (eigenartig) to him that the Jews cheered upon their entrance and gave them flowers and cigarettes. As the Jews heard the soldiers speak, however, they vanished rapidly. One of them upon inquiry finally explained that they had been told that the British were chasing the Germans in front of them, and as another German unit had just passed through the village, they had mistaken the Germans for their British liberators.[98] Sharply asserting hierarchies of both cleverness and power, Riebau and Röhl could rely on readers not just to understand the story but to get it as a joke. In an entirely asymmetric joke relationship, the brutal cleavage between hopeful expectation and gruesome reality was exclusively on the other side.

Summary

The notion of "German humor" was well established before 1914 as a narrative mode of presenting German history and the desired form of subjectivity. It meant the uncritical acceptance of one's (subaltern) position in society and the willingness to achieve German unity and German dominance in Europe by fighting war. These jokes, understood as part of a normative, collective discourse about preferred forms of social order and subjectivity, claimed to be serious and true (even if the stories had not happened), and they asserted the superiority of German civilization. At the same time, they placed particular demands on German citizens.

Humorous stories in both wars, despite their normative character, allowed people to vent fears and frustration, as long as they did not criticize the war effort itself. Still, the emphasis changed. During the First World War, the repetitive stories about everyday hardships could function as stabilizing elements and offer an outlet for fear and pain. During National Socialism, conversely, the effort to block out the war and, at the same time, to target possible internal critics became much more prominent. Also, such narratives harbored conceptions of warfare, soldierly masculinity, and legitimate violence. In both wars, concerning the violence soldiers suffered, the narratives appealed to, and at the same time mirrored, a central notion of soldierly masculinity that became exclusive under National Socialism: the willingness to fight under all circumstances. Regarding the violence perpetrated, however, the difference between the two wars was much clearer. During World War I, derisive descriptions of violence against civilians served to rewrite it as legitimate or to turn it into behavior distinct from war, that is, into hygienic virtues or generous gestures of the victor. Either way, the violence was presented in this manner to a wider audience, which may have fed into widespread opposition to accepting responsibility for nonlegitimate violence during and after the war. During World War II, the violence Germans perpetrated was at the same time a *non-dit* and a rather obvious element of shared social knowledge. It was characterized both by the attempt not to mention it and by authors' utterly casual and derisive tone when they did talk about it. While allowing any reader some glimpses into what happened during the war, this particular configuration of humor reflected and, at the same time, bolstered the attitude of "we never knew anything."

Notes

1. Peter Scher, *Kampf und Lachen* (Konstanz, 1915).
2. For its history before 1914, see Ann Taylor Allen, *Satire and Society in Wilhelmine Germany: "Kladderadatsch" and "Simplicissimus" 1890–1914* (Lexington, 1984).
3. Reproductions in Hans Weigel et al., *Jeder Schuss ein Russ, jeder Stoss ein Franzos: Literarische und graphische Kriegspropaganda in Deutschland und Österreich 1914–1918* (Vienna, 1983); Sigrid Metken, "'Ich hab' diese Karte im Schützengraben geschrieben…' Bildpostkarten im Ersten Weltkrieg," in Rainer Rother, ed., *Die letzten Tage der Menschheit: Bilder des Ersten Weltkrieges* (Berlin, 1994), 137–148, esp. 141–146. Caricatures from all sides are in Eberhard Demm, ed., *Der Erste Weltkrieg in der internationalen Karikatur* (Hanover, 1988).
4. Hermann Bausinger, "Lachkultur," in Thomas Vogel, ed., *Vom Lachen: Einem Phänomen auf der Spur* (Tübingen, 1992), 9–23, here 21.
5. For a discussion of the way soldiers themselves vented their fears and frustrations in ironic jokes in their trench newspapers, at least until 1916 when propaganda became more tightly controlled and the humor articulated in such journals less critical, see Anne Lipp, *Meinungslenkung im Krieg: Kriegserfahrungen deutscher Soldaten und ihre Deutung, 1914–1918* (Göttingen, 2003).
6. See, for example, Klaus Topitsch, "Die Greuelpropaganda in der Karikatur," in Raoul Zühlke, ed., *Bildpropaganda im Ersten Weltkrieg* (Hamburg, 2000), 49–91.
7. Examples also in Otto May, *Deutsch sein heißt treu sein: Ansichtskarten als Spiegel von Mentalität und Untertanenerziehung in der wilhelminischen Ära (1888–1918)* (Hildesheim, 1998), 539–547.
8. Michael Wildt, *Generation des Unbedingten: Das Führungskorps des Reichssicherheitshauptamtes* (Hamburg, 2002), 49.
9. Jay Winter argues that in order to cope with loss and bereavement, people reached back to traditional ways of mourning, as the modern could only express the sense of paradox and alienation: Jay Winter, "The Great War and the Persistence of Tradition: Languages of Grief, Bereavement and Mourning," in Bernd Hüppauf, ed., *War, Violence, and the Modern Condition* (Berlin and New York, 1997), 33–45.
10. Demm, *Der Erste Weltkrieg*; Jean-Yves Le Naour, "Laughter and Tears in the Great War: The need for Laughter / The Guilt of Humour," *European Studies* 31 (2001): 265–275; Stéphane Audoin-Rouzeau, *Men at War 1914–1918: National Sentiment and Trench Journalism in France during the First World War* (Oxford, 1992), 12–20; for truly critical satire in France, see Allen Douglas, *War, Memory, and the Politics of Humour: The "Canard Enchaîné" and World War I*

(Berkeley, 2002); for first results of this project, see Martina Kessel, "Gelächter, Männlichkeit und soziale Ordnung. 'Deutscher Humor' und Krieg (1870–1918)," in Christina Lutter et al., eds., *Kulturgeschichte: Fragestellungen, Konzepte, Annäherungen* (Innsbruck, 2004), 97–116. The number of Allied publications was immense in both wars, but the comparative aspect cannot be dealt with here.
11. Karl Heinz Bohrer, ed., *Sprachen der Ironie—Sprachen des Ernstes* (Frankfurt am Main, 2000); Bausinger, "Lachkultur."
12. Bernd-Jürgen Warneken, "Der sozialkritische Witz als Forschungsproblem," *Zeitschrift für Volkskunde* 74 (1978): 20–39.
13. Jefferson S. Chase, *Inciting Laughter: The Development of "Jewish Humor" in 19th Century German Culture* (Berlin and New York, 2000); for anti-semitism in satirical journals in the nineteenth century, see Ursula E. Koch, *Der Teufel in Berlin: Von der Märzrevolution bis zu Bismarcks Entlassung. Illustrierte politische Witzblätter einer Metropole 1848–1890* (Cologne, 1991), 179–180, 189.
14. See, for example, *Humor im Felde: Heiteres aus dem Deutsch-Französischen Kriege von 1870*, Zweites Heft (Leipzig, 1870); *Humor und Ernst des deutschen Kriegers aus dem Jahre 1866: Piquante, humoristische und interessante Züge des Soldatenlebens aus dem letzten deutschen Kriegs. Ein Gedenkblatt für das deutsche Volk* (Wittenberg, 1866); Kessel, "Gelächter," 102–107.
15. *Humor im Felde*, 54.
16. For the systematic point, see Peter L. Berger, *Erlösendes Lachen: Das Komische in der menschlichen Erfahrung* (Berlin and New York, 1998), 78.
17. Hermann Jahnke, ed., *Humor und Heldentum* (Kottbus, 1888).
18. Artur Moeller van den Bruck, *Lachende Deutsche* (= *Die Deutschen: Unsere Menschheitsgeschichte*, vol. 8), 2nd, enlarged ed. (Minden, n.d. [1910]).
19. Thilo von Trotha, *Der Sommerleutnant: Ein humoristischer Roman* (Berlin, 1899).
20. Reinhard Hippen, *Das Kabarett der spitzen Feder: Streitzeitschriften* (Zürich, 1986), 69.
21. *Vadding in Ost und West*, 27 Original-Zeichnungen von Heinrich Zille (Berlin, 1916).
22. Among others, Benjamin Ziemann, *Front und Heimat: Ländliche Kriegserfahrungen im südlichen Bayern 1914–1923* (Essen, 1997).
23. Jeffrey Verhey, "Krieg und geistige Mobilmachung: Die Kriegspropaganda," in Wolfgang Kruse, ed., *Eine Welt von Feinden. Der Große Krieg 1914–1918*, 2nd ed. (Frankfurt, 2000), 176–183.
24. Gustav Hochstetter, *Wir sind wir: Ernstes und Frohes aus der Weltkriegszeit* (Berlin, 1914), 73.
25. Frietz Mielert, *Bunte Bilder aus dem größten aller Kriege: Ernstes und Heiteres für das deutsche Volk* (Regensburg, n.d.), 26.
26. Hanns Floerke, *Von der Nordsee zu den Dardanellen: Neue Heldentaten unserer Flotte*, 2nd ed. (Munich, 1916), V–VII; see also Georg Müller, Hanns Floerke and Georg Gärtner, eds., *Kriegsanekdoten und Kriegserlebnisse: Heiteres und Ernstes aus dem Großen Kriege*, 4th ed. (Munich, 1915), 215–216.
27. Examples in Kessel, "Gelächter," 109.
28. Albert Brinitzer, *Vom "Kammrad": Feldgraue Kostproben aus meiner Soldatenzeit. Erstes Bändchen erlebten Humors und Stimmungs"zaubers" mit lebensgetreuen Photographien und einigen Liebesgaben, von wohlmeinender Seite beigesteuert, sowie dem Neuen Exerzier-Reglement (nebst Schießvorschrift) als Anhang* (= Tornister-Humor, vol. 27) (Berlin, n.d.).
29. Klaus Latzel, *Deutsche Soldaten - Nationalsozialistischer Krieg? Kriegserlebnis—Kriegserfahrung, 1939–1945* (Paderborn, 1998).
30. Brinitzer, *Vom "Kammrad,"* 24.
31. "Keinem schwant es—keiner ahnt es, Als wir zum Bezirkskommando zogen los im Morgengrau, War uns tristen Zivilisten Doch im Herzen mau und flau. Denn zu Hause ist's am schönsten, und bei Muttern gut es schmeckt, Keinem schwant es—keiner ahnt es, Daß ein Krieger in ihm steckt." Brinitzer, *Vom "Kammrad,"* 2.
32. Brinitzer, *Vom "Kammrad,"* 3.

33. As examples: *Wir halten durch! Saftige Witze und blutige Kalauer aus unserer Kriegsküche*, Aufgetragen von Artur Lokesch (Berlin, n.d.); Günter Mühlen-Schulte, *Die Feldpostbriefe des Gefreiten Knetschke: Mit Erlaubnis der Empfängerin Anna Kwacktüpfel-Neucölle, zusammengestellt und mit würdigen Bildern geschmückt von G. M.-S.* (= Tornister-Humor, vol. 4) (Berlin, n.d.); *Trara, - die Feldpost! Lustiges Allerlei vom feldgrauen Schwager: Zusammengestellt von Artur Lokesch* (= Tornister-Humor, vol. 26) (Berlin, n.d.); *Uns kann keiner: Feine Kosthappen aus der Kriegsküche,* gehamstert von Alfred Brie (=Tornister-Humor, vol. 30) (Berlin, n.d.).
34. See Martina Kessel, *Langeweile: Vom Umgang mit Zeit und Gefühlen in Deutschland vom späten 18. bis zum frühen 20. Jahrhundert* (Göttingen, 2001), esp. 159–238.
35. Brinitzer, *Vom "Kammrad,"* 59.
36. *Trara,—die Feldpost!,* 47
37. Henri Bergson, *Das Lachen: Ein Essay über die Bedeutung des Komischen* (Jena, 1921).
38. Kaspar Maase, "'Wer findet denn so etwas komisch?' Die Massen und ihr Lachen," in Karl Heinz Bohrer and Kurt Scheel, eds., *Lachen: Über westliche Zivilisation,* special issue of *Merkur. Deutsche Zeitschrift für Europäisches Denken* 56 (2002): 874–885, here 883.
39. "Lacht! … Ihr wißt: Ein lachender deutscher Soldat bleibt unbesieglich," in *Das lustige Buechel der Liller Kriegszeitung* (Druck und Verlag der Liller Kriegszeitung, Mai 1916), 5.
40. Karl Arnold, *Arnolds neue Kriegsflugblätter der Liller Kriegszeitung* (Lille, 1917), n.p. ("in stillen und in harten Zeiten [...] mit seinem zwingendem Spott und seinen lustigen Einfaellen die echte deutsche Angriffslust wachzuhalten wusste"; "So moegen denn auch diese neuen Arnoldschen Zeichnungen zu den Kameraden und in die Heimat flattern und ueberall das heilige Lachen wecken, das uns gegen alle Kriegstruebsal feit.")
41. John Horne and Alan Kramer, *German Atrocities 1914: A History of Denial* (New Haven and London, 2001).
42. Regarding the German attitude toward the Hague Convention see Jost Dülffer, *Regeln gegen den Krieg? Die Haager Friedenskonferenzen von 1899 und 1907 in der internationalen Politik* (Frankfurt am Main, 1981), 103–137; see also Alan Kramer, "Kriegsrecht und Kriegsverbrechen," in Gerhard Hirschfeld et al., eds., *Enzyklopädie des Ersten Weltkriegs* (Paderborn, 2003), 281–292.
43. Demm, *Der erste Weltkrieg,* 10, examples also 65, 154; see also *Feldgrauer Humor: Mit zahlreichen Illustrationen.* Hg. v. d. Humoristischen Wochenschrift *Die Muskete,* 2nd. ed. (Vienna, 1916), 76–85.
44. Richard Merker, *'Kriegs-Humor.' Heiterkeit und Satire im Weltkriege 1914/15. Eine Sammlung humorvoller Begebenheiten zur Erheiterung für jetzt und später. Jedem Leser draußen und daheim frohe Stunden bereitend.* Verfaßt, gesammelt und hg. v. R.M. (Dresden 1915), 9. ("alles Männliche und auch alle Schinken- und Speckseiten")
45. See Horne and Kramer, *German Atrocities,* esp. 94–95, 140–153, for the legacy of the war of 1870–71.
46. Mielert, *Bunte Bilder,* 18–19, 32; see also Paul Oskar Höcker, *An der Spitze meiner Kompanie: Drei Monate Kriegserlebnisse* (Berlin and Vienna, 1915), 22–27, 45–46.
47. Mielert, *Bunte Bilder,* 39: "Hoch klingt das Lied vom braven Mann!"
48. *Trara, - die Feldpost!* 48.
49. Aribert Reimann, *Der große Krieg der Sprachen: Untersuchungen zur historischen Semantik in Deutschland und England zur Zeit des Ersten Weltkriegs* (Essen, 2000), 215–219.
50. Vejas G. Liulevicius, *War Land on the Eastern Front: Culture, National Identity and German Occupation in World War I* (Cambridge, 2000), 151–158.
51. See, for example, *Wutki Kraputki: (Leib- und Magentrost aus Väterchens Mordbrennerei.)* Auf Flaschen gezogen und verzapft von Artur Lokesch (= Tornister-Humor, vol. 7) (Berlin, n.d.).
52. Höcker, *An der Spitze meiner Kompanie,* 70–71, also 85, 94; see also Eberhard Buchner, *Kriegshumor* (Munich, 1914), 67.
53. Reinhard Olt, *Krieg und Sprache: Untersuchungen zu deutschen Soldatenliedern des Ersten Weltkrieges* (Giessen, 1980–81).

54. *Papatacci: Südöstlicher Feld- und Etappenhumor. (Bis auf Widerruf letzte Nummer.) Zu Gunsten Angehöriger unserer in Albanien gefallenen Helden,* March 1918, 5–6.
55. Jay Winter, *Sites of Memory, Sites of Mourning: The Great War in European Cultural History* (Cambridge, 1995).
56. For violence in the Weimar Republic, see Dirk Schumann, "Europa, der Erste Weltkrieg und die Nachkriegszeit: Eine Kontinuität der Gewalt?" *Journal of Modern European History* 1 (2003): 24–43.
57. Bernd Hüppauf, "'Der Tod ist verschlungen in den Sieg:' Todesbilder aus dem Ersten Weltkrieg und der Nachkriegszeit," in Bernd Hüppauf, ed., *Ansichten vom Krieg: Vergleichende Studien zum Ersten Weltkrieg in Literatur und Gesellschaft* (Königstein, 1984), 55–91, here 60.
58. Klaus Latzel, *Vom Sterben im Krieg: Wandlungen in den Einstellungen zum Soldatentod vom Siebenjährigen Krieg bis zum II. Weltkrieg* (Warendorf, 1988), 82.
59. See the short remark by Peter Jelavich, *Berlin Cabaret* (Cambridge, 1993), 126, although he concentrates mainly on critical cabaret.
60. Sigmund Graff, *Dicke Luft! Eine neue Ladung Frontwitze* (Magdeburg, 1926); Carl-Albrecht Oertel, *"Hurra, bei Landersch!" Ernstes und Heiteres aus großer Zeit* (Frankenburg, 1932).
61. Sven Reichardt, *Faschistische Kampfbünde: Gewalt und Gemeinschaft im italienischen Squadrismus und in der deutschen SA* (Cologne, 2002), esp. 429–432, 454, 456–457.
62. Manfred Killinger, *Ernstes und Heiteres aus dem Putschleben.* With drawings by A. Paul Weber (Dresden, 1927) (the 11th ed. appeared in 1941); see also Carl Springer, *Auf geht's! Humor aus der Kampfzeit der nationalsozialistischen Bewegung.* Nach Erlebnissen alter Kämpfer erzählt von Carl Springer (Munich, 1939). Publications by members of the SA after 1934 certainly served to underline their role in NS history.
63. Regarding the radio, see Inge Marßolek and Adelheid von Saldern, "Das Radio als historisches und historiographisches Medium: Eine Einführung," in: Marßolek and Saldern, eds., *Zuhören und Gehörtwerden im Nationalsozialismus. I.: Radio im Nationalsozialismus: Zwischen Lenkung und Ablenkung* (Tübingen, 1998), 11–44, here 25–26.
64. Jelavich, *Berlin Cabaret,* 228–282.
65. Meike Wöhlert, *Der politische Witz in der NS-Zeit am Beispiel ausgesuchter SD-Berichte und Gestapo-Akten* (Frankfurt am Main, 1997). Members of party and state institutions argued continuously about the right way to balance the need for diversion and the danger of subversion.
66. Martin Rockenbach, ed., *Hausbuch neuen deutschen Humors,* 3rd ed. (Freiburg im Breisgau, 1942), 286–291, quote 290.
67. Gerd Fricke, "Wie unterhalte ich meine Hörer?" *Der deutsche Sender* 6, 7 (1935): 8.
68. Mario Zeck, *Das Schwarze Korps: Geschichte und Gestalt des Organs der Reichsführung SS* (Tübingen, 2002), 349–352.
69. "Mehr Humor!" *Das Schwarze Korps* 6, no. 6, February 1936: 1.
70. "Lachend seinen Mann stehen, / Lachend seinen Weg gehen, / Lachend vorwärts streben, / Lachend Freude geben - / Lachen zwingt das Leben!" Theo Rausch, *Die drei frohen Gesellen mit der Laterna* (Cologne, n.d. [1935]), quoted in Monica Pater, "Entspannung und Freude für die Hörer" – Heiterkeit als Lebenshilfe, in: Marßolek, Saldern (eds.), *Zuhören,* 187–224, here 207. The night cabaret that the Wehrmacht ran for soldiers passing through Berlin used the slogan "Lachen ist gesund!" (Laughing is healthy), Volker Kühn, *Die zehnte Muse: 111 Jahre Kabarett* (Cologne, 1993), 98, quoted in Pater, "Entspannung," 223, footnote 325.
71. Alfred Schröter, ed., *Hau Dunnerkiel! Heitere Kriegserlebnisse von der Front und aus der Heimat,* 7th ed. (Leipzig, 1943).
72. Joseph Goebbels, "Wunschkonzert," in Joseph Goebbels, *Die Zeit ohne Beispiel: Reden und Aufsätze aus den Jahren 1939–1941* (Munich, 1941), 335.
73. Hans-Eugen Bühler, with Edelgard Bühler, *Der Frontbuchhandel 1939–1945: Organisationen, Kompetenzen, Verlage, Bücher. Eine Dokumentation* (Frankfurt am Main, 2002), 70–71, 83.
74. This is the argument of Tobias Schneider, "Bestseller im Dritten Reich: Ermittlung und Anal-

yse der meistverkauften Romane in Deutschland 1933–1945," *Vierteljahrshefte für Zeitgeschichte* 52 (2004): 77–97.
75. See the correspondence in Bundesarchiv (hereafter BA), NS 18 / 483.
76. For films, Linda Schulte-Sasse, *Entertaining the Third Reich: Illusions of Wholeness in Nazi Cinema* (Durham and London, 1996), 2; for the entertainment of the troops, see the instructive survey in Alexander Hirt, "Die deutsche Truppenbetreuung im Zweiten Weltkrieg: Konzeption, Organisation und Wirkung," *Militärgeschichtliche Zeitschrift* 59 (2002): 407–434.
77. Hans Weis, *Deutsche Sprachspielereien: Gesammelt und erläutert von Dr. Hans Weis*, 2nd rev. ed. (Munich and Berlin, 1942), Introduction (n.p.).
78. For example: Günter Stöve, *Aus vergnügter Feder: Heiteres von ernsten Dichtern*, 2nd. ed. (Bayreuth, n.d. [1942]); Hans Ostwald, *Vom Goldenen Humor in Bild und Wort: Ein Buch des Lachens und der Freude* (Berlin, 1941). Quite a number of collections of war jokes edited after 1939 also avoided references to the actual war.
79. For example: Heinz Kindermann, *Das wunderbare Weinfass: Deutsche Schwänke* (Vienna, 1944); Willy Oeser, ed., *Humor im alten Reichsland: Zwischen Rhein und Vogesen* (Essen, 1944); Karl Lerbs, ed., *Die Drehscheibe: Anekdoten und Schnurren aus allen deutschen Gauen*, 4th ed. (Essen, n.d.194-); Herbert Frhr. v. Oelsen, *Till Eulenspiegels Erben: Der Humor deutscher Landschaften* (Oldenburg, 1943).
80. Hanns-Claus Roewer, ed., *Hamburger Grog: Deftige Begebenheiten aus der alten und neuen Hansestadt* (Berlin, 1943), n.p. [1–2].
81. Laurenz Kiesgen and Wilhelm Spael, eds., *Rheinischer Volkshumor*, 4th ed. (Essen, 1943), 259.
82. However, Richter and Ebeling were bitingly anti-Semitic and typically denied that Jews possessed the ability to fight. Friedrich Richter and Friedrich Ebeling, eds., *Humor in Feldgrau: Erlebtes—Erzähltes aus den Kriegsjahren 1939/1941* (Berlin, 1942), 4.
83. BA R 55/779, Fiche 1, Bl. 14–23, Propaganda-Aktion "Herr Bramsig und Frau Knöterich," Reichsministerium für Volksaufklärung und Propaganda, An die Reichspropagandaämter, 9 October 1941.
84. Herbert Michael, *Sieh dich an! Ein heiteres Buch mit ernstem Inhalt für jung und alt* (Dresden, 1935), esp. 17 (quotes), 26–33, 52–56.
85. Utz Jeggle, "In stolzer Trauer. Umgangsformen mit dem Kriegstod während des 2. Weltkriegs," *Tübinger Beiträge zur Volkskunde* 69 (1986): 242–259, esp. 248ff., 252.
86. Bernhard Poiess, *Soldaten-Geschichten* (=Schriftenreihe zur Truppenbetreuung, H. 29; Die Grauen Hefte der Armee Busch) (n.p., n.d.), 105–110.
87. Such stories sometimes differed markedly from the usual collections of short heroic scenes published earlier in the sense that they offered a real story from beginning to end. They followed a fictional group of soldiers in a complete narrative through the war, giving them names and a distinct history. Gustav Goes, *Die Trommel schlug zum Streite: Ernstes und Heiteres aus dem Krieg*, 6th ed. (Munich, 1944); Josef Stollreiter, *Die Eisernen Fünf: Ernstes und Heiteres um eine Korporalschaft im Weltkriege*, Kleine Wehrmacht-Bücherei, vol. 17 (Berlin, 1940); Fritz Stetefeld, *Kamerad Stetefeld: Humor im Felde. Ein Buch von der lustigen Seite der deutschen Frontsoldaten*, 4th ed. (Nuremberg, n.d.); Latzel, *Vom Sterben*, 84, regarding the "legacy of the dead" as a central part of NS propaganda.
88. Werner Lass and Hans-Adolf Weber, eds., *Landser lachen: Fronthumor dieses Krieges* (= "VB-Feldpost," 4. series), 7th ed. (Berlin, 1944), 6.
89. Cf. Frank Werner, "Massenmord und Männlichkeit. Selbstbilder und Fremdbilder deutscher Soldaten im Vernichtungskrieg, 1941–1944" (Master's thesis, University of Bielefeld, 2004), chaps. 3 and 4.
90. "Das harte Gelächter des 'Dennoch' erklingt, und die Kameradschaft wird umso fester!" Lass and Weber, *Landser lachen*, 5.
91. Omer Bartov, *Murder in our Midst: The Holocaust, Industrial Killing, and Representation* (New York and Oxford, 1996), 26–31.

92. "*Nach Goethe* Über allen Kühlern ist Ruh. Von den meisten Motoren hörest du kaum einen Hauch. Sie fuhren manche Meile, warte nur eine Weile, und die letzten stehen auch." Ludwig Voggenreiter, *Geballte Ladung: Heiteres für alle Fälle. Feldpostausgabe* (Potsdam, 1943), 24.
93. "Aber manchmal sah es böse aus bei uns. Oft wußten wir nicht, wo Deckung hernehmen." Wilhelm Utermann, *Darüber lache ich noch heute: Soldaten erzählen heitere Erlebnisse* (Berlin, 1943), 73.
94. Karl Seibold, *Deutschland lacht* (Munich, 1943), 19–20.
95. Klaus Latzel, "Töten und Schweigen - Wehrmachtssoldaten, Opferdiskurs und die Perspektive des Leidens," in Peter Gleichmann and Thomas Kühne, eds., *Massenhaftes Töten: Kriege und Genozid im 20. Jahrhundert* (Essen, 2004), 320–338, here 322.
96. Hans Riebau, Hans Reimann and Manfred Schmidt, *Lachendes Feldgrau* (Bremen, 1942), 142–143.
97. Riebau et al., *Lachendes Feldgrau*, 145–147.
98. Schröter, ed., *Hau Dunnerkiel!* 81.

Chapter 10

DEATH, SPIRITUAL SOLACE, AND AFTERLIFE
Between Nazism and Religion

Alon Confino

Hitler and die-hard Nazis set out to transform radically German society by providing an alternative to Christian ways of life and thought. An important element of this project was the attempt to create a new Nazi liturgy of death for the national community, or *Volksgemeinschaft*. At the same time, German society was still overwhelmingly religious. Perceptions of death and practices of bereavement were linked to belief in God, to the church, and to notions of redemption and salvation. Nazism as a radical, revolutionary worldview faced traditional rites of death that are, after all, notoriously resistant to change.[1] By looking at the ways people chose to grieve and seek solace, by looking at rites and perceptions of death, we can learn about the impact of Nazi intentions, power, and limits, and we can learn about how people internalized National Socialism.

The historiographical context of this essay is the debate over the relations between Nazism and Christianity. The view that the two worldviews were mutually exclusive has given way to an interpretation that sees—in various ways, terms, and emphasis—adaptation and accommodation.[2] Important in this regard was Sabine Behrenbeck's massive, insightful study, which, focusing on symbols and practices, explored the cult of dead heroes between 1923 and 1945 by showing the continued significance of the Christian churches in the Third Reich.[3] My overall aim is somewhat different: by focusing on death, I would like to understand a mental world that does not begin or end with ideology, and in so doing to think through how to view the Nazi ideology and way of life.

To understand this mental world, we have to begin with ideological intent.

Notes for this chapter begin on page 229.

I

The Nazis attempted to construct a German society based on a new subjective consciousness. Rites of death were central to this new project, whether connected to the violent death of soldiers on the battlefield or to the natural death of members of society. The Nazi idea of death in war was based on the will to battle and on the historic necessity of fighting for the future of the racially pure national community. Dying in war was the highest form of experience (*Erlebnis*) that blended heroism and self-sacrifice.[4] Starting in 1934 the Nazis celebrated Heroes Memorial Day (*Heldengedenktag*), which replaced the Day of National Mourning (*Volkstrauertag*) that had been celebrated since 1925 to remember the fallen soldiers of the First World War. On 16 March 1935, the day before Heroes Memorial Day, Hitler announced universal army conscription; in 1939 Heroes Memorial Day was moved to this date and was also called Day of Military Freedom (*Tag der Wehrfreiheit*). The message of the day changed from one of mourning to one of military strength; flags no longer were flown at half mast.[5]

The poet Ernst Bertram expressed the Nazi idea of death succinctly in his 1943 poem "Aber erst Gräber":[6]

> Aber erst Gräber
> Schaffen Heimat,
> Erst unsre Toten
> Geben uns Licht.
> …
> Erst über Särgen
> Werdet ihr Volk.
>
> Only graves
> Create a Homeland
> Only our dead
> Afford us light.
> …
> Only gathered around coffins
> Do you become a people.

Some soldiers no doubt believed in this. A letter from "Werner," a fallen soldier on the Eastern Front, published in December 1943 in the SS journal *Leitheft* seems genuine: "Should I die in battle at the front, in the company of my comrades until the last minute, then this will be the ultimate fulfillment of my life." When his mother is seized by sadness, he continues, she should "take a walk into the fields, up to the Glössberg and look down at Kallich. No price was too high to preserve our beautiful Sudetenland and the German Reich!"[7] Popular novels propagated the will to fight for the national community. In a book that was widely distributed to Waffen SS troops—Herbert Lange's *The Bridge between Life and Death: A Fallen Soldier's Diary*—the author described a romantic love for Heimat, family, and kin, as the protagonist, SS soldier Schröder, fulfilled his racial biological duty with Veronika. In this context, death was beautiful and rewarding.[8]

But the Nazi idea of death went beyond war, battlefield, and soldiers. It was connected to the larger aim of building Nazism into a cultural system. The journal *Die neue Gemeinschaft*, or *The New Community*, published essays that instructed readers on the correct Nazi ways of living, including attitudes toward music, books, marriage, and death. In a special issue in August 1942 it summarized the "life-cycle rites of the [Nazi] movement," emphasizing elements such as songs, music, aphorisms, and images, and discussed issues of space, decorations, attire, and pertinent traditions.[9] The journal provided examples of model ceremonies of the principle life-cycle rituals of birth, wedding, and obsequies. The obsequies accounted for different life situations, such as a funeral rite for a four-year-old girl or for a wife of a party member.

What were the characteristics of these model obsequies? One notices immediately that they were, in a sense, devoid of religion. But the tension between religion and Nazism is always present in the texts, and is palpable in the only case when religion is mentioned: "An example of an obsequy: the deceased was a religiously unaffiliated [*Gottgläubig*] party member, therefore the church did not participate in the ceremony."[10] The text implies that in other ceremonies the church should or did participate. (These are suggested ceremonies, we should remember). There is no trace of the church in the programs of the ceremonies; God is not mentioned. Instead, Hitler, the Nazi Party, and the people (*Volk*) are the sources of solace and meaning in the face of death. The following funerary eulogy was recommended: "Party member [so and so], we thank you for all that you had done for your family, we thank you for your effort for the Führer and his movement, and we thank you for your life-service for the German people."[11] The ceremonies, to be directed by local party officials, were to be decorated by Nazi and Reich symbols, while being dominated by common icons of German culture such as music by Schubert and Bach, or poems by Goethe.

The New Community conveyed the difficulty the Nazis faced in their attempt to create a new, sacral vocabulary and ritual, as well as the scope of their ambition: "As a result of the diverse characterizations of the life-cycle rites it is already evident how uncertain and unclear are the ideas about them. [For example], a rite to introduce a child into the national community [*Volksgemeinschaft*] is clearly wrong, for a child of German parents is born into the national community, and therefore this kind of a rite is nonsensical and unnecessary."[12] Nazism, as it saw itself, was not simply an ideology with which one could agree or disagree. It was not determined by the individual's will or choice; it was not an opinion, but a state of nature. As such, it produced a break of civilization, or *Zivilisationsbruch*.[13] But this act of rupture was inextricably linked to the act of construction of a racial civilization with its own symbols, rituals, and values. And ideas and rituals of death were at the center of this attempt.

II

And yet, the attempted ideological construction of Nazism was not quite congruent with the way most Germans lived National Socialism. There was a difference between ideological intention and actual experience. Nazism had to negotiate with opposing, contradictory, or simply long-held ways of life and thought in German culture. After 30 January 1933 Nazism was a work in progress, something at once to be culturally, socially, and racially built and to be treated for political reasons as already in existence. How did the attempt to construct Nazism commingle with existing customs about death in German culture? Given the terrible centrality of death in the Third Reich, this is a topic that we still know little about. I would like to articulate some possible lines of inquiry.

Nazism had, first, to take into consideration traditions and popular beliefs about death. Many such beliefs were recorded in the *Atlas of German Folklore* (*Atlas der deutschen Volkskunde*), which was based on a project of the German Research Community (*Deutsche Forschungsgemeinschaft*) that collected popular beliefs in mostly rural and small German localities between 1929 and 1935.[14] Death in Germany, as in every society, was linked to a host of local and regional symbols, superstitions, and prejudices. In some areas, for example, it was believed that letting tears fall on a dead body was a sign of the looming death of the one who cried; it connected the living and the dead and endowed the dead a power over the living. In Württemberg burying the dead on Sunday was considered a sign of forthcoming death. How did popular beliefs about death shape, and how were they shaped by, the war experience of mounting casualties among soldiers and civilians? Some habits must have been changed by Nazi politics and by the conditions of war, the bombings, deprivation, and struggle for survival. At the same time, Nazi policies that contradicted long-held mourning rituals had little chance of being accepted. The Nazis thus found opposition when they revived a policy from the First World War that ordered dead bodies to be buried in clothes made of paper instead of fabric. This was already ordered on 6 June 1939, before the war began. The attempt in the journal *Das Bestattungswesen* to argue that paper clothes could carry "dignity and piety" was unconvincing. Eventually, the dead were buried in paper clothes only out of necessity, as the war was prolonged, the death toll among the civilian population mounted, and deprivation set in.[15]

Regularly, however, the Nazis attempted not to change habits of mind about death, but to endorse them. Far from being innovative, the representation of fallen soldiers on tombstones and other commemorative sites during the war was a continuation of traditional forms. *The New Community*, which emphasized the novelty of Nazi rites, also recommended traditional forms of remembrance such as the *Dorfbuch*, or village book, which was common in small and rural localities. The book was appropriate, according to *The New Community*, because "the village honors its fallen, with whom it has been and still is linked, in a particular way, and the fallen thus remains alive in his Heimat and environment."[16] The *Dorfbuch* stories about the fallen Heimat sons put new wine in old bottles: they placed the swastika and slogans such as "fell for Führer, Volk and fatherland" within traditional forms and topics. In one such story there appeared a map sent to a certain Frau Lübke by the comrades of her fallen husband, showing the journey traversed by Paul Lübke from his native Heimat into Eastern Europe and finally to his grave, indicated on the makeshift map somewhere between Moscow and Leningrad. A cross under a tree made familiar a death that left behind no place of mourning for Frau Lübke.[17]

The New Community presented a picture of Nazi continuity with local, traditional customs of death, be they in the art of tombstones, commemoration within nature, or examples of funerary speeches that emphasized fatherland and localism but not race. Indeed, if the journal pointed out the novelty in Nazi ceremonies, as we have seen at the beginning of this essay, at the same time it emphasized that the "life-cycle rites of the movement" should not be viewed as a norm; they were changeable, and should reflect local conditions. The journal cited Alfred Rosenberg, who wrote in *Richtlinien für die Gestaltung der Lebensfeiern*, a publication linked to *The New Community*, that "On no account is it intended to fix the life-cycle rites in a dogmatic way or to contain them from the start in rigid forms."[18] This is a statement that Nazi ideas about death were, within the framework of racial terror against presumed enemies of the national community, flexible and attuned to local conditions and beliefs. And since the most powerful local beliefs in, and rituals of, death in German culture were religious, the question is raised, How did religion fit within this picture of Nazism as a mixture of new customs and old habits?

III

The New Community may have boldly outlined the contour of Nazi ways of life and thought, but, counseling its readers on how to mourn the death of a loved one, it presented a meek Nazi position in the face of religious rites of death: "When religious rites and the life-cycle rites of the [Nazi] movement are celebrated in proximity, the result is disagreeable disturbances and occasional organizational difficulties. Consequently, life-cycle rites of the movement will be carried out only when *no* religious rite takes place."[19] Not quite the revolutionary rhetoric about replacing Christian with Nazi ways of life and thought. Instead, it presents a revealing acknowledgment of the power of religion in German culture, and of the place of Nazism alongside it—indeed, in the specific case of rites of death, as a secondary player. This was congruent with the ways the majority of Germans were laid to rest. In 1930 in Berlin, for example, 82 percent of Lutherans (who comprised 76 percent of Berlin's population) and 68 percent of Catholics (10 percent of Berliners) were buried with church rituals.[20]

Some Nazi leaders, some soldiers and ordinary Germans, obviously shared the most radical vision that aimed at constructing Nazism as dominating, even replacing, Christianity. Even these die-hard Nazis could not operate totally outside of

Christian language and images, though they did clearly aim at overcoming them. But most other Germans internalized Nazi indoctrination, ideology, or the brutalization of the war in religious metaphors, symbols, and narratives. Hermann Witzmann wrote from the Eastern Front that "I am peaceful ... because I know that even in war and annihilation Jesus Christ is and remains my Redeemer."[21] In a postwar Catholic anthology of letters by fallen soldiers we read the following: "For me the duty as a soldier is the duty as a Christian. It is clear to me, that all my doing and work ... is in God's honor."[22] Others were more perturbed. As defeat and suffering replaced victories and elation, religious agony was evident, as in letters from Stalingrad's last dispatch: "In Stalingrad the question about God was posed, and was answered in the negative." And: "I don't believe in God anymore because He has betrayed us. I don't believe anymore, and you'll see how you will be through with your belief."[23]

These assertions are obviously open to interpretation. Invoking God does not necessarily mean anti-Nazism or human values. The soldier may have lost faith in God because He denied Germany a racial victory over the Russians. But this is precisely the point: most Germans thought and lived Nazism through a commingling with, not a clear-cut opposition to, religious images. The soldiers who lost God in Stalingrad must have assumed before the defeat that God, the war, and a certain understanding of Nazism had a shared mission, for one can lose only that which one has owned in the first place.

Nazi and religious ideas commingled, then. But what exactly do we mean by that? A common explanatory and narrative model in the humanities is based on the notion that "culture" is a web of intertwined relations among different, even opposing, forces. This is a powerful interpretative model. But it can at times obfuscate as much as reveal the exact relations among the various cultural forces. I would like to ask, even without being able to fully answer, Who provided spiritual sustenance to the bereaved?

Here I would like to advance an informed hypothesis. As the war became prolonged and the losses mounted, more Germans had to come to terms with the afterlife and salvation of their loved ones. Significantly, Nazi soldiers died for Hitler and fatherland, but they were buried with Christian rituals. The limits of Nazi ideology were clear: the Party offered a general truth and a national, collective cause, but could not quite offer personal redemption. The Nazi efforts to create new sacred obsequies, and a new sacred language by which to understand death, did not quite succeed, not in Heroes Memorial Day and not in the suggested ceremonies of *The New Community*. As the war went on ever longer, it became clearer that the attempt to replace religious spiritual support for the bereaved with Nazi ideas was not successful. Reports of the Security Service are quite clear about the success of the churches, especially the Catholic Church, in providing solace to the bereaved by endowing their sacrifice—a son, a husband, an uncle—with an everlasting meaning. Die-hard Nazis looked at this with some envy, for they had to use profane representations that also argued for the *Aufhebung* of death, except that the dead entered not into God's kingdom but into the Third Reich of the future, a notion that was satisfactory for Germans on many accounts but not as a spiritual guide for afterlife.[24] Ultimately, it is doubtful that Nazism provided everlasting spiritual support for a society as religious as Germany in the 1930s and 1940s. The spiritual contact with the dead provided in prayer, the spiritual solace offered by talking to God—this the Nazis could not quite provide, and certainly could not match.

This raises another question for reflection and further research: What was the Nazi idea of afterlife? For communists and atheists, the question made no sense; there was no afterlife. But the Nazis were too enamored of myths, blood, race, and death to have the sobriety of communists and atheists (who were not so sober about death and afterlife, after all, though this is a matter for a different discussion). Did the Nazis have an afterlife location (like Heaven or Purgatory), a notion of place and space linked to the afterlife? Some die-hard Nazi thinkers made references to immemorial racial blood as a living organism through the generations; these narratives implied immortality of the racial collectivity, but not a sense of afterlife. Where did the German soldiers end up when they died? If we find no evidence that the Nazis had much to say about it, then for those Germans who felt some links to Jesus a Christian idea of afterlife remained prominent.

What did take place was a coalescing of Nazi general ideas, a national cause, and religious rituals. My point is not that Nazism "lost" or "won" against religion: this is precisely the kind of perspective I reject. It is that whereas Nazism had a die-hard ideological streak that was extremely anti-Christian, lived Nazism, as an actual experience of most Germans, often fit comfortably with common, current traditional ways of life and thought. The Nazis could not monopolize the spiritual element in death in a society that was overwhelmingly religious, while the church provided spiritual assistance in death, but in language that often provided support to the regime.

V

I began this essay by outlining the Nazi revolutionary attempt to construct a new society. In its racial worldview and exterminatory zeal, this project was revolutionary; its aftermath is still with us. But for the historian this only begs the question, What were the elements that gave stability to this revolutionary and exterminatory project? In human affairs, even the most radical transformations are maintained by previous memories, habits, and beliefs. My own view is that Nazism set itself two fundamental limits that gave it tremendous support: the preservation of private property and mass consumption, and of religion. Nazism did provide an ideological alternative and a practical challenge to religion, especially to Catholicism. The conflicts over the euthanasia program and the removal of the Cross from Bavarian classrooms are two notable cases of tensions between Nazism and the established churches in Germany. But they also show the limits of the Nazi intent to eradicate religion in Germany: in both cases Hitler and the Party had to retreat; radical attempts at de-Christianization were not made.

Historical analogies with other revolutionary movements are instructive in keeping the right perspective about the types of relations, and tensions, that existed between National Socialism and religion. The Bolsheviks had a very different attitude toward religion and death. Catherine Merridale describes it in these words in *Night of Stone: Death and Memory in Twentieth-Century Russia*: "The 1920s and 1930s were decades of demolition. Church buildings were prime targets. They were turned into grain stores, cowsheds, arsenals; their roofs were stripped; their stones recycled; and the most annoying were blown up.... A faction in the Bolshevik Party will set out to break the grip of the past ... to supplant traditional languages of mourning....The policies will be inconsistent....But inconsistent as they are, and often unsuccessful, in their own terms, the anti-religious campaigns will ultimately affect every Soviet citizen, will color their attitude toward death, and change the framework of their memories forever."[25] Nazism never seriously considered adopting such policies. And it is open to question how long Nazism would have survived in power had it attempted Bolshevik-like anti-Christian policies.

The argument that elements in the German religious establishment supported Nazism is well known. There is an illuminating scholarship that shows how Christian scholars, clergy, and institutions "betrayed" their mission or used "God's name" in perpetrating genocide.[26] Such studies are insightful, but they are insightful from a particular kind of perspective, one that remains focused on bridging a perceived dissonance between Christian scholars or clergymen and Nazism. My perspective is not so much that Christian scholars and institutions became Nazis, but rather that Nazism, as a lived experience, could be amenable to Christian ways of life and thought in German society. Nazism was supported by Germans, among other things, because it allowed them to remain a certain kind of Christians, even as they became Nazis.

I should say at this point what I am not arguing. The way Germans internalized Nazism in religious notions cannot simply be understood under the term "political religion." This term has often been used, most recently by Michael Burleigh, to interpret National Socialism as "secularized religion" that provided "liturgies, ersatz theologies, vices and virtues."[27] I have no argument here with this position, though my point is different: Germans' religious beliefs should be taken not as a backdrop to a presumed "real" secular ideology, but as a fundamental factor in making Nazism amenable to many Germans who believed in God. At the same time, I obviously do not argue that Germany's religious institutions and beliefs were inherently Nazi or inevitably racist. My argument is that if Germans took their religious beliefs seriously, and if they took Nazi beliefs seriously, we should go beyond the level of ideology to find out how people made the two worldviews interact and, at times, support each other.

This methodological point demands further articulation.[28] The notion of ideology—a more or less systematic set of Nazi ideas about racial superiority and anti-Semitism—has dominated recent understanding of National Socialism. The term "ideology" is broadly used in the historiography to denote Nazi racial-political ideas elaborated by professional and managerial groups such as scientists, psychiatrists, and demographers; supported by the cultural intelligentsia in the arts, academia, and literary circles; refined and legitimized in research institutes and universities; and maintained by German bureaucracy and technology. Recent scholarship has shown how expressions of the regime's racial ideology penetrated all levels of life in the Third Reich. Through ideology—which in current historiography stands in self-conscious contrast to the older understanding of Nazi ideas as a mixture of fuzzy beliefs, vague intentions, or sheer passion and madness—the Nazis aimed at building a racial state, society, and way of life.

It is worthwhile remembering that several decades ago some scholars and laypersons regarded the Nazi regime as a movement without ideas and the very existence of Nazi ideology was denied. Franz Neumann observed in 1944 that "National Socialism has no political theory of its own … the ideologies it uses or discards are mere *arcana dominationis,* techniques of dominations."[29] Hannah Arendt, in a 1945 essay, severed all ties between Nazism and European culture, thus viewing its ideas ahistorically: "Nazism owes nothing to any part of Western tradition, be it German or not, Catholic or Protestant, Christian, Greek, or Roman.… Ideologically speaking, Nazism begins with no traditional basis at all, and it would be better to realize the danger of this radical negation of any tradition, which was the main feature of Nazism from the beginning."[30] This is an astonishing text by a thinker who made ideology a backbone of her interpretation of totalitarianism. The conceptual move to consider Nazi ideas and ideology seriously and historically has therefore been significant. It was a shift in historical consciousness—from viewing Nazism as alien to European history and to such "real" ideologies as liberalism and communism, to viewing it as having a body of ideas that was integral to European history.

This dominant interpretative view, therefore, is fundamentally insightful: namely of National Socialism as radical, revolutionary racial ideology and practice, and of the centrality of Nazi racial ideology in the making of the Third Reich. But it has now reached certain interpretative limits. The notion of ideology, it should be noted first, has been used with various degrees of sophistication and vagueness, and has been more practiced than theorized.[31] It is useful to make explicit what ideology, in the various ways it is used in current literature, cannot quite describe. The simplest argument is the following: the point is not that ideology is marginal to understanding National Socialism, but that, as a guide for values, beliefs, and mentalities, it is insufficient. If ideology is seen as everything and everywhere, then people's tendency to think outside, against, underneath, and above it is left historically unrecorded. Ideology becomes a dominant form of thought when it is supported by a state and a secret police, but it still remains one form of thought among others. In short, ideology is part of culture, not culture itself; it is too cerebral to embrace culture. Germans' collective mentalities existed before, during, and after Nazi ideology, which had to interact with different and older collective representations, such as religion and nationhood. Components of culture like fear, love, murder, salvation, and redemption, and such ideas as justice, liberty, humanity, peace, and morality were constructed in a process of appropriation, change, and reformulation whereby experience, ideology, and collective mentalities agreed with, opposed, and contested each other.

By viewing racial ideas as *the absolute dominant* vehicle in deciding people's actions in the Third Reich, we may risk reducing important beliefs in German culture—such as nationhood and religion—into epiphenomena. The topic of death is instructive. The Nazi way of death and extermination was unparalleled, but it coalesced, as I have attempted to show, with a continuation of traditional forms of bereavement and representation on the home front. In a society where religion and God still held enormous sway over people, regime ideology and racial tenets seem necessary but insufficient to explain actions, motivations, and perceptions of death, which is ultimately a topic mostly linked to morality, religion, and redemption (whatever one thinks of them and whether they exist or not). To think of one interpretative example: the historiography of the perpetrators of the Holocaust has argued that Germans killed at the front because of, among other, habituation, peer pressure, the barbarization of war, and Nazi ideology. This is all correct. But might perceptions of death in German society add to this picture? These perceptions were not the cause of the extermination, but they did exist before it began and therefore certainly had some part in the development, motivation, and consequences of what happened.

Differently put, the Nazi obsession with death resulted in the foundational story of death in the Third Reich, that is, the Holocaust and the extermination of Gypsies, Russian prisoners of war, people slated for euthanasia, and others. What were the relations between, on the one hand, the extermination, and on the other hand, the continuity of representation of death expressed in *The New Community* and in local village books and tombstones? Between extermination at the front and practices of death at the home front? Were they connected at all, and how? Whatever the answers will be, by knowing them we shall be wiser. One possible interpretation is that Planet Auschwitz, to use the words of K. Tzetnik, was possible precisely because so much of traditional German culture and society remained the same under the Nazis. The Nazis attempted to construct a new racial civilization that was based on significant continuities as well as significant ruptures.

To understand how religious and racial beliefs and practices interacted beyond the level of ideology, we need to know much more about rituals of grief and perceptions of death among Germans during the Third Reich.[32] Different levels existed, as I have tried to show. On one level, public ideology propagated death as sacrifice for Hitler and the racial national community in quite revolutionary terms. On a different ideological level, publications such as *The New Community* embraced local customs and religious rites by emphasizing continuity. And on yet another level, most people, without discarding these ideas, privately mourned by turning to God. Differently put, Nazi ideology alone is not enough to explain Germans' mental world, motivations, and belief. After the war, in 1955, the ethnographer Alfred Karasek-Langer collected stories of German expellees from

Eastern Europe. These stories originated, he wrote, "out of the deepest subconscious, legends of the end of the world; predictions and prophesies, future-oriented dreams, signs from heaven and appearances of the Virgin Mary, stories of guilt and atonement, punishments by God, curses and blessings, miraculous salvation, the return of the dead."[33] These sentiments were evident in other cases of mourning, bereavement, death, and extermination in the Third Reich.[34]

This history has implications for German society during the war and the postwar period. Private and public ways of mourning, while not being quite congruent, did intertwine well in the Third Reich. That they were held apart, while being connected, had important consequences. During the war, the fact that private pain could be expressed in terms other than Nazi ideology may have paradoxically added to the support for the regime. After the war, what remained in memory was the private pain, when family and friends remembered the fallen in tender human terms while avoiding the meaning of the exterminatory war. In other words, the history of German private pain during and after the war is fundamental. This history has recently been at the center of controversial debates generated by the works of Jörg Friedrich, Günter Grass, and of course W. G. Sebald.[35] Part of the debate has been thoughtful and elegiac, part polemical. Historians have much to contribute here.

The Third Reich was a break in civilization, and this was manifested in the death it inflicted. It must be unsettling to think that this break was based on much continuity in the rites and perceptions of death in German society of the period.

Notes

1. See the classic work of Philippe Ariès, *The Hour of Our Death*, trans. Helen Weaver (Oxford, 1981) and Michelle Perrot, ed., *A History of Private Life* vol. 4: *From the Fires of the Revolution to the Great War* (Cambridge, 1990).
2. For example, Richard Steigmann-Gall, *The Holy Reich: Nazi Conceptions of Christianity* (Cambridge, 2003).
3. Sabine Behrenbeck, *Der Kult um die toten Helden: Nationalsozialistische Mythen, Riten und Symbole 1923 bis 1945* (Vierow bei Greifswald, 1996).
4. Klaus Latzel, *Vom Sterben im Krieg: Wandlungen in der Einstellung zum Soldatentod vom Siebenjährigen Krieg bis zum II. Weltkrieg* (Warendorf, 1988), 84.
5. For this information, see Latzel, *Vom Sterben im Krieg*, 91.
6. Ernst Loewy, *Literatur unterm Hakenkreuz: Das Dritte Reich und seine Dichtung. Eine Dokumentation* (Frankfurt a/M, 1987 [1966]), 181.
7. Cited in Jay W. Baird, *To Die For Germany: Heroes in the Nazi Pantheon* (Bloomington, 1990), 218. See also Volker Ackermann, *Nationale Totenfeiern in Deutschland: Von Wilhelm I. bis Franz-Josef Strauss* (Stuttgart, 1990).
8. Baird, *To Die for Germany*, 219.
9. *Die neue Gemeinschaft* (August 1942): 275–277.
10. *Die neue Gemeinschaft* (August 1942): 306.

11. *Die neue Gemeinschaft* (August 1942): 309.
12. *Die neue Gemeinschaft* (August 1942): 276.
13. Dan Diner, ed., *Zivilisationsbruch: Denken nach Auschwitz* (Frankfurt, 1988).
14. Matthias Zender, ed., *Atlas der deutschen Volkskunde,* new ed., vol. 2 (Marburg, 1966–1982), 411, 413, 447.
15. Cited in Heidemarie Schade, "Das letzte Hemd—Sterbekleider aus Papier," *Volkskunst.* 8, no. 4 (1985): 40.
16. *Die neue Gemeinschaft* (June 1944): 246.
17. *Die neue Gemeinschaft* (June 1944): 249.
18. *Die neue Gemeinschaft* (August 1942): 275.
19. *Die neue Gemeinschaft* (August 1942): 277.
20. Statistisches Amt der Stadt Berlin, *Statistisches Jahrbuch der Stadt Berlin,* vol. 8 (Berlin, 1932), 158. I owe these figures to Monica Black.
21. Walter Bähr and Hans Bähr, eds., *Kriegsbriefe gefallene Studenten 1939–1945* (Tübingen, 1952), p. 34. I am indebted to Monica Black for this citation.
22. Franz König, ed., *Ganz in Gottes Hand: Briefe gefallener und hingerichteter Katholiken 1939–1945* (Vienna, 1957), 37. Cited in Utz Jeggle's thoughtful article "In stolzer Trauer: Umgangsformen mit dem Kriegstod während des 2. Weltkrieg," *Tübinger Beiträge zur Volkskultur* (1986): 247.
23. *Letzte Briefe aus Stalingrad* (Gütersloh, 1954), 31 and 29.
24. I have followed here Jeggle's analysis in "In stolzer Trauer," 256–257.
25. Catherine Merridale, *Night of Stone: Death and Memory in Twentieth-Century Russia* (New York, 2002), 137, 129.
26. Robert Erickson and Susannah Heschel, eds., *Betrayal: German Churches and the Holocaust* (Minneapolis, 1999); Omer Bartov and Phyllis Mack, eds., *In God's Name: Genocide and Religion in the Twentieth Century* (New York, 2001).
27. Michael Burleigh, *The Third Reich: A New History* (New York, 2000), 5–6. There is a long scholarly tradition that sees fascism as a political religion. Eric Voegelin, *Die politischen Religionen* (Stockholm, 1939); Klaus Vondung, *Magie und Manipulation: Ideologischer Kult und politische Religion des Nationalsozialismus* (Göttingen, 1971); Emilio Gentile, *The Sacralization of Politics in Fascist Italy* (Cambridge, MA, 1996); Uriel Tal, *Religion, Politics and Ideology in the Third Reich: Selected Essays* (London, 2004).
28. I have discussed this issue in "Fantasies about the Jews: Cultural Reflections on the Holocaust," *History and Memory* 17, nos. 1–2 (2005): 296–322.
29. Cited in Shulamit Volkov, "Antisemitism as Explanation: For and Against," in Moishe Postone and Eric Santner, eds., *Catastrophe and Meaning: The Holocaust and the Twentieth Century* (Chicago, 2003), 38.
30. From Hannah Arendt, *Essays in Understanding: 1930–1954,* ed. Jerome Kohn (New York, 1993). Cited in Anson Rabinbach, "The Abyss that Opened up Before Us: Thinking about Auschwitz and Modernity," in Postone and Santner, eds., *Catastrophe and Meaning,* 57–58.
31. There has been little discussion of the definition of the term and how best to use it (whatever approach one would like to adopt, by Karl Marx, Karl Mannheim, Clifford Geertz, or others), and little attempt to consider the relations between Nazi ideology and German culture. For a good introduction to the meaning of ideology, see Terry Eagleton, ed., *Ideology* (London, 1994).
32. There is one fundamental issue I could not discuss here. Protestants and Catholics possibly had different reactions to death and the Nazi view of death, a distinction that might reward careful study. Catholics, after all, continue to believe in purgatory and have a variety of rituals associated with death and burial that have long withered away among Lutherans. On the origins of this divided conception of death see Craig Koslofsky, *The Reformation of the Dead: Death and Ritual in Early Modern Germany, 1450–1700* (New York, 2000) and Koslofsky, "From Presence to Remembrance: The Transformation of Memory in the German Reformation," in Alon

Confino and Peter Fritzsche, eds., *The Work of Memory: New Directions in the Study of German Society and Culture* (Urbana-Champaign, 2002), 25–38.
33. Cited in Robert Moeller, *War Stories: The Search for a Usable Past in the Federal Republic of Germany* (Berkeley and Los Angeles, 2001), 86.
34, For a thoughtful study that focuses on the redemptive narratives that emerged in East and West Germany to explain the war, defeat, genocide, and reconstruction see, Frank Biess, *Homecomings: Returning POWs and the Legacies of Defeat in Postwar Germany* (Princeton University Press, 2006).
35. Jörg Friedrich, *Der Brand. Deutschland im Bombenkrieg 1940-1945* (Berlin, 2002); Günter Grass, *Crabwalk*, trans. Krishna Winston (Orlando, 2002); W. G. Sebald, *On the Natural History of Destruction,* trans. Anthea Bell (New York, 2004).

Chapter 11

YIZKOR! COMMEMORATION OF THE DEAD BY JEWISH DISPLACED PERSONS IN POSTWAR GERMANY

Gabriel N. Finder

Since the slaughter of Jewish communities during the Crusades in the eleventh century, it has been the custom of Ashkenazi Jews—Jews from Central and Eastern Europe—to hold a communal memorial service for the dead on the last day of the three pilgrimage festivals, Passover, Shavuot, and Sukkot, and on Yom Kippur, the Day of Atonement. This service is known by the Hebrew term *yizkor* (*yizker* in Yiddish), which is the opening word of its central prayer. This prayer asks God to remember departed relatives and then all Jewish martyrs. (The word *yizkor* is a form of the verb *zakhor*—"remember.") The *yizkor* service evolved into a defining feature in the life of Jewish communities because, as ethnographer Harvey E. Goldberg explains, "concern for the souls of individuals to whom one had been individually attached when they were alive became inextricably linked to a sense of community. ... When, during the *yizkor* prayer, Jews call upon God to remember the departed, they invoke the intertwined modes of personal and communal memory."[1]

On 17 September 1945, Shmuel Gringauz addressed the congregation assembled in the synagogue of the camp for "displaced persons" (DPs) in the Upper Bavarian town of Landsberg am Lech during the *yizkor* service on Yom Kippur. Gringauz, a former judge in Memel (Lithuania), was postwar chairman of the camp committee in Landsberg and a member of the Central Committee of Liberated Jews in the American Occupation Zone in Germany (*Tsentral-komitet fun di bafrayte yidn in der amerikaner zone in daytshland*). An estimated 50,000–80,000 Jews lived to see liberation of the concentration camps on German soil. By the end of 1946, about 150,000 Jewish refugees had moved into DP camps and

---

Notes for this chapter begin on page 254.

assembly centers in the US zone largely in Bavaria and elsewhere in southern Germany. (Jewish DPs who resided in the British and French zones of occupied Germany and in the American zones of occupation in Austria and Italy do not figure in this essay.) Following biblical references, the mostly Yiddish-speaking Jewish DPs called themselves *sheyres hapleyte* in Yiddish (*she'eirit' hapeleitah* in Hebrew)—"the surviving remnant." They were mainly from Eastern Europe, fleeing anti-Jewish violence and searching for a new home, either in Israel or North America, chiefly the United States. They lived in makeshift installations (former German military barracks, POW and slave labor camps, industrial housing, and the like)—the DP camps. These Jews were distinct, and largely lived separately, from some 15,000 German Jews, a majority of them highly assimilated, who had survived the Holocaust either in hiding or in concentration camps.[2] For the most part, Jewish and non-Jewish DPs in Germany lived in separate DP camps because the Jews insisted on separation from the non-Jewish DP population, since a fair share of Nazi collaborators and anti-Semites could be found in the ranks of the non-Jewish DPs.[3]

Gringauz's address on Yom Kippur was published in the *Landsberger Lager-Cajtung* (*Landsberg Camp Newspaper*), the camp's weekly Yiddish newspaper, on 8 October 1945 under the title—in the Latinized orthography of the time—"Jizker." "Today," he began, "I will for the first time in a free house of prayer say *yizker* for your fallen dearest ones, for your children and parents, for your wives and sisters. And I, in the name of this entire congregation … will say *yizker* for the unidentified and anonymous, for those who have no one left who can say *yizker* for them, … for the six million who lie in the bloody European earth—for all of them I will say *yizker* today." Although Jewish tradition established specific festivals for this purpose, the survivors, he contended, required no specially ordained occasions when the *yizkor* prayer is said:

> We, who lived for six long years in daily contact with the angel of death; we, who saw thousands of the best and dearest fall day in and day out; we, who feel closer to the dead than to the living—we require no special *yizker*. Our *yizker* is a constant and uninterrupted one. We say *yizker* in the morning and in the evening. We say *yizker* by day and by night. We say *yizker* while awake and in our dreams. Our heart beats to the rhythm of *yizker*, and in our brain its melody plays incessantly. We require no special *yizker*.

Gringauz concluded his speech by integrating bereavement into a dual vision of renunciation of Europe on the one hand and national redemption on the other:

> When you have left this accursed European earth and have become citizens of our land in the east, once a year, … on the day of Yom Kippur, go up a mountain in the land, turn with your face to the west, to the country of yesterday, to the bloody European ground, and with the deepest introspection of which your soul is capable, say *yizker* for those who have fallen … for the six million bloodied victims who have fallen—for the

sanctification of God's name, for the sanctification of the nation, for the sanctification of the land [of Israel].⁴

Traditional Jewish rituals of mourning persevered into the aftermath of the *khurbn*, the Yiddish term for "catastrophe," which Jews from Eastern Europe had used already under Nazi occupation to signify the event that came to be known in the 1950s as "the Holocaust." But if Gringauz's assessment from 1947 was accurate, the majority of *sheyres hapleyte* either had lost their faith in God in the concentration camps or struggled to perceive God's imprimatur in the universe. "The solemnity of mass death," he wrote, "aroused a desire for retaliation, but in no case encouraged one to accept what had happened as the verdict of God."⁵

Gringauz's comment brings to mind the biblical narrative in chapter 6 of Judges, where God has delivered the Israelites into the hands of the Midianites. An angel appears to Gideon and appoints him in God's name to lead the Israelites to victory over their enemy. Gideon harbors doubts. "If the Lord is with us, why has all this befallen us?" he inquires of the angel. "Where are all his wondrous deeds about which our fathers told us? ... Now the Lord has abandoned us and delivered us into the hands of Midian!" Gideon asks God for signs of his existence, and God obliges.

The DPs despaired of ever receiving a sign from God. The reason was the veritable avalanche of Jewish corpses. Levi Shalitan, the editor of *Unzer Weg* (*Our Way*), the weekly Yiddish publication of the Central Committee, poignantly expressed what all Jewish DPs must have felt: "The days of our lives have turned into anniversaries of mourning [*yortsaytn*]. There is hardly a date without a remembrance of a specific 'event': ghetto clearances [*aktsies*], selections, transports, liquidations, resettlements and such other horrific terms and bestial workings of the mind."⁶ To borrow from historian Emmanuel Sivan, theirs was a "profane grief." "The aim of the survivors," Sivan writes, "[was] to cope with their grief and make it into a tool for crystallizing a historical consciousness. ... Bereavement [was] integrated into a consciousness of historical continuity, but lack[ed] a transcendental presence. The entity overarching the individuals [was] that of the nation."⁷

Another example among many: In April and May 1946 a cultural delegation dispatched by the American Jewish Congress (AJC) toured the DP camps in an effort to raise the spirits of the survivors. Yiddish poet H. Leivick, the pseudonym of Leyvik Halpern, was a member of this delegation. Leivick opens his memoir of this tour through various DP camps by recalling the words inscribed on memorial plaques—such a plaque is called a *yizker-tovel* in Yiddish, literally a "*yizkor* tablet"—hanging in public areas of every DP camp on his itinerary:

YIZKOR
Remember what the Nazi German Amalek did to your people.
REMEMBER
The six million Jews, who perished for the sanctification of Your name and for the sanctification of the nation
At the hands of the German murderers [and] hangmen.

Remember Treblinka.
Remember Majdanek.
Remember Auschwitz.
Remember Buchenwald.
Remember Dachau.
Remember the gas chambers.
Remember the crematoria.
YIZKOR
6,000,000[8]

Gringauz's speech during the *yizkor* service on Yom Kippur and the words inscribed on the *yizkor* tablets that were ubiquitous in the DP camps—these and countless other expressions of *yizkor* by *sheyres hapleyte* integrated mourning into a political argument for the right of immigration to Jewish Palestine and Jewish statehood. Without a doubt, not all Jews wanted to move to Palestine or, after 1948, to Israel. Many preferred the United States. But intense sentiment in favor of a Zionist resolution to the dilemma of the DPs prevailed in the DP camps and sustained a vibrant Zionist environment in them. Most DPs, regardless of their final destination, were convinced that the *khurbn* could have been averted or at least diminished in scale if a Jewish state had already existed on the eve of the Second World War. Working in tandem with DP leaders, Zionist emissaries from Palestine organized political and cultural activities in the DP camps, and hundreds of young Jews joined Zionist training farms (*kibbutzim*) with a mind to immigrating en masse to Palestine. Anthropologist Katherine Verdery argues for the saliency of the "political lives of dead bodies" in postcommunist Europe.[9] The dead bodies of Jewish victims of Nazism sanctified the DPs' claim to recognition by Americans—and British officials from their zone of occupied Germany—of their right to emigrate to their Jewish homeland. (After the war Britain, the mandatory authority in Palestine, severely impeded Jewish migration to the country and the Jewish path to independence in Palestine.)

By the same token, the intensity of the DPs' grief did not allow for unalloyed transformation of their sorrow into political argument. No antidote, not even the Zionist promise of national redemption, was potent enough to numb the pain of their broken hearts. The politicization of mourning had limits.

In several forms of public commemoration the *sheyres hapleyte* in the American zone of occupied Germany emphatically associated the deaths of Jews in the *khurbn* with Jewish statehood and independence in Palestine. In this article I focus on four such forms: burial and reburial; the memorial assemblies organized by *landsmanshaftn*, which were associations of people from the same locality; the publication of *yizker* (memorial) books by *landsmanshaftn*; and the establishment of an official day of commemoration. In all of these commemorative forms the DPs in varying degrees integrated their bereavement into a political message of compelling moral suasion. However, whether any of these forms of commemoration brought comfort and solace to the mourners is open to question.

I

All Jewish DPs deemed it their solemn responsibility to afford a proper burial to Jewish victims of Nazism who had died on German soil. Since numerous Jewish cemeteries had been ruined during the war, Jewish DP communities were deeply concerned with the establishment and restoration of cemeteries. Thousands of Jews who died either on the eve of liberation or in its aftermath required immediate burial, while the exhumation and reburial of former concentration camp victims deposited pell-mell in mass graves would entail a considerable expenditure of time and effort. Already by the beginning of 1946, many DPs like Levi Shalitan were expressing their impatience with the modest pace of the endeavor to rebury the remains of Jewish victims on German soil, since the honor of the dead required an expeditious burial.[10] That said, what the DPs accomplished in this regard, with the assistance of American Jewish military rabbis, was truly impressive.

In the months prior to liberation thousands of Jewish inmates imprisoned in concentration camps in Germany died while still in the camps, from brutality, disease, and starvation. The inmates who were still alive were evacuated from camps in Germany in the final phase of the war and driven southward in several death marches from the increasingly constricted territory of the Reich in the direction of Tyrol.[11] The survivors of these death marches were liberated en route by American troops, but not before thousands had died either in boxcars or because they were unable to continue on foot. Thousands of liberated concentration camp inmates were too weak to survive much longer and died in the first days and weeks following liberation. Some 20,000 Jews perished within the first few weeks following liberation from the effects of internment in concentration camps.[12] Many perished because after years of malnutrition their impaired digestive systems were unprepared for the fatty military rations that generous American soldiers innocently offered them when they saw their skeletal figures.[13]

In addition, countless DPs died before they were able to migrate from Germany. Years of abuse, starvation, deprivation, and disease took their toll. They suffered from weak hearts, high blood pressure, stomach illnesses, and neurological disorders. Many survivors took their own lives in a state of depression. Tuberculosis in particular was a common ailment and claimed the lives of hundreds of Jewish victims from the moment of liberation to the end of the decade.[14] Jewish doctors struggled to save afflicted survivors and convened a conference in Feldafing in April 1946 to discuss ways to stem the pandemic.[15] But it still exacted a heavy price in lives. The US Army requisitioned the tuberculosis sanitariums of St. Ottilien and Gauting, located in the vicinity of Munich, in April 1945; St. Ottilien was for Jewish DPs and Gauting for all DPs, yet Jews were half of all patients there until the beginning of 1949.[16] From May 1945 through 1949 some 400 Jewish patients died at the Gauting sanitarium.[17]

Among the first Jewish victims to be buried after liberation were two Jews evacuated from a disrupted transport from Dachau under the daring initiative of Zalman Grinberg, a doctor from Kovno who would become the first chairman of the Central Committee, to the hospital of St. Ottilien, which he commandeered from its German personnel before the arrival of American troops. An American captain ordered the German personnel now under Grinberg's supervision to prepare a military funeral with full honors for the two anonymous Jewish men, who had died in the hospital. Standing near the open graves, the captain, in Grinberg's presence, said to the Germans in fluent German: "The two Jews whom we committed to burial today are perhaps the first happy Jews in liberated Europe. Their corpses merited what was denied to millions of their brethren: the right to be buried in their final resting place in purity and holiness according to the rites of their religion."[18] Within only a few weeks after liberation, before the end of May 1945, Grinberg had already buried thirty-five Holocaust survivors, dead of illness, in the cemetery of St. Ottilien.[19]

The liberation of disrupted transports in the last desperate days of the war was frequently followed by spontaneous burials of their dead victims. When Ernest Landau's transport was intercepted by American troops between Tutzing and Feldafing in Bavaria on 1 May 1945, the surviving prisoners removed the corpses, mostly Jews, from the freight cars and dug a grave right on the spot. A Jewish chaplain, Max Braude, arrived on the scene and sought rabbis from among the prisoners. They gathered a few rabbis and held a religious service in the open field, in view of a portable alter. All recited *El male rakhamim,* a memorial prayer for the dead, and many said *kaddish,* a prayer sanctifying God associated with mourning that is recited traditionally on the anniversary of the death of a close relative, while those who still hoped that their parents were still alive refrained. In Landau's estimate, there must have been assembled fifteen hundred or even two thousand men. "It was the most moving religious service I have ever experienced," he recalled in an interview more than forty years later.[20]

In the immediate aftermath of liberation the first task of Jewish chaplains assigned to the US army was to bury the Jewish dead who lay strewn not only in camps but also in and next to open boxcars and on the open roads. The chaplains felt overwhelmed by the large number of unburied corpses and mass graves, yet they deemed it their unique duty to bury the Jewish dead with dignity and according to Jewish ritual.[21] When Chaplain Herschel Schacter arrived at Buchenwald on 12 April 1945, one day after the liberation of the camp, he established a traditional Jewish burial society—*khevrah kadisha*—from among surviving inmates and acquired a plot from the military for use as a cemetery for the burial of the Jewish dead in accordance with Jewish custom.[22] After the liberation of Dachau on 29 April 1945, Rabbi Abraham Klausner supervised the burial of that concentration camp's Jewish victims. Initially, they were placed in common graves on a hill outside the camp, as American military officials were fearful of the spread of disease. Later the dead were buried in individual graves in the Dachau village cemetery. Each day a contingent of German prisoners of war would dig rows of individual graves in the cemetery and trucks would ferry them to the cemetery from Dachau and its nearby satellite camp Allach. At the close of every day Klausner would go to the cemetery, stand at the last grave in which a body had been placed, and recite the *kaddish* prayer. After a while a survivor from the camp accompanied Klausner to the cemetery and recited *kaddish*. Upon returning to the camp, Klausner would record the names of the buried in a military ledger. (Years later Klausner was incensed when he visited the cemetery only to discover that, with few exceptions, the graves had been capped with the Christian cross. He complained to Dachau city officials, asking them to remark the graves as those of Jews on the basis of the military ledger, but to no avail, as they replied that concentration camp inmates buried in the cemetery were of different nationalities and religious beliefs and that the existence of the ledger was unknown to them.)[23]

In Hof in the Bamberg district, Wolf Weil, who was saved by Oskar Schindler, formed a Jewish committee when he arrived from Krakow in mid 1945. When he discovered that more than a hundred dead Jews who had been shot in death marches were strewn in the forests around Hof, he made it his first task to bury them in a mass grave in the town's Jewish cemetery, over the objections of the American commander in charge there. He had a memorial stone erected with an inscription that 142 concentration camp inmates were buried there.[24]

One of the first postwar casualties of tuberculosis was David Zeitlin, the nephew of the Yiddish poet Aaron Zeitlin, who lived in America and was a close friend of the poet Leivick who was visiting DP camps in the spring of 1946. David Zeitlin died in July 1945 at the Gauting sanitarium. Leivick promised Aaron Zeitlin that he would locate his nephew's grave. His was one of six graves arranged helter-skelter on a mound in an open field near the sanitarium. A wooden plaque mounted on a board rising from the ground marked the site of his grave and those of the others.[25]

Beginning in October 1945, the DPs initiated plans for Jewish cemeteries for the victims. The American Joint Distribution Committee (AJDC), which provided legal and material aid to the DPs, lent its support to this process from early on.[26] Through the intervention of the AJDC's Department of Religious Affairs, directed by Rabbi Solomon Shapiro, Jewish DP communities requested permission from American military officials to exhume the remains of Jewish victims who were interred either in mass graves or erroneously in Christian cemeteries.[27] The Department of Religious Affairs appointed Abel Akabas to direct a graves registration office, from which he oversaw the task of identifying mass graves containing the remains of Jewish victims in the vicinity of former concentration camps, near highways, and in forests.[28] Akabas, from Kovno, was a survivor of Dachau who dedicated his life in the immediate aftermath of the genocide to uncovering mass graves.[29] Akabas demanded and obtained financing, labor, and building materials from local German authorities for the establishment and restoration of Jewish cemeteries for victims who died before and after liberation. The military administration put pressure on German officials to expedite the preparation of Jewish cemeteries.[30] The AJDC contributed financially to this project as well. In 1946–47 nine cemeteries for Jewish concentration camp victims and one for the deceased Jewish patients treated at St. Ottilien were erected in the Landsberg district. The total cost for these cemeteries was RM 450,000, including RM 222,000 for the erection of memorials in them.[31] The cemetery established in Schwabhausen in the vicinity of Munich was for Jewish concentration camp inmates who were killed in an air raid while they were being transported in the final days of the war. The cemetery, protected by a concrete wall, was designed to contain a monument adorned by a Star of David made out of bronze, three mass graves containing the remains of the victims, and benches.[32] Hundreds of DPs attended the consecration of the newly erected cemeteries. DPs also sought protection for Jewish cemeteries from desecration, which was a common occurrence after the war.[33] Although the DPs generally demanded separate Jewish cemeteries, there were cemeteries that were shared by Jewish and non-Jewish dead, and even commemoration ceremonies in which Jews and Christian clergy participated together.[34]

A certain Eichler, who was a representative of the AJDC in Bamberg, has left a description of the burial on 12 September 1946 of eighty-six corpses of Jewish concentration camp inmates who were murdered by SS guards in the forest en route from Buchenwald to Theresienstadt. They were buried in the prewar Jewish cemetery in Hof, which escaped the ravages of the war. Former Nazi Party members were forced to prepare the mass grave for the corpses, some of which could be identified, while others remained anonymous. Invited to the ceremony were the American military governor of Hof, representatives of the United Nations Relief and Rehabilitation Administration (UNRRA), local German officials, a clergyman, the secretary of the Communist Party in Hof, and several Jewish dignitaries, among them the chairman of the Jewish committee in Hof, two Zionist representatives, and the AJDC's local representative, Eichler. The majority of those in attendance were fifteen hundred Jewish DPs from the camp in Hof. They were, in Eichler's words, "Poorly clothed pale people, Jews from Poland!" But their humble appearance belied their singularity of purpose. "In the figure of the approximately 1,500 assembled Jews," Eichler wrote, "one sees clearly the seriousness of the hour. The wooden coffins, which contain the remains of the former Jewish prisoners of concentration camp, are conducted by Jews to a mass grave, no loud word is to be heard, all present are obviously moved. Numerous wreaths are laid."

The chairman of the Jewish committee in Hof opened the ceremony with solemn words, followed by the heartfelt prayer of a cantor. The assembled listened with interest to the expressions of sympathy by the non-Jewish guests, but the words of the Jewish speakers deeply moved the DPs. Eichler himself spoke. "Deeply moved with bleeding heart I stand before the remains of our brothers. … How much pain and suffering lies here buried. … You have bequeathed us … a trust. … We will fulfill your trust. … Brothers and sisters! You have to find your peace in this earth we hate so. Before us stands still lies a thorny road. We shall carry out your bequest and struggle for our own home." In a similar vein, a Zionist representative, Horowitz, exclaimed: "The blood of our brothers, their innocent spilled blood calls out and accuses: Where is morality? … These corpses are only a tiny fraction of our six million dead. But they could not and will never break our spirit. We will struggle until we attain our own home." Eisenstadt, another Zionist representative, was even more unforgiving. In Hebrew he said, "Murder after murder was committed against the Jews. ... This cruel destiny will never be repeated in history. We swear to you!" Eichler described the conclusion of the ceremony in poignant terms:

> During the speeches of the Jewish speakers, the assembled were seized with emotion. Sobbing can be heard. We feel miserable as we see these faces, pale from suffering. A woman faints. The ceremony ends with a speech by Cantor Kraus. How heartrending it is when he calls, "Brothers, let us pray." The Jews in attendance say *kaddish* aloud. Many people are crying. Cantor Kraus recites the "*El male rakhamim*," the [Zionist national anthem] "Hatikvah" is sung, and the ceremony is declared ... over. In accordance with the ancient rite, I throw a handful of earth into the grave. People disperse slowly. One man faints; he has had a seizure. A sorry sight was the tired faces from the Hof camp. In bad clothes, undernourished people. They were broken figures. On their faces one could read the tragedy of the Jewish people.[35]

With no expectation of returning to Germany after immigrating to Israel or North America, the DPs, concerned for the maintenance of these cemeteries and enclosed mass graves after their departure, left them without knowing whether anyone would tend them, especially since Germans showed no interest in maintaining them.[36]

II

In the immediate aftermath of liberation the DPs formed *landsmanshaftn*, associations of people from the same town or area in Eastern Europe. Since the turn of the century Eastern European Jewish immigrants had established *landsmanshaftn* in the United States. In America they were mutual aid and fraternal organizations, providing members with the security and familiarity of their tight-knit communities from the "old country."[37] Now in the DP camps *landsmanshaftn* evolved into kinship groups, substitute families for survivors deprived for the most part of their own families, incorporating a few surviving distant relatives, *landslayt* (fellow townspeople), and concentration camp "brothers" and "sisters." One outside observer, a sociologist, was impressed by how "close and intense" these relationships were.[38] Its members were united above all by common grief.

From early on the *landsmanshaftn* throughout occupied Germany organized "assemblies of bereavement" (*troyer akademiyes*) for the victims of their cities, towns, and villages. Anywhere from twenty-five to several hundred survivors from a particular community would gather for speeches by dignitaries and a memorial service usually on the anniversary, or *yortsayt*, of the community's liquidation by the Nazis (Fig. 11.1). The DP press devoted extensive coverage to these assemblies. For instance, on 11 November 1946 about 250 remaining survivors from

Figure 11.1. Survivors from Vilna gather for a memorial service in Munich in 1948. Courtesy of David Rogow. United States Holocaust Memorial Museum Photo Archives.

the town of Rivne in Volhynia (Western Ukraine) convened in the DP camp of Föhrenwald to commemorate the fifth anniversary of the community's liquidation by the Germans, who shot twenty-three thousand of its inhabitants on 7–8 November 1941. The surviving Jews were crammed into a ghetto, which the Germans annihilated on 13 July 1942. A remnant of Rivne's Jews who were put to work for the German economy survived the massacres and subsequent executions. A Rivne native who attended the assembly in Föhrenwald described it:

> On a long table in front of the presidium many candles are burning. The assembled, the remnants of Rivne Jewry, are despondent, hearts burst from grief. There reigns a deathly silence in the hall. In the mind's eye is fixed the horrific image [of] … the graves in which parents, sisters, brothers, and children are driven, they are shot, or they are buried alive!!!! … The assembled rise in honor of the martyrs. The cantor intones the memorial service. … When the cantor recites the words "the souls of the murdered who relinquished their souls for the sanctification of God's name," the assembled see the souls of their dear ones in the burning candles, and their hearts fill with tears; the assembled cannot restrain themselves, and the hall erupts in a wailing lament by all the assembled. The assembly of bereavement is over, [but] the people cannot move, tears gush, the heart is in pain. *Great is the wrath.*

The description of this convocation ends in an afterthought: "Everyone has one wish: Future generations should remember the horrific tragedy that befell our dear brothers, sisters, and children. … *Yizkor!*"[39]

The half-dozen speeches of dignitaries at the assembly held at the DP camp in Landsberg on 20 October 1946 to mark the fourth anniversary of the liquidation of the large ghetto in Częstochowa, Poland (Tshenstokhov in Yiddish) were typical of speeches delivered at such gatherings. The speakers from Częstochowa, who were leaders of its *landsmanshaft*—the other speakers were officials of the Central Committee of Liberated Jews in occupied Germany, including Shmuel Gringauz—reconstructed the community's glory in the annals of Polish Jewry, its destruction at the hands of the Nazis and their accomplices, the hardships endured by its Jewish inhabitants, and the heroic deeds of its Jews in the armed underground resistance. While the speeches looked in large part to the past, they also beckoned to the future. In this spirit Benjamin Orenstein, the cultural director on the central committee of the Częstochowa *landsmanshaft*, concluded with a tribute to the cultural legacy of the town's destroyed community. "The small number of surviving fellow townspeople from Częstochowa," he exclaimed, "constitute the living testimony of the bitter fate of our national tragedy. We all have to unite in spirit with one thought, with one idea, which leads to freedom and justice. Let our hearts beat to the same rhythm and beat, let us close ranks more closely, joined hand in hand and march with identical steps to a free and joyful morning." This dream would be closest to being realized when the survivors would be "free citizens in a free land"[40]—that is to say, Jewish Palestine.

Photographs of these assemblies usually show survivors posing with a memorial plaque or a banner in the shape of a tombstone. Their inscriptions bear similar messages. One group portrait (Fig. 11.2) shows roughly one hundred Jewish DPs from the Polish town of Makow Mazowiecki (Makov in Yiddish) convened at the Fürstenfeldbruck DP camp in Bavaria on 15 December 1947. On the eve of the German invasion of Poland in September 1939, the Jewish community of Makow Mazowiecki numbered 3,500 souls. Shortly after the German invasion another 500 Jews moved to the town. The Germans established a ghetto in September 1941 and transported its Jews in two waves in November and December 1942 to their death in Treblinka. The memorial tablet reads: "In eternal memory of our fathers and families from the city of Makov, who were martyred by the Nazis on 3 Tevet 5703 [11 December 1942]. May God avenge their blood. F[ürstenfeld]bruck, 15 December [19]47."

III

After the war *landslayt* published *yizker bikher* (memorial books), usually written in Yiddish, sometimes in Hebrew, in commemoration of their lost communities. The *yizker* books incorporated various sources and forms of raw material, from town chronicles and folklore to eyewitness testimonies and memoirs "combining," as historian Natalia Aleksiun observes, "in one volume both historical and personal narratives."[41] Occasionally, *landsmanshaftn* commissioned professional Jewish historians, themselves survivors from Eastern Europe, to edit and write

Figure 11.2. Group portrait of Jewish DPs from Makow Mazowiecki convened to commemorate the community's victims of Nazism on the anniversary of the liquidation of its ghetto; December 15, 1947. Courtesy of the YIVO Institute for Jewish Research. United States Holocaust Memorial Museum Photo Archives.

substantial sections of their *yizker* books. In most cases, *landsmanshaftn* recruited the popular labor of its *landslayt* to recount the destroyed worlds of their communities in *yizker* books. As anthropologists Jack Kugelmass and Jonathan Boyarin have observed, "The memorial books are the fruit of the impulse to write a testament for future generations."[42]

While the determination to generate *yizker* books had germinated in DP camps, the dispersion of most DPs to Israel, North American, Argentina, and elsewhere delayed the publication of *yizker* books until they appeared in those countries in the 1950s, 1960s, and 1970s. The library of *yizker* books now contains roughly six hundred volumes. However, nine *yizker* books were published by *landsmanshaftn* in the American zone of occupied Germany between 1947 and 1949.[43] The majority of them were composed by one author, usually a native of the town, but three were the fruit of several native authors. Even when a single author produced a *yizker* book, he relied on the testimony of survivors from the town for information.

The contents of *yizker* books published by *landsmanshaftn* in occupied Germany augured the pattern of later *yizker* books. The Krasnistav (Poland) *yizker* book, which reflects the labor of several authors, contains a chronicle of the town's history, a survey of its interwar Jewish notables, civic associations, political parties, occupational structure, educational system, and reminiscences of its folkways and colorful townspeople. The bulk of the volume describes the destruction of the town's Jewish population. The next section recounts the ordeal of several of the town's survivors after they had left the town. The volume includes a description of the return of a Krasnistav native to the town after the war, where he received a hostile reception from local Poles. In addition, it describes two memorial assemblies held by the town's survivors in the Bad Reichenhall DP camp. The Krasnistav *yizker* book concludes with lists of the town's victims and its remnant of survivors. The volume includes a few photographs.

By contrast, the Częstochowa *yizker* book, which was written by one author, begins with a comprehensive description of the fate of the town's Jews under Nazi occupation from the German invasion to ghettoization, from the internment and exploitation of a significant proportion of the town's Jewish population at the nearby Hasag factory to the deportation of others to various camps, and from the Jewish council to the Jewish underground. The second part describes the path of the surviving remnant from the town from their brief return to Poland to migration to the American zone of occupied Germany, features speeches from convocations of the town's *landsmanshaft* in 1946, and includes poems by survivors from the town. The third part describes numerous luminaries and colorful townspeople from the prewar period, from rabbis, cantors, and communal leaders to healers, journalists, teachers, and athletes, not to mention musicians, thieves, and "crazy people" (*meshugoim*). The *yizker* book ends with a chronology of the most important dates in Jewish life under Nazi occupation, a drawing of a bereaved woman in a synagogue standing under a memorial plaque for the fifty thousand victims from Częstochowa, a list of deceased resisters, and drawings of gravestones for each of them.

In general, then, these *yizker* books, like those published later, contained three parts. First, they immortalized the community by recounting its prewar history, collecting popular anecdotes, depicting its religious and secular institutions, and sketching the biographies of its rabbinical, political, and cultural leaders. Second, they chronicled the community's plight under Nazi occupation, its liquidation, the fate of its inhabitants, and frequently spiritual and armed resistance in it to Nazi rule. Third, they memorialized the community's victims, in part by recording their names.

The funerary function of these *yizker* books published in occupied Germany was exemplary of those published in subsequent years. In anticipation of their resettlement and in view of the absence of graves of their loved ones, these *yizker* books represented, as Kugelmass and Boyarin note for the entire corpus of *yizker* books, "substitute gravestones."[44] Near the end of the Częstochowa *yizker* book, a poem to the victims concludes, "Let this book be your gravestone [*macejwe*]."[45] Indeed, funerary motifs feature prominently in the iconography of these *yizker* books. Thus on the cover of the Radom yizker book one sees the stark outline of a cemetery illuminated by the incandescence of an eternal flame (Fig. 11.3).

In this vein, one ought to mention the publication of *Fun letstn khurbn* (*From the Last Catastrophe*). Published irregularly in Yiddish by the Central Historical Commission of the Central Committee in ten issues between August 1946 and

Figure 11.3 Cover of Radom *yizker* book, *Dos yidishe Radom in khurves* (Stuttgart, 1948). New York Public Library.

December 1948, *Fun letstn khurbn* was the centerpiece of the Central Historical Commission's self-appointed mission, in the words of its director, Moshe Yosef Feygenboim, "to create the documentary basis for the historian ... from which he will be able to draw a clear picture of what befell us."[46] It featured primarily eyewitness accounts collected by the Historical Commission, but it also contained historical studies, songs and poems of the ghettos, camps, forests, and underground resistance, ghetto slang, photographs, and German documents. Notwithstanding its aspirations to create a historically reliable testimony for posterity, *Fun letstn khurbn*, like the *yizker* books, is the fruit of collective memory and marks the last phase in the cultural production of a moribund Yiddish-speaking world. The migration of the DPs from Germany led the Historical Commission to discontinue *Fun letstn khurbn* in 1948 and to transfer its significant collection of documents, testimonies, and photographs to Israel.[47]

IV

Landsmanshaftn would convene to commemorate the destruction of individual communities from mid 1945 until the DP camps were dismantled in the late 1940s and even into the early 1950s. But by early 1946, with the approach of the first anniversary of liberation, leaders of *sheyres hapleyte*, seeking to relieve the psychological stress of endless communal commemorations and to help DPs adjust to life, since the world would not stop just for them, perceived the need for a unified communal day of mourning.[48] The agenda of the weekly meeting of the Central Committee on 5 May 1946 included discussion of a "unified day of remembrance and liberation." Regular members of the Central Committee were joined that day by, among others, Leo W. Schwarz, the director of the AJDC for the American zone of occupied Germany in 1946–47, Levi Shalitan, the editor of *Unzer Weg*, and representatives of the AJC's cultural mission to *sheyres hapleyte*, including the poet H. Leivick and the singer Emma Shaver. The mood was somber. As historian Zeev W. Mankowitz notes, "This was a first attempt to give commemorative form to the European Jewish catastrophe and a special atmosphere hung over the protracted deliberations."[49] Zalman Grinberg, the chairman of the Central Committee who had made the original suggestion to establish a unitary memorial day in the DP camps, believed that it should create, as he wrote in support of creating such a day, "a bond between the past and rebuilding for the future."[50] While some questioned the authority of the Central Committee to establish a memorial day and wanted to leave the decision in the hands of rabbis, the representatives of the cultural delegation endorsed the right of the representatives of *sheyres hapleyte*, the survivors of the tragedy, to decide. A few participants, including Leivick, who was mindful of the suffering of the living after a visit to the tuberculosis sanitarium in Gauting, wanted to limit the commemoration to mourning. But the majority, led by Grinberg and Gringauz, supported a day of commemoration marked by celebration of liberation.[51] The decision to have this day be embossed by both mourning and celebration seems to have struck a responsive chord in the DP community in general.[52]

The participants decided to fix the date of the day of commemoration on the fourteenth day of the Hebrew month of Iyar. In fact, the end of the war, 8 May 1945, coincided with 25 Iyar. Nevertheless, 14 Iyar was chosen because it related to a minor festival in the Jewish calendar: the Second Passover (*Pesach Sheni*). According to the Hebrew Bible (Num. 9:6–13), any person who because of ritual impurity was unable to offer the Passover sacrifice on 14 Nisan, the traditional beginning of Passover, is supposed to offer it one month later on 14 Iyar. Some people eat matzah, the ritual unleavened bread of Passover, on this Second Passover as a symbolic remembrance of the exodus from Egypt. Passover in 1945 took place before liberation of concentration camps in southern Germany, but since the DPs were liberated by the Second Passover, observance of the memorial day on this date was a symbolic Jewish marker of redemption.[53] In 1946 it coincided with 15 May.

Pursuant to its decision, the Central Committee issued a declaration, which enjoyed the public support of the camps' Council of Union of Rabbis, calling on the surviving remnant to commemorate liberation on 14 Iyar according to the Hebrew calendar. The first part of the declaration reviewed the Nazi regime's reign of terror and its assault on Europe's Jews, which "turned the continent into a Jewish mass grave." Because of its unprecedented policy of annihilation, "[s]ix million Jews were slaughtered." The remainder of the declaration, however, looked with hope to the future:

> On 8 May 1945, the [Nazis'] diabolical might was finally defeated, and during the first week of May the remnants of European Jewry were liberated by the allied armies. The *sheyres hapleyte* proclaims the fourteenth of Iyar—this year 15 May—the unified, official liberation day, a holiday, now and for future generations. This day represents not only the liberation of the small living remnant; this day is also the liberation of the martyrs because their mass grave, degraded and desecrated, on this day has been transformed into a monument of the singular holy martyrdom of a nation. This day will remain forever in Jewish history as a historically symbolic date of the liberation from Hitler's yoke.[54]

The fourteenth of Iyar was celebrated at a large commemorative meeting in Munich and in local DP camps. Schwarz attended the ceremony in Munich. The DPs filled the auditorium the American government provided to overflowing. Blue and white flags, representative of the Zionist movement, were the only outward symbol of their feelings. As Schwarz recollected, "*Yizkor* ran like a fugue through all the addresses." After the recitation of prayers of mourning, Grinberg requested two minutes of silence. In Schwarz's words, "The people stood with bowed heads and wept. The hall was wrapped in a deathly stillness. The men and women were like trees whose roots have been laid bare." But, as its architects had intended, the ceremony expressed not only bereavement but also hope. As Schwarz observed, "Out of the sorrow and stillness emerged another grand theme, lifting the collective spirit of all present toward a renascent Zion." In this vein, several speakers urged the assembled to rebuild Jewish life, particularly in Jewish Palestine. As reported by Schwarz, Abraham Reisman, a survivor of Treblinka, said: "No other people has shed as much blood as Israel. Hence we demand a secure home for our future generations, and it can be only in Eretz Israel [the Land of Israel]." At the end of the ceremony, everyone stood and sang a Zionist hymn. Schwarz concluded his description of this assembly in an upbeat mood: "A high note of promise. I had the feeling that, despite the profound memorial, spring had broken through the paralyzed joy of these men and women and stirred the roots which blossomed three years later in the heroic deeds of another spring."[55]

The commemoration of liberation in Landsberg was perhaps the most elaborate of all in the DP camps. On the eve of the commemoration an assembly was held on the camp's sports field. Invited guests included officials of the US military and representatives of the AJDC and UNRRA. Half a dozen Zionist *kibbutzim* whose members were preparing to migrate to Palestine were represented. A large number of residents from the DP camp in Landsberg attended. Illuminated by the light of torches, Gringauz, representing the Central Committee, underlined the dual meaning of the commemoration for the past and the future, not to mention for the *sheyres hapleyte* and (optimistically) for the entire Jewish world. A parade followed in which kibbutz members waved their flags. After the parade the kibbutz members led the singing of nationalistic songs in Hebrew and Yiddish.

On the morning of 14 Iyar the camp's entire DP population, including kibbutz members, attended a memorial service in a gymnasium. Presiding over the ceremony were elected representatives of Landsberg's DP community and two rabbis. The sermon (*droshe*) of one of the rabbis, Rabbi Hurwitz, launched the substantive portion of the ceremony. Rabbi Hurwitz compared the condition of the *sheyres hapleyte* to the state of Jews after their return from Babylonian exile to the Land of Israel in biblical times. Under the direction of Ezra the scribe, the returnees built the Second Temple to replace the destroyed First Temple. According to Rabbi Hurwitz, those among the returnees who remembered the First Temple lamented its destruction, while the youth among them, who had no memory of the First Temple, rejoiced in the inauguration of the new house of worship. In a similar fashion, even as the survivors mourned the loss of their loved ones and communities, their survival from the clutches of an enemy who was determined to kill all Jews represented a divine miracle, for which a prayer of thanksgiving in joy was appropriate. Jewish destiny from time immemorial to the present knew both mourning and joy. But in their moment of joy it was the survivors' duty to remember those who died in sanctification of God's name. Yet while Ezra foresaw the tragic arc of Jewish history, he did not prevent the youth from celebrating the consecration of the Second Temple. In other words, "the Jewish people, when they live to see their restoration, have to exert themselves to allow joy into their hearts so that they can express thanks to God." Rabbi Hurwitz alluded further to the verse in Ecclesiastes calling attention to "a time for mourning and a time for dancing." According to the rabbi's interpretation of this verse, "It is clear that when we want to thank God for a miracle that happened to us we really must accept a little joy into our hearts." "For the few Jewish survivors," he concluded, "must be applicable the old Jewish commandment … to take heart [and] to continue living." Thus Rabbi Hurwitz's sermon integrated the destruction of Europe's Jews into the trajectory of Jewish history, while, in line with how DP leaders sought to shape collective memory on this day, it instructed the survivors, in their bereavement, to be mindful of the future for which their lives were spared. After the conclusion of Rabbi Hurwitz's sermon, the cantor intoned the *El male rakhamim* prayer for the dead. According to the account of the ceremony, "All those in attendance are deeply moved, one hears silent, suffocating crying and sees tears in their eyes." Even if many, if not a majority, of those present harbored intense religious doubt, the old religious ways clearly stirred the survivors.

The program included additional speakers. The Zionist representative urged those present to unite in their grief for the sake of their struggle—that is to say, to create a Jewish state. Abel Akabas reviewed for those in attendance the effort led by the Central Committee with the support of the military administration and in cooperation with local German officials to rebury victims left in mass graves. Thirty-five thousand Jews, he reported, were still lying in mass graves in the vicinity of Landsberg alone. He appealed for help in completing the "holy labor" of ensuring the "dignity [*kowed*] of the martyrs." The assembly closed with a stirring communal singing of "Hatikvah," the anthem of the Zionist movement (and the national anthem of Israel after its establishment in 1948).

In the evening of the same day, three thousand DPs attended an assembly in the gymnasium. Gringauz was the evening's main speaker. He likened the day's commemoration to a "holy task," akin to erecting a "gravestone" (*macejwe*) for the victims of the catastrophe. Another important objective of the commemorative events was to signal to Jews in the rest of the world "a warning that as long as the Jewish people do not have their own country such catastrophes are unavoidable." And yet Gringauz was sensitive to the universal import of what had befallen the Jews of Europe. Instead of being perceived as confined to Jews living at a specific time in a specific place, this memorial day was a "holiday for the victory of progressive humanity, of human morality and human ethics." The artistic part of the evening included recitations, a choral performance of Jewish folk songs, and the orchestral rendition of songs from both the Yiddish and Hebrew repertoires. Like the morning program, the evening assembly closed with a communal singing of "Hatikvah."[56]

The commemoration in Landsberg contained motifs that recurred in the celebrations held locally throughout the DP camps. As historian Zeev W. Mankowitz observes, in general "the assemblies opened or closed with the singing of *Hatikvah*, the intoning of the memorial *Yizkor* and *El malei rachamim* prayers, standing in silence in honor of the *kedoshim*—martyrs, public addresses, victory marches and community singing." At other commemorations, memorial candles, Zionist and American flags, and banners were evident. In addition to Jewish notables, US army officers and UNRRA officials attended the ceremonies, and, on occasion, local German officials. In camps that were located in the vicinity of mass graves, the assembled marched to them and laid wreaths on memorial tablets.[57]

One year later, in 1947, 14 Iyar fell on Sunday, 4 May. Local committees in the communities of Garmisch and Mittenwald had proposed reenacting the American rescue there in April 1945 of three thousand Dachau prisoners, the survivors of a death march to Tyrol. This demonstration was intended in part to thank the Americans for their role in the liberation. The Central Committee appropriated the idea and expanded it from a local event to a memorial observance for the entire occupied zone. The centerpiece of the observance was a march to Mittenwald (Fig. 11.4). Four to five thousand marchers participated, including many former prisoners who had actually traversed the same route on the death march from Dachau to Tyrol two years earlier. They marched for almost two hours to the assembly point. The podium, surrounded by the Alpine mountains, was decorated with American flags, the blue-white flags of the Zionist movement, and large trilingual placards exclaiming "Exodus, [the Jewish militia

Figure 11.4. Jewish DPs march to Mittenwald for a memorial observance, May 14, 1947. Courtesy of Lieb Sultanik. United States Memorial Museum Photo Archives.

in Palestine] Haganah, Settlement will liberate Palestine!" The assembled heard survivors of the original Mittenwald march, including the new chairman of the Central Committee, Dovid Treger, who urged them to assume the struggle for the establishment of a Jewish homeland in Palestine. Lieutenant James Charles Rooin especially drew cheers and applause when he declared his admiration for and sympathy with the goals of the marchers. When the speeches were over and the throng descended onto the roads to return, the members of the Central Committee assembled in the corner of Mittenwald's Catholic cemetery, where those who died in the Tyrol march had been buried. Treger laid a wreath in the midst of the martyrs' grave.[58] Commemorations on a smaller scale were held in several individual DP camps.

On 9 May 1948 liberation was commemorated in the Landsberg DP camp. One thousand DPs attended. After the conclusion of prayers, a number of speeches, and the singing of "Hatikvah," the assembled marched to the camp's main square to hear criticism, by both German and Jewish speakers, of denazification policy. They then drove to several mass graves in the vicinity, where Philipp Auerbach, a prominent leader of the Jewish communities in Germany, and other dignitaries, including a German politician, laid wreaths and said the *kaddish* prayer.[59]

Leo W. Schwarz, a participant at the meeting of the Central Committee on 5 May 1946 at which it was decided to declare 14 Iyar as a day of commemoration, described his emotions on that day: "What befell me in May, 1946, was an experience which was momentous for our entire people. It was the first attempt to formulate the meaning of liberation of the Jewish survivors by the Allied armies in the spring of 1945. I was deeply conscious that I was witnessing the birth of a holiday which probably would be engraved on the heart and the calendar of the Jewish people."[60] Schwarz's impression was characteristic of the expectation of many DPs that this day would be acknowledged by Jews everywhere as a memorial day for the victims of the *khurbn*.[61]

This was not, however, to be the case. The date determined by the DPs was ignored by the rest of the postwar Jewish world. In 1951 the Israeli legislature (Knesset) established its own memorial day, Yom Hashoah Vehagvurah. In tune with the Israeli interpretation of Jewish history, which in the spirit of Zionism recasts the ruins of Jewish history into myths of national redemption, the symbolic link of the catastrophe (*Shoah*) with heroism (*gvurah*) transformed the Holocaust into the ultimate stage of Jewish life in exile on whose ruins arose the restoration of a Jewish state in Israel. The Knesset decided to fix the commemoration on the twenty-seventh day of the Hebrew month of Nisan because that date in Jewish history was linked to the massacre of Jews by the Crusaders and was close to the anniversary of the Warsaw ghetto uprising on 19 April. Yom Hashoah also inaugurated a series of three related national commemorations. Yom Hashoah is followed within one week by the Memorial Day for Soldiers Fallen in Israel's Wars and Israel's Independence Day. As historian Saul Friedländer notes, through the close association of these three commemorations "the traditional [Israeli] mythic pattern of catastrophe and redemption is forcefully reaffirmed."[62]

By contrast with 14 Iyar, the Jewish Diaspora enthusiastically adopted Yom Hashoah. In fact, the DP memorial date had already faded from view by 1948, when it had to compete for attention with events in Palestine and then Israel and fell into desuetude after the establishment of the state of Israel in May 1948 and the dismantlement of all but a handful of DP camps by 1950. The DP commemoration was still being observed in April 1950, but it was a modest affair, marked by the laying of a wreath at a memorial for the Jewish victims of Nazism at the Jewish cemetery in Munich.[63]

Indeed, in the DP camps, liberation day competed for attention with commemoration of the anniversary of the Warsaw ghetto uprising, which was assiduously observed with pomp and circumstance in the month of April in most, if not all, DP camps. Observance of this anniversary carried overt political overtones, since resistance and revolt were now needed to overcome British policy in Palestine. While commemoration of the Warsaw ghetto uprising vied in popularity with 14 Iyar in 1946 and 1947, the former overshadowed the latter by 1948. On 18 April 1946, the Central Committee of Liberated Jews in the American occupied zone in Germany organized a well-attended convocation at a theater in Munich in commemoration of the uprising. The podium was decorated in Zionist banners and stars of David. According to a report on the event, when the cantor intoned the prayer for the dead, there were "visible tears in eyes and audible stifled sobs from the men and women present." Several Jewish dignitaries spoke, and well-known Jewish artists conducted the cultural part of the ceremony.[64] In his speech, Grinberg emphasized the "historical significance" of the uprising because it represented a "struggle ... in the name of Jewish honor." "Our task," Grinberg concluded, "is now to continue the uprising, for it depends now on us whether the Warsaw fighters won or not." It was incumbent on the surviving remnant to cultivate "the heroic spirit of the Warsaw fighters" in "our old-new fatherland."[65]

The uprising commemoration in the Landsberg DP camp, which followed a similar format, drew three thousand people in 1946 and two thousand in 1947.[66] These ceremonies invariably ended with communal singing of "Hatikvah." And while coverage of the events on 14 Iyar competed with many others in the pages of the DP press, even in 1946 when it was first celebrated, many DP newspapers devoted most or even all of their issues to remembering the Warsaw ghetto uprising in mid April from 1946 to 1950.[67] Even in 1950, when the liberation day merited only a modest ceremony, commemoration of the Warsaw ghetto uprising earlier the same month in Munich was much more elaborate by comparison.[68]

It is interesting to compare the commemorations organized by the Eastern European DPs on the one hand and German Jews on the other. German Jews integrated their memory of the Holocaust into public commemorations of the "victims of fascism" (*Opfer des Faschismus,* OdF), which fell on the second Sunday in September and on 8 May, the anniversary of the defeat of Nazi Germany. Both of these events exhibited a universal, antifascist character. As Y. Michal Bodemann notes, "At first, at least, until the Cold War finally succeeded in dividing them, they were commemorative events that included all victims, Jewish and non-Jewish alike."[69] Two thousand German Jews, joined by Eastern European Jewish DPs from DP camps in the Berlin area, marched on OdF day in Berlin in September 1946.[70] The German Jewish community in Berlin exhibited its ingenuity for casting its particular observance of OdF day in Jewish terms. In September 1949 it sponsored a commemoration at the Weissensee Jewish cemetery in East Berlin. While the first part of the memorial service was conducted by an American rabbi and included a speech by Heinz Galinski, the head of the West Berlin Jewish community, the second part, which was officiated by two Jewish communists, featured the transfer of the remains of Herbert Baum, the communist resistance fighter killed by the Nazis. Bodemann describes the character of these observances in the following terms: "Most importantly, then, the early commemorations were events sponsored and conducted by the antifascist/Jewish spectrum, commemorations of a small, and often closed, community, and it was this community that invited outsiders, albeit in the second row." [71]

Although Eastern European DPs' observance of 14 Iyar in Bavaria was articulated in a Zionist idiom, not all of their leaders conceived liberation as being limited to the Jewish victims of Nazism, either. The decision to associate the DPs' official memorial day with liberation rather than a date with a compelling Jewish significance—or at least more compelling than Second Passover—demonstrated the residual attachment of some DP leaders, notwithstanding Zionist arguments to the contrary, to the European cultural legacy. Recall Gringauz's speech on the eve of liberation day in Landsberg in 1946. "We, who are the victims of this [European] civilization," Gringauz subsequently wrote, "have been called upon to discover the positive basis on which we can unite with it. ... We cannot and will not turn away from it. ... Our experience must serve to redirect the Jewish people. Our tragedy must become the starting point of a new humanism."[72] If Gringauz's assessment was correct, many DPs hoped to restore universal ideals to European culture, which had collapsed during the Holocaust, from their new homes in Israel and with the nascent state's encouragement. But the Jewish establishment in both Israel and the United States, after the destruction of Europe's Jews the undisputed center of Jewish life in the Diaspora, would have rejected the DPs' memorial day if it had not simply ignored it, because in the aftermath of the Holocaust universal celebration of the victory over Nazism was eclipsed by the politicization of Jewish memory in service to a nationalistic narrative of the Holocaust.[73]

V

Notwithstanding the prevailing Zionist environment in DP camps, the politicization of Jewish memory in occupied Germany was also the result of a practical impediment to mourning. Traditional mourning rituals represented a highly structured rite of the gradual separation of the bereaved from close relatives. The expansion of a private form of bereavement to a public form was impelled by a terrible paradox: a torrent of bodies, but not those of any of the survivors' immediate loved ones. Their remains were scattered in the killing fields of Eastern Europe, never to be returned to those who loved or knew them. Jewish tradition, moreover, obliges Jewish mourners to recite *kaddish*. Since most Holocaust survivors could not know the date of a relative's death at the hands of Germans or German allies, they came to say *kaddish* on festivals when *yizkor* was recited, or on specially ordained occasions of communal memorial for victims of the genocide.[74] By necessity, then, the DPs commemorated absent relatives and buried fellow Jews who were strangers to them. By and large the DPs buried and commemorated largely unidentified and unidentifiable corpses. This upending of the traditional mourning process prescribed by Judaism enabled the DPs to evacuate Jewish mourning of its traditional meaning and to fill this void with a positive collective meaning. In the absence of the graves of loved ones, personal grief was parlayed rather seamlessly into public memorialization, which became the occasion, in light of what had befallen European Jewry and of the struggle for Jewish statehood in Palestine, for political argument.

DPs represented the soul of Jewish experience after the Holocaust. Yet the legacy of their forms of commemorating the Holocaust recedes into oblivion. The graves of the Jewish victims of Nazism who are buried in Germany are unvisited. *Landsmanshaftn* have disbanded, for most of the surviving *landslayt* are now dead. Hardly anyone nowadays can read the *yizker* books because Yiddish has become the linguistic patrimony of a tiny fraction of Jews. And no one observes or even remembers the DPs' memorial day commemorating liberation. The realm of these particular dead, whom the DPs were the last to remember, recedes ever further into the past.

Notes

1. Harvey E. Goldberg, *Jewish Passages: Cycles of Jewish Life* (Berkeley, 2003), 203, 204.
2. Abraham Peck, "Zu den Anfängen jüdischen Lebens nach 1945," in Andreas Nachama and Julius H. Schoeps, eds., *Aufbau nach dem Untergang: Deutsch-jüdische Geschichte nach 1945* (Berlin, 1992), 229–230; Michael Brenner, *After the Holocaust: Rebuilding Jewish Lives in Postwar Germany*, trans. Barbara Harshav (Princeton, 1997), 41–51; and Michael Brenner, "The Transformation of the German-Jewish Community," in Leslie Morris and Jack Zipes, eds., *Unlikely History: The Changing German-Jewish Symbiosis, 1945–2000* (New York, 2002), 51.
3. For excellent recent studies of Jewish DPs in Germany, see, among other sources, Michael Brenner, *After the Holocaust;* Angelika Königseder and Juliane Wetzel, *Waiting for Hope: Jewish Displaced Persons in Post–World War II Germany*, trans. John A. Broadwin (Evanston, IL, 2001); Zeev W. Mankowitz, *Life between Memory and Hope: The Survivors of the Holocaust in Occupied Germany* (Cambridge, 2002); and Atina Grossmann, *Jews, Germans, and Allies: Close Encounters in Occupied Germany* (Princeton, 2007).
4. Shmuel Gringauz, "Jizker," *Landsberger Lager-Cajtung*, 8 October 1945, 3; quoted in part in Mankowitz, *Life between Memory and Hope,* 193.
5. Samuel [Shmuel] Gringauz, "Jewish Destiny as the DP's See It," *Commentary* 4, no. 6 (December 1947): 507; see also Mankowitz, *Life between Memory and Hope,* 223.
6. Levi Shalitan, "Gedenk dem tog!" *Unzer Weg,* 11 November 1945, 1.
7. Emmanuel Sivan, "Private Pain and Public Remembrance in Israel," in Jay Winter and Emmanuel Sivan, eds., *War and Remembrance in the Twentieth Century* (Cambridge, 1999), 188.
8. H. Leivick, *Mit der sheyres hapleyte* (New York, 1947), 7–8; see also Mankowitz, *Life between Memory and Hope,* 193.
9. Katherine Verdery, *The Political Lives of Dead Bodies: Reburial and Postsocialist Change* (New York, 1999).
10. Levi Shalitan, "Vehahalisi es atsmotsay mize," *Unzer Weg,* 18 January 1946, 2.
11. Several survivor testimonies collected in volume 5 of *Fun letstn khurbn,* the publication of the Central Historical Commission of the Central Committee of Liberated Jews in the American Zone of Occupation in Germany, describe the death marches from Nazi camps in Bavaria in the direction of Tyrol in the final months of the war. For the introduction to this volume, see Y[osef] K[aplan], "Der katsetler-marsh keyn Tirol," *Fun letstn khurbn* 5 (May 1947): 3–7.
12. Leonard Dinerstein, *America and the Survivors of the Holocaust* (New York, 1982), 28.
13. Speech by Zalman Grinberg, chairman of the Central Committee of Liberated Jews in the American Zone of Occupation, [undated], YIVO Institute for Jewish Research (hereafter YIVO), Leo W. Schwarz Collection (hereafter LWSC) RG 294.1, folder 129, fol. 729; for a description of a similar occurrence in the British zone, see Judith Tydor Baumel, *Kibbutz Buchenwald: Survivors and Pioneers* (New Brunswick, NJ, 1997), 9.
14. Lucy Dawidowicz, *From that Place and Time* (New York, 1989), 301.
15. Sz. Mirjami, "Baratung fun jidisze doktorim," *Landsberger Lager-Cajtung,* 26 April 1946, 9.

16. Königseder and Wetzel, *Waiting for Hope*, 227–228, 243.
17. UNRRA (United Nations Relief and Rehabilitation Administration) Sanitarium for DP's Gauting, "Liste von allen verstorbenen jidischen patienten," 20 February 1947, YIVO, LWSC, folder 244, fols. 408–11; and "Bescheinigung über Sterbefälle," YIVO, LWSC, folder 357, fols. 245, 275, and 312. .
18. Zalman Grinberg, *Shukhrarnu mi-Dachau* (n.p. [Israel], 1947 or 1948), 45.
19. "Speech by Z[alman] Grinberg, M.D., Head Doctor of the Hospital for Political Ex-Prisoners in Germany at the Liberation Concert in St. Ottilien on May 27, 1945," The National Archives (London), FO 371/55705.
20. Brenner, *After the Holocaust*, 81–82.
21. Julius Carlebach and Andreas Brämer, "Flight into Action as a Method of Repression: American Military Rabbis and the Problem of Jewish Displaced Persons in Postwar Germany," *Jewish Studies Quarterly* 2, no. 1 (1995): 63–64.
22. Alex Grobman, *Rekindling the Flame: American Jewish Chaplains and the Survivors of European Jewry, 1944–1948* (Detroit, 1995), 39–40.
23. Abraham J. Klausner, *A Letter to my Children from the Edge of the Holocaust* (San Francisco, 2002), 11–13.
24. Brenner, *After the Holocaust*, 115–116.
25. Leivick, *Mit der sheyres hapleyte*, 188–190; a photograph of Zeitlin's grave can be seen on 190.
26. Rabbi Alexander S. Rosenberg to Leo W. Schwarz, "Report for Month of June 1946," 9 July 1946, YIVO, LWSC, folder 268, fol. 441.
27. Rabbi Solomon Shapiro to Charles Passman, Report of Religious Activities for the Month of June 1947, 30 June 1947, YIVO, LWSC, folder 243, fol. 377.
28. Rabbi Solomon Shapiro, Report of the Religious Department for the Months of October and November 1947, no date, YIVO, LWSC, folder 243, fol. 354; Rabbi Solomon Shapiro, Director for Religious Affairs, AJDC Germany to Dr. J. Eagan, Director of Religious Section, OMGUS (Official Military Government of the United States), Munich, 28 November 1947, YIVO, LWSC, folder 268, fol. 427.
29. Marian Zhid, "Der kdoyshim-greber," *Jidisze Cajtung*, 7 May 1948, 5–6.
30. Dr. Gerbl, Landrat des Kreises Landsberg/Lech to Michael Schmid, 10 January 1946, YIVO, LWSC, folder 242, fol. 359.
31. F. A. Koch, Kreisbaumeister, "Beschreibung der im Bau befindlichen Friedhöfe für KZ–Häftlinge und Judenfriedhöfe in Kreis Landsberg/Lech," 18 June 1947, YIVO, LWSC, folder 268, fols. 421–425.
32. Kreisbaumeister F. A. Koch, "Betreff: Friedhof für KZ-Häftlinge in Schwabhausen, Landsberg," 18 June 1947, YIVO, LWSC, folder 173, fol. 1005.
33. Captain M. G. Karsner, Office of Military Government for Bavaria to Rabbi Rosenberg, Jewish Liaison Representative, 24 May 1947, YIVO, LWSC, folder 244, fol. 405.
34. Jehuda Pfefer, "Troyer-fajerung cum 2-tn jorcajt fun der befrajung in Niderbayern," *Jidisze Cajtung*, 13 May 1947, 7. See also the photographs of a common Jewish and Christian cemetery for concentration camp victims in Mühldorf in *Jidisze Cajtung*, 20 May 1947, 8.
35. Eichler, report on the burial service in Hof, no date (September 1946), YIVO, LWSC, folder 532, fols. 656–658. For photographs of the service, see fol. 659.
36. Zhid, "Der kdoyshim-greber," 6.
37. See Daniel Soyer, *Jewish Immigrant Associations and American Identity in New York, 1880–1939* (Cambridge, MA, 1997).
38. Leo Srole, "Why the DP's Can't Wait," *Commentary* 3, no. 1 (January 1947): 16.
39. Y. Marguliets, Z. Finkelsteyn, and Y. Shvartsapel, eds., *A zikorn far Rovne* (n.p. [American Zone of Occupied Germany], n.d. [1947]), 35 (emphasis in original).
40. Benjamin Orenstein, *Churban Czenstochow–The Destruction of Czenstokov–Khurbn Tshenstokhov* (n.p. [American Zone of Occupied Germany], 1948), 321.

41. Natalia Aleksiun, "Gender and Nostalgia: Images of Women in Early *Yizker Bikher*," *Jewish History and Culture* 5, no. 1 (2002): 70.
42. Jack Kugelmass and Jonathan Boyarin, eds., *From a Ruined Garden: The Memorial Books of Polish Jewry*, 2nd ed. (Indianapolis, 1998), 17.
43. These *yizker* books are Marguliets et al., *A zikorn far Rovne*; A. Meirantz and H. Nemlich, eds., *Sierpc: Khurbn Sierpc 1939–1945: Zikhroynes fun di ibergeblibene landslayt vos gefinen zikh in der amerikaner Zone in Daytshland* (Munich, 1947); Aryeh Shtunzeyger, ed., *Yizker tsum ondenk fun di kdoyshey Krasnistav* (Munich, 1948); Mordekhay Bokhner, *Seyfer Kzhanov [Chrzanow]: Lebn un umkum fun a yidish shtetl* (Munich, 1949); Y. Frenkel, S. Lelonek, Y. Nemlik, M. Raykhgot, and R. Yurish., *Zaml-bukh fun Sherptser sheyres hakhurbn 1939–1945* (n.p. [American Zone of Occupied Germany], 1948); Benjamin Orenstein, *Khurbn Otvotsk, Falenits, Kartshev* (n.p. [American Zone of Occupied Germany], 1948); Benjamin Orenstein, *Churban Czenstochow*; Avraham Vaysbrod, *Es shtarbt a shtetl: Megiles Skalat* (Munich, 1948); anonymous, *Dos yidishe Radom in khurves: Ondenkbukh*, pt. 1. (Stuttgart, 1948).
44. Kugelmass and Boyarin, *From a Ruined Garden*, 34.
45. Benjamin Orenstein, *Churban Czenstochow*, 411.
46. Moshe Yosef Feygenboim, "Tsu vos historishe komisyes?" *Fun letstn khurbn* 1 (August 1946): 2.
47. On the Central Historical Commission and *Fun letstn khurbn*, see Mankowitz, *Life between Memory and Hope*, 214–222; Philip Friedman, "European Jewish Research on the Holocaust," in Philip Friedman, ed., *Roads to Extinction: Essays on the Holocaust* (New York and Philadelphia, 1980), 500–524.
48. Shalitan, "Vehahalisi es atsmotsay mize," 2; Zalman Grinberg, "Der 14-tn Iyar," *Unzer Weg*, 10 May 1946, 2; Mankowitz, *Life between Memory and Hope*, 194–195.
49. Mankowitz, *Life between Memory and Hope*, 195.
50. Grinberg, "Der 14-tn Iyar," 2; quoted (in a slightly different translation) in Mankowitz, *Life between Memory and Hope*, 195.
51. Mankowitz, *Life between Memory and Hope*, 195–197; Leo W. Schwarz, "Memorial in Munich," *Congress Weekly* 22, no. 15 (18 April 1955): 6–7.
52. See, e.g., Jojsef Gar, "14-ter Ijar—a wichtike jid[ishe] date," *Landsberger Lager-Cajtung*, 17 May 1946, 2.
53. For this explanation see Gar, "14–ter Ijar—wichtike jid[ishe] date," 2. On observance of Second Passover, see Moritz Zobel, *Das Jahr des Juden in Brauch und Liturgie* (Berlin, 1936), 188.
54. "Deklaracje fun Central Komitet fun di bafrayte Jidn in der amerik[aner] Okupacje Zone in Dajczland!" *Undzer Wort*, 10 May 1946, 2; quoted in part (in a slightly different translation) in Mankowitz, *Life between Memory and Hope*, 197.
55. Schwarz, "Memorial in Munich," 7; see also Dovid Kovay, "Yud-daled Iyar—yizker farzamlung in Minkhen," *Unzer Weg*, 24 May 1946, 3–4.
56. M[oshe] F[ridenzon], "Di fayerlechkajtn fun 'jud-dalet Ijar'–yom-tow in Landsberg," *Landsberger Lager-Cajtung*, 17 May 1946, 2; Mankowitz, *Life between Memory and Hope*, 199–201.
57. Mankowitz, *Life between Memory and Hope*, 197–198, quote on 197.
58. Anonymous, "Troyer-fajerlechkajtn fun di KZ-ler in Mittenwald," *Undzer Wort*, 8 May 1947, 1; anonymous, "Impozanter befrajungs-fajerung in der amerikaner zone," *Jidisze Cajtung*, 9 May 1947, 1; and Leo W. Schwarz, *The Redeemers: A Saga of the Years 1945–1952* (New York, 1953), 230–232.
59. Anonymous, "Grojse bafrajungs-fajerung in Landsberg," *Jidisze Cajtung*, 11 May 1948, 2.
60. Schwarz, "Memorial in Munich," 6; quoted in part in Mankowitz, *Life between Memory and Hope*, 202.
61. See Grinberg, "Der 14-tn Iyar," 2; Gar, "14-ter Ijar—a wichtike jid[ishe] date," 2; see also Mankowitz, *Life between Memory and Hope*, 202.
62. Saul Friedländer, "Afterword: The Shoah between Memory and History," in Efraim Sicher, ed., *Breaking Crystal: Writing and Memory after Auschwitz* (Urbana, 1998), 347; see also Mankow-

itz, *Life between Memory and Hope,* 202–203; Roni Stauber, *Halekakh ledor: Shoah ugvurah bamakhshavah hatsiyonit baarets bishnot hakhamishim* (Jerusalem, 2000), chap. 2.

63. Philipp Auerbach, "Tsu der yid[isher] bafelkerung in Minkhen," *Unzer Weg,* 28 April 1950, 6.
64. Anonymous, "Troyer-akademie lekowed der 3-ter jorcajt fun warszewer ojfsztand in München," *Landsberger Lager-Cajtung,* 3 May 1946, 8.
65. "Referat fun Dr. Grinberg zu der trojer-akademije fun Warschawer getto, gehalten dem 18 April 1946 in Prinz-Regentn Theater, München," YIVO, LWSC, folder 129, fols. 804–806. On the symbolic importance of the Warsaw ghetto uprising to the Jewish DPs, see also Mankowitz, *Life between Memory and Hope,* 209–213.
66. Anonymous, "Grandjeze trojer-akademie lekowed dem 3-tn jor-tog fun jid[isher] ojfsztand in Warsze," *Landsberger Lager-Cajtung,* 3 May 1946, 8; anonymous, "Grandjeze akademie lekowed dem 4-tn jortog fun warszwer geto-ojfsztand in Landsberg," *Jidisze Cajtung,* 25 April 1947, 7. The *Landsberger Lager-Cajtung* was renamed *Jidisze Cajtung* in 1947.
67. For an example of coverage of the Warsaw ghetto uprising in the DP press, see *Jidisze Cajtung,* 23 April 1948, and *Moment,* 3 April 1947.
68. Moshe Fridenzon, "S[heyres] H[apleyte]—yidn baern dem ondenk fun di gvurim un kdoyshim fun varshever geto-oyfshtand," *Unzer Weg,* 28 April 1950, 7.
69. Y. Michal Bodemann, "Reconstructions of History: From Jewish Memory to Nationalized Commemoration of Kristallnacht in Germany," in Y. Michal Bodemann, ed., *Jews, Germans, Memory: Reconstructions of Jewish Life in Germany* (Ann Arbor, 1996), 191.
70. Atina Grossmann, "Home and Displacement in a City of Bordercrossers: Jews in Berlin, 1945–1948," in Leslie Morris and Jack Zipes, eds., *Unlikely History: The Changing German-Jewish Symbiosis, 1945–2000* (New York, 2002), 76, 82.
71. Bodemann, "Reconstructions of History," 192.
72. Gringauz, "Jewish Destiny as the DP's See It," 506.
73. Orna Kenan, *Between Memory and History: The Evolution of Israeli Historiography of the Holocaust, 1945–1961* (New York, 2003), 25–26.
74. Goldberg, *Jewish Passages,* 221.

Part IV

RUINS

Chapter 12

THE IMAGINATION OF DISASTER
Death and Survival in Postwar West Germany

Svenja Goltermann

For some time now, the concept of trauma has enjoyed an inflationary career in public discourse as well as in historical studies. It is no longer just the Vietnam veteran or the Jewish survivor of the Holocaust who can count on being counted among the "traumatized." "Trauma" appears to have taken over almost everywhere. This is not to deny that the Holocaust is still regarded, again and again, as the defining and most outstanding traumatic event of the twentieth century. But, as Andreas Huyssen argues in a recently published article, the discourse of trauma "radiates out from a multi-national, ever more ubiquitous Holocaust discourse, is energized, at least in the USA, by the intense interest in witness and survivor testimonies, and then merges with the discourses about AIDS, slavery, family violence, and so on."[1]

This observation is not far from the mark, but it should be complemented on two counts at least. For one, Huyssen's take on the development cannot be restricted to the United States. We can see that the Holocaust is used as a venue to talk about the world's other catastrophes in Europe as well. In Peter Fritzsche's words, "local traumata are being memorialized by way of remembering the Holocaust and by transferring the knowledge of someone else's trauma."[2] Yet, and this is my second point, this all-inclusive Holocaust memory is not sufficient to explain the rapid expansion of the concept of "trauma" in public discourse. Rather, this expansion is in itself part of an extensive and wide-ranging "trauma industry" with an ever increasing output since the 1980s.[3] I cannot look into the reasons for this in detail here. But it needs reminding that the original thrust of this development—also in the US—was due not to the Holocaust but to the politically and morally shored up "invention" of "Post-Traumatic Stress Disorder" (PTSD) in the course of the Vietnam War and the official acknowledgement

---

Notes for this chapter begin on page 271.

of this diagnosis by the American Psychiatric Association in 1980. It is still not well known how the establishment of this diagnosis might have changed our understanding of the Holocaust and of its survivors. In her book on "Trauma: A Genealogy," Ruth Leys has pointed out one connection that deserves further consideration: she claims that the results of the otherwise rather isolated psychiatric research on concentration camp survivors have been assimilated to the findings on PTSD. Leys describes the major effects of this inclusion and homogenization as follows: "This process of viewing the literature of the Holocaust through the lens of Vietnam and PTSD has produced a simplification that works for the former"—i.e., the Holocaust literature—"in the sense that it can now be seen to have contributed to the development of current research on PTSD." And, she concludes, for this reason "the Holocaust now appears, retroactively so to speak, not only to have been *the* crucial trauma of the century, but also the one that can fully be understood only in the light of our knowledge of PTSD."[4]

This, of course, is not to say that the idea of the Holocaust as the most outstanding and destructive event of the twentieth century—an idea that has long been held as unquestionable at least in the Western world[5]—could only be traced to the establishment of a psychiatric diagnosis or the construction of some sort of linear progress in scientific rationality. Leys' pointed argument does lead, however, to a central and much neglected problem: How are we to judge the degree to which theories, assumptions, and explanations of present-day humanities and natural sciences—such as the diagnosis of PTDS or other concepts of trauma—work on our perception and interpretation of past events and problems and change the frame of reference for our understanding of attitudes and actions at the time?

This field of enquiry has been well mapped in historical studies on the early modern period or the nineteenth and even the early twentieth centuries. In many cases they have charted the importance of scientific knowledge and the scientific mind in general for the setup and reformulation of social and legal, political and moral concepts of social order. At the same time, some have made clear the extent to which moral values, social needs, and political contingencies feed into the construction and uses of scientific concepts.[6] This was the case, for example, in studies on "inventing the criminal," hysteria, or war neurosis.[7] It has to be said, however, that contemporary historians have only rarely addressed these issues in the period since 1945. Contemporary historians were even instrumental in extending the uses of the everyday concept of "trauma" in the description and explanation of historical phenomena that are clearly prior to its scientific "invention." By increasingly falling back on this concept, contemporary history seems to accept the timeless validity of a scientific notion, which needs, first of all, to be put in historical perspective itself.

It is nothing new for contemporary history to take on board current scientific notions without much consideration; in so far as this was done by the historiography in earlier periods it is not unusual. (The concept of race, which was embraced by the historiography in the late nineteenth and early twentieth centuries without much ado in order to construct some sort of "natural" world and social order in the dual sense of the word, is just one example.[8]) No doubt, there are enormous difficulties involved in controlling historical knowledge against the categories currently in circulation and the established contemporary worldview. This may never be fully possible nor necessarily desirable. Yet, wherever current categories of analysis are projected back onto historical evidence we are never far from some unmitigated idea of progress. This is particularly so—as in the case of "trauma"—when the relevant categories are taken from the field of the medical or the natural sciences. In a way, the recourse to the official recognition of PTSD by the American Psychiatric Association—and thus by "expert" knowledge—seems to be "proof" enough of one's own historical argument. This has the effect of a foregone conclusion: Wherever the notion of "trauma" is employed, the reality and imagination of anxiety, violence, and brutality of a particular event are being called up, as if they were already defined. This is equally true for the aftereffects on the daily lives of those who have experienced these events.

This is not to belittle the effects of trauma research on historiography. In acknowledging the concept of "trauma"—whether based on psychoanalysis or neurobiology—new venues were opened up for reflecting on the impact of violent events in new ways. Recent studies on German postwar society—and I will concentrate on the post-1945 period—can be seen as part of a more general trend to question the long-established view that many European societies simply returned back to "normal" without much rupture in evidence.[9] Thus, the lasting presence of the violence of war in the private lives of individuals comes more and more into view.[10] Also, the perception and characterization of events of violence as such have profited from the circulation of the "trauma" coinage. This can be seen not only in the framing of recent events, but also in the way we focus on an ever increasing number of violent phenomena in the past. I am well aware that a number of other factors also come into play, but I would like to argue that the notion of "trauma" has come to occupy center stage in our historical imagination and by doing so has rerouted our understanding of the past and its consequences for our lives.

An evident point in case, here, is the current debate on the effects of the Second World War on German society. The confrontation of the mass of German society, soldiers and civilians alike, with the violence of war and mass death has come to the fore of the public consciousness to a degree that would have seemed impossible only a few years ago.[11] Until very recently, at least in the case of German history, "trauma" had been primarily related to the effects of the First World War and certainly to the Holocaust. Now the Second World War is regularly upgraded into a "traumatic experience" as well, which reflects the fundamental shift of its place in memory. To quote from the introduction of the recent publication *Life After Death*: "Many more people than in the First World War had been traumatized both by what they had endured and by what they had done: the violence of the war—of its battles along its vast and constantly shifting front lines, its incessant air attacks, the brutal acts of population policy—neither spared nor could go unnoticed."[12]

Above all, this blanket assertion of "trauma" marks the newly established acknowledgement of loss and pain as well as a new understanding for a difficult, often persistently painful attempt to come to terms with mass death, which surfaces in many of the recent accounts of war veterans. But this is no real evidence of how the survivors actually lived with the wartime experience of mass death and killing after the event, nor does it show that the way they tried to do this was necessarily directly related to the event itself—as the concept of "trauma" would have it, even in its metaphorical sense. Using the concept of "trauma" does not help here, though not because it would call into question the veracity of the currently held view that violent situations might have long-lasting "traumatic" effects on the mental disposition and constitution. What is crucial is that the way people think of their own past and make sense of their former behavior heavily depends on whether or not those direct links are acknowledged by scientific experts and publicly accepted.[13] In this respect, we should keep in mind what the philosopher of science Ian Hacking observed: individuals who are able to interpret their behavior in a different way also develop a new kind of self-awareness, see themselves differently, and even feel different as a person.[14] This is also why the concept of "trauma" is a problematic tool for historians: it transports particular notions of how memory works and in particular of how pain and shocking events are being processed in memory. In the words of Allan Young: "Our sense of being a person is shaped not simply by our active memory …, it is also a product of our conception of 'memory.'"[15]

"Trauma" is, therefore, not just historical as a scientific concept with all sorts of cultural and moral assumptions; it is also historical as experience.[16] When we try to look—as I will do in the following—at the way in which the presence of the countless war dead and murdered victims may have rocked the lives of the veterans and survivors, it is thus essential not to forget that concepts of "trauma" were simply unavailable at the time. If we were to write the history of society and memory in those days in terms of "trauma," we would most likely end up doing philosophy of history through the back door, as Andreas Huyssen has remarked with regard to the psychoanalytical approach—"not via Hegel or Marx, to be sure, but via Freud."[17] The same is true for the backward projection of PTSD. In the words of the Harvard psychologist Richard McNally: "Retrospective historical diagnosis of PTSD constitutes a psychiatric version of the 'Whig interpretation of history.'"[18]

There is certainly no lack of studies that try to trace the impact of Nazi crimes and the carnage of war on postwar German society. But for some time now, they have focused primarily on public memory construction by analyzing public discourse in the media, the symbolic politics of remembrance, and the public display of memorials. In this way, they have established the extent to which the memory of the Nazi war and its deadly harvest was socially acceptable and politically useful.[19] It has been shown repeatedly that by remembering Nazi atrocities selectively, the memory construction of German victims of war tended to be one-sided, and that this has to be seen against the background of paramount "national" self-victimization.[20] But the constraints on what could publicly be remembered did not necessarily govern the individual memory of those who lived through the war. How was death present in their very personal memory construction? Who of the dead was actually memorized? Is it really true, as was argued in a recent article, that German atrocities and crimes were forgotten as a result of the foregrounding of Soviet violence in East Germany, the painful ordeal of expellees and refugees, and the abject sight of POWs returning from the Soviet Union?[21]

What sort of contemporary sources should we look at when asking these questions? After sifting through hundreds of psychiatric files recorded between 1945 and 1960 I have come to the conclusion that we might actually be able to cover new ground here, under one condition: we must not allow ourselves to be carried away by the suggestion that evident strange behavior and massive psychological derangement, or just of unidentified problems at home or at work, is directly caused by the experience of war and violence.[22] In a number of cases it is indeed tempting to question the diagnoses of the psychiatrists at the time who failed to acknowledge the possible causal link between the confrontation with violence and long-term psychological consequences. This situation changed only gradually, as more and more returnees from Soviet POW camps had to be treated for physical and psychological complaints. But no historian—nor, I would claim, any psychiatrist—is in a position to conclude in retrospect from this evidence that the symptoms and complaints documented in these files are due solely to the experience of war and captivity. Yet, in analyzing in detail these medical files, which also record conversations, curriculums vitae, and letters of patients as well as of their family and friends, we can retrieve a wide range of memory constructions much richer than, and often contrary to, public discourse. We can see "memory spaces" emerging, allowing the dead to be present in a way that was not compatible with the public memory construction of the day. The internal presence of the dead spoke in many voices and took many forms, but speak it did. It surfaced in records written by the patients themselves, and it broke through in bouts of out-of-control narratives during vehement mental breakdowns. The tangible presence of the dead was "embodied" in actual behavior during the day, and it took shape in the dream world of the night. At times the knowledge of the dead also erupted in nightmares and hallucinations. Like dreams, these sights cannot be taken as the true reading of real experience. They are fictional in character. But they can be read as historical sources because they are part and parcel of violence perceived and in this respect function like "internal mental snapshots," as Reinhart Koselleck has argued with regard to the dreams of the "Third Reich."[23]

In analyzing these fragments of memory, therefore, we cannot claim to get at the past experience of war as such. We can only hope to detect ways of dealing with it in the present, and thus in general terms we are not dealing with the history of the war but with the history of postwar imagination of disaster. This is not a history of "trauma" given and discovered, but of an open-ended process of negotiation, public and private, in which unsettling experiences, even if only experienced from hindsight, may be settled or not. There were, of course, different sorts of survivors, for example the vast majority of ex-soldiers and female civilians, or the tiny minority of Jewish citizens. I will look at examples of all these three cases here, albeit necessarily in an uneven manner. This is not to say that these groups were confronted with death during the war in ways that were equally threatening.[24] These differences in experience are evident in the memory fragments to be retrieved from the files. But all are the product of a past that left their life stories inescapably bound up with each other after the war. Many examples can be given for this in the aftermath of the war, for the individual memory of all groups of survivors was shot through with an "imagination of disaster" that in some cases fed on prior, in other cases on ex-post knowledge of mass death and mass murder and thus combined memories and imagination of war, violence, and death. To look at these allegedly unconnected tales of suffering in context, as I will do in the following, is in no way to disparage the suffering of the victims of Nazi persecution, as the notion of German "self-victimization" would have it.[25] On the contrary, it should shed some light on the criss-crossing presence of death and account for the inherent contradictions in West German memory construction.

Many observers have failed to see these contradictions, noting instead the rapidity with which West German society set itself to the task of reconstructing the country while removing places of memory for Nazi crimes out of sight and even blotting out their memory altogether. The next generation was somewhat disturbed by the obsession with ever more affluence and the yearning for consumption and leisure. It appeared as if the backdrop of deliberate mass destruction of life only a few years ago had had no effect of any importance: German crimes and atrocities in particular seemed completely wiped out in individual memory.[26] This judgment by the '68 generation, however, is misguided. In evaluating the specific way the dead were dealt with, it saw only the orchestrated silence of the postwar years. Certainly, the language available for confronting death was limited. But the causes for this are not readily apparent, nor is this interpretation sufficient to give a true picture of the realities of life for survivors, or their family and friends.

The real story of how postwar West Germans dealt with their dead is far from coherent, for the injection of death into life often came suddenly and in manifold ways. The moment of danger in which the individual was forced to wrestle with death could never be revealed to the full or in the same way, even to the closest family. Their knowledge of these moments may have varied by degrees, but in principle it was detached, for an autobiographic sense of suffering is transferable into some one else's mind only to a very limited extent.[27] This is borne out clearly by the following case studies of communication in psychological crises, which will show tentative conclusions, sudden shifts of perception, utter incomprehension, and only occasionally, some degree of accommodation on all sides.

Margaret M., whose family had fled to the West from Silesia, had regularly attended school for some years when she suddenly "collapsed" in 1951, in the middle of her exams.[28] On the next day, as her mother reported, she was "full of fear" that the Russians might get her. She insisted on an answer to her question as to "why she had had to leave the house and the shop," and she kept retelling "all events from 1945" without ever getting "beyond 1947." As her mother explained to the doctor, her daughter "had taken the loss of home and property very much to heart" and had since been "somewhat depressed." But she insisted that up to the day of her being taken in, Margaret had been a "very lively and jolly child," even "exuberant." Of her daughter's nightmares she had nothing to report. Margaret, on the other hand, confided to the doctor that she had been troubled again and again by her dreadful experience—for example, when Russian soldiers had "selected some girls from her trek, bound them top down onto trees and slit their stomachs open," or when a neighbor had been bludgeoned to death with the butt of a rifle, when her own father was later beaten, or when all around her mines went off in a forest across which she had to run for her life in fearful frenzy. She had felt that she had overcome it after all, until on a normal school day this confidence was suddenly shattered by a discussion of the "amputated territories probably lost for ever." At that moment—in her own words—"all the plight of the loss and the shocking experience suddenly re-surged in her mind." During the day she could never get rid of these thoughts again, and more and more they seeped into her dreams at night as well.

Margaret M. only spoke once to her doctor about this, and after a few days of observation she was registered as "free of symptoms." In fact she had redirected her thoughts to the oral exams ahead, taken part in the conversation, and even played the piano in the ward, which was all registered as "positive" in the file. There was nothing strange for the doctor in Margaret's obvious desire and her quickly mobilized ability to practice respectable "normality." She had won control over the pain and grief again and with it over the dead as well, and this was regarded as essential proof of her mental "normality." Meanwhile, it would have been a sign of "abnormal constitution" with the likelihood of pathological reactions if Margaret had "hung her head" or even enjoyed telling the inmates about the "bad experience during her Russian time." These behaviors were observed in Anna S., who was taken into psychiatric care on her own account after having spent years in Russian detention.[29] For Anna's doctors, her detention story certainly did not warrant any such behavior—although she had been beaten regularly during interrogation to start with, was raped several times in 1945, and attempted suicide twice when she was molested again by Polish officers three years later. Her doctors' approach was to collect information about her former behavior. They even confidentially questioned Anna's sister-in-law, whom Anna had characterized as "harsh" and "hysterical" and who obviously had only reluctantly given her shelter after her release. Anna S., who dreamt in "ever more dreadful pictures" about her relatives who had died in the war and who burst out in tears upon seeing pictures of the Korean War in the cinema, was quite convinced: it was the "prevailing conditions" in the home of her sister-in-law that had made her feel "depressed." The latter, who had lost her husband as a soldier in the war and was now living with a Jew, would constantly belabor Anna with the reproach that her detention was but a just atonement "for what German officers had done to the Jews."

It may well be that such open confrontation with German crimes was a rare occurrence in families.[30] But since the fate of German POWs in Soviet captivity was commonly regarded in private as some kind of "atonement" it would be a mistake to believe that their tales of suffering were not related to and shot through with the knowledge of German crimes. The same is true of the fact that the bombing of German cities and the Russian barbarity in warfare was often regarded as some kind of vengeance, as Michael Geyer has pointed out.[31] The knowledge of mass murder committed by Germans, which was acquired in a number of ways at different points in time and at different occasions, could not easily and totally be removed from German memory. It is true, there might be all sorts of reasons for mental transformation, but the rush of anxiety that was articulated in great numbers up to the end of the 1940s almost leads to the conclusion that this was a society driven by angst in many different ways.[32] This applies to ex-soldiers of all ranks and civilians as well. So, for example, Gertrud S. could find no rest any more after having seen a film on "circumstances" in the concentration camps, as she called it. She was driven by the fear that she might have to endure the same horrors as the inmates in the film. And she firmly believed that she was followed by a policeman in the street, and one day she was haunted by the premonition that her brother, who was out on the streets at night, would be taken up by the police.[33] In another case, Adolf W., who in 1948 confessed his former *völkisch* beliefs and his dismay at the outcome of the war, was haunted ever after by the fear that now the "tables would be turned" and they would get him in the end. Driven by additional hallucinations, he eventually took fright at the idea that the time had come for everybody "unworthy and unfit" like himself to be "wiped out."[34]

In some cases these feelings of paranoia were long in coming and hard to pin down to any particular exposure to fear, shame, or anger in war and captivity. Günter B. had already suffered from such fits of anxiety during the war, and their reoccurrence after the war fed on a whole range of possible emotional triggers.[35] From his side, he could only think of one possible reason: his failure to defuse a live hand grenade in time had caused some injury to his fellow-soldier. For a while Günter B. recovered, so that even his wife found him almost "completely restored," but his delusions of persecution caught up with him again. They had never fully disappeared, he now confessed to his doctor. He claimed to have heard different voices calling him "rascal and dirty dog" and urging, "Beat him up and hang him!" Some days later he admitted that while at home he had always been worried "that he might be snatched up and brought into the Russian zone of occupation which is why he was glued to the window and took down the numbers of all the cars which passed by." He did not mention any reason why he should have been in such a state of fear. Some weeks later, again he heard voices that denounced him openly as "Nazi, Nazi"; this, at least, led him to conclude that everybody wanted to insinuate that he had been a Nazi, although he protested this was far from the truth, maybe rightly so. Yet his imagined accusations, like his defense, show the degree to which being a Nazi had become a taboo and a stigma in the aftermath of the war. After the Germans were publicly confronted with the evidence of their mass crimes it was hard to believe that the Allies really meant the denazification procedures to show and prove individual responsibility and not collective guilt.[36] "Being a Nazi" had become a code for the crimes committed, which in some cases imbued the memories of returnees with full knowledge, in other cases with the nagging suspicion, of these horrors. The reactions of the German population were not long in coming, as Hans S. had to note after returning home from four years of captivity in Egypt. As he recounted, he had tried to "frighten the English with Hitler" out of a sense of distress and persecution while detained in a military hospital, so "that they dare not do as they wish to us." But when he arrived back in Hamburg only to meet people who denounced his overcoat as a "Nazi-coat" and wanted to "spit on it," he felt as if he had been deprived of any possible reaction by this gesture of repulsion and disdain. It may be disputed whether the charge of collective guilt was indeed leveled at the Germans by the Allies, or, as Norbert Frei has argued, whether it was a foregone conclusion on the side of the Germans on account of their "widespread feelings of personal implication."[37] In any case, the change functioned as a moral regulator that closely circumscribed the limits of public speech acts.

Many more cases like these could be added. Frequently, the files speak of the uneasy and sometimes even disgusted feeling of shared responsibility for the crimes, either on account of one's own collaboration or simply as a human being. This could be read as a sign of shame in one case, as secret acknowledgement of guilt in another.[38] In both cases, however, these feelings demarcated the limits within which the dead could be dealt with. They provided the frame of reference for the articulation of the violence of war, but also of the suffering and the mourning attached to it.

Even in the fragmentary and admittedly highly selective narratives of death, and even more so of killing, there was still a lurid reflection of this double confrontation. From these narratives families could at least get a vague idea of how painful survival must have been. "You have no idea how much I suffered. Why don't you just club me to death!" When the ex-soldier Rudolf R. suddenly shouted these sentences at his family in a private conflict, he burst out in tears. His mother reported to the doctor that he had lived through what she called the "chaos of retreat" from January 1945 in different combat units. But she gave no information as to what these experiences might have been. His angry and desperate outburst left her helpless and above all irritated. She never asked to know any more.[39]

This reaction was no exception. Whenever horrors of war were hinted at, relatives preferred to stay silent. Some may have shrunk from acquiring certainty about what they knew about the crimes at the back of their minds or what they suspected about the horrors. But it is telling that in many cases, what was extremely disturbing for the relatives was to see their men in tears. This may be seen as proof of a special ideal of masculinity, but the gender argument will not suffice as an explanation. Many of the cases under review here clearly show that women felt equally duty-bound to exercise self-control in face of war death as a way of coping. In part this may be put down to the effects of the Nazi cult of the dead,[40] which had framed the face of mourning and, by idealizing death and even killing, had restricted the imagination as to what memory impact the face of death could actually have. In the case of Private Hans S., however, the closeness of death did sink in.[41] As he told his doctor, he had "exposed himself openly to Russian fire" in a seemingly desperate situation of encirclement. But, as he said, "since he escaped unscathed he had taken this as a sign from above that nothing could happen to him during the war." As if to demonstrate again his invincibility to his doctor and himself, he told the story of his getaway: "In the course of this battle he had broken through the ice of a river repeatedly and could only make it back to quarters after hours. In the meantime his feet had turned black and he was sent off to hospital." However, it was the moment of imminent death in the fire of the machine guns that kept coming back in his dreams. In addition, Hans S. reported, "he had become a shy person compared to his former self, prone to think seriously about everything and even today he tended to brood." Also, he added, "he was easily moved to tears but could equally well be cheerful and even hilarious."

It is not clear, however, to what degree the Nazi cult of the dead actually played itself out in the frequent recourse to speechlessness in face the of death and the dead. The problem of continuity is highlighted, for example, in a story told by Luise F., who in 1954 went to see a doctor in a welfare office for a psychiatric opinion.[42] Luise F. was Jewish and had survived in a major German city. She had worked there well into the war, then gone into hiding together with her child, surviving in dire poverty. Her mother and one of her brothers had perished in the camps. Luise F. shied away from other people and lived a life of quiet seclusion for many years. But at night, haunted by nightmares, she often shouted aloud. She told the doctor that she often dreamed about her mother, and "then someone is trying to get me and then I shout." Her son, she said, "was afraid that people would think that he would mistreat her when she was shouting." At first it appears as if her son was heeding the limits within which he thought that West German society was prepared to deal with the lasting presence of the dead in their midst. But there is more to it. His fear of being wrongly associated with some cruel act against his mother carried a sense of shame for her behavior. Maybe this was simply due to his desire to live a life of peaceful and respectable "normality."

To come to a conclusion: All these cases show a particular urgency and despair in dealing with the dead, but it seems clear from the multidirectedness of these narratives that the concept of "trauma" gives a misleading answer as to causes and consequence. In the first place, there is no foregone conclusion linking "evidence" and "experience," nor is there an automatic response to suffering. The recall of horrible events, imagined or not, is "the event," and this is the only thing we can historically investigate. This event in time cannot be defined in terms of any past "traumatic experience" because it was filled with all sorts of experience, past and present, as well as with fear, justified or not. It was an open-ended process that could not feed on the concept of "trauma," which was simply unavailable at the time. Even more, this process was mediated by public and private circumstances, for example by accepted languages and moral codes, psychiatric knowledge, and considerations of political opportunity. In spite of an increasing number of studies on postwar Germany, we still lack the requisite knowledge of the dominant discourses at the time in order to fully understand these circumstances. We might advance in this direction, I would like to suggest, if we were ready to question again the commonly held notion that men are only able to express themselves within the framework of accepted opinions. In other words, this would mean redirecting our attention more closely to the way in which the dominant discourse might have been fractured by individual languages that, in a way, broke the ground for a new conceptualization and a new idiom of suffering and pain. It may have to be left undecided whether the cases under investigation here did in fact speak of the threatening experience of postwar collapse that was read back into the imagined horrors of war, or whether personal wartime experience itself sought expression in a tangled language not provided for by public discourse.

In any case, these examples show the surfacing of irritating fragments of memory, which were bound to challenge the accepted mode of speaking about the experience of war and death. Of course, this did not happen right away. As I have shown elsewhere, this also required shifting ground in the language and practice of psychiatry itself.[43] But in these private cases we can see how moral regulations and widespread assumptions about the "normality" of man and even of political conditions are at work in the personal constellation in which the "imagination of disaster" was modeled by different ways of speaking about the dead. These were not in unison; they were dissonant voices. Some efforts at speaking of unspeakable horrors triggered the "imagination of disaster" as a family secret, while others led to the projection of personal or professional coping strategies outside the family. But in the end it may be questionable whether there was a personal escape, even if it meant falling silent. For this reason alone the majority of survivors who never made it into the files might have thought that they had a right to silence after all that had happened. This certainly did not mean that the dead or the killing had disappeared from their memory. On the contrary, they surfaced in public consciousness in different languages that were thought to be appropriate at the time. The language of "trauma" is one of them, but not necessarily the one appropriate to this time.

Notes

I am grateful to the Alexander von Humboldt Foundation for supporting me in 2003/04 as Feodor Lynen Research Fellow at the University of Southampton, where this paper was written.

1. Andreas Huyssen, "Trauma and Memory: A New Imaginary of Temporality," in Jill Bennett and Rosanne Kennedy, eds., *World Memory: Personal Trajectories in Global Time* (New York, 2003), 16–29, 16.

2. Peter Fritzsche, "Volkstümliche Erinnerung und deutsche Identität nach dem Zweiten Weltkrieg," in Konrad Jarausch and Martin Sabrow, eds., *Verletztes Gedächtnis. Erinnerungskultur und Zeitgeschichte im Konflikt* (Frankfurt am Main, 2002), 75–97, 95.
3. Carol Tavris, "Just Deal with it," *Times Literary Supplement*, 15 August 2003, 10–11, 10.
4. Ruth Leys, *Trauma: A Genealogy* (Chicago, 2000), 15–16.
5. See, for example, the critical discussion of this position in Mark Mazower, "Violence and the State in the Twentieth Century," *American Historical Review* 107 (2002): 1158–1178.
6. See, among others, the articles in Lorraine Daston, ed., *Biographies of Scientific Objects* (Chicago, 2000). For a survey on the nineteenth and twentieth centuries see also Lutz Raphael, "Die Verwissenschaftlichung des Sozialen als methodische und konzeptionelle Herausforderung für eine Sozialgeschichte des 20. Jahrhunderts," *Geschichte und Gesellschaft* 22 (1996): 165–193.
7. See, for example, Richard F. Wetzell, *Inventing the Criminal: A History of German Criminology, 1880–1945* (Chapel Hill, 2000); Paul Lerner, *Hysterical Men: War Psychiatry and the Politics of Trauma in Germany, 1890–1930* (Ithaca, 2003); Mark Micale and Paul Lerner, eds., *Traumatic Pasts: History, Psychiatry and Trauma in the Modern Age, 1870–1930* (New York, 2001); Doris Kaufmann, "Science as Cultural Practice: Psychiatry in the First World War and Weimar Germany," *Journal of Contemporary History* 34 (1999): 125–144.
8. See, among others, Paul Weindling, *Health, Race, and Politics in Germany between National Unification and Nazism 1870–1945* (Oxford, 1989); Mary Poovey, *Making a Social Body: British Cultural Formation 1830–1864* (Chicago, 1995); Daniel Pick, *Faces of Degeneration: A European Disorder, 1848–1918* (Cambridge, 1989).
9. See, for example, Alice Förster and Birgit Beck, "Post-Traumatic Stress Disorder and World War II: Can a Psychiatric Concept Help Us Understand Postwar Society?" in Richard Bessel and Dirk Schumann, eds., *Life After Death: Approaches to a Cultural and Social History of Europe During the 1940s and 1950s,* (Cambridge, Mass., 2003), 15–38; Niels Birbaumer and Dieter Langewiesche, "Neuropsychologie und Historie – Versuch einer empirischen Annäherung. Posttraumatische Belastungsstörung (PTSD) und Soziopathie in Österreich nach 1945," *Geschichte und Gesellschaft* 32 (2006): 153–175; Frank Biess, *Homecomings: Returning POWs and the Legacies of Defeat in Postwar Germany* (Princeton, 2006), 70–94.
10. For Great Britain, see Pat Thane, "Family Life and 'Normality' in Postwar British Culture," in Bessel and Schumann, *Life After Death,* 193–210; for Spain, see Angela Cenarro, "Memory beyond the Public Sphere: The Francoist Repression Remembered in Aragon," *History and Memory* 14 (2002): 165–188.
11. As Thomas Kühne points out: "even at the beginning of the 1990s the question of social and in particular mental effects of war was irrelevant also for the self-definiton of contemporary history." See Thomas Kühne, "Der nationalsozialistische Vernichtungskrieg und die 'ganz normalen' Deutschen: Forschungsprobleme und Forschungstendenzen der Gesellschaftsgeschichte des Zweiten Weltkriegs," *Archiv für Sozialgeschichte* 39 (1999): 580–662, 582.
12. Richard Bessel and Dirk Schumann, "Introduction: Violence, Normality, and the Construction of Postwar Europe," in Bessel and Schumann, eds., *Life After Death,* 1–13, 4.
13. See Ian Hacking, *Multiple Persönlichkeit: Zur Geschichte der Seele in der Moderne* (Munich, 1996), chap. 4, esp. 93; Hans Pols, "The Repression of War Trauma in American Psychiatry After World War II," in Roger Cooter, Mark Harrison, and Steve Sturdy, eds., *Medicine and Modern Warfare* (Atlanta, 1999), 251–276.
14. Hacking, *Multiple Persönlichkeit,* 93.
15. Allan Young, *The Harmony of Illusions: Inventing Post-Traumatic Stress Disorder* (Princeton, 1995), 4.
16. Young, *Harmony of Illusions;* Leys, *Trauma;* Hacking, *Multiple Persönlichkeit;* Richard McNally, *Remembering Trauma* (Cambridge, MA, 2003); Paul Lerner, *Hysterical Men.*
17. Huyssen, "Trauma and Memory," 18.
18. McNally, *Remembering Trauma,* 283. See also Michael Geyer, "Das Stigma der Gewalt und das Problem der nationalen Identität," in Christian Jansen et al., eds., *Von der Aufgabe der Freiheit:*

Politische Verantwortung und bürgerliche Gesellschaft im 19. u. 20. Jahrhundert (Berlin, 1995), 673–698, 678.
19. See, among others, Sabine Behrenbeck, "Between Pain and Silence: Remembering the Victims of Violence in Germany after 1949," in Bessel and Schumann, *Life After Death,* 37–64.
20. See especially Robert G. Moeller, *War Stories: The Search for a Usable Past in the Federal Republic of Germany* (Berkeley and Los Angeles, 2001); Frank Biess, "Survivors of Totalitarianism: Returning POWs and the Reconstruction of Masculine Citizenship in West Germany, 1945–1955," in Hanna Schissler, ed., *The Miracle Years Revisited: A Cultural History of West Germany* (Princeton, 2000), 57–82. In this context see also the interesting suggestions in Pieter Lagrou, "The Nationalization of Victimhood: Selective Violence and National Grief in Western Europe, 1940–1960," in Bessel and Schumann, eds., *Life After Death,* 243–257, who charts the development of different and selective forms of memory construction. There also seems to be more to the high profile of German POWs still in Soviet captivity in German public discourse well into the 1950s than can be explained merely in terms of German self-victimization. As Neil Gregor rightly points out, it was also, and for many Germans most of all, a sign of hope for the return of those loved ones who had disappeared in the East. Neil Gregor, "'Is he still alive or long since dead?' Loss, Absence and Remembrance in Nuremberg, 1945–1956," *German History* 21, no. 2 (2003): 183–203.
21. Peter Reichel, "Helden und Opfer. Zwischen Pietät und Politik: Die Toten der Kriege und der Gewaltherrschaft in Deutschland im 20. Jahrhundert," in Michael Th. Greven and Oliver von Wrochem, eds., *Der Krieg in der Nachkriegszeit: Der Zweite Weltkrieg in Politik und Gesellschaft der Bundesrepublik* (Opladen, 2000), 167–182, 177.
22. See also the recent discussion of psychiatric records as historical sources as exemplified in a particular case in Greg Eghigian, "Der Kalte Krieg im Kopf: Ein Fall von Schizophrenie und die Geschichte des Selbst in der sowjetischen Besatzungszone," *Historische Anthropologie* 11 (2003): 101–122.
23. Reinhart Koselleck, "Terror und Traum: Methodologische Anmerkungen zu Zeiterfahrungen im Dritten Reich," in Reinhard Koselleck, *Vergangene Zukunft: Zur Semantik geschichtlicher Zeiten,* 2nd ed. (Frankfurt am Main, 1992), 278–299, 287.
24. See, among others, Lagrou, "Nationalization of Victimhood," 245, 250.
25. See esp. Moeller, *War Stories;* and Thomas Kühne, "Die Viktimisierungsfalle: Wehrmachtsverbrechen, Geschichtswissenschaft und symbolische Ordnung des Militärs," in Greven and von Wrochem, eds., *Der Krieg in der Nachkriegszeit,* 183–196.
26. See, for example, Wolfgang Benz, "Postwar Society and National Socialism: Remembrance, Amnesia, Rejection," *Tel Aviver Jahrbuch für deutsche Geschichte* 19 (1990): 1–12. The general assumption about the "repression" of German guilt in postwar society has recently been critically assessed in Anthony D. Kauders, "'Repression' and 'Philo-Semitism' in Postwar Germany," *History and Memory* 15 (2003): 97–122.
27. Reinhart Koselleck, "Formen und Traditionen des negativen Gedächtnisses," in Volkhard Knigge and Norbert Frei, eds., *Verbrechen erinnern: Die Auseinandersetzung mit Holocaust und Völkermord* (Munich, 2002), 21–32, esp. 23–24, denies this altogether. See also Elaine Scarry, *Der Körper im Schmerz* (Frankfurt, 1992), who claims that pain cannot be properly communicated.
28. Hauptarchiv der von Bodelschwinghschen Anstalten Bethel (HAB), Bestand Kidron, Reg. Nr. 4124. The following quotations are from this case.
29. HAB, Bestand Kidron, Reg. Nr. 4017.
30. See, for example, Harald Welzer, "Krieg der Generationen: Zur Tradierung von NS-Vergangenheit und Krieg in deutschen Familien," in Klaus Naumann, ed., *Nachkrieg in Deutschland* (Hamburg, 2001), 552–571; for the GDR: Dorothee Wierling, "Nationalsozialismus und Krieg in den Lebens-Geschichten der ersten Nachkriegsgeneration der DDR," in Elisabeth Domansky and Harald Welzer, eds., *Eine offene Geschichte: Zur kommunikativen Tradierung der nationalsozialistischen Vergangenheit* (Tübingen, 1999), 35–56.

31. Geyer, "Stigma der Gewalt," 683.
32. A thoughtful and stimulating essay in this context is Michael Geyer, "Cold War Angst: The Case of West-German Opposition to Rearmament and Nuclear Weapons," in Schissler, *The Miracle Years,* 376–408.
33. HAB, Bestand Kidron, Reg. Nr. 2888.
34. HAB, Bestand Morija, Reg. Nr. 4559.
35. HAB, Psychiatrieakten Morija, Karton 41 (4524).
36. See Norbert Frei, "Von deutscher Erfindungskraft oder: Die Kollektivschuldthese in der Nachkriegszeit," in Gary Smith, ed., *Hannah Arendt Revisited: "Eichmann in Jerusalem" und die Folgen* (Frankfurt am Main, 2000), 163–176.
37. Frei, "Von deutscher Erfindungskraft," 163–165.
38. Shame, according to Hannah Arendt, can be seen as a still rather private and apolitical expression of the deeper understanding that one needs to carry responsibility as a human being for all crimes committed. Guilt, on the other side, presupposes some awareness of individual culpability. Hannah Arendt, "Organisierte Schuld" (1946), in Hannah Arendt, *In der Gegenwart. Übungen im politischen Denken II* (Munich, 2000), 26–37, 31, 37. For a more detailed discussion see Svenja Goltermann, "Im Wahn der Gewalt: Massentod, Opferdiskurs und Psychiatrie 1945–1956," in Naumann, *Nachkrieg in Deutschland,* 343–363.
39. HAB, Bestand Morija, Reg. Nr. 3959.
40. Geyer, "Stigma der Gewalt," 681–682.
41. HAB, Bestand Morija, Reg. Nr. 5589.
42. Historisches Archiv der Stadt Köln, Acc. 627, 11. Gutachten für die Landesversicherungsanstalt 1954.
43. See Svenja Goltermann, "Psychisches Leid und herrschende Lehre: Der Wissenschaftswandel in der Psychiatrie der Nachkriegszeit," in Bernd Weisbrod, ed., *Akademische Vergangenheitspolitik: Beiträge zur Wissenschaftskultur der Nachkriegszeit* (Göttingen, 2002), 263–280.

Chapter 13

European Melancholy and the Inability to Listen
Sebald, Politics, and Death

Daniel Steuer

Prologue: Standing on the Shore

When we contemplate this display of passions, and consider the historical consequences of their violence and of the irrationality which is associated with them (and even more so with good intentions and worthy aims); when we see the evil, the wickedness following from it, and the downfall of the most flourishing empires the human spirit has created; and when we are moved to profound pity for the untold miseries of individual human beings—we can only end with a feeling of sadness at the transience of everything. And since all this destruction is not the work of mere nature but of the will of man, our sadness takes on a moral quality, for the good spirit in us (if we are at all susceptible to it) eventually revolts at such a spectacle. Without rhetorical exaggeration, we need only compile an accurate account of the misfortunes which have overtaken the finest manifestations of national and political life, and of personal virtues or innocence, to see a most terrifying picture take shape before our eyes. Its effect is to intensify our feelings to an extreme pitch of hopeless sorrow with no redeeming circumstances to counterbalance it. And we can only harden ourselves against it, or escape from it, by telling ourselves that this is the way it was, it was ordained by fate and nothing can be done about it now. And by then returning from the boredom caused by such reflexions of sorrow to our feeling for life, into the presence of our aims and interests, in short: by returning to that selfishness which stands upon a calm and safe shore and from there appreciates the distant spectacle of confusion and wreckage.[1]

This passage from Hegel's lectures on the philosophy of world history, published under the heading of 'Reason in History,' far from corroborating its title, displays

---

Notes for this chapter begin on page 293.

Hegel's deep ambivalence toward history: the calm and safe shore is not provided by reason but by self-interest; our moral and spiritual outrage at the ongoing catastrophe is nowhere answered; the rift between the meaningless destruction, be it natural or man-made, and the human quest for meaning remains unhealed. Thus, the hopeless sorrow and boredom can only be overcome by a trick reason plays on itself, an emotional and intellectual distancing that assumes a vantage point outside the raging sea of history. Reason emerges as ambivalent in itself: it is empathy that forces it to perform the trick, yet the trick abolishes empathy in the process, turning suffering into a distant spectacle and making reason concentrate solely on its own present interests and aims.

This ambivalence of reason, and that toward history, finds a parallel in Hegel's characterization of the novel as the place where "the poetry of the heart and the opposing prose of circumstances and the accidents of external situations" collide.[2] The resulting "complex and ceaseless interplay of materiality and mentality," it has been suggested, is typical of the German narrative and intellectual tradition, including the work of Sebald, in which "precisely that interplay, in shifting configurations" provides the heart of the "creative achievement."[3] And his literary scholarship, too, is said to be informed by it: "In Sebald's criticism, then, physical description becomes a mental world which is understood as an instance of both psychological and socio-political cognition."[4] If so, and if Sebald's writing really presents "materiality made eloquent by the implied 'metaphysical lining,'" what becomes of the unredeemed rift we find in Hegel? Does Sebald, the author, leave the safe vantage point of selfishness and plunge into "the untold miseries of individual human beings"? It may seem so.

It should be obvious that any historian, by definition, is faced with the same choice of remaining on firm ground, or taking a leap that is not supported by the methodological and factual assurances that the academic discipline and its institutions seem to offer. To say so is no more than a reminder that, ultimately, all interpretations and judgments are ours. Historians, as historically embedded subjects, write history from perspectives that, in turn, correspond to forms of historically produced consciousness. If their work is meant to exceed a repetition of the social, political, and moral configurations that have shaped their way of thinking, they must take into consideration, with as little prejudice as possible, the 'poetry of the heart' as much as 'the prose of circumstances.'

Sebald's Natural History of Destruction and the Memory Industry

In the case of German history, and perforce when combined with the theme of death, this task of the historian is fraught with particular difficulty. It is not surprising then that in W. G. Sebald's work, that of a German born in 1944 who, as an adult, lived and worked in England, Germany and death stand in a tense relationship. Here is an author who, by nationality, belongs to the group of perpetrators, and in his writing evokes sentiments of loss, and a dense atmosphere of sadness, mourning, and empathy with the victims of history. Yet, ever since Susan Sontag, in her review of *Vertigo,* declared him to be one of the few examples of "literary greatness" today, someone "registering evidence of the mortality of nature, recoiling from the ravages of modernity," complaints about the fact that a descendant of the perpetrator nation assumes the role of narrating Jewish lives have been rare.[5] And his constant interweaving of human suffering and death with the destruction and death of nonhuman nature also is met with fascination rather than being seen as a cause for concern.[6]

On the Natural History of Destruction, published in 2003, is based on a series of lectures that Sebald, by then a university professor and renowned writer, gave at the university of Zurich in 1997. These lectures discussed the relative absence of the Allies' bombing campaign in postwar German literature,[7] a theme that occupied Sebald at least as early 1982, when he published a scholarly article on it.[8] In 1982 as well as in 1997 his verdict on most of the anyhow scarce literary attempts to describe the effects of the bombing raids on human and nonhuman material had been negative: the descriptions fail to capture the traumatic horror.[9] Yet, there are differences. It has been suggested, e.g., that between the two occasions "[t]he aesthetic verdict transmutes into a political commentary and the adoption of a moral position."[10] However, I would argue, this is only a shift in degrees; Sebald's aesthetic and moral position have always been of one piece, and there is no fundamental change to be found in his attitude toward Germans and German literature as displaying "the moral failure of the very refusal to remember."[11] The blame for the "narrative void" is firmly placed on the Germans themselves.[12] But why this inflexibility on Sebald's part?

According to Wilms, the answer lies with a "political taboo on criticising the Allies for the attacks on civilians," a taboo that is Sebald's "blind spot" and that is responsible for the fact that his "interpretive wings are clipped from the start."[13] This may be part of the truth, but it ignores the discourse between the poetry of the heart and the accidental circumstances in which postwar Germans, including Sebald, found themselves: they were told to feel ashamed and guilty, and they had reason to feel ashamed and guilty. Thus, Wilms's argument misses the mark precisely because it repeats the limitation of historical truth to political expediency; it remains partisan, this time 'against' the Allies and 'for' the Germans, whereas the narrative void is more likely the result not only of the political consensus that ruled the Cold War, in which 'the evil of German Nazism defeated' played an important and legitimizing role,[14] but also of a psychological dynamic within and between the war and postwar generations of Germans, a dynamic that would have taken place in some form with or without the re-educational efforts of the Allies. Both aspects put Sebald in a moral double-bind, which he tried to escape by taking what could be described as an exterritorial historiographical position.

This historiographical attempt is also the interesting aspect of Sebald's writing, providing a perspective in which the destruction and the fragments of his texts emerge as both the process and "the ruins of the dialectic of Enlightenment."[15] It is the development of the corresponding aesthetic strategy, as Ward argues, what really distinguishes Sebald's scholarly article of 1982 and his lectures of 1997. In the latter (as in Sebald's literature),[16] "[t]he process of artistic production is a conscious act of destruction, but also a natural eruption of material; a self-conscious art that is also, in part, a natural product. And so, while Sebald's texts may contain a metaphysics of the natural history of destruction (with the danger of relativisation and mystification this implies), his response to that metaphysics is not resignation, but is to be found in the production of an art which understands itself as part of nature, but only partly, and thus is able to offer resistance through its conscious process of simultaneous construction and ruination."[17]

This succinctly expresses Sebald's philosophico-aesthetic project. However, Sebald's lectures in 1997 must be seen also within the context of a new, united Germany, the anxieties that were then still associated with it, and controversial discussions concerning a false normalization of German self-understanding and German identity. Yet, Sebald's interventions in these debates are based on a norm established in the 1960s and epitomized by the Mitscherlichs' book on the German's alleged inability to mourn.

Thus, in his Zurich lectures, there are at stake at least three very general issues: the relationship between emotion and history, the relationship between public and private memory, and the relationship between academic and personal discourse. The last two of these raise the question of the political function of the memory and culture industries (of which Sebald's work forms a part). The first two raise the question whether there can be such a thing as 'critical mourning,' or even 'critical melancholy,' in the face of historical evidence, and a mode of writing that would be an adequate expression of it. My thesis will be that there is ultimately an ambivalence in Sebald, between the historical specificity of the writings by a post-1945 German author (and here, he does not quite shake off the emotional and intellectual baggage of his generation) and a metaphysical project that aims, indeed, at an impartial historiography. With respect to the latter, Sebald combines in very interesting ways some nineteenth-century thoughts on the implications of physical laws for natural history on the one hand, and on the other Benjamin's ideas on philosophical writing and a materialist historiography, and Adorno's views on the proper, essayistic task of philosophy.[18] Sebald's work is ultimately informed by an ideal of unintentionality, of writing from a neutral perspective, which is not unlike the early Adorno's characterization of philosophy, following Benjamin, as the interpretation of unintentional reality. This ideal gives it an authoritative voice, and at the same time, as Sebald does not grow tired of reminding the reader in his highly self-referential way, that s/he is faced with the constructed narrative of an individual, it has an emotive appeal as well. The consciousness of the highly personalized narrator in Sebald's texts functions as a lens that projects all material of all ages onto a single chronological plane, thus, in a sense, suspending temporality but not form. The present as such seems to possess little value apart from its function as the memory screen for the past. However, Sebald's empathy not only has temporal limits, but it also, as we shall see, ends where he comes across his fellow Germans.

The Germans

In his Zurich lectures, Sebald combines, in a peculiar way, what could be called the continuity and rupture models of German history in taking as crucial the years between the end of the moral bombing campaign and the economic miracle.[19] The "purely immaterial catalyst" for the latter was, in his words: "the stream of psychic energy that has not dried up to this day, and which has its source in the well-kept secret of the corpses built into the foundation of our state, a secret that bound all Germans together in the post-war years, and indeed still binds them, more closely than any positive goal such as the realization of democracy ever could."[20]

This passage establishes a continuity provided by the corpses that are the result of the first half of the century and still determine the second. Yet, there is rupture in so far as the communal bond is no longer provided by public and political ideas and traditions, but by a subterranean flow of psychic energy that has its source in communal silence. Preceding this passage, Sebald attests to the West Germans an "almost entire absence of profound disturbance to the inner life of the nation" and "an almost perfectly functioning mechanism of repression."[21] Amongst the objective conditions for Germany's reconstruction, he sees "the unquestioning work ethics learned in a totalitarian society, the logistical capacity for improvisation shown by an economy under constant threat, experience in the use of 'foreign labour forces,' and the lifting of the heavy [architectural] burden of history that went up in flames between 1942 and 1945 ..., a historical burden ultimately regretted by only a few."[22] At least the last claim is a strong one, indeed, and so is the following equivocation of the German currency of the 1990s with the German Wehrmacht of the 1930s and 1940s: the project to create a greater Europe, Sebald reminds us, "is entering a new phase, and the sphere of influence of the Deutschmark—history has a way of repeating itself—seems to extend almost precisely to the confines of the area occupied by the Wehrmacht in the year 1941."[23]

Sebald's emotive attitude toward Germany and Germans comes out with even more clarity in his discussion of letters he received in response to his Zurich lectures. In his selection from these wartime memories, he rather predictably picks on mentionings of *Gemütlichkeit,* and the German shepherd dog Alf makes an appearance too. While I do not doubt that some of the mail Sebald received may have been politically and morally disturbing, and that much of it may not have done justice to the realities of war, the question remains why Sebald chose to ignore possible interpretations of these letters as, e.g., masking desperation or even trauma, or simply showing lack of narrative competence or command of language, etc., and instead uses them to produce a rather conventional image of not-to-be-trusted, ugly, self-gratifying, and potentially dangerous Germans. To the suggestion, made in one of the letters, that memories of the destruction had not been published because the media erected, and still maintain, a "wall of taboo," he reacts by saying that the letters he received cannot be said to represent a mighty if subterranean echo of the collapse of the Reich and the destruction of its cities. They tend instead to be rather cheerful reminiscences, marked by those characteristic turns of phrases that unintentionally express a certain social alignment and state of mind, and fill me with the utmost uneasiness wherever I come upon them. We have here the glorious world of our mountains, ..., Alf the shepherd dog, quite beside himself when Dorle Breitschneider calls for his mistress ('Frauchen' is the frightful term used) and they all go for a walk; with scarcely concealed nostalgia the writers dwell on their past lives and emotions: the sense of togetherness enjoyed over *Kaffee und Kuchen*. We are told how Granny still works all hours in house and garden, and hear of various gentlemen who came for dinner and—most hair-raising of all German clichés—*zum gemütlichen Beisammensein* ... .[24]

The striking fact is that Sebald, in this ironic and scornful passage, repeats a structure that, as we shall see, also characterizes the work that provides his theoretical foundation, the Mitscherlichs' *Inability to Mourn*.[25] He attests the letter writer "a faint touch of paranoia,"[26] and then goes on to provide justification for this faint touch by ridiculing what are, however inapt, attempts at memory. Whatever one's opinion of *Kaffee und Kuchen,* it is unlikely that you get someone to talk openly by suggesting that his memories are monuments of psychosocial pathology, and that he had better not mention his dog.[27] Sebald's response to certain German phrases and Germans, as well as his wholesale acceptance of the Mitscherlichs' work, is a permanent feature of his writing, from earlier academic essays[28] to *Vertigo* (where the narrator is tortured by the noise of German tourists who enjoy themselves on a terrace overlooking Lake Garda), to the description of Bad Kissingen and its population in *The Emigrants*.[29]

Memory Production: Made in Germany

Sebald's choice not to concentrate on the "attempts at self-criticism, and moments when the dreadful truth makes its way to the surface," which, he admits, are also to be found in the mail he received,[30] is particularly important when looking at his academic and fictional writing under the aspect of memory production. Wulf Kansteiner recently argued that "[m]ost studies on memory focus on the representation of specific events within particular chronological, geographical, and media settings without reflecting on the audiences of the representation in question. As a result, the wealth of new insights into past and present historical culture cannot be linked conclusively to specific social collectives and their historical consciousness."[31] This, he claims, is aggravated by the "metaphorical use of psychological and neurological terminology, which misrepresents the social dynamics of collective memory as an effect and extension of individual, autobiographical memory." In fact, according to Kansteiner, we have three historical agents: (1) cultural memory producers, producing in the light of (2) more or less persisting memory traditions, and (3) cultural memory consumers who are, one is not to forget, potentially subversive in their interests: "The negotiations among these three different historical agents create the rules of engagement in the competitive arena of memory politics ...."[32]

Like all models, this model is incomplete. In particular, it leaves out a first stage of memory production that could be termed 'semiprivate,' that area where, according to psychological research,[33] primary memory material is transformed through repeated narration into lasting memories—or not. However, the model is rich enough to allow us to suggest a different, albeit still rough and schematic, pattern for the post-1945 stages in German memory politics, one that deviates from the model of continuous and community-producing repression: we find a first phase of attempted cultural and traditional restoration (on all political sides), which, from the 1960s onwards, gave way to a debate on war crimes and genocide, and, as a consequence, an opposition between (perceived) victim memory and submerged (perceived) perpetrator memory. This necessary bringing out into the open of the NS legacy was paralleled by a lack of communication between different political factions as well as a generational rift (associated with Germany's recent past, but also with the emergence of an international youth culture), and it took place against the backdrop of the Cold War. This phase thus ended only with the fall of the iron curtain and German unification in 1989.

Within this schema, Sebald, as a memory producer, even in 1997, falls squarely within the logic of the second of these two phases. In this phase the memory producers and consumers were increasingly divided into two groups: those who considered themselves progressive, and those who were seen as revisionist and backward-looking. As a result the translation of private into public memory, a social process of great importance, was as distorted in the second phase as it had been in the first—if for different, one may say opposed, reasons. In either case, the war generation (however defined) suffered what could be termed 'narrative exile.' Neither the politics of revisionist regeneration nor those of wholesale condemnation gave them a public, or—and here is the generational aspect—unregulated private, space to tell a story.

The difficulty even today of leaving behind the dual logic of victim or perpetrator in favor of more flexible frameworks can be seen in contributions that aim to do just that. The title of Lothar Kettenacker's volume on the air war illustrates this in striking fashion: *Ein Volk von Opfern? Die neue Debatte um den Bombenkrieg 1940–45*.[34] Notwithstanding the quality of the contributions contained therein, 'A people of victims?' forecloses a qualified answer—it rules out any discrimination between parts of the population—and only allows itself to be read as a rhetorical question: of course not. And in fact, the volume turns out to possess a strong hint of the old debate, i.e., the one over the necessity and efficiency of the Allies' strategy.

An example of a different nature is the research by Welzer and his co-workers on the transmission of wartime memories in the family context and between the generations.[35] This research is carried out with substantial psychological sensitivity, and it is based on a relatively subtle model of intergenerational memory- and biography- production. But the analysis of this process does not take into account the ways in which the private intergenerational communication is always already influenced by an established public political and moral framework. Thus, e.g., reluctance by a younger interviewer to question critically the older interviewee does not necessarily indicate that there is a "Tradierungstyp Überwältigung" in which the younger listener is overwhelmed and taken captive by the authority of primary memory.[36] This and similar conclusions run the risk of underestimating the communicative and interpretive skills of the younger generation. They may well play along and show themselves to be impressed, yet reserve their judgment and continue to collect information.

The material presented in these studies is extremely rich, and yet the form in which it is presented is undeniably influenced by suspicion: stories about a real threat of rape are turned into stories about fear of rape;[37] stories about nonviolent encounters with enemy soldiers are disqualified as Landser-type narratives, possibly serving to cover up actual killing;[38] war wounds are said to be routinely used to impress and silence.[39] The list, finally, of the narrative mechanisms and roles by which memories are passed down is exclusively negative: preparedness for self-sacrifice, self-justification, self-distancing, fascination, induced identification and empathy (*Überwältigung*). Even if these were really the only mechanisms in operation, and if the German "master narrative" is really one in which one's own family never had any real Nazis and the real Nazis were always somewhere else,[40] then that situation is not originary, or a natural constant, but derives from postwar developments. It certainly does not adequately characterize the relationship between the '68-generation and the war generation that forms the backdrop against which the findings of Welzer et al. would need to be interpreted. In saying this, I do not wish to devalue their work. Rather, I would suggest that this work itself is expressive of a postwar polarization that is not helpful in opening up communicative spaces. Within that polarization, to put it bluntly, there were either guilty Nazis or innocent non-Nazis, a perspective that does not allow a differentiating view of the social, political, and psychological processes relevant to this historical period.[41]

The difficulty in freeing German memory and going beyond a dual logic emerges in all clarity in a recent article by Aleida Assmann, despite her liberal intention to create a wider space for memory. The year 2003, she writes, saw a "flood of memories, whose intensity and scope nobody, …, could have predicted. … The themes included flight and expulsion from the East, the carpet-bombing of German cities, and the mass rapes of German women at the end of the war."[42] According to Assmann, the thematization of German suffering is nothing new *per se:* "For in fact, immediately after the war it was the Germans' self-perception as victims that prevented them from taking into account the suffering of others." And after a period during which "the prioritisation of Jewish suffering pushed aside acknowledgement of the suffering of non-Jewish Germans," today, perhaps, she continues, "it is German suffering which once again pushes aside memories of the Holocaust and blunts the consciousness of German guilt."[43] This is indeed a strange "psycho-logic,"[44] in which such heterogenous phenomena as guilt and suffering (in one and the same or in different individuals) are conflated, and the sufferings of different individuals are not added to, but subtracted from each other.

Assmann goes some way toward a resolution of these strange equivocations. "Every generation," she says, "must develop its own relationship to the past and the previous generation cannot dictate the way in which this should be done." An increase in the diversity of social memory is to be welcomed, while "historians are challenged in their hegemonic and monopolistic authority in the reconstruction of the past."[45] However, in the same breath Assmann relates this liberalization of 'social' (i.e., private) memory to norms governing national (i.e., public) memory: "The insistence on norms at the level of national memory allows for greater flexibility on the level of social memory."[46] Of course, a question arises straightaway: Who does the insisting, and which are the norms? The first question is not answered; the second is: "The norm of German national memory, as established in the 1960s and reconfirmed in the 1980s, is the Holocaust, the recognition and working-through of German guilt, involving the assumption of historical responsibility for the atrocities of the Nazi-regime. … As long as this framework remains in place, the diverse memories of suffering, guilt and resistance can co-exist side by side without necessarily cancelling each other out. Integration into the overall framework does not mean that memories lose their distinctively individual perspectives. It means to narrate and assess them within the larger context of the recklessly started and criminally conducted war."[47]

Assmann admits frankly that this is a hierarchical model in which national memory sets the standard. What remains unclear is who sets the standard, and where the power for change actually lies. Anything that makes "a claim to public representation and general validity must show itself capable of being reconciled with, indeed integrated into, national memory," but meanwhile, in a democracy, social memory can help "national memory to gain greater complexity."[48]

Thus constructed, power is situated precisely at the interface between social (private) and national (public) memory. Assmann's proposal grants a certain liberalism at this interface, as long as the consensus of the 1960s remains in place as the touchstone permitting public representation and general validity. What informs Assmann's well-meant suggestion is a fear of what might emerge if access to the public realm and to validity claims is not controlled. In other words, the extreme case, e.g., of Holocaust denial, rules the attitude toward memory in general.

Between Polemic, Irony, and Melancholy

Repressed memory causes melancholy, and Sebald considered himself a melancholic man. The ice rings of Saturn circled his heart and settled in his writing. His idea of history was a marriage of Benjamin's angel of history and the nineteenth-century entropic vision of inevitable decline.[49] Combustion drives and consumes the cultural process from the very first moment, as he points out in the *Rings of Saturn*.[50] His metaphysical project could bear the same name as the English title of his book on air war and literature; it attempts, indeed, a natural history of destruction, of the disappearance of nature. It is truly metaphysical because the act of writing, Sebald's own included, is seen as part of the natural or cultural process that turns living nature into death. Writing, according to Sebald, produces an artificial order that, taken to its extreme, results in paranoia; i.e., the elements of one's experience are put into relations that, strictly speaking, they do not possess in reality. This results in a delusional vision. Importantly, though, Sebald did not see the relation between writing and madness in the form of a dialectic, but rather as an ambivalence.[51]

Writing first isolates and then arranges its objects into a fixed immovable pattern. Thus, crystallization is a key metaphor for Sebald, as is, in contrast to it, combustion. He is a collector of crystallized artefacts, a bricoleur constructing labyrinthine texts that become metafictional not only through their historical content and references, but also through the author inserting himself and other 'real' characters into them. Most of all, they are metafictional through their form, which aims at dissolving the boundary between natural object and artifact, between nature and culture. The natural history of destruction becomes one with the history of the destruction of nature; and here the term 'nature' could easily be replaced with 'culture.' Everywhere in his literature, Sebald performs the transition from physical nature to mental and emotional life, fictional narrative and autobiography, while at the same time reflecting on the unreliability of memory as well as writing: "Combustion is the hidden principle behind every artefact we create. ... Like our bodies and like our desires, the machines we have devised are possessed of a heart which is slowly reduced to ember."[52] And: "Whenever a shift in our spiritual life occurs and fragments such as these surface, we believe we can remember. But in reality, of course, memory fails us. Too many buildings have fallen down, too much rubble has been heaped up, the moraines and deposits are insuperable."[53] Yet his interest, ultimately, would be to understand the context that exists "between the so-called witnesses of the past made of stone and this something which keeps itself in existence—as a vague longing, with the help of our bodies—in order to populate these stones and the dusty landscapes and flooded fields of the future."[54]

This metaphysical project is at odds with Sebald's theoretical stance as an academic. The sensitivities of the melancholic who registers the process of destruction, of course, do not need to be in conflict with the conceptual tools of a critical theorist, but the tensions between them flare up at Sebald's sensitive spot: the Germans, Germany, and his own Germanness. Here, his ambivalence lets him abandon empathy, melancholy, and irony, including his well-developed self-irony, in favor of the polemical. Thus, within the concert of imagined voices of those crushed in the course of history, German voices mostly appear as the threat of cacophony, as far as his fiction is concerned. And his point of departure in the essays and lectures on the air war is the apparent absence of voices, the questions why there are no literary works that give expression to the experience of the Allied bombing campaign, and why there are also no historical studies on the subject (despite, as he adds, the proverbial industriousness of the guild of German historians).

In his attempts at answering these questions, his ambivalence turns into contradiction. With respect to expressive, literary texts, Sebald admits that the events in question (a) do not allow for adequate description, and that (b) the traumatized victims of these raids can not easily be expected to write or talk about their experiences any more than the victims of Hiroshima. Mentioning Dieter Schäfer's attempts to come to terms with the experience and Biermann's remark about the clock stopping for him at the moment of the raids, he concludes: "Neither Schäfer nor Biermann, nor presumably various other people whose clock also stopped at that time, could bring themselves to go back over their traumatic experiences … for reasons probably to be sought partly in the subject itself, partly in the psychosocial constitution of those affected."[55] It is worthwhile spelling this out: following his own graphic description of the air war victims' experiences, he still sees the need to explain their silence *partly* as a result of the same psychosocial constitution that, apparently unique to German society, results in the catastrophe of National Socialism, conflating those who were victims of the raids with those who contributed to the rise of fascism and to the silence thereafter. Implicit in Sebald's argument is a thesis not of collective guilt, but even worse, of collective inescapable nature. Inescapable, of course, also for himself. The paranoia of the system-building intellectual writer is, after all, not categorically distinct from the spirit that leads to "this German land, cleared up and straightened out into the last vestiges, that, since time immemorial, has been incomprehensible for me."[56]

But what about the historians' unusual restraint? Sebald, in a different passage, gives a quotation from Karl Marx used by Alexander Kluge as a caption underneath the picture of a bombed city:

'We see how the history of *industry* and the now *objective* existence of industry have become the open book of the *human consciousness* [der menschlichen Bewußtseinskräfte], human *psychology* perceived in sensory terms…' (Kluge's italics) [Sebald continues:] This is the history of industry as the open book of human thought and feeling—can materialistic epistemology or any other such theory be maintained in the face of such destruction? Is the destruction not, rather, irrefutable proof that the catastrophes which develop, so to speak, in our hands and seem to break out suddenly are a kind of experiment, anticipating the point at which we shall drop out of what we have thought for so long to be our autonomous history and back into the history of nature?[57]

Sebald's vision of natural history is indeed that of a process in which human agency plays a role on a par with that of other natural forces, a process that happens to be temporarily, but need not be necessarily, reflected in human consciousness. Where this differs from scientific evolutionism is when he wonders about the context of "the so-called witnesses of the past made of stone and this something which keeps itself in existence as a vague longing with the help of our body" (see above).

In any case, we can draw some conclusions from this passage. It seems, what is needed in the face of the atrocities of the twentieth century is a new kind of historiography, of philosophy, and of writing, if descriptive and/or explanatory justice is ever to be done. Traditional theorizing and narration are no longer adequate. Neither unbridled sentimentality nor unbridled theoretical aloofness will do. Sebald's own work, to a certain point, is such a new form of writing, and he practices it in the most impressive passages of *On the Natural History of Destruction*. But the theoretical underpinning of the text reads like an appendix, a mechanical continuation of *The Inability to Mourn*, uncovering a German conspiracy of silence as the basis for the economic miracle and the FRG's constitution.

The "Inability to Mourn": Final Verdict or Diagnosis?

In 1992, Tilman Moser published a reevaluation of the Mitscherlichs' *Inability to Mourn*. His argument is highly differentiated, and he qualifies many of his statements in subtle ways. But the general points are the following. Firstly, contrary to psychoanalytic praxis, the authors demand a recognition of guilt from 'the patient' prior to an understanding of him and his condition, based on empathy.[58] Secondly, the actual situation in which many, if not most, Germans found themselves after 1945, and in which their capacities for mourning and feelings of moral guilt were exhausted, is ignored.[59] The patients, he concludes, are taken as repulsive examples of Germans as a species and serve as a pretext for a general slandering of the German people. Upon reading the text again, Moser is particularly surprised by the hateful and persecuting attitude taken by the authors.

It is not difficult to back up his claims with textual evidence. Not only the level of generalizing, but also the direct association of psychological theory with practical politics is striking: German *Ostpolitik* is delusional,[60] and is based on "this German way of wanting the strictly impossible."[61] Germany's official policies are described as "tied up with fictions and wishful thinking," and there is said to be no real attempt at coming to terms with the past, the result being "a far-reaching isolation from the outside, and a striking clumsiness when it comes to questions of manners and taste. Urbanity is lacking."[62] The Germans—in 1967—are still on the level of "infantile denial" about the past,[63] while all "libidinal energy" is channeled into the economic sector.[64] Any confrontation of the past happened exclusively because of outside international pressure.[65] The orientation toward the West is solely a result of changing the symbiotic partner from National Socialism to democracy, which is easily done because Germans identify uncritically with their guardian, whoever it is. But in case the FRG should experience difficulties of a magnitude similar to those of the Weimar Republic, the next *Führer* is already in the cards.[66]

The expellees' position is described—in an afterword added in 1970—as playing the role of a "perverted conscience."[67] By not accepting that the eastern parts of the former Germany are lost for good, they want to paint over the Nazi atrocities. This is the hidden agenda: not a geopolitical, but a psychohygienic one.

As far as the relationship between the generations is concerned, the text suggests that the children of 1967 must be educated by the historical experts in order to control the influence of the mad ideas of their parents, and to be able to educate them in turn.[68] In short: the parent generation is morally discredited, and emotionally deranged, and their memories (i.e. their version of reality and history) are to be treated with categorical skepticism. The task of the postwar generation is to pass on the truth about the past—which they have learned from specific memory producers—to their parents.

Moser concludes that, as a consequence of this line of argument, the second, '68-generation "entrenched themselves behind outrage and accusation, and the parents, by now even older, closed themselves off yet again." He calls it "tragic" that the second generation delayed the coming-to-terms in the sense of being able to speak in a protected space for another decade or two: "They felt safe, as a condemning collective with *The Inability to Mourn* ready at hand on their march."[69]

And yet, this was an important book. The tragic structure is produced by the perhaps inevitable form in which the postwar generation finally forced the past into the public debate; a form that was—how not?—confrontational, that pulled the Germans to pieces and thus effected polarization. As a result the next generation saw itself in opposition to their parents, and the third, as Moser points out,[70] developed a tendency to revert to and share the silence of their silenced grandparents.[71]

The Inability to Listen

The inability to mourn was neither exclusively nor in all cases a consequence of intrapsychic or mass psychological processes. It is also maintained—and Sebald demonstrates this by contributing to this maintenance work—by a political, psychological, and cultural rhetoric that is quick to identify revisionist motivations when the fate of Germans is discussed. In this context, denazification and reeducation, whatever else their use was, have set a pattern for the postwar era. Every cure, as we know, has its side effects. Thus it is not only the concrete architecture of the hastily rebuilt cities that has made public debate of certain aspects of the past difficult, it is also the moral position in which generic Germans were kept. It is likely that denazification created little faith in official justice; the proverbial 'Persilschein' suggests that it was seen as a kind of 'conscience laundering' of little moral relevance.

What was arguably established, though, was a set of implicit rules for public conduct—a first appearance of the politically correct—and as a result, a narrative underground in which outdated political and historical mythologies probably found it much easier to survive. Sebald's and my own generation have contributed to this situation by holding the war generation at arm's length. They did not speak—except, perhaps, amongst themselves—not least because we didn't listen.

In Sebald's argument there is a distinction to be found between generic Germans and unknown German victims. This distinction crumbles where he talks about his own experiences as a boy playing in the garden of a villa in Sonthofen that had been destroyed in an air raid:

> As children we often spent whole afternoons in this wilderness created in the middle of town by the war. I remember that I never felt at ease going down the steps to the cellars. They smelled of damp and decay, and I always feared I might bump into the body of an animal or a human corpse. A few years later a self-service shop opened on the site of the Herzog-Schloss, an ugly, windowless single-storey building, and the once beautiful garden of the villa finally disappeared under the tarmac of a car park. That, reduced to its lowest common denominator, is the main theme of the history of post-war Germany.[72]

Even including the final sentence, the tone is completely different from the one Sebald uses when talking about the corpses in the foundation of the FRG. Limiting himself to the description of his experiences, including his emotions, the subsequent symbolic interpretation does not express blame so much as sadness. The possible corpses under the self-service shop are not accusations, but are individuals to be mourned; they almost have a name.

Another writer of Sebald's generation, Peter Schneider, in his article on 'Germans as Victims? Concerning a Taboo amongst the Post-War Generation,' speaks of the "moral and aesthetic impossibility," particularly in the eyes of those post-war authors who were politically and historically aware, of presenting Germans as victims.[73] Their fear of contributing to a myth of victimhood, not considered as a possible motive by Sebald, was surely one reason for their silence; however, I would argue, 'moral and aesthetic' here also covers for the term 'emotional.'[74]

Schneider points out several features that characterized the '68-generation: silence about the expelled, silence about the dead civilians in the cities, and silence about the parents, all part of an attempt to rid themselves of guilt by denouncing the parent generation wholesale as perpetrators. This was made possible by theory. The abstract catch-phrase that everything private is always already political meant in practice that what was really personal could be excluded from discussions. There was an unwritten law that one should not talk about personal biographical matters *as* personal. What is excluded as a result is emotional involvement. "The 'private,' familial experiences and conflicts of these sons and daughters," Schneider says, "did not play a role in the endless discussions within the communes."[75] And he sums up the spirit of the age thus: the accusation of being fascist could be used either side of the political fence; it became more a means of denouncing a political enemy, and less a word signifying a specific historical phenomenon. Thus, it led to a derealization of history and to an almost magic attitude. The '68-generation tried to pacify the gods of history on the altar of antifascism. In short, critical consciousness turned into mythological thinking.[76] Most likely, this attitude was the result of internal as well as external pressure. The tragic paradox Moser is concerned with in his article may be described as an 'identity double-bind,' produced by the overlapping of the need to drag the past into the open on the one hand, and the specific form this took—had to take—in the hands of those who suffered and survived in the Nazi era on the other. The resulting double-bind reads thus: 'To the extent that you are truly German, you are evil, if you do not want to be evil you have to give up on being German.'

According to Schneider, "[i]t is as if" Sebald could only gather the courage for his risky enterprise of showing Germans also as victims of the world war they unleashed, by performing the breaking of a taboo, and accusing the generation of authors who avoided the topic for good reasons of a massive repression."[77] There is indeed an emotional double-bind in Sebald's long essay: he can neither soothe nor punish 'the Germans.' This double-bind could be traced down to the level of grammar by looking at the contexts in which Sebald uses the communal 'we' and 'us' to invoke the generic German. He does not use it when he talks about victims or survivors: "This is the necropolis of a foreign, mysterious people, torn from its civil existence and its history, thrown back to the evolutionary stage of nomadic gatherers."[78] He does use it when he talks about Germans who made it past pure survival: "In spite of strenuous efforts to come to terms with the past, as people like to put it, its seems to me that we Germans today are a nation strikingly blind to history and lacking in tradition. We do not feel any passionate interest in our earlier way of life and the specific features of our own civilization, of the kind universally perceptible, for instance, in the culture of the British Isles."[79] This is still the Mitscherlich line of argument, and it is cast in the same style that characterized their *Inability to Mourn*, a book whose authors' declared "enlightening intention" it was "to improve the likelihood of a friendly German."[80]

An alternative to the Mitscherlichs' and Sebald's polarizing narrative stance can be found in Adorno. Adorno, throughout his writing, avoids any form of collective accusations or condemnation. A section from *Minima Moralia*, titled 'Miles off the firing line,'[81] begins by spelling out the interests of industrial companies, then outlines the anonymity, the exterritoriality to human experience, of the reality of killing in this war, as a result of the industrial and administrative nature of warfare and the derealization of the events in the media on all sides. The war remains "phony" throughout.[82] He mentions Hitler's robot bombs as quasi-symbols of world spirit, but without putting particular emphasis on the fact that they are being developed in Germany. (After all, no country would have shied away from developing them if able to do so, and in fact the same people who worked on the rockets for Hitler later won the space race for the United States.) Statements like "What is this culture still waiting for?" and "The logic of history is as destructive as the human beings it produces: wherever its center of gravity tends to move it reproduces the equivalent of the past disaster"[83] keep a balance, neither playing down Germany's role (though Adorno prefers to talk of Hitler and National Socialists, rather than Germans), nor sweeping under the carpet that Auschwitz has a European dimension.

Thus, the section moves from the larger context of the administrative, technical, industrial status quo of modern warfare, to Europe and Germany, and then, crucially, to a very personal paragraph where Adorno asks the question of what to do with Germany after it has lost the war. His only answer is that neither would he, under any circumstances, want to be the hangman, or provide a legal or moral justification for hangmen; nor would he want to stop anyone who attempted to take revenge. This, he readily admits, is unsatisfactory, contradictory, and impracticable. "But," he says, "maybe the error lies already with the question and not with me."[84] He then ends the section by drawing a parallel between the fate of the Jews under fascism and that of the individual in warfare: in both cases the subject is turned into material.

Where this short piece of prose differs from Sebald is not in its greater 'objectivity,' but in its admission of emotionality and moral and cognitive helplessness. The moral rage, the desire for revenge, are perceptible, and at the same time used to demonstrate the limits of reflection: revenge, Adorno says, would turn whole nations into subjectless subjects, mercy would let fascism get away scot-free.

As a German of Jewish descent, Adorno is precise about the contribution that German qualities, i.e., qualities resulting from the specificity of German history, made to the possibility of Auschwitz, but neither does he turn Auschwitz into a unique, nor a uniquely 'German,' atrocity. Rather, he contextualizes it without relativizing it: "The consideration can not be ignored that the invention of the atomic bomb, which can literally kill hundreds of thousands in an instant, belongs to the same historical context as the genocide."[85] And in his lectures of 1965 on *Metaphysics. Problems and Concepts,* he aligns Auschwitz and Vietnam as symptoms of "the natural catastrophe of society, spreading towards totality."[86] He remains faithful to his own philosophical premises, even where the temptation to be sweeping in his argument must have been considerable. Thus, he begins his radio talk "On the Question: What Is German?" by rejecting notions of collective identity and national stereotypes. Although he uses the example of a reemerging narcissistic Germanic identity, the argument at the same time makes clear that there can be no negative stereotypes either. This is further strengthened by his juxtaposing of a positive understanding of German tradition (in the wake of Kant's notion of autonomy) with those who, in the past and at present, pretend to defend this tradition but in fact fail to understand it, or deliberately abuse it.[87]

His verdict on the relationship between German qualities and National Socialism remains dialectical and qualified: on the one hand, without "German seriousness, deriving from the pathos for the absolute," neither Hitler nor the best of German culture would have been possible.[88] On the other hand, the thesis that ascribes all responsibility to the Germans as a people must seem strange, he says, to someone who understands fascism in socioeconomic terms.[89] In accordance with his own version of the categorical imperative—to act so that Auschwitz, or anything similar, may never happen again—and his ethics of resistance,[90] he rejects any absolute generalization, even concerning Germany and the Germans. His ethical stance is based on the values of maturity, *Mündigkeit,* understood as self-critical awareness and epistemological humility (that could be summarized in the directive to always reckon with the possibility that you may be wrong, even in your self-critical reflection), as well as the ability to be affected by and show affection toward others (a kind of determinate negation of bourgeois indifference and coldness, which he takes to be the one necessary condition that made Auschwitz possible).

A fundamental moral as well as epistemological uncertainty, assumed to be everyone's condition under late capitalism, together with historical contextualization, thus allows Adorno to be discriminatory in his condemnation. He can be ruthless in his moral judgment, precisely because he does not erect any kind of categorical barrier between the guilty and the innocent.[91] From his aphoristic statement in *Minima Moralia*—"There is no good life in the false"[92]—he also draws the conclusion, that no one, as long as the whole of life is not right, can be totally condemned: "That fact that even Hitler and his monsters, according to our psychological knowledge, are slaves of their early childhood, products of mutilation; and that yet those few that we could lay our hands on must not be acquitted if the atrocious deeds are not to be repeated endlessly, ... this can not be smoothed over with auxiliary constructions such as a utilitarian necessity which contradicts reason."[93] Call this the antinomy of practical reason after Auschwitz. We cannot abandon the principle of individual responsibility, even though we know that it is not a natural given, nor is it in the power of the individual alone to bring it about. The antinomy remains unresolved. But in the context of the present argument, the short look at Adorno has shown that, in contrast to Sebald's and the Mitscherlichs' criticism, Adorno leaves a door open for those criticized. He does not argue from the safe shore of self-interest, but provides arguments against those who think they can retreat to such grounds.

If life histories are "representing individual biographies as subject to irrational forces beyond one's control, which allows individuals the role of merely coping, trying to muddle through, or hoodwinking fate,"[94] then this "reactive fashion" of telling these histories may correspond to what Adorno calls *Verhängnis,* the "withered space of experience, the vacuum between people and their undoing, which, in essence, constitutes this undoing."[95] It is not impossible that this vacuum includes the experience, or rather the lack thereof, of one's own agency, and this possibility needs to be kept separate from individual repression, self-styled passive or active resistance, systematic exclusion of one's own responsibility, and other such retrospective distortions. Nor is it impossible that the narrative desert of generational, and political, conflict—of which the relentlessness of Sebald and the Mitscherlichs are examples—has contributed to this vacuum.

Epilogue: Mourning and Death outside History?

> History, in any case, is a highly dubious construction; the assumption that it has a meaning and a goal is purely based on faith, and to assume that there are methods of useful intervention amounts to religious madness. All great crimes of mankind have been, and continue to be executed by individuals who are conscious of history, and who feel that they act 'in the name of history'; and this feeling abolishes all scruples. ... If there is a 'scrap heap' of history, then what should most urgently be put there is our concept of history itself.
>
> But what would we be without 'history'? We would be contemporaries.[96]

The question is indeed: "What should historians do with these old men's and women's tales?"[97] Two tentative answers: they should refrain from interpreting them according to a single schema of guilty repressor and innocent victim with the appropriate pattern of truth values for each of them. And they should refrain from doing what my generation, on the advice of the 1960s generation, by and large, has done: not listen to them at all. *Trau keinem über 30* (Don't trust anyone older than 30). Don't listen, you might get infected. What we didn't consider—and this, today, seems to me as much the reason for any deficiency in German historical consciousness, lamented by Sebald, as anything the war generation did—was that this attitude may lead to a certain vacuum in our own lives once we are past 30 ourselves. There was the simple not listening, and there was the listening and waiting for the phrase that gave it away. We became amateur psychoanalysts detecting repressed fascisms without ever having heard of Freud.

Would I, twenty-five years ago, have listened to one of the expellees? Did I draw a difference between those who simply were expelled, and those who were revanchistic about it? I remember well my reaction to television news reports on the annual meetings of their organisations: They were nothing short of Martians to me. If the telling and retelling of stories is part of the natural process that makes experiences intelligible, then public attitudes and the private attitudes of their own children forced the war generation into a form of narrative exile that did little to help them understand events that under the best of circumstances remain almost incomprehensible. We, those born at the end and after the war, have debunked a whole generation, and in the light of one part of me—the one that holds it to be too much trouble to buy a house that needs redecorating and is annoyed when the supermarket has run out of my favorite brand of organic milk—I can only laugh about the link established by Sebald between *Ordnungswut* and *Wiederaufbaustolz* on the one hand, and repression of the past on the other. Sebald rightly felt deprived of something. But it is less the trees under the tarmac than the silence, the "multiple gaps and odd silences in personal narratives," that leads to a feeling of void.[98]

What I have tried to make plausible is that the silence of the war generation was partly produced by the postwar generation, and by attempts to lock them into a particular history, one that contained important truths but also untenable generalizations. The resulting gaps, the rupture of an affirmative relationship with the past, are dangerous: they constitute a vacuum of individual knowledge, knowledge that plays an important role in social and emotional intelligence as a counterbalance to abstract and monolithic accounts. To fill these gaps, or rather, to discontinue their production, historians can do little but to avoid imposing further restrictions on the flow of deregulated communication. Strangely enough, this is the effect Sebald's books can have on a reader—as long as he doesn't talk about the Germans. His reading of ruins can also bring about—as in a flash—the realization that the lives and buildings of today are the memories and ruins of tomorrow, and that the only way to know anything about them is, in an adaptation of Wittgenstein's image for philosophers, not to look in the Baedeker when standing in front of the building, but rather to look at the actual building.

The word 'death' has not taken a prominent position in this essay. And yet, it is about little else but the effects of death on those who brought it about, witnessed it, just about escaped it, and not least on those who experienced the death of people close to them. My reflections are an attempt to throw some light on a type of silence that may be particular to German history. Imre Kertész, I think, must have felt it while walking through German cities: "Germany, since God's punishment, is completely devastated. These cities, these roads, all these rebuildings and new buildings are nothing but the scarred over surface of an enormous wound. No one knows it, everyone finds it nice."[99] Here, we have an image of the silence in rebuilt Germany that differs significantly from Sebald's views on it. This wound seems to possess the necessary complexity; it includes repression of guilt as much as of sadness and loss, sometimes in the same, sometimes in different persons. And the silence is as complex as the wound; it is made up of being silenced, not being able to speak, not wanting to speak. It ranges from trauma to conveniently leaving the skeleton in the cupboard. I think, however, that in the final sentence of the quotation Kertész is taken in too much by an outwardly displayed attitude; that sentence could also be reversed: Everyone knows it, and no one finds it nice. And, I would suspect, following Adorno's interpretation of National Socialism and fascism, we may find that such a reversal between official and unofficial consciousness lies not only in Germany and with Germans. We live in a post-Auschwitz world, and whether we want to or not, in one sense our perspective is Hegel's: standing on the shore, still on the other side of the catastrophe, even if Adorno is right, and it is continuously unfolding. But we are not allowed to make sense of the catastrophe, to enjoy the heap of rubble from a safe distance, or even pretend to understand it, the way Hegel attempted to make sense of history. Instead, we have the responsibility to find and enable ways of mourning that do not rest on, and do not fall back into the logic of, self-interest, into the logic of moral or political self-righteousness. Here would lie our task in writing history. My use of a generic plural must be a hopeful one.

Notes

I would like to thank Michal Ben-Horin for her comments on an earlier version of this essay, as well as the editors for their encouragement.

1. Georg Wilhelm Friedrich Hegel, "Introduction: Reason in History," in *Lectures on the Philosophy of World History* (Cambridge, 1975), 68–69; trans. modified.
2. Georg Friedrich Wilhelm Hegel, *Aesthetics: Lectures on Fine Art* (Oxford, 1975), quoted after Martin Swales, "Theoretical Reflections on the Work of W. G. Sebald," in J. J. Long and Anne Whitehead, eds., *W. G. Sebald: A Critical Companion* (Edinburgh 2004), 23–28, 25.
3. Ibid., 25–26.
4. Ibid., 26–27.

5. Susan Sontag, "A Mind in Mourning: W. G. Sebald's Travels in Search of Some Remnant of the Past," *The Times Literary Supplement,* 25 February 2000, 3. For an introduction to Sebald's work (and a short chronology) see Long and Whitehead, *Critical Companion,* XI–XII, and 3–15. In a reversal of the original German publications, *Vertigo* (1999), a more autobiographically based text, was published after *The Emigrants* (1992), narrating the lives of Jewish exiles. *Austerlitz,* the fictional story of a member of the 'Kindertransport,' appeared in 2001. Sebald has sometimes been criticized for unacknowledged use of documentary sources, but not for his narrative approach as such. It is also worth mentioning that his work has received much less attention in the German-speaking countries than in the Anglo-Saxon world, despite the fact that Sebald never stopped writing in German.
6. The most striking example of this interweaving is *The Rings of Saturn,* trans. Michael Hulse (London, 1998).
7. W. G. Sebald, *On the Natural History of Destruction. With essays on Alfred Andersch, Jean Améry and Peter Weiss,* trans. Anthea Bell (London, 2003). The original German edition of 1999 was titled *Airwar and Literature* and did not contain the essays on Améry and Weiss.
8. "Zwischen Geschichte und Naturgeschichte: Versuch über die literarische Beschreibung totaler Zerstörung mit Anmerkungen zu Kasack, Nossack und Kluge," *Orbis Litterarum,* 37 (1982): 345–366. The Allied bombing of civilians also appears in a prominent position in Sebald's first literary publication, the tryptic prose poem *Nach der Natur,* where the last section of the third part refers to the narrow escape of the author's pregnant mother. *After Nature,* trans. Michael Hamburger (London 2002).
9. Notable exceptions mentioned in the Zurich lectures include Gerd Ledig's *Vergeltung* (Frankfurt/Main, 1956 [1999]), and the work of the historian Jörg Friedrich, as well as passages from Hubert Fichte and, of course, the work of Alexander Kluge, which was one of Sebald's inspirations. Predictably, attempts to disprove Sebald's thesis on the literary silence regarding the air war soon followed: see Volker Hage, *Zeugen der Zerstörung. Die Literaten und der Luftkrieg. Essays und Gespräche* (Frankfurt/Main 2003), and Volker Hage, *Hamburg 1943: Literarische Zeugnisse zum Feuersturm* (Frankfurt/Main 2003).
10. Wilfried Wilms, "Taboo and Repression in W. G. Sebald's On the Natural History of Destruction," in: Long and Whitehead, *Critical Companion,* 175–189, 180.
11. Ibid., 182.
12. Ibid., 188.
13. Ibid.
14. This role is by now becoming increasingly obsolete in the face of, on the one hand, the FRG's accrued democratic merits and increasing contributions to EU and UN policy-making and policy implementation, and, on the other hand, the 'war against terror.'
15. Simon Ward, "Ruins and Poetics in the Works of W. G. Sebald," in: Long and Whitehead, *Critical Companion,* 58–71, 65.
16. Here we ignore, for convenience's sake, that Sebald aims to undermine the distinction between literary and academic writing as well, most notably in *Logis in einem Landhaus* (Munich, 1998).
17. Ward, *"Ruins and Poetics,"* 70. Ward's perceptive analysis of Sebald's self-referential writing also convincingly defends him against Huyssen's charge that Sebald, in his 1997 lectures, naturalizes man-made catastrophe (thereby denying agency and responsibility), and—just as much as those authors he criticizes for this—hides the real terror behind abstraction and a fake metaphysics; see Andreas Huyssen, "On Rewritings and New Beginnings: W. G. Sebald and the Literature about the Luftkrieg," *Zeitschrift für Literaturwissenschaft und Linguistik* 124 (2001): 72–90.
18. See Theodor W. Adorno, "The Actuality of Philosophy," *Telos* 31 (Spring 1977): 120–133, and Theodor W. Adorno, "The Essay as Form," in Adorno, *Notes to Literature,* vol. 1 (New York, 1991), 1–21.
19. On the dimensions of continuity and rupture see Konrad H. Jarausch and Michael Geyer, *Shattered Past: Reconstructing German Histories* (Princeton, 2003), esp. Introduction, 1–33.

20. Sebald, *Natural History of Destruction*, 13.
21. Ibid., 11–12.
22. Ibid., 12–13.
23. Ibid., 13.
24. Ibid., 83–84.
25. Alexander and Margarete Mitscherlich, *Die Unfähigkeit zu trauern: Grundlagen kollektiven Verhaltens*, new ed. (Munich, 1977). On postwar literature, see 56–57. (All translations from this and other German texts are mine, unless otherwise noted.)
26. Ibid., 83.
27. Sebald aligns the Mitscherlichs' case histories with the letters he receives, saying that the assumption of "psycho-social origins to the aberration which developed with such momentous consequences" seems increasingly plausible to him the more "of these reminiscences" he reads (ibid., 84–85).
28. See his 1983 "Konstruktionen der Trauer," in W. G. Sebald, *Campo Santo* (Munich and Vienna 2003), 101–127, which calls *The Inability to Mourn* one of the most plausible explanations of the inner constitution of West German postwar society.
29. W. G. Sebald, *Schwindel. Gefühle* (Frankfurt/Main, 1994), 111. W. G. Sebald, *The Emigrants* (London, 1996), 218–221; this time, incidentally, the "loyal Alsatian" is called "Prinz" (p. 220). For a German shepherd apparently not under any moral suspicion, the dog-loving reader may be referred to a picture of "Peter," Agathe Calvelli-Adorno's best friend, in Reinhard Pabst, ed., *Theodor W. Adorno: Kindheit in Amorbach. Bilder und Erinnerungen* (Frankfurt/Main 2003), 103.
30. Sebald, *Natural History of Destruction*, 85.
31. Wulf Kansteiner, "Finding Meaning in Memory: A Methodological Critique of Collective Memory Studies," *History and Theory* 41 (May 2002): 179–197, 179.
32. Ibid.
33. See, e.g., Ulric Neisser and Robyn Fivush, eds., *The Remembering Self: Construction and Accuracy in the Self-narrative* (Cambridge, 1994) and David C. Rubin, *Remembering Our Past: Studies in Autobiographical Memory* (Cambridge, 1996).
34. Lothar Kettenacker, ed., *Ein Volk von Opfern? Die neue Debatte um den Bombenkrieg 1940–45* (Berlin, 2003).
35. Harald Welzer, Robert Montau, and Christine Plaß, *"Was wir für böse Menschen sind!" Der Nationalsozialismus im Gespräch zwischen den Generationen* (Tübingen, 1997) and Harald Welzer, Sabine Moller, and Karoline Tschugnall, *"Opa war kein Nazi": Nationalsozialismus und Holocaust im Familiengedächtnis* (Frankfurt/Main, 2002).
36. Welzer et al., *Böse Menschen*, 198–211.
37. Welzer et al., *Opa war kein Nazi*, 32–35.
38. Welzer et al., *Böse Menschen*, 204–206.
39. Welzer et al., *Böse Menschen*, 208: "The historical witnesses make no big fuss about them, but show them almost without commentary, as if those scars spoke for themselves, and as if they embodied all the suffering or heroism which produced them. They are ultra-short stories—narrative abbreviations—by virtue of saying what must not and can not be said." The last difference, it seems, would deserve further attention.
40. See Welzer et al., *Opa war kein Nazi*, 205–206.
41. Within a different context, Paul Haggis' 2004 film 'Crash' on racial relations in Los Angeles shows far more psychological differentiation.
42. Aleida Assmann, "On the (In)Compatibility of Guilt and Suffering in German Memory," *German Life and Letters* 59, no. 2 (April 2006): 187–200, 188.
43. Ibid., 193.
44. Ibid.
45. Ibid., 199.
46. Ibid.

47. Ibid.
48. Ibid.
49. See Anson Rabinbach, *The Human Motor: Energy, Fatigue, and the Origins of Modernity* (no place, 1990), and David Baguley, *Naturalist Fiction: The Entropic Vision* (Cambridge, 1990).
50. W. G. Sebald, *The Rings of Saturn* (London, 1998), 170–171.
51. See ibid., 181–182: "For weeks on end one racks one's brains to no avail, and, if asked, one could not say whether one goes on writing purely out of habit, or a craving for admiration, or because one knows not how to do anything other, or out of sheer wonderment, despair or outrage, any more than one could say whether writing renders one more perceptive or more insane. Perhaps we all lose our sense of reality to the precise degree to which we are engrossed in our own work, and perhaps that is why we see in the increasing complexity of our mental constructs a means for greater understanding, even while intuitively we know that we shall never be able to fathom the imponderables that govern our course through life."
52. Ibid., 170.
53. Ibid., 177.
54. W. G. Sebald, *Vertigo*, trans. Michael Hulse (London, 2002), 106f. Trans. modified.
55. Sebald, *Natural History of Destruction*, 94.
56. Sebald, *Vertigo*, 253, trans. mod.
57. Sebald, *Natural History of Destruction*, 67. The quotation from Alexander Kluge, "Der Luftangriff auf Halberstadt am 8 April 1945," in Alexander Kluge, *Chronik der Gefühle*, vol. 2, chap. 8, no. 2 (Frankfurt/Main 2000), 27–82, 79.
58. Tilman Moser, "Die Unfähigkeit zu trauern: Hält die Diagnose einer Überprüfung stand? Zur psychischen Verarbeitung des Holocaust in der Bundesrepublik," *Psyche* 46, no. 5 (1992): 389–405, 394.
59. Ibid., 396.
60. Mitscherlich and Mitscherlich, *Unfähigkeit*, 14.
61. Ibid., 16.
62. Ibid., 20.
63. Ibid., 27.
64. Ibid., 23.
65. Ibid., 41.
66. Ibid., 64.
67. Ibid., 362.
68. Ibid., iii.
69. Moser, *Diagnose*, 401.
70. Ibid., 401–402.
71. In 1987, five years prior to Moser's criticism, Margarete Mitscherlich-Nielsen had published a book titled *Erinnerungsarbeit: Zur Psychoanalyse der Unfähigkeit zu trauern* (Frankfurt/Main, 1987). In it, she also mentions the young generation's adoption of the silence; however, she sees it as the result of an unbroken reproduction of fascist structures in society (p. 14) and holds out little hope for the future: "A sadomasochistic education and attitude, a submissive identification with power, a loathing of the weak, have, indeed, persisted throughout large parts of our society, including the relation of the sexes. Character deformations of this kind, and the corresponding disguises and misinformation, pass on the evil [Übel] of the Hitler era for an indefinite time" (p. 16).
72. Sebald, *Natural History of Destruction*, 76–77.
73. Peter Schneider, "Deutsche als Opfer? Über ein Tabu der Nachkriegsgeneration," in Kettenakker, *Ein Volk von Opfern?*, 158–165, 159.
74. I suspect that the exclusion of certain forms of emotional discourse in the context of Germany and Germans contributed to the stability of the postwar consensus, in so far as it fitted well into the simple distinction between morally good and bad. And it probably still is useful for maintaining the moral superiority of 'the West,' as Hitler/Saddam comparisons illustrate. This

fact interacts in complicated ways with the postwar generation's 'Inability to Listen' and the war generation's mixture of denial, trauma, repression, and the sheer need to survive, but none of this can be understood in isolation.
75. Schneider, *Deutsche als Opfer?,* 164.
76. Ibid., 165. Schneider's perceptions are confirmed by scholarly work. Edgar Wolfrum argues that the 1960s saw a second repression in the form of an anonymization and derealization of all victims, and Axel Schildt describes how the Nazi past was functionalized, not least under the influence of growing medialization, for the cultural conflicts between the generations. Edgar Wolfrum, "Die Suche nach dem 'Ende der Nachkriegszeit': Krieg und NS-Diktatur in öffentlichen Geschichtsbildern der 'alten' Bundesrepublik Deutschland," in Christoph Cornelißen, Lutz Klinkhammer, and Wolfgang Schwentker, eds., *Erinnerungskulturen: Deutschland, Italien und Japan seit 1945* (Frankfurt/Main, 2003), 183–197. Axel Schildt, "Die Eltern auf der Anklagebank? Zur Thematisierung der NS-Vergangenheit im Generationenkonflikt der bundesrepublikanischen 1960er Jahre," in Cornelißen et al., *Erinnerungskulturen,* 317–332.
77. Schneider, *Deutsche als Opfer?,* 165.
78. Sebald, *Natural History of Destruction,* 36.
79. Ibid., viii–ix.
80. Mitscherlich and Mitscherlich, *Unfähigkeit,* 11.
81. Theodor Adorno, *Minima Moralia* (Frankfurt/Main, 1969), 62–66; written autumn 1944.
82. Ibid., 64.
83. Ibid., 65.
84. Ibid., 66.
85. Theodor Adorno, "Erziehung nach Auschwitz," in Theodor Adorno, *Gesammelte Schriften* 10.2 (Kritische Modelle 2), ed. Rolf Tiedemann (Frankfurt/Main, 1997), 675.
86. Theodor Adorno, *Metaphysik. Begriffe und Probleme,* ed. Rolf Tiedemann (Frankfurt/Main, 1998), 160–164. The English translation is Adorno, *Metaphysics. Concept and Problems,* ed. Rolf Tiedemann, trans. Edmund Jephcott, Polity Press 2000. I refer to the passage on pp. 101–105 and the quotation is on p. 105.
87. Theodor Adorno, "Auf die Frage: Was ist deutsch?" in Adorno, *Gesammelte Schriften* 10.2, 692.
88. Ibid., 695.
89. Ibid., 696.
90. Adorno, *Negative Dialektik* (Frankfurt/Main 1970), 358. On Adorno's ethics see James Gordon Finlayson, "Adorno on the Ethical and the Ineffable," *European Journal of Philosophy* 10, no. 1 (2002): 1–25.
91. Adorno, *Negative Dialektik,* 241.
92. Adorno, *Minima Moralia,* 42.
93. Adorno, *Negative Dialektik,* 261–262.
94. Jarausch and Geyer, *Shattered Past,* 322.
95. Adorno, *Minima Moralia,* 64.
96. Robert Menasse, "'Geschichte' war der größte historische Irrtum," in Robert Menasse, *Hysterien und andere historische Irrtümer* (Vienna, 1996), 21–36, 29.
97. Jarausch and Geyer, *Shattered Past,* 29.
98. Ibid., 338.
99. Imre Kertész, *Ich—ein anderer* (Berlin, 1998), 37.

Chapter 14

A Cemetery in Berlin

Peter Fritzsche

Between Südwestkorso and Laubacher Strasse, in the Berlin district of Wilmersdorf, there is a cemetery surrounded by tall brick walls and shaded by comfortably old trees. It is a peaceful place and looks like a garden. Some of the dead buried there died young, but the number who died in the prosperity of old age is much greater. Their graves are carefully, sometimes whimsically attended, so that the cemetery has a warm, harmonious feel to it. But only on first glance. There are two outlying parts of this burying ground that are different and distinguish it from so many other neighborhood cemeteries in bourgeois districts around the world. One quadrant holds row upon row of heavy stone crosses packed closely together. They mark the graves of some of the thousands of Berliners killed in the first months of World War I. Each stone cross has the name and rank of the victim, and the precise date of his birth and of his death. They are all relatively young men:

Kriegswilliger Friedrich Abendroth
25.2.1896
8.1.1915

Leutnant Walter Lorenz
22.9.1886
26.8.1914

Hauptmann Kurt Helf
1.1.1873
2.9.1914

In another quadrant near the main entrance are two broad arrays of small rectangular stones set in the ground. Most of the stones are inscribed with at least

---

Notes for this chapter begin on page 312.

a fragment of a name: an initial and a last name, or simply a family name. Some give the birth year, and almost all have the date of death, some time in late April or early May 1945. These are the last of Berlin's World War II casualties, men and women, young and old, German and non-German, soldiers and civilians, killed by bombs and streetfighting. A few gravestones commemorate the names of foreigners, most likely conscript laborers from Poland or the Soviet Union. The provenanced order of the World War I dead has completely unraveled in World War II:

Gertrud Andree
*
1945

Willie Herse
4.8.1886
1945

Jan Anyska
*
1945

Sometimes the stone face is empty except for the summary word "Unknown."

These two quadrants of war dead are different from one another. The dead of World War I are a known, named, and recognized cohort whose early death was memorialized by municipal authorities in a systematic way, while the dead of World War II comprise a heterogeneous, sometimes nameless group that conjures up not sacrifices in the name of the nation but rather the vast losses of total war. But the two quadrants work together to disrupt the generally solitary aspect of the graveyard as a whole. They give evidence of the violent, untimely deaths that interrupted lives in twentieth-century Germany, and they give evidence also of the larger collective fates in which individuals have found themselves and with which they have identified. Germans have not just died as members of families but as the designated warriors and intended victims of larger political enterprises. Moreover, the orderly rows and columns of the mass graves recall the audacious lines of national authority that enabled the vast energies of mass mobilization and patriotic feeling in the world wars. World War I and World War II did not just happen to people in Wilmersdorf, or interrupt their lives as outside forces, but were coproduced by them. In Germany's struggles in World War I (1914–18) and during the Third Reich (1933–45), Berliners participated in collective politics and choreographed their commemoration. The cemetery, then, testifies not simply to the dispersion of single lives, but to the intensification of collective lives in fearsome political mobilizations.

The quadrants of war cannot be overlooked, and they report on the uneasy presence of Germany's national past. Yet it is the other parts, which make up the much larger ground of individual graves, that today are tended by mourners with flowers. What is the relationship between the two places in the Wilmersdorf cemetery? Does the evidence of war continue to disrupt and complicate the private rhythm of life and death, or have the private deaths, a lifetime after the end of World War II, finally overwhelmed the graves of the war and, in effect, contributed to a normalization of history? Are the war dead largely forgotten, or does the strangeness of their different placement in the cemetery remain jarring to observers? The contradictory narratives of private grief and collective death are held together by the same cemetery walls, but their relationship to one another is not certain.

For those who know the cemetery well, there is, at the place marked 34/28, a grave inscribed "Marlene." This is where Marlene Dietrich, born *in* Berlin but for sixty years not *of* Berlin, is buried (she died in 1992). A fresh flower or two testifies to her cult status in circumscribed subcultures, but only an occasional flower indicates as well how this melancholic figure has in fact been disdained by most Germans because, the fact is, she sang for the Allies. The gravesite is a chilling reconfirmation that to this day people continue to be moved by the collective allegiances of wartime and are not simply exercising individual choices about taste. And yet a few flowers do confirm the existence of associations beyond the solidarities of war and the loyalties to nation. Again and again, the placement of the graves plays optical tricks, shadowing moments of freedom with ghostly habits of the past and casting orderly ensembles into neglected, overlooked ruins. What exactly is in view in the cemetery in Wilmersdorf?

From one perspective, the German past and the dead of the world wars it has buried appear only along the margins. A shelf of young German writers, so *The New York Times* informed its readers in summer 2003, neither takes inspiration from acclaimed older writers such as Günter Grass or Bernhard Schlink nor tinkers with their wartime themes.[1] They are more introspective, as in the acclaimed case of Judith Hermann, or they explore niches in the new urban scene. When the past does appear it does so, more often than might be imagined, as just another piece of urban collage.[2] In an apartment on Neukölln's Thomasstrasse, in Tanja Dückers' well-known novel *Spielzone,* the TV broadcasts a show about Plötzensee, the prison where the 20 July 1944 plotters against Hitler were executed. Laura's parents want her to look at the memorial site: "'No thanks!' I say loudly:" "I myself personally have already been to Plötzensee twice, once with school and once, if they even remember it, with my parents. Each time I had nightmares, I cared, even if Wolf blamed me for not caring, just because I ate a bag of chips inside, which for some reason he found 'totally inappropriate.'"[3] The television is also on when Lehmann wakes up one evening in Sven Regener's comic masterpiece, *Herr Lehmann:* "The afternoon news was on—some sort of demonstrations. Next to him, Katrin lay on her back and snored quietly." Lehmann is ultimately caught by surprise by the events he hears but does not register: "Ach du Scheisse"—"holy shit"—he remarks upon hearing that the Berlin Wall has fallen.[4] Judith Hermann composes a similar scene in her acclaimed collection, *Sommerhaus, später*: "I said: 'Christian has fallen in love,' and you said, 'Nothing new there,' and then we were silent. I could hear the quiet voices from the television set, war noise, air-raid alarm; I knew that it was cold in your room, frost flowers on the window. You hung up."[5] While historical references to the war and the division of Germany litter the descriptions of these confined urban spaces, they reappear in various degrees of decay. They are barely noticeable in the present time of distraction and self-indulgence.

From another perspective, however, "war noise" and "air-raid alarms" have been getting louder and louder, demanding the attention of television viewers and forcing a consideration once again of the quadrants of graves in the quiet cemetery on Laubacher Strasse. Since the late 1990s, more than a dozen documentaries have investigated the military engagements and leading generals of World War II and the explusion of German refugees from Eastern Europe; they are among Germany's leading television exports.[6] The German war dead have been reappearing in massive numbers in the last years, given voice in Walter Kempowski's complex documentation *Das Echolot,* published in 1999, which tracks the movement of camp inmates, refugees, and soldiers in January and February 1945; analyzed in Jörg Friedrich's controversial 2002 study of the air raids; recalled in Joachim Fest's and Anthony Beevor's best-selling accounts of the final months of the *Reich,* both of which appeared in 2003; and thematized in important new novels published over the course of recent years: Günter Grass's *Crabwalk,* which places at its center the sinking in January 1945 of the *Wilhelm Gustloff,* a boat crowded with soldiers and refugees, Reinhard Jirgl's *Die Unvollendeten,* which tracks the bitter fate of Sudeten Germans driven from their homes, and Stephan Wackwitz's *Ein unsichtbares Land,* in which Germans do not see and then slowly come to see the ghosts of Auschwitz.[7] The novels, in particular, are interesting because they cast considerable doubt on *The New York Times*'s summary. Their narratives span the entire twentieth century, taking place across three generations before and after World War II, and they move around the reunified, formerly divided, and now Polish parts of Germany and cross borders into adjacent countries in order to compose a new hyphenated or hybrid knowledge about identity. Unlike the up-close portraits developed by Hermann or Regener, Grass, Jirgl, and Wackwitz have taken an unmistakably national perspective and echoed vexed discussions about the role of German victims—millions of refugees and thousands of air raid victims—in the narration of German history. Is all this attention to German victims in 1945 a signal that a conventional nationalization of German history is taking place, for which the serried graves of World War I soldiers in Wilmersdorf might provide a visual symbol, or is German history being explored and written up in rather more messy, uncertain ways, as the admixtures and gaps and unanswered questions in the improvised graves of the World War II dead might indicate? Sixty years later, what are all these German victims—from Sudetenland, the *Wilhelm Gustloff,* and Dresden—being made to say?

For many commentators there is an unmistakable normalization of memory, in which German victims can finally be recognized and German suffering find a place alongside the national narratives of the French, the Poles, and the Israelis. A self-satisfied undertone of "now it can be told" is audible even as critics warn against the perils of relativizing the crimes of the Germans; this certainly characterizes the public reception of Friedrich's *Der Brand*. There is undoubtedly an intimate link between the recognition of suffering and the authority of the nation, and the evidence of German memory work confirms how strong the organizing form of the nation remains sixty years after the end of World War II and how much more coherent and confident it is in the years since reunification. The distinctive ability of the nation to commemorate loss and suffering needs to remain in view, and it is no surprise that reunification in 1990 vastly elaborated memory work.

But what Pieter Lagrou has referred to as the "national epics" of the postwar years, which overrode particular differences in war experiences to create broad antifascist coalitions, are now complemented by more searching, self-exposing histories in which encounters with anticommunist victims or anti-fascist victims break down the binary opposition of perpetrator and victim and invite more complicated, ambiguous remembrance. In turn, the European scale to recovering a variety of narratives of victimhood and perpetratorship has legitimated the open retrieval of Germany's war dead and the commemoration of Germany's civilian victims. In other words, both the conventional national narrative and the acknowledgement of its insufficiency in the post-Cold War context have reanimated German narratives of suffering.[8] At the turn of the twenty-first century, notions of German identity are no longer held together simply by a particular narrative of remembering in which Germans feature as victims, but by the difficult work of remembering as such, in which the acquisition of the status as victim is contested. This often tendentious, highly personal genre of the memory of suffering has opened up important new political spaces for understanding the fracture lines of complicity and victimhood.

The voices of German victims have been around since the very end of World War II. Far from suppressing the past, which has been the misleading conventional interpretation, Germans selectively embellished it and even obsessed over it. Over *Stammtische* and around *Skatspiele*, and in popular novels and television documentations, veterans, war widows, refugees from the East, and their families shared stories that recognized the wartime suffering of German individuals and gradually constructed a story of Germany's tragic ordeal, epitomized in the nation's division for forty years. The frame remained national, a complement to the more boldly heroic antifascist "epics" in France, Poland, and Czechoslovakia. Popular renditions of twentieth-century history have been told and retold around the particular themes of the suffering of German soldiers, particularly prisoners of war ("Stalingrad"); around the bombing and destruction of German towns and cities ("Dresden"); and around the expulsion of some twelve million Germans from traditionally German homelands in Eastern Europe ("Vertreibung"). It was not until the systematic research of Robert Moeller and Klaus Naumann that historians became aware of this extensive work of vernacular memorialization.[9]

What was constructed in domestic settings in the 1950s, 1960s, and 1970s was a shared national history. Without the narration of German history—evident in the flood of postwar histories, memoirs, chronicles—material distress could not have been interpreted as of one piece or identified as an encompassing historical passage that elevated parochial tragedies into a meaningful, legible, and common national fate and recognized them as national sacrifices. The vernacular register of the national ordeal of war and postwar was a crucible for enfranchisement and entitlement, recognition and empathy. Without this national tale, individual tragedies would not so easily have found a collective echo. War stories, writes Robert Moeller, bolstered "one of the most powerful integrative myths of the 1950s." They "emphasized not German well-being but German suffering," and they "stressed that Germany was a nation of victims, an imagined community defined by the experience of loss and displacement during the Second World War."[10] That Stalingrad, Dresden, and *Vertreibung* remain specifically national memories, even if not critically acceptable accounts of German history, indicates the degree to which the nation throughout the postwar years served as a nexus of popular memory, commemoration, and grief, which recognized suffering but also blurred questions of complicity.

In the last ten years, "war stories" continue to replenish collective memory, and they do so in ways that are both conventional and innovative. In the first place, the new familiarity with "Stalingrad," "Dresden," and "*Vertreibung*" should be seen as much as an effort to remember as an effort to forget.[11] This German history, and these German memories, resist "Vergangenheitsbewältigung," the confrontation with the past, by being an extreme form of it. Their wide circulation may even expose the uselessness of the term and the quixotic nature of the efforts of professional historians to enforce its norms. As Rudy Koshar argues in his book *Germany's Transient Pasts,* the memory work of the nation is predicated on the ability "to arouse remembrance per se, rather than to remember something specific." In other words, it is designed "to help the German people 'recognize itself,'" and to see a "most natural connection" between past and present. People do not remember in order to expose their own complicity. National memory thus has done little to encourage Germans "to remember specific events or injustices" such as Nazism, and it tends to elide over "unusable" individual memories.[12] A good example of all of this is the recent film *Das Wunder von Berlin* (2003), in which the reconciliation of a family in the midst of Germany's victory in the 1954 World Cup enables the resurrection of the nation by restoring the place of fathers, dreams, and national myths.[13]

Surely one of the reasons for the popular success of Kempowski's *Das Echolot,* and of the more popular television programming around refugees and air raid victims, is that it recuperates German suffering and represents this suffering as a shared national fate. Although Kempowski's method of juxtaposition and collage works against a compulsive identification with German victimhood, the emotional centerpieces of the documentation are horrific accounts of German suffering: the treks from East Prussia, Pommern, and Silesia; the encirclement of Breslau and Königsberg; the torpedoing of the KdF cruise liner *Wilhelm Gustloff,* with the loss of 5,600 lives (this is Grass's topic), and the successive bombings of

Dresden on the nights of 13 and 14 February 1945, which conclude the fourth and final volume. Kempowski's vividly detailed texts, as well as the pastoral photographs that accompany them, recall for readers well-remembered incidents and cherished images of a "world we have lost." Moreover, Kempowski's texts, like the testimonies collected by the West German government after the war and the commemorations surrounding the fiftieth anniversary of the end of the war, mostly record the attempts to escape death. They thereby embellish the sense of victimhood rather than an understanding of complicity.[14]

It is not clear whether the war stories being told at the beginning of the twenty-first century are more prolific than those that circulated forty or fifty years ago. Government commissions investigated the fate of the *Vertriebene* in a long series of documentations in the 1950s and 1960s. Much of this material about "German suffering in the East" was worked over by popular novelists such as Jürgen Thorwald and Theodor Plievier. Nonetheless, in the absence of pressure not to destabilize the postwar division of Europe, the difficult histories of Germans vis-à-vis the Russians, the Czechs, or Anglo-American bombers have been more easily told in the years since 1989 than before. At the same time, the stories of the refugees that were more suitable in West Germany (because the Russians were the culprits) and the stories of Allied bombings, which were more congenial in East Germany (in which the British and Americans were the perpetrators), have spilled across the former borders of the Cold War divide. The full articulation of German political subjectivity since reunification has invited imaginative and historical accounts of a shared national fate, setting aside for a moment the question of how tendentious or critical these can be. "Now it can be told," a phrase that accompanied some of the reception of Jörg Friedrich's book on the German civilian experience of the air war, is not accurate, but accurately captures the way the idea of nation and the narrative of national ordeal are inextricably linked with one another. German unification and full German sovereignty enabled the production of more stories of German victims, which emotionally upholstered the new national subject. In a more precise way, Friedrich's book also served as emotional support for Germany's opposition to US intervention in Iraq in 2003 and to US foreign policy generally. "This happened to us in this way" is, in any case, a remarkably strong marker of national identity.

A more nuanced version of the argument that the return of the war dead has something to do with Germany's robust international role is that Germany's specific national identity and the specific international role it plays rely on Germany's critical engagement with the Nazi past. The question could be rephrased as follows: Is it not precisely because Germans have accepted and explored their roles as perpetrators in World War II that they can and do support mulitlateral, reconciliationist, and even pacifistic foreign policies? In this case, the identity of Germans as "Gutmenschen," a newly acquired virtuous identity, requires the presence of historical victims who can warn against new international dangers. Of course, (non-Jewish) German victims are more convenient when arguing against intervention, as in the case of the 1991 and 2003 Iraq wars, while (not only German-) Jewish victims served to justify Germany's support of US intervention in Bosnia and Kosovo in 1999. There is no doubt that the vigorous opposition to what is regarded as US imperialism in the present sanctioned public sympathy with Germany's own victims of US air wars in the past.

The concession that the identity of Germans as "Gutmenschen" is, to some extent, self-serving and ends up providing moral cover for economic and political differences with the United States, should not, however, obscure the kind of historical work it presupposes. What distinguishes the "Gutmenschen" of the present day is that they have quite explicitly accepted the broad complicity of even ordinary Germans in the 1930s and 1940s in the Holocaust and in the military occupations and human disaster of World War II. Their credibility rests on the long record of confronting the German past in ways that oppose any easy division between the German people and the Nazi elite, which had remained authoritative for at least a generation after the war.[15] What Helmut Dubiel calls the "historicization" of the German past has proceeded in different registers in the last twenty years, but it does not amount to a whitewash. It set the stage for the release of narratives of German suffering, this time at the turn of the twenty-first century, in a new context that acknowledges that victims can be perpetrators and perpetrators victims.

To my mind, the close analysis of the terms of German complicity in mostly domestic, family settings, particularly after 1968, reveals the ordinariness and density of German perpetrators and also the inadequacy of the black-on-black depictions that had been hitherto reserved for an understanding of the brutal actions of the Nazi elite. Even though most Germans continue to insist that their "Opa" was not a Nazi, they are increasingly open to the revelations of others, revealing both engagement with and displacement of the difficult past.[16] The reconstruction of the entanglement of non-Jewish Germans in the racial project of the Nazi state entailed recognizing the bitter consequences of that entanglement when the war came home in a direct and ferocious way. German victims reemerged as well when other European historiographies began to examine the collaboration of non-Germans in Germany's military occupation and their complicity in the forcible expulsion of German settlers.

All this is not to suggest that German suffering relativizes German crime. On the contrary, I think what characterizes the confrontation with the Nazi past in Germany today is the huge effort to break down the distance that had been established between ordinary Germans and Nazi actors and thus the easy absolutism of the categories of victim and perpetrator. In so far as German identity rests less on imagined and self-contained continuities and more on acknowledging questions of complicity at specific times in specific places, then it is possible to imagine that memory work can proliferate to recover all the war dead. This activity will produce narratives of German suffering, but against a larger understanding of the terms of complicity in the rise of the Nazis, the appeal of the *Volksgemeinschaft*, and readiness to accept and act on the racial categories that distinguished Jews and Slavs as racial others, which I think explains the popular success of Daniel

Goldhagen as well as Jörg Friedrich. Precisely because of the precise nature of the work necessary to establish itineraries of complicity, and the imperative to sift and return and reexamine, in which the work as well as the object of memory remains in view, literature rather than history has been more successful in realizing this archeological task.[17]

There is always the fear that with so much complicity and so much suffering, memory work will end up creating a false universal in which we all recognize each other as sinners and know each other through sinning, a universal that elides the asymmetries of power and causality and evades the specific ecologies of fascism and antifascism. The denationalization or Europeanization of memory may end up echoing this false universal.[18] But what it avoids, or rather overcomes, is what remains fundamental to the memories of so many nations, which is the reconciliationist narrative that in the United States, for example, remains authoritative and conceptualizes the Civil War as a war between states and brothers rather than as a still incomplete struggle for racial emancipation in which many Americans remain unrecognized.[19]

German victims have become more audible both with the stability of German sovereignty and with its authority in European politics. But I do not think the attention to the victims is simply or only a playing out of the standard lament "we were victims too," in which Germany can now indulge. The introduction of the voices of German victims functions to expose national myths and certitudes, primarily the myth of antifascism, which Pieter Lagrou notes for former occupied European states, and the persistence of Nazi-era indifference in the two Germanies. In the years after 1945, Italy, France, Holland, Belgium, Czechoslovkia, and Yugoslavia homogenized the experience of national victim and national combatant and thus brushed away distinctions between resistance, acquiescence, and collaboration. The voices of the victims in contemporary texts also undermine the easy oppositions by which the generation of 1968 enforced and policed the distinction between itself and the *Tätergeneration*. And finally the voices of the victims help problematize how memories are furled and unfurled, how they become frayed, and how they are reused. They usefully expose the fabrications of history and the frailities of the collective myths that had once worked so well to shush and comfort the victims. I want to explore the reemergence of the war dead in contemporary Germany by way of two important novels that appeared in 2003.

Stephan Wackwitz's acclaimed novel *Ein unsichtbares Land* is about how Germans have learned to talk about the war. It is thus relevant to an exploration of the reappearance of the German dead sixty years later. In this semi-autobiographical account, we learn that for years Stephan's grandfather, Andreas, lectured his family about his German Nationalist views and his discontent with the postwar country he inhabited as a stranger, and when sons and grandsons no longer listened, he then typed out the reminiscences of life in dozens of single-spaced sheets. This is exactly the sort of self-righteous, self-pitying father figure that occupied narratives of German suffering in the 1950s and 1960s, that the generation of

1968 rebelled against, and that the "Vatertexte" of recent German literature in the 1970s and 1980s so fearsomely indicted. Indeed, Stephan, the grandson, joined Marxist groups as a young literature student in Stuttgart and even undertook a study tour of the GDR. Eventually, however, Stephan breaks with the contemptuous certainties of the rebellers. He takes joy in the generosity of life as a cultural diplomat for the Federal Republic of Germany in Japan and Poland, and becomes more curious about his now deceased grandfather and his typescript memoir. He encounters his grandfather's past in a new way.

As Stephan reads the memoirs in the 1990s, his understanding of his grandfather's life becomes more complex. There is no revising the deeply held German nationalism, the old man's racism, or his nostalgia for the "endless German Reich of hunting lodges, Kaiser portraits, and stag antlers," typified by the country house in Laskowitz that is the grandfather's Silesian birthplace.[20] Stephan is also astonished that no one in his family had ever brought up the fact that Anhalt, the small German town where his grandfather served as German parson in what had become Poland from 1921 to 1933, and where his own father spent his first ten childhood years, was just a few kilometers from the Polish town of Oswiecim. Wackwitz takes note of the discipline of not talking about certain things, a common theme in other recent novels such as Grass's *Crabwalk* that take the German past as their theme. Perhaps, he wonders, his father has a right to a childhood without history and his memories of Anhalt need not be revised by knowledge of Auschwitz.

This is certainly the position of Martin Walser, who in the first lines of his novel *Ein springender Brunnen* recalls "past as the present": "as long as something is, it is not what it will have become" ("Solange etwas ist, ist es nicht das, was es gewesen sein wird").[21] Again and again, Walser resists retrospective instruction: "my memory is different," he insists.[22] His is a defense of the world of the child and the innocent and self-contained nature of intentions, ambitions, and desires of a moment in the past, including moments dated 1941, 1942, and 1943. Wackwitz, however, does not want to guard a particular experience of the past. Such a posture of defense had, after all, alienated his grandfather from post-1945 Germany and alienated Stephan from his grandfather, creating more than one "unsichtbares Land," another invisible country.

What Stephan comes to reject in himself and in his grandfather's German Nationalism are "the rhetorics of earnestness" (183) spoken by self-appointed prophets, whether in the Weimar-era German National People's Party or, as Wackwitz suggests, the Red Army Faction in the 1970s. This is quite a leap. It is easy to join up with Wackwitz in criticizing what he tellingly refers to as the "*fichtehaft*" language of German nationalism: "courageous, immature, unassailable, a mighty fortress" (172). The comparison to 1968 seems more of a stretch, yet Wackwitz pursues the argument: he and his generation were also iterative, substituting for the grandfathers they rejected the grandparents they wanted: Rosa Luxemburg, Karl Liebknecht, Erich Mühsam. This substitution restored the voices of Jewish radicals to German history, which Wackwitz commends, but locked the students of 1968 into a repetitive cycle, which he now condemns. "We became them," Stephan remembers: "in my own time, I was fighting against Goebbels, the SA, and my grandfather" (264). In each case, the German Nationalists and the student radicals found and held on to an identity; both generations were obsessed with "origins" (*Ursprünglichkeit*) and "demarcations" (*Abgrenzung*). Against this "*fichtehaft*" tradition, which for Wackwitz is embodied by the Romantic nationalist philosopher Johann Gottlieb Fichte, he counterposes Friedrich Schleiermacher, Fichte's great antagonist in early nineteenth-century Berlin, who stressed the "invention" of tradition rather than the "discovery" of origins. Fichte stays in and guards one place, Schleiermacher is playful and moves around.

Wackwitz was prepared for Schleiermacher's message, admiring as he had in his years abroad a "*richardrortyhaft*" way of looking at things, but then he discovers that Schleiermacher had, in fact, grown up in the very same parsonage his father had in Anhalt one hundred years earlier. With Schleiermacher in German history and with Schleiermacher inside his grandfather's parsonage, Wackwitz returns to the family story with a new sensibility. He begins to ask why his grandfather sought out places outside Germany: Anhalt in 1921, Southwest Africa in 1933. And he asks why he himself discovered his professional vocation as a cultural diplomat outside Germany. Stephan reads Andreas's text against the grain and discerns a moment of unsettlement as the grandfather arranges for his overseas voyage in the German capital on what happens to be the fateful day of 30 January 1933. Energetic voyagers both, the grandfather and the grandson emerge "less Protestant, dry, reactionary, and oppressive" (275). Wackwitz finds something commendable in their energetic, inquisitive pioneer spirit, which he sees in Protestant settlements such as Anhalt in the midst of Catholic Silesia, and which anticipate the westward movement of free American settlers that Wackwitz so admires in Hollywood moves such as *Red River*. Here Wackwitz loses his critical edge, and he relishes the identification with the grandfather that needs to be recognized as a qualification of my argument; nostalgia for the acts of improvisation of this "first" generation echoes elsewhere as well.[23]

Wackwitz overlooks the monstrous costs of colonization, whether in Poland three hundred years ago or in the United States one hundred and fifty years ago, but more importantly, he wants to possess the new knowledge that we "do not just come from somewhere, but rather we have always arrived sometime, somewhere" (195). This is the insight gained from rereading the reactionary grandfather's memoirs, placing the old man's blind spots against his own in an effort to let in some light, and peopling the "confusing, concealed, and complex twists and turns of a family novel" with his relatives (18). What is necessary is to "reinvent oneself and others in friendly, continuous, and collective telling of stories" (182), which is Wackwitz's answer to Walser. It is an answer in which the acknowledgement of the blindspots and the struggle to turn "*fichtehaft*" narratives into "*richardrortyhaft*" ones are central parts of the story. The "settling of accounts" with the father figures has given way to an encounter and a partial reconciliation with the grandfathers. Wackwitz's story covers new ground, thus steering away from the cycle of murderous returns that forms the unconvincing theme of Günter Grass's *Crabwalk,* which concludes: "It doesn't end. Never will it end."

The departures and new beginnings that are the basis of new knowledge in Wackwitz's novel are the painful and unchosen realities in Reinhard Jirgl's extraordinary novel of a family of Sudenten Germans newly settled in East Germany. Like Wackwitz, Jirgl has written a strong autobiographical novel in which the costs of staying to care for one's family—*Pflicht* (duty)—and the costs of leaving to start anew—*Abschied* (leaving)—are accounted for in the rhythmic suspense of "'*schied-Pflicht*—,—'*schied-Pflicht*" (208). The pain of the expulsion from Komotau one day in autumn 1945 detonates across the generations and into the unsettled language by which Jirgl forces the reader to imagine his protagonists. The two sisters only slowly realize the terms of their banishment: "Long Time Now Hanna must have realized that *Home* was forever gone, *FOR=EVER*. And found herself woven into an Alfabet of someone else's conditions" (206).[24]

FOR=EVER is also the inability of the sisters to settle down where they are and the permanence of their refugee identity. They are always ready to appear at the train station hours too early in order to be sure to catch the last train, even when they go on a trade-union holiday many years after the war. For the daughter Anna, however, "*Home: that is nothing but 1 rawrubbed heel*" (39).[25] She leaves for (East) Berlin to build a new life, but her overwhelming desire for a normal family settles her in an unhappy marriage and alienates her from her own son, who has no use for her. "What I can still hear from Mother=Today are just little noises, involuntary noises o. noises of a phlegmatic=pensioners existence, like the scratches at the end of 1 long-playing record."[26] What is the knowledge carried away? "MOTHERS ARE TO BE FORGOTTEN BY THEIR CHILDREN" (242). The son is also abandoned, unable to make the transition into the new Berliner Republic, and is dying of cancer, the pathologization of the bitterness across three generations. The bitterness and rage that Jirgl brings the reader to hear and see in the brilliant technique of his self-fashioned typography prohibit any sentimentalization of the *Vertriebene* but also demand by shouting, a measure of postponed empathy for these "leftovers," unwanted and unseen.

> When they arrived there, April rained down in grey filaments on seeming endless black stretchedout earth, which with every step stuck to the shoes in lumps, in the glittery, frothy water of plowed furrows. And along the horizon, as if smeared on by a dark grease pencil, pine forests which appeared as the black border of a condolence card for a land flat as a table top (11).

In this family story, the truth that emerges is "*Flüchtling immer Flüchtling*" ("once a refugee, always a refugee," 63, 223). As Jirgl pushes these women from Komotau into the history of the German Democratic Republic, it becomes plain that their ordeal is echoed in all sorts of subsequent postwar disappointments; their suffering is not exceptional, but corresponds to so many other humiliations in Germany after the war. At an old age, the two sisters are finally completely dispossessed through the chicanery of the East German bureaucracy. Apartments assigned to civil servants are taken away from them once they are retired, so Hannah and Marie are exiled to the white-concrete edge of town without the means to move their furniture, which is left behind: "Now the two refugees were com=pletely expropriated" (247). Moreover, the scarcity of apartments in Berlin in the 1960s forces Anna to continue to live with the ex-husband she has divorced. The narrator himself, Anna's son, Reiner, experiences his own history as abandonment: his erstwhile girlfriend is the wife her husband has left for the West; as a dentist in the late 1980s, Reiner has plenty of patients because so many doctors have left East Germany—the broken friendships are now "deader than dead" (242); opening a hip bookstore after the *Wende* exposes him to the faddish, unforgiving world of the consumer city; and his inoperable cancer leaves him enslaved to high-end technology. The *Vertriebene* from Komotau in 1945 are the means to get to all the refugees who inhabit "The 20th Century, the Century of Camps & Expulsions" (250).

While Jirgl's story is much darker than Wackwitz's, both authors deploy multiple layers, perspectives, and generations to create spaces where empathy is possible and self-pity and self-righteousness are blocked. In Jirgl's novel the violence of 1945—the beatings, rapes, executions, and bombings—continues to detonate across the decades, but there is no prior idyll that war has destroyed, and there are no heroes. The pain is passed along in myriad forms from mother to daughter to son in a way that keeps the reader from readily identifying victims and perpetrators. Rather, the horrors of the twentieth century act as a forcefield that smashes families, distorts memories, and propels the protagonists forward between the blades *"'schied-Pflicht—,—'schied-Pflicht."* *Heimat* is not a place out of Eichendorff, but a power effect out of Foucault. Guilt and innocence are not positions the author seeks to determine; they are the false certainties mothers and sons have to endure.[27]

However, Jirgl almost pushes his argument about the effects of real history over the edge by pursuing the pain across the generations so relentlessly that political catastrophe begins to seem like a natural disaster. This naturalization of human fate, which the immediate postwar era reported on in the pairing of Auschwitz with Hiroshima, works against the production of new ways of representing the past.[28] In similar fashion, the epic tone of Dieter Forte's acclaimed trilogy, which describes what happens to people rather than what they actually do in demarcated historical spaces, also runs the risk of turning history into a series of stylized effects. In these cases, the process of remembering across the generations is short-circuited.[29]

Iris Radisch has written in *Die Zeit* that "the time of settling accounts has passed. And with it the time of the single, sovereign individual," a reference to the explorations of self in the "Vatertexte" of the 1970s and 1980s. There are no secure and proper moral positions that individuals can inhabit, which is also the insight that Stephan Wackwitz takes away from his confrontation with 1968. "Back into the lap of the novel of generations and back to discovery of the traces of the grandparents," Radisch notes: "Never in the last decades have there been as many family stories as there are now." There is a distinct reconciliationist mood in some of these novels, particularly in Wackwitz, and in so far as nobody is any worse or sicker than anyone else, in Jirgl too. But I do not think that the hand is extended to the grandparents in order to simply forgive or to integrate the generation of the perpetrators into the normalized future of the Bundesrepublik, although this is certainly what motivates some readers. In my view, the play of three or more generations creates multiple perspectives and voices that destabilize any moral authority, whether it comes from the past, 1968, or the present. It also produces the parallelism that Wackwitz notes between himself and his grandfather, which guards against both self-pity and self-righteousness.

The family novel also has a tremendous capacity to introduce unexpected lineages—Jewish grandfathers, Polish grandfathers, Nazi grandfathers—to move around and cross borders as sons and daughters leave places or are left behind in places such as Anhalt or Komotau or Berlin. It is thus prepared to stage the transnational contexts of the tragic history of the twentieth century. Border crossings are as important as generational confrontations, and they enhance the dialogic operations of the novels. This is not to say that everything is connected and connectable, as Tanja Dückers remarks about her own novel of the sinking of the *Wilhelm Gustloff*. There are no "blind alleys of history," she notes, only "nodal points in dense networks."[30] What this "go anywhere" conception leaves out are the silences, taboos, the denials, and the strong narratives that make up the engagement of every generation with the past. Yet it is just these points of rupture, loss, and partial recovery that have become the central part of the story, the incompleteness that Günter Grass reports on in his memoirs, *Beim Häuten der Zwiebel*.[31] In some ways the German war dead are with us again because of what they do not say and cannot say; the recognition of that silence is useful knowledge. Each quadrant of the cemetery—the messy, sad intertwined fates of refugees, civilians, and soldiers from across Europe; the orderly crosses of fallen soldiers; the cultivation of peace with more timely deaths—each poses questions that none alone can resolve. The neat rows of the dead of World War I do not look the same when seen from the perspective of the dead of World War II.

The national frame to memory remains remarkably sturdy. Yet what distinguishes memory work at the beginning of the twenty-first century is the insinuation of individual counternarratives. These not only register the full force of the destruction of total war, which ravaged domestic and family settings in a way World War I did not, but also begin to reveal the messy intertwinedness of complicity and suffering. Memory work scrutinizes itself not so much to say what had been for so long unspeakable, but to show that taboos, silencing, and blind spots are also the materials of our histories, that our suffering is also inscribed with guilt, and that we begin to think of our losses through the losses of others. The occasional flower on Marlene Dietrich's grave is perhaps a sign of this fragile empathy beyond the epic narratives of the nation-state.

Notes

1. Nora Fitzgerald, "For Young German Writers, All is Ich," *The New York Times*, 24 July 2003, pp. B1, 5.
2. See Peter Fritzsche, "History as Trash: Reading Berlin 2000," *Studies in 20th and 21st Century Literature* 28 (winter, 2004), 76–95.
3. Tanja Dückers, *Spielzone* (Berlin, 1999), 20–21.
4. Sven Regener, *Herr Lehmann* (Frankfurt, 2001), 153, 294.
5. Judith Hermann, "Bali-Frau," *Sommerhaus, später* (Frankfurt, 1998), 98.
6. Michael Th. Greven and Oliver von Wrochem, eds., *Der Krieg in der Nachkriegszeit: Der Zweite Weltkrieg in Politik und Gesellschaft der Bundesrepublik* (Opladen, 2000).
7. Walter Kempowski, *Das Echolot: Fuga furiosa* (Munich, 1999); Jörg Friedrich, *Der Brand: Deutschland im Bombenkrieg, 1940–1945* (Munich, 2002); Joachim Fest, *Der Untergang: Hitler und das Ende des Dritten Reiches* (Berlin, 2002); Anthony Beevor, *The Fall of Berlin 1945* (New York, 1945); Günter Grass, *Crabwalk* (New York, 2002); Reinhard Jirgl, *Die Unvollendeten* (Munich, 2003); Stephan Wackwitz, *Ein unsichtbares Land* (Frankfurt, 2003). One can add: Ulla Hahn, *Unscharfe Bilder* (Munich, 2003) and Wibke Bruhns, *Meines Vaters Land: Geschichte einer deutschen Familie* (Munich, 2003).
8. Pieter Lagrou, *The Legacy of Nazi Occupation: Patriotic Memory and National Recovery in Western Europe, 1945–1965* (Cambridge, 2000); and also Tony Judt, "The Past Is Another Country: Myth and Memory in Postwar Europe," in Istvan Deak, Jan T. Gross, and Tony Judt, eds., *The Politics of Retribution in Europe: World War II and Its Aftermath* (Princeton, 2000). On narrative, see Peter Fritzsche, "What Exactly Is *Vergangenheitsbewältigung*? Narrative and Its Insufficiency in Postwar Germany," in Anne Fuchs et al. eds., *German Memory Contests: The Quest for Identity in Literature, Film, and Discourse since 1990* (Rochester, NY, 2006), 25–40.
9. Robert G. Moeller, *War Stories: The Search for a Usable Past in the Federal Republic of Germany* (Berkeley, 2001); Klaus Naumann, *Der Krieg als Text: Das Jahr 1945 im kulturellen Gedächtnis der Presse* (Hamburg, 1998); and Naumann, ed., *Nachkrieg in Deutschland* (Hamburg, 2001).
10. Moeller, *War Stories*, 6.
11. See, for example, Klaus Naumann, "Die Presse als Gedächtnisort des Krieges: Narrative Zeugnisse von Schockerfahrungen," in Elisabeth Domansky and Harald Welzer, eds., *Eine offene Geschichte: Zur kommunikativen Tradierung der nationalsozialistischen Vergangenheit* (Tübingen, 1999), 184–187.
12. Rudy Koshar, *Germany's Transient Pasts: Preservation and National Memory in the Twentieth Century* (Chapel Hill, 1998), 8, 259, 331.
13. The advertising for the film was as follows: "Jedes Kind braucht ein Vater; jeder Mensch brauch einen Traum; Jedes Land braucht eine Legende."
14. Peter Fritzsche, "Walter Kempowski's Collection," *Central European History* 35 (2002).
15. Helmut Dubiel, *Niemand ist frei von der Geschichte: Die nationalsozialistische Herrschaft in den Debatten des Deutschen Bundestages* (Munich, 1999).
16. Harald Welzer, Sabine Moller, and Karoline Tschugnall, eds., *"Opa war kein Nazi:" Nationalsozialismus und Holocaust im Familiengedächtnis* (Frankfurt am Main, 2002); Wibke Bruhns, *Meines Vaters Land;* and Uwe Timm, *In My Brother's Shadow: A Life and Death in the SS* (New York, 2005).
17. Nicholas Stargardt, *Witnesses of War: The Third Reich through Children's Eyes* (London, 2004) uses multiple perspectives, but does not examine the production of representations.
18. This is also Tony Judt's argument in "The Past is Another Country: Myth and Memory in Postwar Europe."
19. David Blight, *Race and Reunion: The Civil War in American Memory* (Cambridge, 2001).
20. Sabine Rohlf, "Von Auschwitz nach Afrika und zurück," *Berliner Zeitung*, 24 March 2003.
21. Martin Walser, *Ein springender Brunnen* (Frankfurt am Main, 1998), 9.

22. Walser, "Über Deutschland reden," cited in Aleida Assmann and Ute Frevert, *Geschichtsvergessenheit—Geschichtsversessenheit: Vom Umgang mit deutschen Vergangenheiten nach 1945* (Stuttgart, 1999), 38. Dagmar Barnouw, *The War in the Empty Air: Victims, Perpetrators, and Postwar Germans* (Bloomington, 2005) should now be added to this genre.
23. On identification, see also Bruhns, *Meines Vaters Land* and Thomas Medicus, *In den Augen meines Grossvaters* (Munich, 2004); on nostalgia, Uwe Timm, *The Invention of Curried Sausage* (New York, 1997).
24. Jirgl's idiosynractic, self-fashioned style of writing is part of the message and difficult to translate, so I will provide the original German: Seit-Längerem musste Hanna erkannt haben, dass *die-Heimat* verloren blieb, *FÜR=IMMER*. Und fand sich unversehens ins Alfabet fremdbestimmter Zugeständnisse verstrickt."
25. "*Heimat: das ist nichts als 1 wundgeriebene Ferse*"
26. "Was ich von der Mutter=Heut noch höre, sind entweder unwillige od rentnerhaft=behäbige Daseinsgeräusche, allsamt wie nach dem letzten Ton Kratzer auf 1 Schallplatte"; "DIE MÜTTER SIND VON IHREN KINDERN ZU VERGESSEN."
27. On this point, Christina Nord, "Vererbte Fluchtreflexe," *die tageszeitung*, 19 July 2003.
28. See also W.G. Sebald's *The Rings of Saturn* (New York, 1998) and my analysis, "Sebald's Twentieth-Century Histories," in Scott Denham and Mark McCulloh, eds., *W. G. Sebald: History, Memory, Trauma* (New York, 2006), 291–299.
29. Dieter Forte, *Das Haus auf meinen Schultern* (Frankfurt, 2003); and see also Peter Weiss, *Ästhetik des Widerstandes* (Frankfurt, 1975).
30. Dückers quoted in Gerrit Bartels, "Die totale Erinnerung," *die tageszeitung*, 29 March 2003. See also Dückers, *Himmelskörper* (Berlin, 2003).
31. (Göttingen, 2006).

Contributors

Simone Ameskamp teaches Modern European History at the University of Tennessee, Knoxville. Her research interests focus on the social and cultural history of Germany, questions of mortality, and intelligence history. She co-authored *Alliance of Enemies: The Untold Story of the Secret American and German Collaboration to End World War II* (New York, 2006) with Agostino von Hassell and Sigrid MacRae. She is now working on a study of the making of the Berlin-Rome-Tokyo Axis.

Richard Bessel is Professor of Twentieth-Century History at the University of York. He has taught at the University of Southampton and the Open University, and currently is Chair of the German History Society. His most recent books are *Life after Death: Approaches to a Social and Cultural History of Europe during the 1940s and 1950s* (edited, with Dirk Schumann, Cambridge, 2003) and *Nazism and War* (London and New York, 2004). He is working on a study of Germany in 1945.

Paul Betts is Reader in Modern German History at the University of Sussex in Brighton, England. He is the author of *The Authority of Everyday Objects: A Cultural History of West German Industrial Design* (Berkeley, 2004) and co-editor of *Pain and Prosperity: Reconsidering 20th Century German History* (Stanford, 2003). He is also Joint Editor of the journal *German History*.

Monica A. Black is Assistant Professor of History at Furman University. She is revising a manuscript for publication based on her dissertation, "The Meaning of Death and the Making of Three Berlins," which won a Fritz Stern Prize from the German Historical Institute (Washington, D.C.) as one of the two best dissertations in German history for 2006.

Alon Confino is Professor of Modern German and European History at the University of Virginia. He has written extensively on memory, nationhood, and historical method. He is the author of *The Nation As a Local Metaphor: Württemberg, Imperial Germany, and National Memory, 1871–1918* (Chapel Hill, 1997) and most recently *Germany as a Culture of Remembrance: Promises and Limits of*

Writing History (Chapel Hill, 2006), and the forthcoming study *Foundational Pasts: An Essay on the Holocaust and Historical Understandings*.

Gabriel N. Finder teaches at the University of Virginia. He studies the Holocaust and the rebuilding of Jewish life in its aftermath. He is guest co-editor of volume 20 of *Polin;* the theme of this issue is divided Jewish and Polish memories of the Holocaust.

Peter Fritzsche is Professor of History at the University of Illinois at Urbana-Champaign, where he has taught since 1987. He is the author of numerous books including *Stranded in the Present: Modern Time and the Melancholy of History* (Cambridge, 2004), *Nietzsche and the Death of God* (New York, 2006), and the forthcoming study *Life and Death in the Third Reich*.

Michael Geyer is Samuel N. Harper Professor of Modern German and European History at the University of Chicago. He has written on the history of war as well as various aspects of German, European, and global history. He is the co-author (with Konrad Jarausch) of *Shattered Past: Reconstructing German Histories* (Princeton, 2002) and most recently author of "Rückzug und Zerstörung 1917," *Die Deutschen an der Somme 1914–1918: Krieg, Besatzung, verbrannte Erde*, ed. Gerhard Hirschfeld, Gerd Krumeich, and Irina Renz (Essen, 2006).

Svenja Goltermann teaches Modern European History at the University of Freiburg. She has published several articles in the field of German nationalism, the representation of the body, the history of psychiatry, and post-war memory. She is the author of *Körper der Nation. Habitusformierung und die Politik des Turnens* (Göttingen, 1998), and the forthcoming book *Gegenwärtige Vergangenheiten: Kriegsheimkehrer, Psychiatrie und Erinnerung in der westdeutschen Gesellschaft, 1945–1970* (München, 2009).

Tim Grady teaches Modern European History at the Universities of Portsmouth and Southampton, where he is also an Honorary Fellow of the Parkes Institute for the Study of Jewish/non-Jewish Relations. He is currently completing a book on the history and memory of the German-Jewish soldiers killed in the First World War.

Martina Kessel is Professor of Modern History and Gender History at Bielefeld University. In 1996–1997 she was Fellow at the Institute for Advanced Study, Princeton, and in 2005–2006 held the German Chair at the University of Toronto. She is the author of *Langeweile: Zum Umgang mit Zeit und Gefühlen in Deutschland vom späten 18. bis zum frühen 20. Jahrhundert* (Göttingen, 2001).

Kay Schiller teaches Modern European History at Durham University. His research interests are twentieth-century German-Jewish and German intellectual history, social movements in postwar Europe, sports history, and the history of the "old" Federal Republic, in particular its memory culture. His books include *Gelehrte Gegenwelten* (Frankfurt, 2000) and, co-edited with Gerald Hartung, *Weltoffener Humanismus* (Bielefeld, 2006).

Felix Robin Schulz teaches Modern German History at the Universities of York and Lancaster. He has a long-standing academic interest in death, disposal, and commemoration. He is currently conducting research on identity, space, and the Alps and is working on a monograph that explores death in East Germany.

Dirk Schumann is Professor of History at Jacobs University, Bremen, Germany. His most recent books are *Politische Gewalt in der Weimarer Republik* (Essen, 2001; English translation New York, 2008) and *Life After Death: Approaches to a Social and Cultural History of Europe during the 1940s and 1950s* (edited, with Richard J. Bessel, Cambridge, 2003) and *Violence and Society after the First World War* (edited, with Andreas Wirsching, first issue of *Journal of Modern European History*, Munich, 2003).

Daniel Steuer is Senior Lecturer in the Department of English at the University of Sussex, and a member of the Center for Social and Political Thought. He is currently writing a book on the role of natural history in critical theory. He has published books and articles on Wittgenstein, Goethe's science, Thomas Bernhard, Otto Weininger, Ernst Mach and Robert Musil, Freud, and others.

Select Bibliography

Ackermann, Volker. *Nationale Totenfeiern in Deutschland: Von Wilhelm I. bis Franz-Josef Strauß.* Stuttgart, 1990.
AFD. *Raum für Tode: Die Geschichte der Friedhöfe von den Gräberstraßen der Römerzeit bis zur anonymen Bestattung.* Braunschweig, 2003.
Adorno, Theodor W. *Metaphysics: Concept and Problems.* Ed. Rolf Tiedemann. Trans. Edmund Jephcott. Stanford, 2000.
Ariès, Philippe. *Western Attitudes toward Death from the Middle Ages to the Present.* Baltimore, 1974.
Assmann, Aleida. "On the (In)Compatibility of Guilt and Suffering in German Memory," *German Life and Letters* 59 (April 2006): 187–200.
Atze, Marcel, and Franz Loquai, eds. *Sebald: Lektüren.* Eggingen, 2005.
Audoin-Rouzeau, Stephane, and Annette Becker. *14–18: Understanding the Great War.* Trans. Catherine Temerson. New York, 2002.
Baird, Jay. *To Die for Germany: Heroes in the Nazi Pantheon.* Bloomington, 1990.
Barnouw, Dagmar. *Germany 1945: Views of War and Violence.* Bloomington, 1996.
Bartov, Omer, and Phyllis Mack. *In God's Name: Genocide and Religion in the Twentieth Century.* New York, 2001.
Bauman, Zygmunt. *Mortality, Immortality and Other Life Strategies.* Stanford, 1992.
Becker, Hansjakob, ed. *Im Angesicht des Todes. Ein interdisziplinäres Kompendium.* Vol. 1. St. Ottilien, 1987.
Behrenbeck, Sabine. *Der Kult um die toten Helden: Nationalsozialistische Mythen, Riten und Symbole 1923 bis 1945.* Vierow, 1996.
Bessel, Richard. *Nazism and War.* London, 2004.
——— . "Hatred after War: Emotion and the Postwar History of East Germany." *History & Memory* 17, nos. 1/2 (2005): 195–216.
Bessel, Richard, and Dirk Schumann, eds. *Life After Death: Approaches to a Cultural and Social History of Europe during the 1940s and 1950s.* New York, 2003.
Betts, Paul. "Germany, International Justice, and the 20th Century." *History & Memory* 17, nos. 1/2 (2005): 45–86.
Betts, Paul, and Greg Eghigian, eds. *Pain and Prosperity: Reconsidering Twentieth Century German History.* Palo Alto, 2003.
Biess, Frank. *Homecomings: Returning POWs and the Legacies of Defeat in Postwar Germany.* Princeton, 2006.
Blasius, Tobias. *Olympische Bewegung, Kalter Krieg und Deutschlandpolitik 1949–1972.* Frankfurt am Main, 2001.
Blumenthal-Barby, Kay. *Betreuung Sterbender: Tendenzen, Fakten, Probleme.* Berlin-Ost, 1982.
Borneman, John, ed. *Death of the Father: An Anthropology of the End in Political Authority.* New York and Oxford, 2004.

Bourke, Joanna. *An Intimate History of Killing: Face-to-Face Killing in Twentieth-Century Warfare.* New York, 1999.
Brenner, Michael. *After the Holocaust: Rebuilding Jewish Lives in Postwar Germany.* Trans. Barbara Harshav. Princeton, 1997.
Dubiel, Helmut. *Niemand ist frei von der Geschichte: Die nationalsozialistische Herrschaft in den Debatten des Deutschen Bundestages.* Munich, 1999.
Dückers, Tanja. *Spielzone.* Berlin, 1999.
Duménil, Anne. "1918, l'année de la 'Grand Bataille': Les facteurs militaires de la défaite allemande." In Nicolas Beaupré, Anne Duménil, and Christian Ingrao, eds., *1914–1945: L'ère de la guerre—violence, mobilisations, deuil.* Paris, 2004, 229–255.
Eisenberg, Christiane. *"English Sports" und deutsche Bürger: Eine Gesellschaftsgeschichte 1800–1939.* Paderborn, 1999.
Ferguson, Niall. *The Pity of War.* New York, 1999.
Fischer, Norbert. *Vom Gottesacker zum Krematorium: Eine Sozialgeschichte der Friedhöfe in Deutschland seit dem 18. Jahrhundert.* Cologne, 1996.
———. *Geschichte des Todes in der Neuzeit.* Erfurt, 2001.
Forte, Dieter. *Das Haus auf meinen Schultern.* Frankfurt, 2003.
Franz, Ansgar. "Alles hat am Ende sich Gelohnt? Christliche Begräbnisliturgie zwischen Tradition und säkularen Riten."*Liturgisches Jahrbuch* 51 (2001): 204–205.
Friedrich, Jörg. *Der Brand: Deutschland im Bombenkrieg 1940–1945.* Berlin, 2002.
Fritzsche, Peter. "History as Trash: Reading Berlin 2000." *Studies in 20th and 21st Century Literature* 28 (winter, 2004), 76–95.
———. "What Exactly Is *Vergangenheitsbewältigung*? Narrative and Its Insufficiency in Postwar Germany." In Anne Fuchs et al., eds., *German Memory Contests: The Quest for Identity in Literature, Film, and Discourse since 1990.* Rochester, NY, 2006, 25–40.
Geyer, Martin H. "Der Kampf um nationale Repräsentation. Deutsch-deutsche Sportsbeziehungen und die 'Hallstein-Doktrin.'" *Vierteljahrshefte für Zeitgeschichte* 44 (1996): 55–86.
Geyer, Michael. "Das Stigma der Gewalt und das Problem der nationalen Identität." In Christian Jansen et. al., eds.,*Von der Aufgabe der Freiheit. Politische Verantwortung und bürgerliche Gesellschaft im 19. u. 20. Jahrhundert.* Berlin, 1995, 673–698.
Gleichmann, Peter, and Thomas Kühne, eds. *Massenhaftes Töten. Kriege und Genozid im 20. Jahrhundert.* Essen, 2004.
Görner, Rüdiger, ed. *The Anatomist of Melancholy: Essays in Memory of W. G. Sebald.* Munich, 2003.
Gorer, Geoffrey. "The Pornography of Death." *Encounter* 5, no. 4 (1955): 49–52.
Gregor, Neil. "'Is he still alive, or long since dead?' Loss, Absence and Remembrance in Nuremberg, 1945–1956." *German History* 21, no. 2 (2003): 183–203.
Groschopp, Horst. "Weltliche Trauerkultur in der DDR: Toten- und Bestattungsrituale in der politischen Symbolik des DDR-Systems." *Zeitschrift für Sozialwissenschaften* 29 (2000): 109.
Hacking, Ian. *Rewriting the Soul: Multiple Personality and the Sciences of Memory.* Princeton, 1995.
Happe, Barbara. "Urnengemeinschaftsanlagen: Zur Friedhofs- und Bestattungskultur in der DDR." *Deutschlandarchiv* 3 (2001): 436–446.
Herf, Jeffrey. *Divided Memory: The Nazi Past in the Two Germanys.* Cambridge, 1997.
Herzog, Dagmar. *Sex After Fascism: Memory and Morality in Twentieth-Century Germany.* Princeton, 2005.
Hillmann, Jörg, and John Zimmermann, eds. *Kriegsende 1945 in Deutschland.* Munich, 2002.

Hoffmann, Christhard. "Between Integration and Rejection: The Jewish Community in Germany 1914–1918." John Horne, ed., *State, Society, and Mobilization in Europe during the First World War*. Cambridge, 1997, 89–104.

Houlbrooke, Ralph, ed. *Death, Ritual, and Bereavement*. London and New York, 1989.

Hüppauf, Bernd. "Das Schlachtfeld als Raum im Kopf mit einem Postscriptum nach dem 11. September 2001." In Steffen Martus, Marina Münkler, and Werner Röcke, eds., *Schlachtfelder. Codierung von Gewalt im medialen Wandel*. Berlin, 2003, 207–33.

———, ed. *War, Violence, and the Modern Condition*. Berlin and New York, 1997.

Hull, Isabel V. *Absolute Destruction: Military Culture and the Practice of War in Imperial Germany*. Ithaca and London, 2005.

Huyssen, Andreas, "Trauma and Memory: A New Imaginary of Temporality." In Bennett and Rosanne Kennedy, eds., *World Memory: Personal Trajectories in Global Time*. New York, 2003, 16–29.

Jarausch, Konrad H., and Michael Geyer. *Shattered Past: Reconstructing German Histories*. Princeton, 2003.

Jirgl, Reinhard. *Die Unvollendeten*. Munich, 2003.

Judt, Tony. "The Past is Another Country: Myth and Memory in Postwar Europe." In Istvan Deak, Jan T. Gross, and Tony Judt, eds., *The Politics of Retribution in Europe: World War II and its Aftermath*. Princeton, 2000, 293-323.

Jupp, Peter. *From Dust to Ashes: Cremation and the British Way of Death*. London, 2005.

Kempowski, Walter. *Das Echolot: Fuga furiosa*. Munich, 1999.

Kessel, Martina. "Gelächter, Männlichkeit und soziale Ordnung: 'Deutscher Humor' und Krieg (1870–1918)." In Christina Lutter, ed., *Kulturgeschichte. Fragestellungen, Konzepte, Annäherungen*. Innsbruck, 2004, 97–116.

Klein, Aaron J. *Striking Back: The 1972 Munich Olympics Massacre and Israel's Deadly Response*. New York, 2005.

Knoch, Habbo. "Die Grenzen des Zeigbaren: Fotografien der NS-Verbrechen und die westdeutsche Gesellschaft, 1955–1965." In Sven Kramer, ed., *Die Shoah im Bild*. Munich, 2003, 87–116.

Königseder, Angelika, and Juliane Wetzel. *Waiting for Hope: Jewish Displaced Persons in Post-World War II Germany*. Trans. John A. Broadwin. Evanston, 2001.

Koselleck, Reinhart. "Terror und Traum: Methodologische Anmerkungen zu Zeiterfahrungen im Dritten Reich." In Reinhart Koselleck, *Vergangene Zukunft: Zur Semantik geschichtlicher Zeiten*. 2nd ed. Frankfurt, 1992, 278–299.

Koshar, Rudy. *From Monuments to Traces: Artifacts of German Memory, 1870–1990*. Berkeley and Los Angeles, 2000.

Lagrou, Pieter. *The Legacy of Nazi Occupation: Patriotic Memory and National Recovery in Western Europe, 1945–1965*. Cambridge, 2000.

Latzel, Klaus. *Deutsche Soldaten - Nationalsozialistischer Krieg? Kriegserlebnis – Kriegserfahrung, 1939–1945*. Paderborn, 1998.

Leisner, Barbara, ed. *Vom Reichsausschuss zur Arbeitsgemeinschaft Friedhof und Denkmal*. Kassel, 2002.

Le Naour, Jean-Yves. "Laughter and Tears in the Great War: The Need for Laughter / The Guilt of Humour." *European Studies* 31 (2001): 265-275.

Leys, Ruth. *Trauma: A Genealogy*. Chicago, 2000.

Long, J. J., and Anne Whitehead, eds. *W. G. Sebald: A Critical Companion*. Edinburgh, 2004.

Lüdtke, Alf. "Histories of Mourning: Flowers and Stones for the War Dead, Confusion for the Living. Vignettes from East and West Germany." In Gerald Sider and Gavin Smith, eds., *Between History and Histories: The Making of Silences and Commemorations*. Toronto, 1997, 149–179.

Lüdtke, Alf, and Bernd Weisbrod, eds. *No Man's Land of Violence: Extreme Wars in the 20th Century*. Göttingen, 2006.
Mankowitz, Zeev W. *Life between Memory and Hope: The Survivors of the Holocaust in Occupied Germany*. Cambridge, 2002.
Marcuse, Harold. *Legacies of Dachau: The Uses and Abuses of a Concentration Camp, 1933– 2001*. Cambridge, 2001.
Marßolek, Inge, and Adelheid von Saldern, eds. *Zuhören und Gehörtwerden im Nationalsozialismus. I.: Radio im Nationalsozialismus: Zwischen Lenkung und Ablenkung*. Tübingen, 1998.
Menasse, Robert. "'Geschichte' war der größte historische Irrtum." In Robert Menasse, *Hysterien und andere historische Irrtümer*, Vienna, 1996, 21–36.
Mendes-Flohr, Paul. "The 'Kriegserlebnis' and Jewish Consciousness." In Wolfgang Benz, Arnold Paucker, and Peter Pulzer, eds., *Jüdisches Leben in der Weimarer Republik / Jews in the Weimar Republic*. Tübingen, 1998, 225–237.
Moeller, Robert G. *War Stories: The Search for a Usable Past in the Federal Republic of Germany*. Berkeley and Los Angeles, 2001.
Moser, Tilman. "Die Unfähigkeit zu trauern: Hält die Diagnose einer Überprüfung stand? Zur psychischen Verarbeitung des Holocaust in der Bundesrepublik." *Psyche* 46, no. 5 (1992): 389–405.
Mosse, George. *Fallen Soldiers: Reshaping the Memory of the World Wars*. Oxford, 1990.
Mosse, Werner E., ed. *Deutsches Judentum in Krieg und Revolution: 1916–1923*. Tübingen, 1971.
Naumann, Klaus. *Der Krieg als Text: Das Jahr 1945 im kulturellen Gedächtnis der Presse*. Hamburg, 1998.
Niehaus, Michael, and Claudia Öhlschläger, eds. *W. G. Sebald: Politische Archäologie und melancholische Bastelei*. Berlin, 2006.
Overmans, Rüdiger. *Deutsche militärische Verluste im Zweiten Weltkrieg*. Munich, 1999.
Paulmann, Johannes, ed. *Auswärtige Repräsentationen: Deutsche Kulturdiplomatie nach 1945*. Vienna, 2005.
Purseigle, Pierre. "Mirroring Societies at War: Pictorial Humour in the British and French Popular Press during the First World War." *European Studies* 31 (2001): 289–328.
Regener, Sven. *Herr Lehmann*. Frankfurt, 2001.
Reichardt, Sven. *Faschistische Kampfbünde: Gewalt und Gemeinschaft im italienischen Squadrismus und in der deutschen SA*. Cologne, 2002.
Ruck, Michael. "Ein kurzer Sommer der konkreten Utopie: Zur westdeutschen Planungsgeschichte der langen 60er Jahre." In Axel Schildt, Detlef Siegfried, and Karl Christian Lammers, eds., *Dynamische Zeiten: die 60er Jahre in den beiden deutschen Gesellschaften*. Hamburg, 2000, 362–401.
Rugg, Julie. "Defining the Place of Burial: What Makes a Cemetery a Cemetery." In *Mortality* 5, no. 3 (2000): 259–275.
Samuels, Martin. *Command or Control? Command, Training and Tactics in the British and German Armies 1888–1918*. London, 1995.
Sarasin, Philipp. "Subjekte, Diskurse, Körper: Überlegungen zu einer diskursanalytischen Kulturgeschichte." In Wolfgang Hardtwig and Hans-Ulrich Wehler, eds., *Kulturgeschichte heute*. Göttingen, 1996, 131–164.
Schildt, Axel, Detlef Siegfried, and Karl Christian Lammers, eds. *Dynamische Zeiten: die 60er Jahre in den beiden deutschen Gesellschaften*. Hamburg, 2000.
Schiller, Kay. "The Presence of the Nazi Past in the Early Decades of the Bonn Republic." *Journal of Contemporary History* 39 (2004): 285–294.

Schumann, Dirk. "Europa, der Erste Weltkrieg und die Nachkriegszeit: eine Kontinuität der Gewalt?" *Journal of Modern European History* 1 (2003): 24–43.
Schwarz, Leo W. *The Redeemers: A Saga of the Years 1945–1952.* New York, 1953.
Sebald, W. G. *The Rings of Saturn.* Trans. Michael Hulse. New York, 1998.
———. *On the Natural History of Destruction. With essays on Alfred Andersch, Jean Améry and Peter Weiss.* Trans. Anthea Bell. London, 2003.
———. *Campo Santo.* Munich and Vienna, 2003.
Strachan, Hew. "Ausbildung, Kampfgeist und die zwei Weltkriege." In Bruno Thoß and Hans-Erich Volkmann, eds., *Erster Weltkrieg—Zweiter Weltkrieg: Krieg, Kriegserlebnis, Kriegserfahrung in Deutschland.* Paderborn, 2002, 265–286.
Tatar, Maria. *Lustmord: Sexual Murder in Weimar Germany.* Princeton, 1995.
Thalmann, Rolf. *Urne oder Sarg? Auseinandersetzungen um die Einführung der Feuerbestattung im 19. Jahrhundert.* Bern, Frankfurt, and Las Vegas, 1978.
Tomlinson, Alan, and Christopher Young, eds. *National Identity and Global Sports Events: Culture, Politics, and Spectacle in the Olympics and the Football World Cup.* Albany, 2006.
Wackwitz, Stephan. *Ein unsichtbares Land.* Frankfurt, 2003.
Wegner, Bernd. "Hitler, der Zweite Weltkrieg und die Choreographie des Untergangs." *Geschichte und Gesellschaft* 26 (2000): 493–518.
Welzer, Harald, Sabine Möller, and Karoline Tschugnall, eds. *"Opa war kein Nazi:" Nationalsozialismus und Holocaust im Familiengedächtnis.* Frankfurt am Main, 2002.
Winter, Jay. *Sites of Memory, Sites of Mourning: The Great War in European Cultural History.* Cambridge, 1995.
Winter, Jay, and Emmanuel Sirvan, eds., *War and Remembrance in the Twentieth Century.* Cambridge, 1999.
Wöhlert, Meike. *Der politische Witz in der NS-Zeit am Beispiel ausgesuchter SD-Berichte und Gestapo-Akten.* Frankfurt am Main, 1997.
Wolfrum, Edgar. "Die Suche nach dem 'Ende der Nachkriegszeit': Krieg und NS-Diktatur In öffentlichen Geschichtsbildern der 'alten' Bundesrepublik Deutschland." In Christoph Cornelißen, Lutz Klinkhammer, and Wolfgang Schwentker, eds., *Erinnerungskulturen: Deutschland, Italien und Japan seit 1945.* Frankfurt am Main, 2003, 183–197.
Young, Allan. *The Harmony of Illusions: Inventing Post-Traumatic Stress Disorder.* Princeton, 1995.
Ziemann, Benjamin. *Front und Heimat: ländliche Kriegserfahrungen im südlichen Bayern 1914–1923.* Essen, 1997.
———. "Die Eskalation des Tötens in zwei Weltkriegen." In Richard van Dülmen, ed., *Erfindung des Menschen: Schöpfungsträume und Körperbilder 1500–2000.* Vienna and Cologne, 1998, 411–429.

INDEX

Abendbroth, Friedrich, 298
Ackermann, Volker, 152
Adenauer, Konrad, 15, 151–162, 168-176
Adenauer, Paul, 158
Adorno, Theodor, W., 8, 278, 289–91, 293
Afterlife, 17, 225
Aicher, Otl, 137
Akabas, Abel, 238, 248–49
Aleksiun, Natalia, 242
American Civil War, 7
Ameskamp, Simone, 15
Anderson, Benedict, 201
Andree, Gertrud, 299
Andrianov, Konstantin, 134
Anhalt, 307–8, 311
Anyska, Jan, 299
Arendt, Hannah, 62–63, 227, 274n38
Argentina, 243
Ariès, Philippe, 5, 7, 15, 18, 19n21, 95, 109
Arndt, Ernst Moritz, 7
Aschenbach, Gustav von, 4, 6
Assmann, Aleida, 282–83
Auer, Fritz, 138
Augstein, Rudolf, 162
Auschwitz/Oswiecim, 107, 228, 290–91, 293, 301, 307, 310
Austro-Hungarian-Empire, 191

Bach, Johann Sebastian, 117, 221
Bad Reichenhall (DP camp), 244
Baden, 7
Bamberg, 238–39
Bartov, Omer, 210
Barzel, Rainer, 134

Baum, Herbert, 252
Bausinger, Hermann, 197
Bavaria, 7, 96, 103, 131, 135, 138, 143, 190–91, 233, 237, 242, 254n11
Becher, Johannes, 167
Beethoven, Ludwig van, 117, 134, 167, 188
Beevor, Anthony, 301
Behrenbeck, Sabine, 219
Belgium, 9, 11, 204, 211, 306
Ben-Gurion, David, 156, 159–60
Ben-Horin, Elyashiv, 141
Benjamin, Hilde, 74
Benjamin, Walter, 1, 8, 283
Bergen-Belsen, 60,
Bergson, Henri, 203
Berlin Wall, 12, 171–2
Berlin, 14–15, 22n61, 52, 54–55, 60, 69–87, 101, 103, 107, 114, 115, 118, 121, 124–25, 128n40, 131, 136–38, 154, 158, 160, 162–68, 181–83, 188, 201, 223, 252, 298-311
Berlin, Isaiah, 1
Bessel, Richard, 14
Betts, Paul, 15, 137
Bismarck, Otto von, 8, 153, 158, 160, 161, 163, 168
Black, Monica, 14
Bloch, Ernst, 8
Blumenthal-Barby, Kay, 119
Bodemann, Y. Michal, 252
Bohrer, Karl Heinz, 199
Bojanovo, 184
Bonn, 140, 142, 143, 153, 158–9, 161, 189
Bosnia, 305
Bourke, Joanna, 26

Boyarin, Jonathan, 243–44
Brandt, Willy, 132, 133, 136, 143–44, 151, 160, 173n1
Braude, Max, 237
Brecht, Bertolt, 179
Bremen, 97, 103
Breslau, 52, 54–56, 65n34, 189, 303
Brezhnev, Leonid, 165–66
Brinitzer, Albert, 202
Bruck, Moeller van den, 200
Brundage, Avery, 134, 139, 141, 145
Buber, Martin, 182
Buchenwald, 60, 239
Büchner, Georg, 7
Burg, Yossef, 143
Burial, 5, 83
  and cremation, 98–9, 103–104
  in East Germany, 15, 115, 121–2
  at end of Second World War, 59–60, 69, 72–73, 76
  of Jewish DPs, 237–40
  notion of proper burial, 79–81, 85
  and race, 71, 74
  See also cemeteries, corpses, death, Federal Republic of Germany, First World War, German Democratic Republic, funerals, Holocaust, mourning, Nazism

Carlos, John, 134
Caucasus, 28,
Celan, Paul, 1, 151
Cemeteries, 5, 81
  in Berlin Wilmersdorf, 298–300
  in East Germany, 122–24
  Jewish, 79, 116
  and opposition to cremation, 96
  See also burial, death, Federal Republic of Germany, First World War, German Democratic Republic, funerals, Holocaust, mourning, Nazism
Chamberlain, Neville, 138
Charlemagne, 94
Chestochowa, 242, 244
Chile, 152
China, 10
Chopin, Frederic, 117
Churchill, Winston, 153, 158
Coburg, 96
Coffins, 73, 115, 153, 166

Cohen, Hermann, 182
Cold War, 63, 152, 172–3
Cologne, 58, 155–57, 159, 161, 182
Confino, Alon, 16
Corpses,
  and cremation, 102
  in 1945, 55–58, 60–61, 75, 77
  in Second World War, 70
  See also burial, cemeteries, death, Federal Republic of Germany, First World War, German Democratic Republic, funerals, Holocaust, suicide
Cottbus, 55
Coubertin, Pierre de, 134
Craig, Gordon, 160
Cremation, 15
  and attitude toward mortality, 94–95
  and Catholics, 98, 102–103
  in East Germany, 118, 122
  and idea of progress, 105–106, 109
  long term patterns of, 97, 109
  and Protestants, 103
  and urbanism, 96
  See also burial, cemeteries, death, Federal Republic of Germany, German Democratic Republic, Nazism
Czechoslovakia, 114, 116, 302, 306

Dachau, 60, 107, 135–36, 142–44, 236–38, 249
Daladier, Édouard, 138
Daume, Willi, 132–35, 137, 139, 141, 144–46
Day of National Mourning (Volkstrauertag), 189, 220
De Gaulle, Charles, 156, 160
Death
  continuities of perceptions of, 2, 4–7, 13, 109, 113–14, 229
  and German nationalism, 6, 8, 170
  and ideology, 5, 17, 115–6, 219, 222, 226–27
  and humor, 201–12
  and hygiene, 58, 100–101
  mass and individual death, 4–5, 10, 13, 17
  and mentalities, 5–6, 94, 219, 222, 226–27
  politicization of, 5, 190, 246–53

and private sphere, 5, 63, 264–65, 299–300
and public sphere, 51, 63, 264–65, 299–300
short term cataclysm, 4–5, 229
and religion, 5–6, 15, 98, 109, 118–19, 185, 188, 223–25
repression of, 15, 17, 109, 266–71
rituals of, 5, 7, 17, 59, 117–19, 232–25
See also burial, cemeteries, corpses, Federal Republic of Germany, First World War, German Democratic Republic, funerals, grief, Holocaust, humor, memory, mourning, Nazism, suicide
Demm, Eberhard, 204
Demmin (Pomerania), 55
Diesing, Rudolf, 76
Dietrich, Marlene, 300, 311
Dilke, Charles Wentworth, 93–95
Dönitz, Karl, 54
Dresden, 3, 52, 59, 94, 120, 121, 126, 127n18, 301, 302–4
Dress, Walter, 82
Dubiel, Helmut, 305
Dückers, Tanja, 300, 311
Duménil, Anne, 48n31
Dziadek, Rudi, 210

Eban, Abba, 143
Ebert, Friedrich (1871–1925), 153
Ebert, Friedrich, (1894–1979), 166
Egypt, 246, 269
Eichendorff, Joseph von, 310
Eichsfeld, 116
Einstein, Albert, 182
Eisenhower, Dwight D., 60
Elbing (West Prussia), 54
Elias, Norbert, 51, 95
Enzensberger, H.M, 132
Erfurt, 107
Erhard, Ludwig, 151, 160
Erickson, John, 63n7
Eshkol, Levi, 159

Federal Republic of Germany,
and 1972 Olympic Games, 129–50
and Adenauer funeral, 153–62
and coming to terms with the past, 275–313
and private memory of Second World War, 261–74
See also burial, cemeteries, death, German Democratic Republic, funerals, Holocaust, memory, mourning, Nazism
Feldafing (Bavaria), 237
Ferguson, Niall, 27
Fest, Joachim, 301
Feygenboim, Moshe Yosef, 245
Fichte, Johann Gottlieb, 199, 308
Finder, Gabriel, 17
First World War, 2, 5–6, 14, 151,
Fliegerbauer, Anton, 140, 143
Floerke, Hans, 202
Flossenbürg, 107
Föhrenwald (DP camp), 241
Forte, Dieter, 310
Foucault, Michel, 310
France, 7, 11, 15, 21n51, 204, 302, 306
Franco, Francisco 135, 171
Frank, Manfred, 170
Frankfurt (am Main), 58
Frankfurt (am Oder), 55, 118
Franz, Ansgar, 118
Frei, Norbert, 269
Freud, Sigmund, 264, 292
Fricke, Gerd, 207
Friedeburg, Hans Georg von, 54
Friedländer, Saul, 251
Friedrich II, 106, 198
Friedrich Wilhelm II, 90n76
Friedrich, Jörg, 3, 12, 70, 229, 294n9, 301, 302, 304, 306
Frings, Josef Richard, 156
Fritzsche, Peter, 18, 261
Funerals,
in East Germany, 117–19
of Konrad Adenauer, 15, 153–62
of state, 158
in Third Reich, 221–23
of Walter Ulbricht, 15, 163–69
See also burial, cemeteries, death, Federal Republic of Germany, German Democratic Republic, grief, Holocaust, mourning, Nazism
Fürstenfeldbruck (DP camp), 242
Fürstenfeldbruck (military airport), 145
Fürth, 58
Fussell, Paul, 6

Galinski, Heinz, 252
Garmisch, 249
Gavin, James, 60
Gebhardt, Hertha von, 73
Geertz, Clifford, 230n31
Genscher, Hans-Dietrich, 140, 141
German Democratic Republic, 11–12, 15
   Sepulchral culture, 113–14, 123, 126
   Marxism and idea of death, 115–16, 125
   See also burial, cemeteries, death, Federal Republic of Germany, funerals, Holocaust, memory, mourning, SED
Gerstenmaier, Eugen, 160
Geyer, Michael, 10, 14, 268
Giesler, Paul, 54
Glössberg, 220
Goebbels, Joseph, 10, 54, 132, 158, 179, 208, 211, 308
Goethe, Johann Wolfgang von, 111n28, 210, 221
Goldberg, Harvey E., 232
Goldhagen, Daniel Jonah, 21–22n61, 305–6
Gollancz, Victor, 88n31
Goltermann, Svenja, 17
Goppel, Alfons, 143
Göring, Hermann, 54, 211
Görlitz, 56
Gotha, 95, 96
Gottwald, Georg, 57
Grabbe, Christian Dietrich, 7
Grady, Tim, 16
Grass, Günter, 3, 12, 53, 229, 300, 301, 303, 307, 309, 311
graves, 77, 82
Great Britain, 97, 98, 121. *See also* United Kingdom
grief, 5, 180, 228
   among Jews in First World War, 184–87
   after 1918, 187–92
Grimmelshausen, H. J. Ch. von, 7
Grinberg, Zalman, 236–37, 246, 252
Gringauz, Shmuel, 232–35, 246, 248–49, 253
Grotewohl, Otto, 165, 167, 170
Grünberg (Lower Silesia), 57

Haas, Ludwig, 183
Hacking, Ian, 264

Hager, Kurt, 165
Halle, 188
Hamburg, 16, 67n71, 95, 181, 184, 186–90, 192, 269
Hamburger Fremdenblatt, 185
Haydn, Joseph, 156
Hegel, G. W. F., 7, 264, 275–76, 293
Heidegger, Martin, 8
Heidelberg, 95
Heilbronner, Emil, 183–84
Heine, Heinrich, 200
Heinemann, Gustav, 138–39, 141–44
Helf, Kurt, 298
Henning, Willi, 75
Herf, Jeffrey, 78
Hermann, Judith, 300–301
Heroes Memorial day (Heldengedenktag), 220, 224
Herse, Willie, 299
Herzog, Dagmar, 82,
Heuss, Theodor, 153, 159
Himmler, Heinrich, 53–54, 211
Hindenburg, Paul von, 153, 202
Hiroshima, 285, 310
Hirsch, Julius, 184–85
Hitler, Adolf, 1, 3, 4, 9, 53–54, 70, 73, 78, 138, 151–52, 158, 161, 167–8, 172, 211, 219, 221, 228, 247, 269, 289–91, 296n73, 300
Hobsbawm, Eric, 1
Hochsteter, Gustav, 201
Höcker, Paul Oskar, 203–4
Hoffmann, Christhard, 183
Holland, 11, 152, 306
Hollywood, 308
Holocaust, 10, 29, 84, 97, 228, 283
   and 1972 Olympic Games, 129–31, 140
   commemorated by DPs, 240–42
   and cremation movement, 107–109
   memorial books, 242–46
   and Zionism, 246–53
   See also death, Federal Republic of Germany, German Democratic Republic, memory, mourning, Nazism
Hölscher, Lucian, 71
Honecker, Erich, 151–52, 163–68
Hook, Sidney, 171
Horne, John, 204
Hull, Isabel, 31

Humor,
  in First World War 201–206
  in Second World War, 206–12
Hussein, Saddam, 296n73
Huyssen, Andreas, 261, 264

Iraq Wars, 304
Israel/Palestine, 16–17, 142, 159, 235, 240,
  243, 245, 247, 253
Italy, 306

Japan, 62, 161
Jarausch, Konrad, 10
Jeggle, Utz, 209
Jirgl, Reinhard, 18, 301, 309–10, 313n24
Johnson, Lyndon B., 156, 160, 162, 172
Jüdische Rundschau, 182–83

K. Tzetnik, 228
Kallich, 220
Kalthoff, Albert, 97
Kansteiner, Wulf, 280
Kant, Immanuel, 290
Karasek-Langer, Alfred, 228–29
Keane, John, 8
Kempowski, Walter, 301, 303–4
Kertész, Imre, 293
Kessel, Martina, 16
Kettenacker, Lothar, 281
Khrushchev, Nikita, 167
Kiesgen, Laurenz, 208
Kiesinger, Kurt Georg, 132, 151, 160
Killinger, Manfred Freiherr von, 207
Kinkel, Gottfried, 97, 99
Klausner, Abraham, 237–38
Kleve, 58
Kluge, Alexander, 285, 294n9
Knoch, Habbo, 78
Koch, Joseph, 189
Koch, Robert, 100
Koerner, Theodor, 7
Komarov, Vladimir, 172
Komotau, 310, 311
König, Fritz, 145
Königsberg, 56, 58, 303
Kori, Heinrich, 107
Koselleck, Reinhart, 265
Koshar, Rudy, 82, 180, 303
Kosovo, 305
Kovno, 238

Krakow, 238
Kramer, Alan, 204
Krasnistav (Poland), 243–44
Kraus, Karl, 167
Krebs, Hans, 54
Krolikowski, Werner, 165
Kronawitter, Georg, 142–43,
Krummacher, Friedrich Wilhelm, 83
Kugelmass, Jack, 243–44
Kursk, 52
Kushner, Tony, 129

Lagrou, Pieter, 302, 306
Lalkin, Shmuel, 141
Lamm, Hans, 141
Landsberg (DP camp), 232–33, 238–39,
  242, 248, 252
Lange, Herbert, 220
Langemarck, 34
Laskowitz (Silesia), 307
Lass, Werner, 210
Latzel, Klaus, 202
Leipzig, 9, 54, 120, 127n19
Leivick, H. (Leyvik Halpern) 234, 238, 246
Leo XIII, Pope, 102
Lessing, Gotthold Ephraim, 111n28,
Ley, Robert, 54
Leys, Ruth, 262
Liebknecht, Karl, 152, 167, 307
Liulevicius, Vejas, 205
Löchner, Friedrich, 75–76
Lorenz, Walter, 298
Lübke, Paul, 223
Ludwigslust, 60
Luebke, Heinrich, 153, 160
Luft, Georg, 183–84
Lustigen Blätter, Die, 197
Luxemburg, Rosa, 152, 167, 307

MacDonald, Kevin, 130
Madrid, 134
Magdeburg, 52,
Makow Mzowiecki (Poland), 242–43
Mankowitz, Zeev W., 246, 249
Mann, Golo, 153
Mann, Klaus, 198
Mann, Thomas, 4–6, 20n37
Mannheim, Karl, 230n31
Marne, Battle of the, 38
Maron, Karl, 80

Marschwitz (Lower Silesia), 57
Marx, Karl, 3, 230n31, 264, 285
McNally, Richard, 264
Mehring, Franz, 167
Meir, Golda, 140, 142, 144
Memel (Lithuania), 232
memory, 5, 187–191
   of air bombing in post 1945 Germany, 3, 52, 276–81
   and death in post 1945 West Germany, 266–71
   of German victimhood, 14, 18, 62, 78, 84, 281–82, 287–91, 300–303
   and melancholy, 17, 283–86
   and psychology, 265–66, 286–67
   and repression, 4, 280–83
   See also death, Federal Republic of Germany, German Democratic Republic, Holocaust, Nazism
Mendes Flohr, Paul, 181
Menzel, Matthias, 74
Merker, Richard, 204
Merridale, Catherine, 226
Metternich, Prince Klemens Wenzel von, 161
Mexico City, 134, 137, 139
Mielert, Fritz, 202, 204
Mielke, Erich, 165
Minsk, 62
Mitscherlich, Alexander and Margarete, 4, 17, 278, 280, 286–87, 289–91
Mittenwald, 249–50
Model, Walter, 54
Moeller, Robert, 11, 133, 302–3
mortality,
   statistics of, 114–15
Moscow, 52, 73, 116, 121, 166, 172
Moser, Tilman, 286–87
Mosse, George L., 10, 179–80
mourning, 5
   after 1918, 187–92
   in First World War, 184–87
   inability to, 17, 278, 280, 286–87
   Jewish traditions of, 17, 232–35
   See also burial, cemeteries, death, Federal Republic of Germany, First World War, German Democratic Republic, grief, Holocaust, memory
Mühsam, Erich, 307
Müller, Heiner, 12

Munich, 6, 15, 50n62, 66n55, 107, 129–146, 183, 236, 239, 241, 247
Murr, Wilhelm, 54
Musil, Robert, 12

Nannen, Henri, 142
Napoleon Bonaparte, 7
Naumann, Klaus, 302
Nazism
   coming to terms with in 1972 Olympic Games, 130–31, 137–38
   and cremation, 106–107
   and death, 4, 9, 10, 77–78, 220–29, 270
   death and religion, 16, 219–25
   and idea of proper burial, 71, 74, 85–87
   private memory of, 264–65
   See also burial, cemeteries, corpses, death, Federal Republic of Germany, First World War, German Democratic Republic, funerals, grief, Holocaust, humor, memory, mourning, suicide
Neubrandenburg, 115
Neue Gemeinschaft, Die (*The New Community*), 221–25, 228
Neue Zeit, 78
Neuengamme, 108
Neues Deutschland, 163, 170
Neumann, Franz, 227
Neumark (Brandenburg), 61
New York City, 98
New York Times, The, 300, 301
Nuremberg Trials, 2, 11, 151

Ohnesorg, Benno, 152
Ollenhauer, Erich, 153, 159
Olt, Reinhard, 205
Orenstein, Benjamin, 242
Ostrowski, Nicolai, 117
Otto, Frei, 138

Pasteur, Louis, 100
Pauly, Max, 101
Peikert, Paul, 54, 56
Peres, Shimon, 144
Pforzheim, 52
Pieck, Wilhelm, 165, 167, 170
Plivier, Theodor, 304
Plötzensee, 300
Poland, 52, 61, 115, 239, 242, 299, 302, 307, 308

Pommern, 303
Potsdam, 113
Prussia, 96
   East Prussia, 52, 303
   Prussian Military, 7
   West Prussia, 54
Puttkamer, Jesko von, 143–44

Radisch, Iris, 310–11
Radom, 244–45
Rathenau, Walter, 152
Reclam, Carl, 94
Reeve, Simon, 130
Regensburger, Karl August, 192
Regneer, Sven, 300, 301
Reimann, Hans, 211
Reims, 157
Reisman, Abraham, 247
Rhine/Rhineland, 153, 208
Rhöndorf, 153–4, 158
Riebau, Hans, 211
Riess, Curt, 72
Rivne (in Volyhnia, Western Ukraine), 241
Röhm, Ernst, 152
Romano, Yossef, 139
Rome, 102
Rooin, James Charles, 250
Rosenberg, Alfred, 223
Rossellini, Roberto, 88n27
Rostock, 115
Rotterdam, 62
Russia, 52, 198. *See also Soviet Union*
Rust, Bernhard, 54

Sachsenhausen, 107
Samaranch, Juan Antonio, 135
Sarajevo, 1
Schacter, Herschel, 237
Schäfer, Dieter, 285
Scher, Peter, 197
Schieder, Theodor, 57
Schildt, Axel, 297n75
Schiller, Friedrich, 111n28, 199
Schiller, Kay, 15
Schindler, Oskar, 238
Schleiermacher, Friedrich, 308
Schlink, Bernhard, 300
Schmidt, Fritz, 57
Schneider, Peter, 288–89, 297n75
Scholem, Gerschom, 182, 184

Scholem, Werner, 184
Scholl, Hans and Sophie, 137, 152, 171
Scholz, Franz, 56
Schreiber, Manfred, 139, 141
Schröter, Alfred, 208
Schubert, Franz, 221
Schulz, Felix Robin, 15
Schumann, Robert, 117
Schwarz, Leo W., 246–47, 250–51
Schwarze Corps (Black Corps), 208
Schwerin, 123–24
Sebald, W. G., 3, 11–13, 17, 229, 276–293
Second World War
   consequence for burial culture, 69–87
   mass death at end of, 51–63
   German way of war, 25–31
   humor in, 206–12
   See also burial, cemeteries, corpses, death, Federal Republic of Germany, First World War, German Democratic Republic, funerals, grief, Holocaust, memory, mourning, Nazism, suicide
SED, 11–12, 15–16
Seghers, Anna, 170
Seitz, Walter, 74
Serov, Ivan Alexandrovich, 55
Shalitan, Levi, 234, 236, 246
Shapiro, Solomon, 238
Shaver, Emma, 246
Siemens, Friedrich, 94
Sievers, Max, 97
Silesia, 55–56, 266, 303
Simon, Ernst, 187
Simon, Gustav, 54
Simplicissimus, 197
Sindermann, Horst, 166
Smith, Tommie, 134
Somme, Battle of the, 27, 31, 41
Sontag, Susan, 277
Sonthofen, 288
Soviet Union, 2, 28, 29, 163–6, 265, 299
Spael, Wilhelm, 208–9
Spain, 135, 171
Spiegel, Der, 133, 141, 160–62
Spielberg, Steven, 129
Sprenger, Jakob, 54
Springer, Axel, 142
Stalin, Joseph, 1
Stalingrad, Battle of, 11, 52, 224, 302–3
Stargarder Tageblatt, 53

Stauffenberg, Claus Schenk Graf von, 152
Steeg, Ludwig, 71
Stern, Carola, 167
Stern, Der, 142, 161
Steuer, Daniel, 17
Stolph, Willi, 166
Streicher, Julius, 76
Stresemann, Gustav, 153, 161
Stürmer, Der, 76
Stuttgart, 50n62, 138
suicide, 267
   in 1945, 54–5, 57
Sweden, 97, 121, 126
Swinemünde, 52

Tallyerand, 161
Tel Aviv, 143
Telchow, Otto, 54
Terboven, Josef, 54
Teterow (Mecklenburg), 55
Thälmann, Ernst, 152, 167
Theresienstadt, 239
Thierack, 54
Thirty Years War, 3, 7, 13
Thompson, Henry, 98
Thorwald, Jürgen, 304
Topf, J.A. und Söhne, 107
Tonel, Ulrich, 78
trauma, 5,
   critique of concept of, 261–65, 271
Treblinka, 242, 247
Treger, Dovid, 250
Tucholsky, Kurt, 206
Tutzing (Bavaria), 237
Tyrol, 236, 250, 254n11

Ulbricht, Lotte, 167
Ulbricht, Walter, 15, 151, 152, 163–73
Ulm, 137, 190
Unification Wars, 1864–1871, 7, 200
United Kingdon, 126, 276, 289. *See also* Great Britain
United States, 156, 159, 161, 233, 240, 253, 261, 305, 308
Unzer Weg, 234, 246
Utermann, Wilhelm, 210

Verdery, Katherine, 235
Verdun, Battle of, 31, 41
Versailles, Treaty of, 2, 151

Victoria, Queen, 158
Vietnam War, 261–62, 290
Vilna, 241
Vogel, Hans-Jochen, 132, 135, 141–42, 145
Volga, 28
Völkische Beobachter, Der, 209–11

Wackwitz, Stephan, 18, 301, 306–11
Walser, Martin, 307–8
Wars of Liberation, 7
Ward, Simon, 277
Warsaw Ghetto, 133, 251–52
Warsaw Pact, 132, 166
Warsaw, 133
Weber, Hans-Adolf, 210
Weil, Wolf, 238
Weimar Republic, 8, 9, 16, 95, 108, 151, 158, 189, 191, 206, 211, 286
Weinberg, Moshe, 142
Weiss, Peter, 18
Welt, Die, 161, 172
Welzer, Harald, 282
Wessel, Horst, 152, 158
Wieck, Michael, 56
Wilhelm II, Emperor of Germany (1888–1918), 181–82
Wilms, Wilfried, 277
Wilson, Harold, 156
Winter, Jay, 180, 185
Winzer, Otto, 80
Wittgenstein, Ludwig, 293
Witzmann, Hermann, 224
Wöhlert, Meike, 207
Wolf, Georg, 141
Wolfrum, Edgar, 297n75
Württemberg, 7, 222
Würzburg, 16, 52, 59, 66n55, 181, 185–86, 190

Young, Allan, 264
Yugoslavia, 1, 306

Zeit, Die, 161, 310
Zeitlin, Aaron, 238
Zeitlin, David, 238
Zetkin, Clara, 167
Zille, Heinrich, 201–2
Zurich, 277–79,
Zweig, Arnold, 170

www.ingramcontent.com/pod-product-compliance
Lightning Source LLC
Chambersburg PA
CBHW051418290426
44109CB00016B/1343